Journeys to Empire

This fascinating study of two British missions to Tibet in 1774 and 1904 provides a unique perspective on the relationship between the Enlightenment and European colonialism. Gordon Stewart compares and contrasts the Enlightenment-era mission led by George Bogle and the Edwardian mission of Francis Younghusband as they crossed the Himalayas into Tibet. Through the British agents' diaries, reports, and letters and by exploring their relationships with Indians, Bhutanese, and Tibetans, Stewart is able to trace the shifting ideologies, economic interests, and political agendas that lay behind British empire-building from the late eighteenth century to the early twentieth century. This compelling account sheds new light on the changing nature of British imperialism, on power and intimacy in the encounter between East and West, and on the relationship of history and memory.

GORDON T. STEWART is the Jack and Margaret Sweet Professor of History at Michigan State University. His previous publications include *The Great Awakening in Nova Scotia 1760–1791* (1982), *The Origins of Canadian Politics* (1986), and *Jute and Empire: The Calcutta Jute Wallahs and the Landscapes of Empire* (1998).

Frontispiece Hoisting the British flag at the top of the Tang La. As the British forces crossed the Tang La in January 1904 they paused to raise the Union Jack. It was scenes such as this that convinced Tibetans, and observers in other countries, that the British intended to occupy parts of central Tibet. © Royal Geographical Society.

Journeys to Empire

Enlightenment, Imperialism, and the British Encounter with Tibet, 1774–1904

Gordon T. Stewart

CAMBRIDGE
UNIVERSITY PRESS

CAMBRIDGE UNIVERSITY PRESS
Cambridge, New York, Melbourne, Madrid, Cape Town, Singapore, São Paulo, Delhi

Cambridge University Press
The Edinburgh Building, Cambridge CB2 8RU, UK

Published in the United States of America by Cambridge University Press, New York

www.cambridge.org
Information on this title: www.cambridge.org/9780521735681

First published 2009

Printed in the United Kingdom at the University Press, Cambridge

A catalogue record for this publication is available from the British Library

Library of Congress Cataloguing in Publication data
Stewart, Gordon T. (Gordon Thomas), 1945–
Journeys to empire : enlightenment, imperialism, and the British encounter with Tibet,
1774–1904 / Gordon Stewart.
    p.   cm.
Includes bibliographical references and index.
ISBN 978-0-521-51502-3 (alk. paper) – ISBN 978-0-521-73568-1 (pbk. : alk. paper)
1. Great Britain – Foreign relations – China – Tibet.   2. Tibet (China) – Foreign
relations – Great Britain.   3. Younghusband, Francis Edward, Sir, 1863–1942.
4. Bogle, George, 1746–1781.   5. Great Britain – Colonies.   I. Title.
DS786.S787   2009
327.41051′509033 – dc22   2009005582

ISBN 978-0-521-51502-3 hardback
ISBN 978-0-521-73568-1 paperback

Thou art in the Ka'ba at Mecca
as well as the [Hindu] temple
of Somnath.
Thou art in the monastery,
as well as the tavern.

Thou art at the same time the light
and the moth,
The wine and the cup,
The sage and the fool . . .

Dara Shukoh, "The Compass of
Truth," in K. R. Qanungo, *Dara Shukoh*
(Calcutta: S. C. Sarkar, 1952)

Contents

Illustrations

Acknowledgments

Let's begin with libraries and librarians, archives and archivists. Most of the research for this book was done in the Manuscript Reading Room and the Asian and African Reading Room in the British Library. It is hard to imagine a more congenial place for researchers than this wonderful repository of historical and contemporary information. The staff in the Asian and African Room, which houses the India Office and Oriental Collections, were unfailingly courteous and efficient in spite of the heavy demands placed upon them. I particularly wish to thank Burkhard Quessel, the Curator of Tibetan Collections, who kindly helped a Tibet neophyte like me track down Albert Grunwedel's 1915 German translation of the Third Panchen Lama's treatise *The Way to Shambhala* (1775). The staff at the Public Record Office at Kew (now the National Archives) and the Mitchell Library in Glasgow were also considerate and helpful. In India I spent many useful hours at the National Archives in New Delhi being supplied with the records of the East India Company and the Foreign Department of the Government of India in connection with the two British missions to Tibet in 1774 and 1904. The British bibliographer in the Michigan State University Libraries, Agnes Widder, proved once more to be inventive and indefatigable in meeting all my requests. The financial support provided by the Jack and Margaret Sweet Endowed Professorship in the History Department at Michigan State University helped support some of my research travel to these libraries and archives in England, Scotland, and India.

Research trips to India were made even more pleasant by the warm hospitality in Delhi and Chandigarh of Justice and Mrs. Manmohan Singh Gujral and their extended family and many friends. Their introduction to contemporary India and to the recent history of India was a most informative and enjoyable complement to my academic endeavors. During my stint as a Visiting Scholar at Jawaharlal Nehru University I was very kindly received (and entertained to a memorable dinner) by Professor Sabyasachi Bhattacharya. There is surely no more pleasant place to stay in India's capital than the International Center, nestled against the Lodi

Gardens. In delightful surroundings that are normally the perquisites of only the rich or privileged, relatively penurious academics can survive very nicely indeed on dal, tea, and biscuits. All the staff in the Annexe Building of the Center were exceptionally kind and considerate. In connection with travel matters, I would like to thank Dr. Lilianet Brintrup and other organizers of the "International and Interdisciplinary Conference on Alexander von Humboldt and Zheng He" held at Xian in China in 2006. The invitation to present a paper on the first British mission to Tibet helped me make an early test of some of my ideas in a stimulating international setting.

Many people were kind enough to read and comment on the manuscript at various stages in its development. Professor Jyotsna Singh was invariably patient as she tried to keep me abreast of the rich variety of work being done by literature scholars on travel narratives and imperialism. Amrita Sen from Kolkata provided helpful insights on Bengal in the 1770s in the course of her work in an interdisciplinary graduate seminar on cultural encounters in the medieval and early modern eras organized by the College of Arts and Letters at Michigan State University. Several of my colleagues in the History Department provided sound advice after their reading of the manuscript. I would particularly like to thank Donald Lammers, Lewis Siegelbaum, and Lisa Fine for their thorough readings and occasionally trenchant comments. Other colleagues, Kristie Macrakis and Karrin Hanshew, advised on a translation issue; Peter Knupfer and Shawn McBee helped me with computer-imaging matters. Warren Cohen, now at the University of Maryland, and Linda Johnson helped on matters Chinese. Mark Kornbluh has provided unstinting support and encouragement throughout his tenure as Chair of the History Department.

In a work of this kind my debt to a whole host of other scholars and writers is obvious. I have attempted to acknowledge that fully not only in the footnotes and bibliography but within the body of the text as well. This was particularly the case in connection with the Tibetan side of the story. While the notes will record many of my obligations to scholars who have written on Tibet, I single out here the three-volume collection of articles (with introductions and commentary) compiled and edited by Alex MacKay. For beginners like me this overview of modern history writing on Tibet was invaluable. In his Preface MacKay noted ruefully that friends had warned him that editing such specialized tomes would be a thankless task because no one beyond the small community of Tibetan scholars would take notice. These volumes are of immense help for anyone trying to build up an understanding of Tibet's complex history. I made extensive use of the information and insights provided.

The lifetime of research and writing by Alastair Lamb on India's northern borderlands and British policies towards Central Asia has also been of inestimable help for my understanding of British involvement in these regions.

My greatest debt is to J who acted as an exacting but loving editor through several versions of the manuscript. She has also been my helpmate and steadfast companion not only on trips to faraway places, and on mountain trails, but in the other more challenging journeys that make up life.

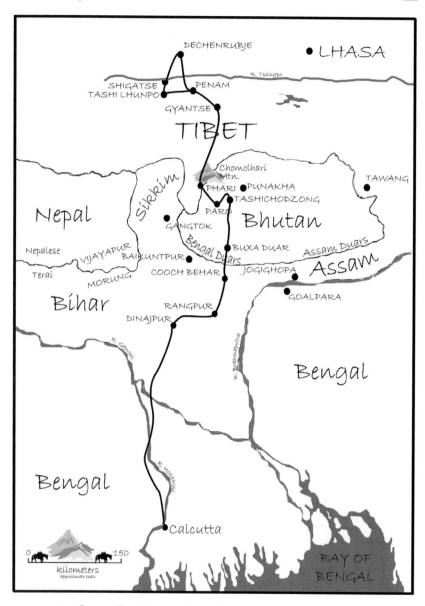

1   George Bogle's route from Calcutta to Tashilhunpo 1774

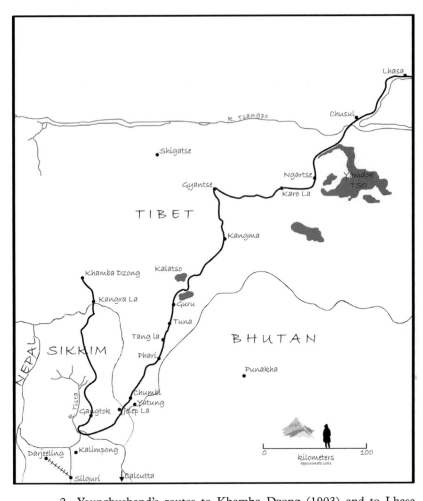

2   Younghusband's routes to Khamba Dzong (1903) and to Lhasa (1904)

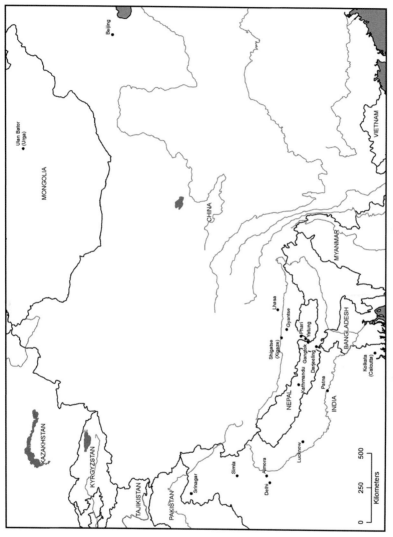

3 Overview of India's Northern Borderlands and China with modern boundaries

Introduction

"We passed the wall into Tibet"

"This is the proudest day of my life and I shall never forget it. We passed the wall into Tibet – which no European had gone through before without opposition." This exultant message was sent on December 13, 1903 by Colonel Francis Younghusband, the leader of the Tibet Frontier Commission, despatched by the British government in India to bring Tibet to heel. It was written as Younghusband and his officers moved up past Yatung in the Chumbi valley towards the high Tibetan plateau. A stone wall had been built to mark the last boundary and Younghusband was relieved to pass it without incident. This sense of excitement about being first into Tibet continued as the armed diplomatic mission fought its bloody way to Lhasa. As Younghusband stood on the mountain pass looking down into the Tsangpo valley, knowing that he was finally within striking distance of "the Forbidden City," he felt another strong surge of anticipation: "This is a day to be remembered. Such a beautiful sight it was. Such a labyrinth of mountains, and down in the valley bottom 4000 feet below us numbers of villages with cultivated lands and trees all round." Once he finally reached Lhasa he was delighted to receive on September 13, 1904 a telegram from the Viceroy of India: "Clear the line. His Majesty the King-Emperor commands me to express to you and all the officers of the Mission his high approval of the admirable manner in which you have brought your difficult Mission to a happy conclusion."[1]

Younghusband misrepresented the historical record in these vaunting letters to his wife Helen. Many Europeans had entered Tibet before him.[2]

---

[1] Francis Younghusband to Helen Younghusband, Camp Rinchingong, December 13, 1903, Younghusband Papers, MSS. EUR. F197/174, British Library [hereafter BL]; Same to Same, Camp on Yamdok Tso, July 23, 1904, F197/177, BL; Same to Same, with a copy of the Viceroy's Telegram, Lhasa, September 13, 1904, F197/177, BL.

[2] A useful one-volume summary of exploration in Tibet is provided in John MacGregor, *Tibet. A Chronicle of Exploration* (London: Routledge and Kegan Paul, 1970). There is a thorough and comprehensive annotated bibliography of Britain's connections with Tibet

Jesuit missionaries had traveled into Tibet from India and China in the 1600s. The Capuchins had even succeeded in briefly establishing a mission at Lhasa in the mid-eighteenth century. In the 1790s Tibet closed its borders with India in an attempt to prevent Europeans meddling in their country. Only then did Tibet become for the West the mysterious land beyond the Himalayas, and Lhasa the forbidden city. When Younghusband wrote of entering Tibet by a route no European had used before he was reflecting a post-1790s European fascination with getting into Tibet. As Donald Lopez observes in *Prisoners of Shangri-La*, Tibet became "an object of imperial desire, and the failure of the European powers to dominate Tibet politically only increased European longing, and fed the fantasy of the land beyond the Snowy Range."[3] By the late nineteenth century "a veritable stampede of Westerners, fired by the tantalizingly incomplete tales of earlier sojourners, had begun to compete to be 'the first' to breach its sacred heart."[4]

Westerners had only a confused understanding of this little-known land. The cover illustration for this book is from a painting by William Alexander, a member of the Royal Academy, who accompanied the Macartney mission to China in 1793. The painting, now held by the Victoria & Albert Museum, is titled "Poo Ta La or Great temple of Fo, near Zehol, Tibet, China." All readers will notice at once that this is not the Potala in Lhasa, which is now perhaps the most instantly recognizable building in the world. It is the Potala temple at Chengde which was completed by the emperor Qianlong (1735–1796) in 1771 and modeled on the real Potala. It was built, as was the rest of the Chengde summer palace complex in the cool mountains north-east of Beijing, to pay homage to Lamaist Buddhism and to symbolize Manchu imperial claims over Tibet and Mongolia.[5] But as the garbled title suggests, it was conflated in Alexander's mind, and by many British viewers at the time, with the actual Potala – or at least it was accepted as an exact replica. No one in Britain knew for sure what the Potala, the seat of the Dalai Lamas, looked like. There were no realistic representations to rival Alexander's finely colored image of the Chengde imitation. To penetrate the Tibet

---

in Julie G. Marshall, *Britain and Tibet 1765–1947. A Select and Annotated Bibliography of British Relations with Tibet and the Himalayan States including Nepal, Sikkim and Bhutan* (London: Routledge Curzon, 2005).

[3] Donald S. Lopez, *Prisoners of Shangri-La. Tibetan Buddhism and the West* (University of Chicago Press, 1998), pp. 5–6.

[4] Orville Schell, *Virtual Tibet. Searching for Shangri-La from the Himalayas to Hollywood* (New York: Henry Holt, 2000), p. 153.

[5] Philippe Forêt, *Mapping Chengde. The Qing Landscape Enterprise* (Honolulu: University of Hawaii Press, 2000), pp. 15, 25, 51, 125.

mystery the British resorted to sending Indian spies, often disguised as Buddhist pilgrims, north across the mountains.[6]

Being the first to get into Tibet – and to see the Potala at first-hand – became an obsession for European travelers and explorers. Younghusband succumbed to this melodramatic mode of thinking when sharing his excitement with his wife. But his mission was not even the first British one to enter Tibet. An expedition had been despatched across the Himalayas as far back as 1774. That mission had been led by George Bogle, a young servant in the East India Company service, who had entered Tibet from the pass at the head of the Pachu valley about thirty miles to the east of the Chumbi route taken by Younghusband. The two routes came together at the small frontier town of Phari to which Younghusband was headed as he wrote these rousing letters to his wife.

During Bogle's four-month sojourn in Tibet, in the winter and spring of 1774–1775, he participated in a series of friendly meetings with the Third Panchen Lama, Lobsang Palden Yeshes (1738–1780), at Tashil-hunpo monastery near Shigatse. The armed diplomatic mission led by Younghusband forced its way into Tibet and, at a ceremony held in the Potala Palace at Lhasa, compelled Tibetan officials to sign a treaty. The first mission took place just as Britain was beginning to establish its empire in India; the second, when British imperial power in India was at its height. When Bogle crossed the Himalayas, the Enlightenment played a significant role in shaping British views of geography and of other peoples and cultures; when Younghusband's invasion took place, a popular imperial ideology modulated British views of the world.

My encounter with the two Tibet missions came in the India Office and Oriental Collections Reading Room (now the Asian and African Reading Room) at the British Library. It was one of those unexpected discoveries that make research in such a rich archive a delightfully rewarding experience. I was reading in the India Office Records about the events of 1903–1904 when I came across a strange incident. Younghusband described a scene in July 1903 at Khamba Dzong, a tiny Tibetan village at the head of a valley just over the Sikkim border. This region was under the administrative authority of the Sixth Panchen Lama, Chokyi Nyima (1883–1937). Urged on by Lhasa, the Panchen Lama sent a delegation to demand that Younghusband dismantle his armed camp and return across the frontier to India. In the course of this meeting Younghusband produced from his baggage a copy of Bogle's narrative describing the 1774 mission (edited and published in 1876 by Sir Clements Markham)

---

[6] D. J. Waller, *The Pundits. British Exploration of Tibet and Central Asia* (Lexington, KY: University of Kentucky Press, 1990).

and flourished the volume in front of the Tibetans. Younghusband told Badula, the chief delegate from the Panchen Lama, that he was following in the friendly footsteps of Bogle. Badula replied that no one at Shigatse had even heard of George Bogle.[7]

This awkward moment of incomprehension about the first official contact between Britain and Tibet back in 1774 surprised me. I wondered what Younghusband was up to. Presumably he claimed a kinship with the Bogle mission because he believed that establishing such a link would provide some reassuring legitimacy to his expedition. In adopting this pose he conveyed the impression that he had embarked on the same kind of peaceful project as Bogle's journey across the mountains. Were these two British missions to Tibet, separated by 130 years, cut from the same cloth? And had Tibetans at Shigatse really forgotten all about the 1774 mission?

Trying to figure out what Younghusband had in mind by yoking himself to the 1774 mission meant following the trail of George Bogle. That trail became even more interesting on a winter afternoon in the Mitchell Library in Glasgow when, working through the Bogle papers, I came across a reference to Bibi Bogle (the lady Bogle), a woman Bogle had apparently married in Bengal. She appeared in the correspondence between Bengal and Scotland because she was still receiving money from Bogle's estate forty years after Bogle himself had died, and the Bogle family lawyers in Glasgow were making pointed enquiries about the pension.[8] Bogle's Indian (or Tibetan) wife and family in Bengal added another intriguing dimension to the story. The possible Tibetan family link has been investigated by Hugh Richardson, the great British

[7] Francis Younghusband to Louis W. Dane, Khamba Jong, July 29, 1903; Diary of Captain O'Connor, Tibet Frontier Mission, Khamba Jong, July 29, 1903 and August 3, 1903, Government of India. Foreign Department. Secret-E. Proceedings, September 1903, Nos. 189–235, Tibet Negotiations, National Archives of India [hereafter NAI]; Younghusband to Helen Younghusband, Khamba Jong, July 30, 1903, Younghusband Collection, MSS. EUR. F197/173; Younghusband to his Father, Khamba Jong, August 2, 1903, Younghusband Collection, MSS. EUR. F197/145, BL. The British always used the form "Khamba Jong." There is still no agreed-upon standard for the transliteration of Tibetan words into English but "Khamba Dzong" is the more common rendering now. "Dzong" means "fort" (although by the 1700s and 1800s many of these forts had fallen into disrepair and had long lost their military function). They often still served as centers for local or regional administration. Since the British used the form "Khamba Jong" that form is retained throughout the text and notes when British sources are cited. It would be tedious and distracting for the reader to change the form every time it comes up. When the British sources are not speaking to us the form "Khamba Dzong" is used.

[8] Colvin Barrett and Company (Calcutta) to Robert Brown (Messrs. Brown and Watson, Glasgow), Calcutta, September 18, 1820, Bogle Papers, Folder George Bogle Miscellaneous [marked 88], Mitchell Library, Glasgow.

Tibetologist, who served as the last British and Indian representative in Lhasa in the 1930s and 1940s before the Chinese invasion of 1950. We shall follow Richardson's pioneering detective work in Tibet and Scotland in an attempt to track down the true story of Bogle's mysterious Bengal marriage.

Bogle's putative wife or wives – Tibetan or Indian or both – introduce the fascinating topic of relationships between British men and Indian women during the imperial era. There is a lively debate about sex, marriage, and concubinage in British India. The issues involved lie at the core of colonial encounters in all their cultural and gendered dimensions. William Dalrymple, the highly respected writer and independent scholar, in his evocative writings on this topic, especially *The White Mughals. Love and Betrayal in Eighteenth-Century India*, depicts the eighteenth century as an era when English and Indians interacted in more mutually respectful ways in sexual and cultural matters than they did in the following century, when more prejudiced attitudes took over. Gyan Prakash, Professor of South Asian Studies at Princeton, and widely admired for his expertise on colonial India, has argued that all these seemingly equal male–female relationships in the 1700s have to be understood in the context of the unwelcome pressure of East India Company power in Bengal which placed all Indians, women and men alike, in subordinate positions.[9] Examining the behavior of Bogle and his friends with respect to Indian (and Tibetan) women – and how things had changed by Younghusband's time – provides illuminating insights into this controversial aspect of empire.

The case of George Bogle raises other big questions about imperialism. Bogle "was a product of the Scottish Enlightenment."[10] He was also an agent of the British empire. His case presents the opportunity for investigating the relationship between the Enlightenment and empire. This relationship has been a central issue in writings on European imperialism ever since the publication of Edward Said's *Orientalism*, one of the seminal books of twentieth-century humanities scholarship, which argued that the West developed stereotyped views of Asian peoples and cultures in the course of justifying their colonial impositions.[11] This book has had an enormous influence on how historians and literature scholars understand the myriad cultural encounters between East and West. The

---

[9] William Dalrymple, "Plain Tales from British India," *New York Review of Books*, April 26, 2007, pp. 47–50; Gyan Prakash, "Inevitable Revolutions," *The Nation*, April 30, 2007, pp. 25–30.

[10] Alastair Lamb, ed., *Bhutan and Tibet. The Travels of George Bogle and Alexander Hamilton 1774–1777* (Hertingfordbury, Hertfordshire: Roxford Books, 2002), vol. I, p. 9.

[11] Edward Said, *Orientalism* (New York: Pantheon, 1978).

word "orientalism" has become almost unavoidable when reading and writing about empires and about Western views of non-Europeans.

An unexpected example of Said's ubiquitous influence on our understanding of the British empire erupted into public view when the National Maritime Museum at Greenwich opened its permanent gallery on the empire. There was an almighty public row when the exhibition was promoted by a poster of a Jane Austen-like figure sipping tea, with a bowl of sugar on the table at her side. On the floor below her, a black hand stretched in supplication through the hatch of a slave ship. The unmistakable message was that polite society in imperial Britain depended on the cruelty of slave labor.[12] This picturing of the empire was derived from a chapter in Said's *Culture and Imperialism* which used Jane Austen's *Mansfield Park* to argue that polished and enlightened English society benefited from slavery in the empire while generally ignoring its existence. When Fanny Price, the dependent poor relation staying with the family in the comfortable country house of her more refined cousins, dared to raise the topic of slavery there was "a dead silence" at the dinner table. It is only by reading the silences in such iconic sources as Jane Austen's novels, argued Said, that we can appreciate what the empire wrought within European cultures and how non-British "others" were viewed – or not viewed.[13] The Empire Exhibition controversy over the faceless slave brought out critics of Said but his theories about empire lay at the center of the heated public debate in British newspapers at the time – as they are at the center of many scholarly debates on European imperialism.

But as often happens in scholarship (and in life generally) what was an illuminating conceptual breakthrough has turned into a confining orthodoxy. Said was sophisticated and open-ended in his thinking. Much of the derivative scholarship has promoted a dogmatism which too easily designates the Enlightenment as the protean causal force behind all European empires. By privileging European science and rationalism over other ways of knowing, so the argument runs, the Enlightenment led Europeans to adopt superior, condescending, and prejudiced attitudes to peoples they encountered round the world. This led into the Orientalist mentalities of the nineteenth century which viewed Asian cultures and states (and by extension, all non-European peoples) as stagnant, backward, and exotic in contrast to the energetic, progressive, and normal developments in Europe. Thus, the "Enlightenment project" led to European colonial impositions round the world. Shelley Walia's *Edward Said and the Writing of History* is a characteristic example of this approach. It is a

---

[12] "Empire Show Arouses Pride and Prejudice," *The Guardian*, August 23, 1999.
[13] Edward Said, *Culture and Imperialism* (New York: Alfred A. Knopf, 1993), pp. 80–97.

useful and clearly written book directed at an international audience. Walia sums things up in a matter-of-fact manner (with the suspects identified by capital letters): "the Enlightenment project emphasised Reason and Progress which could only issue forth from the Western mind. Said shows that the Enlightenment ideals of Reason and Progress had a hidden agenda: that of creating a successful imperial practice."[14]

Such propositions about the Enlightenment and empire have become axiomatic in many scholarly circles round the world, but there have been some challenges to this piece of conventional wisdom. Sankar Muthu's *Enlightenment Against Empire* has drawn attention to major Enlightenment-era writers (Denis Diderot, Immanuel Kant, and Johann Herder) who "attacked the very foundations of imperialism."[15] Jennifer Pitts in *A Turn to Empire. The Rise of Imperial Liberalism in Britain and France* has noted that many of the key intellectual figures of the late eighteenth century, such as Adam Smith and Jean-Antoine-Nicolas Condorcet, launched "a critical challenge to European conquest and rule."[16]

On both sides of the debate the issues have been defined by the ideas of major European thinkers. The learned commentaries by J. G. A. Pocock on the connections between eighteenth-century philosophers and European imperial ideologies are an example of how complex and erudite the discussion can become.[17] In the four volumes of his *Barbarism and Religion* series, Pocock traces the intellectual genealogies of historians and philosophers, beginning with an examination of "the Enlightenments of Edward Gibbon" and continuing on with Voltaire, David Hume, William Robertson, and many other greater and lesser stars in the intellectual firmament of eighteenth-century Europe. The title of Pocock's grand enterprise refers to the "Enlightenment narrative" which eighteenth-century writers thought they were engaged in – the story of Western society's descent from the bright world of classical antiquity into the darkness of barbarism and religion before emerging into the new dawn of the Renaissance and enlightened civil society of the 1700s.[18]

---

[14] Shelley Walia, *Edward Said and the Writing of History* (Duxford, Cambridge: Icon Books, 2001), p. 36.

[15] Sankar Muthu, *Enlightenment Against Empire* (Princeton University Press, 2003), p. 258.

[16] Jennifer Pitts, *A Turn to Empire. The Rise of Imperial Liberalism in Britain and France* (Princeton University Press, 2005), p. 1.

[17] J. G. A. Pocock, *Barbarism and Religion*, vol. IV *Barbarians, Savages and Empires* (Cambridge University Press, 2005). Three previous volumes of this *magnum opus* on *Barbarism and Religion* were published by Cambridge between 1999 and 2003.

[18] W. Clark Gilpin, "Enlightened Genealogies of Religion: Edward Gibbon and His Contemporaries," *The Journal of Religion* 84 (April 2004), p. 257. This is a review article of Pocock's first three volumes.

According to this view of the course of history, Europe was now inter-acting with regions of the world where barbarism and religion still per-sisted in varying degrees of intensity. This encounter between Europe (now seen as enlightened) and the rest of the world captured the imagi-nation of intellectuals in the eighteenth century. Pocock's own narrative is a densely complex one. He agrees with the view that there was not one single Enlightenment but "a plurality of Enlightenments which cannot be appropriately grouped together and unified by the employment of the definite article."[19] As in all his work, Pocock is meticulous in showing the intricate histories of the phrases and concepts behind the specu-lations and theories of eighteenth-century thinkers. But even Pocock's sympathetic critics admit his books are a challenge. As Robert Booth of the University of Wisconsin kindly put it, Pocock's work "is hardly for the general reader." All his volumes are "magnificently learned" and "knowingly allusive." B. W. Young of Christ Church College, Oxford, admiringly sums up Pocock as "an historian's historian . . . [and] not, in any sense, an easy read."[20]

We shall return to some of Pocock's observations later when dealing with Bogle's views on India and Tibet, but my simple point here is that the writings of even such formidable scholars as Pocock offer only one window into understanding the relationship between the Enlightenment and European expansion overseas. It is hard to imagine an agent of the British empire carrying in his intellectual baggage all the subtle under-standings of history and philosophy that are featured in Pocock's four volumes, or for that matter, in Sankar Muthu's close study of his three philosophical giants. It is in this context that George Bogle is such a treasure. His view of the world was certainly shaped by the Enlighten-ment but he was no Gibbon or Voltaire or Diderot. Through him we can see Enlightenment ideas in day-to-day action rather than as they are painstakingly delineated in learned treatises.

These two moments of British imperial contact with Tibet therefore provide a less rarefied but, as we shall see, a revealing perspective on the relationship between the Enlightenment and the British empire. Con-trasting the Enlightenment-era Bogle with the Victorian and Edwardian imperialist Younghusband will bring into sharper focus some of the key issues at stake. Was the Enlightenment the source for the exclusionary and destructive aspects of imperial ideologies? Both Bogle and Younghusband wrote extensively about their encounters with Tibet but neither one was

---

[19] Pocock, *Barbarism and Religion*, vol. I *The Enlightenments of Edward Gibbon 1737–1764* (Cambridge University Press, 1999), p. 138.

[20] Robert Booth's review of *Barbarism and Religion* vols. I and II, in *American Political Science Review* 94, 2 (2000), p. 451; B. W. Young's review of *Barbarism and Religion* vol. III, in *Albion* 36 (Autumn 2004), pp. 528–529.

a study-bound thinker. They were merchants, diplomats, and soldiers. Through these two workaday emissaries of empire we can explore the relationship between Enlightenment and empire in more down-to-earth terms. We can understand the way the relationship worked in real historical circumstances rather than in the theories of philosophers.

The northern borderlands of India run along the Himalayas, the highest mountain range in the world. For many Tibetans and Indians much of this mountain landscape is spiritualized by myth and religious belief as the home to gods, demons, and spirits. For many British and other Westerners the Himalayas have become a place to demonstrate prowess in exploration or mountain climbing. For the peoples who lived in the shadow of the Himalayas the mountains were never a barrier closing off communication. Humans have often migrated across the mountain passes between Tibet, Nepal, Sikkim, Bhutan, and Ladakh, a well-known example being the Sherpa people who made their way from Tibet to the Solo Khumbu region of Nepal south of Chomolungma (Mother Goddess of the World) in the 1500s. The British later named this mountain Everest and employed Sherpas like Tenzing Norgay to help them make the first ascent in 1953. This "conquest of Everest" allowed many British newspapers at the time to claim a grand late-imperial triumph at the dawn of a new Elizabethan age.

In spite of its inaccessibility, the region has also often been fought over, most recently in 1962 as China and India clashed over disputed sections of their Himalayan boundary. During the British era, the Indian border with Tibet was pushed to the outer limits of Kashmir, Garwhal, Sikkim, and Assam. The Himalayas were never a barrier to trade as commercial routes snaked their way up high valleys and passes into Tibet from towns in north India and Nepal. The Bogle and Younghusband missions were (among other things) attempts by the British to insert themselves into these ancient trans-Himalayan trade routes connecting India with Central Asia and China.

In a lifetime of meticulous scholarship devoted to these northern borderlands of India, Alastair Lamb has made himself a respected authority. I have made use of all his writings including his two great framing narratives, *Britain and Chinese Central Asia. The Road to Lhasa 1767 to 1905* and *British India and Tibet 1766–1910*. More recently Lamb has edited a volume of primary-source material on Bogle himself – *Bhutan and Tibet. The Travels of George Bogle and Alexander Hamilton 1774–1777*.[21]

---

[21] Alastair Lamb, *Britain and Chinese Central Asia. The Road to Lhasa 1767 to 1905* (London: Routledge and Kegan Paul, 1960); Lamb, *British India and Tibet 1766–1910* (London: Routledge and Kegan Paul, 1986); Lamb, ed., *Bhutan and Tibet*, vol. I *Bogle and Hamilton Letters, Journals and Memoranda*.

I have also learned a great deal from Alex McKay's three-volume *History of Tibet*, which brings together most of the significant modern writings on the history of that country, its cultures, and its regions.[22] McKay's comprehensive introduction to the history of Tibet, and his informative commentaries in each volume, have been extremely useful. As we shall see, what McKay has to say about the current state of history writing about Tibet, particularly the vexed topic of Tibet's relationship to China, can be surprisingly helpful in achieving a clearer perspective on Eurocentric discourses about the motivating ideologies behind empires.

Shortly after I began following the trail of George Bogle, I discovered that Kate Teltscher was already well ahead of me. All of her insights have been brought together in her book *The High Road to China. George Bogle, the Panchen Lama, and the First British Expedition to Tibet*.[23] After she had spoken to a mutual friend, Professor Jyotsna Singh (who writes on Renaissance travel writing and empire), I shared with her one of my then unpublished papers on Younghusband's theatrical invocation of Bogle which she made use of in her own book. I am greatly indebted to Kate Teltscher for her informative commentary on Bogle. The Younghusband Expedition of 1903–1904, which turned into the British invasion of Tibet, is a much better-known episode in British imperial history than Bogle's mission. There are two highly readable books which provide vivid descriptions – Peter Fleming's swashbuckling account *Bayonets to Lhasa*, and Patrick French's compelling biography *Younghusband. The Last Great Imperial Adventurer*.[24] First-rate books by Indian, British, and Tibetan scholars (all taking a less ethnocentric approach than Fleming) have explained the broader imperial and Asian contexts for understanding the British march to Lhasa in 1904.[25]

The Bogle and Younghusband missions to Tibet were widely separated episodes in imperial history, but they were brought into the same frame of reference at Khamba Dzong in July 1903 when Younghusband chose to make use of Bogle in his meeting with the Tibetan delegates sent by the

[22] Alex McKay, ed., *The History of Tibet*, 3 vols. (London: Routledge Curzon, 2003).

[23] Kate Teltscher, *The High Road to China. George Bogle, the Panchen Lama, and the First British Expedition to Tibet* (London: Bloomsbury, 2006).

[24] Peter Fleming, *Bayonets to Lhasa. The First Full Account of the British Invasion of Tibet in 1904* (New York: Harper, 1961); Patrick French, *Younghusband. The Last Great Imperial Adventurer* (London: HarperCollins, 1994).

[25] Parshotam Mehra, *The Younghusband Expedition. An Interpretation* (Bombay: Asia Publishing House, 1968); Premen Addy, *Tibet on the Imperial Chessboard. The Making of British Policy towards Lhasa 1899–1925* (London: Sangam Books, 1985); Alex McKay, *Tibet and the British Raj. The Frontier Cadre 1904–1947* (Richmond: Curzon Press, 1997). Tsepon W. D. Shakabpa, *Tibet. A Political History* (New Haven: Yale University Press, 1967), pp. 154–155, 204–223, briefly situates both missions in a general account of Tibetan political history.

Panchen Lama. I delve further into the linkage in this study because of the conceptual issues that swirl around these two British-Tibetan encounters. Bogle's mission was about trade and economics; Younghusband's was about the defense of British India, and the Great Game between Britain and Russia for influence in Central Asia. The missions were inspired by two of the most famous proconsuls who ruled British India. Bogle was sent by Warren Hastings who survived the denunciations of Edmund Burke and Richard Brinsley Sheridan during his impeachment trial in Westminster Hall to become admired in Victorian Britain as the founder of the British empire in India. Younghusband was sent by George Curzon, the most ostentatious of the Viceroys, who sometimes ruled the British *Raj* in the style of a Mughal emperor, and proudly declared he was "an imperialist heart and soul."[26] Hastings and Curzon initiated these missions and remained closely involved as they followed the progress and wrote letters of encouragement to the agents they had despatched across the Himalayas. These two British–Tibetan encounters speak to all the major topics associated with imperialism – trade and economics, war and geo-politics, ideologies and cultural assumptions, and sexual relationships between colonizers and colonized.

There is one more intriguing dimension to all this. The Panchen Lamas, operating from their monastic seat at Tashilhunpo (which misled the British into calling them the "Tashi" or "Teshoo" Lamas), were deeply revered spiritual figures but they also played important political, administrative, and diplomatic roles in Tibet. They had to deal with the sometimes rival authority of the Dalai Lamas in Lhasa; they had to negotiate with Chinese power in Tibet; they had to oversee routine administrative tasks in their region of Tibet, the southern districts of the province of U-Tsang. As we shall see, the two British envoys engaged with them in mundane political and diplomatic matters. The prime concern of the Panchen Lamas however was to promote spiritual wisdom. As major figures in Tibetan Buddhism, incarnations of Amitabha, the Buddha of Wisdom, they were leading exemplars of, and commentators on, the path to enlightenment. So in the first of these British encounters with Tibet we have a meeting of two versions of enlightenment – one largely secular, the other entirely spiritual. This confrontation between two human attempts at enlightenment will also tell us something significant about the shaping forces behind empires.

Tibet was never part of the British empire, of course, but it lay along the northern frontier of the British *Raj* in India. E. M. Forster once observed that "only what is seen sideways sinks deep." Alan Bennett,

---

[26] David Gilmour, *Curzon* (London: John Murray, 1994), p. 164.

author of *The History Boys*, that captivating exploration of the nature of history, and the teaching of history – which played to packed houses in London and New York, and has since been turned into a movie – likes this Forsterian observation, and confesses his "great faith in the corner of the eye."[27] Looking at these two encounters with Tibet is looking at the British empire from outside – from beyond its edge. From that corner-of-the-eye perspective we may arrive at deeper insights into the great debate about the Enlightenment and imperialism. The comparison will also reveal the evolving nature of the British empire. Besides, following this journey of the British empire to the roof of the world is a good story. Both Bogle and Younghusband were prolific correspondents. In addition to the lengthy official reports to their imperial masters, they wrote many letters to family and friends attempting to convey their immediate impressions as they made their way across the Himalayas to Tibet. At times the letters read like adventure narratives. As Herodotus showed us over two thousand years ago, telling seemingly odd stories about history can be an effective way of recapturing the past.

[27] Alan Bennett, *Untold Stories* (London: Faber and Faber, 2005), p. 476.

1   An Enlightenment narrative 1774

The first contact between Britain and Tibet took place in March 1774 when a letter from Lobsang Palden Yeshes, the Third Panchen Lama, was delivered to Warren Hastings, the Governor of Bengal. The Panchen Lama, whose monastic seat of Tashilhunpo was near Shigatse, was acting as a peacemaker in the war between the East India Company and the small Himalayan state of Bhutan. The Panchen Lama had intervened because Bhutan had many cultural and political ties to Tibet, its very name deriving from the Sanskrit word "Bhutanta" meaning "end of Tibet."[1] By the time the letter was received in Calcutta hostilities had already ended, but Hastings decided to take advantage of the Panchen Lama's intervention to open broader negotiations between Bengal and Tibet, the ultimate goal being to use Tibet as a back door to the Chinese empire. George Bogle, the young Scotsman who was sent by Hastings to meet the Panchen Lama, left an array of writings about his Tibet mission. He kept a journal, he sent letters to friends and family, and he compiled memoranda and reports for Hastings and the governing Council at Calcutta. The narrative which emerges from many parts of these writings seems to represent the Enlightenment at its best.

Bogle was tolerant, curious, and open-minded. He viewed Bhutanese and Tibetan cultures as interesting examples of human achievement. He avoided thinking in terms of superior or inferior, backward or advanced. Bogle's attitude was that Tibetan and Bhutanese cultures presented new ways (for the British) of understanding the universal human condition. During his time in Bhutan, Bogle wrote that lamas "enlighten this corner of the world."[2] Three months into his stay at Tashilhunpo, he sent a letter home criticizing some earlier accounts of Tibet, such as John Bell's *Travels from St. Petersburg in Russia to Diverse Parts of Asia* (1763), which

---

[1] Nirmala Das, *The Dragon Country. The General History of Bhutan* (Calcutta: Orient Longman, 1974), p. 1.

[2] George Bogle, "History and Government of Bhutan," in Lamb, ed., *Bhutan and Tibet*, p. 96.

had taken a dim view of Lamas and their influence throughout Central Asia. Bogle attempted to open the eyes of his correspondents to the achievements and status of these major figures in Tibetan society. "The Teshoo Lama is taken note of in Bell's *Travels*," Bogle informed his father, "but the disrespectful Manner in which he, and most Writers, speak of the Lamas, appears to me highly unjust." He explained that "the Lamas in Thibet are not only Pontiffs: they are also Temporal Princes." In Bogle's view they possessed all the virtues and worldly knowledge that Europeans would expect to see of men in such elevated positions.

Bogle took on directly the argument that European learning, since the Renaissance and the invention of printing, had surged ahead of other regions of the world. He pointed out that Europeans esteemed the thinkers of ancient Greece who were now viewed as important contributors to the new knowledge that had been created and disseminated since the 1400s. He put the Panchen Lama in the same august company:

A Lycurgas or a Solon are justly called wise although they were ignorant of all those Arts, and all that Learning with which Printing and Geography have deluged the world. In this light Teshoo Lama will appear to be endowed with very superior Parts, and an enlarged mind. He is well acquainted with the State of China, of all the different countries of Tartary, and also of Hindostan. He has the more Merit in his knowledge on account of the difficulty of acquiring it.[3]

Bogle's respectful observations during the 1774–1775 mission stand in stark contrast to the commentaries made during the 1903–1904 British expedition to Tibet. An editorial in *The Times* referred to "these obstinate ecclesiastical potentates" who dared defy the British, and Younghusband told the Viceroy, Lord Curzon, that the Tibetans were "nothing but slaves in the power of the selfish and ignorant monks who hold the supreme authority at Lhasa."[4]

Bogle was not an intellectual but he was shaped by Enlightenment culture. From the books he had in his Calcutta library, and from references he made in his letters and journals, it is evident he had at least a partial knowledge of some of the major writers of the era. He knew something of Charles-Louis de Secondat Montesquieu (1689–1755) on methods of cultural comparison, and of the ideas of Hugo Grotius (1583–1645) and Samuel Pufendorf (1632–1694) on international law. He had some acquaintance with Georges-Louis Leclerc de Buffon's (1708–1788)

---

[3] George Bogle to his Father, Tashilhunpo, January 8, 1775, Bogle Papers, MSS. EUR. E226/77(i), BL.

[4] *The Times*, August 8, 1904, p. 7; Francis Younghusband to George Curzon, Camp Chumbi, Tibet, January 1, 1904, Younghusband Collection, MSS. EUR. F197/80, BL.

Histoire naturelle on the history of the earth and geographical explanations for the variation of species in nature; and he had read William Robertson's (1721–1793) *History of the Reign of Charles V*, with its influential analysis of the impact of the Spanish empire in the Americas. When Bogle died at Calcutta in 1781 his library contained most of the standard works that we associate with Enlightenment Europe.[5]

But Bogle was also an agent of empire. He worked to expand British trade into Tibet and, as he and his patron Warren Hastings hoped, on into China. His last post in Bengal was as Collector at Rangpur, near the border with Bhutan, where he meted out Company justice and used Company troops to enforce revenue collection.[6] His various writings on his experiences in India and Tibet present us with an opportunity to investigate the relationship of the Enlightenment to empire by moving away from an elite intellectual context, and looking at some of the core issues through the eyes of an ordinary participant in Britain's imperial enterprise in India. If Bogle can be taken as a modestly representative figure of the Enlightenment, his commentaries on India, Bhutan, and Tibet will open up common or garden perspectives on how the Enlightenment and empire were intertwined.

Bogle was born in 1746, the same year that the Jacobite clans from the Scottish Highlands were defeated at Culloden in the last military challenge to the Hanoverian dynasty. Like many mercantile and landowning families in lowland Scotland, the Bogles had fully committed themselves to the 1707 union with England, and to the Hanoverian succession in 1714. They felt no kinship with the savage Highlanders who had disturbed the peace in the 1715 and 1745 Jacobite uprisings. They were benefiting economically from the union with England, above all by participating in the English colonial system. Bogle's father and grandfather had made their fortunes in the North American trade, like many Glasgow family businesses, profiting from the tobacco shipped to Glasgow from the Chesapeake colonies and sent on to markets throughout Britain and Europe.

On the other side of the world from America there were plenty of openings for young Scots in the ranks of the East India Company. They could

---

[5] Account Sales of the following Effects belonging to the Estate of the late George Bogle Esq. deceased, sold at public auction the 18th, 19th, and 20th September last by orders of Claud Alexander and David Anderson Esq. the Administrators, Bogle Papers, Folder GB [marked 9], Mitchell Library, Glasgow.

[6] Warren Hastings and Council to George Bogle, Collector at Rangpur, Fort William, October 10, 1779, *Bengal District Records. Rangpur*, vol. I *1770–1779*, ed. W. K. Firminger (Calcutta, 1914), BL.

serve as Writers (clerks) in the Company, and hope to make money, as they worked their way up the Company's seniority system, by trading on their own behalf within India. They could also enlist as officers or surgeons in the Company's army, military service being a favorite route for former Jacobites to work themselves back into legitimacy. No one in the Bogle family in the mid-1700s would have insisted on being called Scottish. They were Scottish by birth and culture (Bogle found "the Berwickshire 'r' which I inherit from my mother" a problem when attempting to speak to the Bhutanese[7]) but the class of Scottish society which George Bogle came from sought opportunities in London and the empire. One of Bogle's descendants complained in a letter to *The Sunday Times* in 1948 that Bogle was Scottish rather than English, and that he should be so described in all writings pertinent to the first British contact with Tibet.[8] But this was a later sensibility about Scottishness. George Bogle and his family had no difficulty in describing themselves as English, or perhaps North British, as they benefited from full participation in the expanding economy at home and in the colonies.

The Bogles were a typical entrepreneurial and landed family of lowland Scotland. The wealth of Bogle's grandfather, earned from the Atlantic economy, including some participation in the slave trade, had enabled him to buy a country estate at Daldowie about eight miles up the Clyde valley from Glasgow. Bogle's father continued to make money in the Atlantic trading system and played a prominent role in the life of the city. He was educated at Leyden University in the Netherlands and was elected three times as Lord Rector of Glasgow University. By the time of Bogle's birth the family had been a significant presence in the Glasgow merchant community for three generations. The family's prosperity was intimately linked to the ups and downs of empire. The London company associated with the family was dissolved in 1769 during the dislocation in the Atlantic networks caused by the non-importation strategy of the American colonists in response to the Townshend duties. George's eldest brother Robert (called Robin within the family) then went to Grenada to run a sugar plantation but suffered a series of commercial losses in the early 1770s. By 1773, the estate at Daldowie was faced with severe debt problems because its accounts were entangled with Robert's debts.

When the family fortunes hit this rough patch in the 1770s, Bogle's father expected his son George to send home remittances from Bengal to help extricate the estate from its financial woes. During his time in

---

[7] George Bogle to David Anderson, Lambaolong, Bhutan, June 20, 1774, David Anderson Papers, Add. 45421, f. 30, BL.

[8] *The Sunday Times*, February 15, 1948, pp. 2, 6 and February 22, 1948, p. 6.

India, Bogle sent back money every year for this purpose – by 1781 he had managed to remit £4,500.[9] For the Bogles, as for many Scottish families making their way in the commercial world of post-1707 Britain, the empire was not an ideological construct but a practical place where opportunities abounded to make (and lose) fortunes.

The family was also typical in valuing education as a necessary means of gaining knowledge and skills to advance in the world of business, and as an essential aspect of being part of polite society. Bogle attended the University of Edinburgh for one year in the 1760–1761 session, and then moved to London where he completed a three-year commercial course at Enfield, north-east of London, to prepare him for work in accounting, book-keeping, and general business practices. The family was not wealthy enough to be able to send its sons on the grand tour of Europe to complete their education, but in 1764 Bogle did spend several months in France accompanying a sick friend.

At Edinburgh Bogle took courses in logic. He also read Montesquieu – or at least his father thought he was doing so.[10] He did not stay long enough to graduate but that was not unusual during these years at Edinburgh. Most of the young men who attended simply took courses that interested them, or courses delivered by professors reported to be popular. Alexander Grant, in his history of the university, noted that

after 1708 it was not in the interest or concern of any Professor in the Arts faculty (except for the Professor of Natural Philosophy who got fees for laureating his class) to promote graduation... This became most decisively apparent in the middle of the eighteenth century; in 1749 there were only three graduates, and after that date down to the very end of the century only one or two persons were admitted in each year to the Master of Arts degree.

Since graduation was not a goal, students simply took courses as their interests swayed them. "The main subjects of Arts teaching were there but each Student attended such classes as he or his friends might think advisable."[11] Thus no significance should be read into Bogle's partial attendance and the absence of graduation – though that meant his scholarly knowledge was more limited than would have been the case had he attended for the full four years.

Nor should his stint at the Enfield commercial academy be dismissed as merely practical. The stadial theory of human history, developed

<hr/>

[9] Lamb, *Bhutan and Tibet*, pp. 5, 6.

[10] George Bogle (father) to Bogle, Daldowie, September 19, 1761, Bogle Papers, Box: India and Tibet, Folder George Bogle 1762–1769 [marked 49], Mitchell Library.

[11] Alexander Grant, *The Story of the University of Edinburgh* (London: Green & Co., 1884), pp. 265, 277.

by Scottish thinkers in the 1700s, posited that human societies moved progressively through successive phases – from hunting and gathering, to pastoral, to feudal, to commercial. In this taxonomy of history there was ever greater refinement and civilization, culminating in the modern commercial stage (which English society was now enjoying). All aspects of society involved in these transformations were worthy of study – indeed, a major postulate of the theory was that at each stage there were identifiable features of society produced by the material circumstances at that moment of development. One of the characteristic products of the Scottish Enlightenment was the three-volume *Encyclopedia Britannica* brought out "by a Society of Gentlemen in Scotland" in 1771. In that first edition of the *Encyclopedia Britannica* the subject of "Book-Keeping" took up thirty-eight pages where "Botany" occupied only twenty-six.[12] All those taken on as Writers in the Company were required to produce "a certificate of proficiency in commercial arithmetic and book-keeping."[13] In the polite and commercial world of eighteenth-century Britain, mastery of such subject matter was esteemed – and Bogle worked to achieve it.

This era was the golden age for the Scottish universities, above all Glasgow and Edinburgh, and for Scottish writers and intellectuals. In these years the Scottish Enlightenment was respected throughout Europe. The ideas that flowed from all the intellectual energy shaped many of the fields in our modern social scientific systems for understanding the world, so much so, that one author has claimed that the Scots "invented the modern world."[14] Bogle attended Edinburgh just before the principalship of William Robertson, the historian whose works on *Europe in the Age of Charles V* (1769) and *History of America* (1777) had a profound impact on how the European world understood historical change. Robertson's tenure was the high-water mark for Edinburgh's reputation across Europe. Bogle's stint at Edinburgh came too early for him to have attended any of Robertson's lectures, but he referred to Robertson briefly in one of his Tibet letters – and he had several of Robertson's volumes in his Calcutta library.

From other references in his Tibet journals, we also know that he had an acquaintance at least with the works of Grotius and Pufendorf on natural law and the law of nations. In October 1774, for example,

---

[12] *Encyclopedia Britannica or A Dictionary of Arts and Sciences Compiled upon a New Plan*, 3 vols. (Edinburgh, 1771), vol. I, pp. 582–620, 627–653.

[13] Suresh Chandra Ghosh, *The Social Condition of the British Community in Bengal 1757–1800* (Leiden: E. J. Brill, 1970), p. 28.

[14] Arthur Herman, *How the Scots Invented the Modern World* (New York: Crown Publishers, 2001).

after Bogle crossed his last Himalayan pass and entered the Tibetan village of Phari, he learned of a lively legal dispute over the fate of some Bhutanese rebels who had sought refuge in Tibet. The question was whether they should be allowed to remain in Tibet or be sent back to Bhutan to face punishment. In this remote spot on the Tibetan border Bogle casually revealed that he had done some reading in these classic sources on international law. He reported that the debate "was as full of the principles of government and the law of nations, as if it had been conducted by Grotius and Pufendorf."[15]

Bogle was never a scholar, however. His student diary mentions night escapades in Edinburgh but no books or lectures. He always carried whatever learning he had lightly. When referring to philosophers and famous writers in his own letters, he typically wrote in an ironic, light-hearted manner (as in this incident at Phari). But that posture is what makes him so interesting. Although not an intellectual, he was a rough-hewn product of the Enlightenment culture of contemporary Scotland – and for that reason he is perhaps more representative of his times than the intellectual coteries who spent their lives in learned investigations and discussions of Montesquieu, Grotius, and Pufendorf.

After finishing his studies at Enfield, Bogle worked for a time in the Bogle & Scott firm in London. The business connections there, along with the family network, helped him secure an appointment as a Writer in the East India Company. These posts usually went to gentlemanly candidates. The directors of the Company were "businessmen, merchants or bankers, or professional men, or members of the gentry [and] they selected candidates . . . from among their own kind. Thus the Writers and cadets recruited for Bengal between 1757 and 1800 had a similar class background."[16] Bogle's ancestry and the estate at Daldowie qualified him on that score. His grandmother was a daughter of Sir John Lockhart who had held high legal office under Charles II; his mother was the daughter of Sir John Sinclair, who could claim descent from James I. The family did not move in such exalted court and aristocratic circles by the time Bogle appeared on the scene but that background was one factor in their claim to gentility. Once in Bengal he would be assigned duties either in Calcutta or in one of the Company posts up country. His name was duly noted in the little red book which listed all the Company's employees with their date of appointment – seniority mattered in the Company. He arrived in Calcutta on the East Indiaman the *Vansittart*, on August 19, 1770.

---

[15] Bogle's Journal, October–November 1774, Lamb, *Bhutan and Tibet*, p. 139.
[16] Suresh Ghosh, *British Community in Bengal*, pp. 30, 32.

The East India Company had begun as a trading enterprise, relying on a royal monopoly in the trade between India, south-east Asia, China, and Britain. By 1770 the three main trading posts or factories in India were at Calcutta, Madras, and Bombay (now Kolkata, Chennai, and Mumbai). By the middle decades of the eighteenth century, as the Mughal empire weakened and regional powers began emerging, the Company transformed itself into a territorial power in India as it tried to protect and improve its position in an increasingly unstable setting. The expansion was most rapid in Bengal. Following the attempt of the local ruler, the Nawab of Bengal, Siraj-ud-daula, to expel the Company, the British used local allies such as Mir Jafar to manage a victory at the battle of Plassey in 1757. The Company then installed Mir Jafar as a compliant nawab, enabling the British to play a dramatically larger role in the province. In the aftermath of the battle of Buxar in 1764, the weakened Mughal emperor Shah Alam II recognized the Company as the *diwan* of Bengal. This gave the Company the legal right to collect revenue and administer the province. Bengal became a territorial bridgehead for the British from which they would eventually expand their rule across much of the subcontinent.[17]

Bogle's early career in Bengal reflected the new position of the Company as the government of the province, and as a new regional power in India. His first post was in the office of the Select Committee at Fort William in Calcutta. This committee was responsible for the political affairs of the Company in Bengal, and for its "foreign relations" – that is, for relations with the neighboring powers, from the Mughal emperor in Delhi, to the Company's ally, the Nawab Vizier of Oudh, to small polities, such as Cooch Behar, on the northen border of Bengal. The Select Committee was "in effect the Secretariat to the Bengal Governor." Bogle's work in that office immediately forced him to begin learning the necessary languages – Hindi (Hindustani), Bengali, and, above all, Persian, the language of the Mughal court and of diplomacy between the regional states in north and central India.

Bogle's linguistic accomplishments were one of the things that Warren Hastings noted when he took over in 1772 as Governor and President of the Council in Bengal. In that year Bogle was appointed private secretary to Hastings, and Assistant Secretary to the Board of Revenue, which enabled him to develop expertise in the revenue-gathering practices throughout the province. The following year he was made Registrar of the newly created Sadar Adalat Court in Calcutta which heard appeals

---

[17] P. J. Marshall, *Bengal. The British Bridgehead. Eastern India 1740–1828* (Cambridge University Press, 1987).

in civil cases involving revenue issues from all over the province.[18] These multiple offices held by Bogle graphically show how the Company had taken over executive, revenue-raising, and legal power in Bengal. About one year after Hastings' arrival in Calcutta, Bogle's promotion to Secretary of the Select Committee gave him a prime position in which he could learn about the complex relations in which the Company was engaged with all surrounding states and rulers.

The mission to Tibet was a direct consequence of what was happening in one of these neighboring states. Dharendra Narayan, the Raja of Cooch Behar, a small state lying between Bengal and Bhutan, requested assistance from the Company to expel Bhutanese invaders. In return for this military help, he agreed to enter into a treaty relationship with the Company. Under the terms of the treaty, signed in April 1773, the Raja of Cooch Behar agreed "to acknowledge subjection to the English East India Company upon his country being cleared of its enemies, and will allow the Cooch Behar country to be annexed to the province of Bengal." The Company was also permitted to retain one half of the revenues of Cooch Behar.[19] In such ways did the Company expand its possessions in eighteenth-century India, while being able to claim, with a degree of plausibility, that it was doing so in concert with Indian rulers.

Cooch Behar became one of the 500 or so princely states that remained loyal clients of the British right down to 1947. The 1773 treaty made with Raja Dharendra Narayan set the tribute at half the annual revenue but in 1780 it was fixed at 67,700 rupees. By 1867 the British had awarded the rulers of Cooch Behar a thirteen-gun salute, and in 1884 granted them the titles of Maharaja and Bahadur. The Maharajas of Cooch Behar reciprocated as expected by remaining loyal supporters of the British *Raj*. Buckland's *Dictionary of Indian Biography* of 1906 noted approvingly that the current ruler, Maharaja Sir Nripendra Bhup Bahadur of Cooch Behar, GCIE [Grand Commander of the Indian Empire], "has visited England several times; is a keen sportsman and has excelled in polo, tennis, and other games."[20] From the British point of view he had become an ideal Indian prince. These were some of the manifold ways of acquiring and maintaining power for the British in their Indian empire. Back in 1773 the future rise of the British *Raj* across the entire subcontinent was

---

[18] Lamb, *Bhutan and Tibet*, pp. 5–6.

[19] Lamb, *Bhutan and Tibet*, p. 29; *Memoranda on the Indian States* (New Delhi, 1940), pp. 102–103, BL; Amba Prasad, ed., *Fort William-India House Correspondence and Other Contemporary Papers Relating Thereto. Secret and Select Committee 1752–1781*, vol. XIV (New Delhi: National Archives of India, 1985), pp. lxxvii, 299.

[20] C. E. Buckland, *Dictionary of Indian Biography* (London, 1906), p. 92, BL.

anticipated by no one. Dharendra Narayan simply needed British help urgently to expel the Bhutanese soldiers, and he got it – for a price.

In response to this plea for help, the Company sent troops northwards and successfully defeated the forces of the Deb Rajah of Bhutan. It was this military campaign against Bhutan that led to the intervention of the Panchen Lama. At this time, the Panchen Lama was a highly significant figure in Tibet. He had considerable room to play an almost autonomous role. The current Dalai Lama (Jampal Gyatso [1758–1804], the Eighth Incarnation) was still a minor, and a regent ruled at Lhasa. The Panchen Lama's letter to Warren Hastings implied that he was in charge of Tibet. "The said Deb Rajah," he informed Hastings, "is dependant upon the Dalai Lama who rules this country with unlimited sway (but on account of his being in his minority, the charge of the government and administration for the present is committed to me)."[21] The question of who exercised power in Tibet was more complicated than that phrasing suggests, but at the time Hastings took it at face value and thought he was dealing with the ruler of Tibet. The Panchen Lama stated in his letter that he was "the rajah and Lama of this country with which you have no doubt been acquainted by travellers from these parts."[22] The letter was delivered to Calcutta by Padma, a personal representative of the Panchen Lama, and Purangir Gosain, a Hindu pilgrim and trader who was to prove of immense help as the British tried to open up communications across the Himalayas.

The Panchen Lama, or the Panchen Rimpoche – "the precious gem of wisdom" – was the incarnation of the Dhyani Buddha, Amitabha. There has always been some controversy over this incarnation. One tradition that prevailed in Lhasa, and reflected Lhasa's commitment to the primacy of the Dalai Lama, was that the incarnation was first recognized by the Fifth Dalai Lama, Ngawang Lobsang Gyatso (1618–1682), and named Abbot of Tashilhunpo monastery. As Alastair Lamb explains,

the essential point in this tradition is that the Panchen Lama was more concerned with compassion and meditation rather than with issues of practical government. However, in the Tashilhunpo tradition it was held that the Incarnation identified by the Dalai Lama was the third appearance of the incarnation who had already appeared three times.

Thus Lobsang Palden Yeshes could either be referred to as the Third Incarnation (by Lhasa's count), or the Sixth (by the Tashilhunpo count). The issue has become intensely political in recent times because the

[21] Letter from the Tashi (Panchen) Lama to Warren Hastings (received in Calcutta, March 29, 1774), Lamb, *Bhutan and Tibet*, pp. 37, 38.

[22] *Ibid.*, p. 37.

Chinese use the Tashilhunpo tradition while "those influenced by current movements of Tibetan separateness from China adhere to the other [the Lhasa tradition]."[23] The nomenclature issue was further complicated when the British referred to the Panchen Lama as the "Tashi Lama" because of his monastic seat at the monastery of Tashilhunpo. Other foreigners sometimes adopted the same usage. When the British Resident at Kathmandu attended meetings during the Younghusband mission, the Nepalese and Chinese diplomats he spoke to referred to the Panchen Lama in the same way, and for parallel reasons spoke of the Dalai Lama as "the Potala Lama" because of his seat at the Potala palace at Lhasa.[24]

In his letter to Hastings, the Panchen Lama presented himself as a simple religious figure, distressed by warfare between Bhutan and the Company troops, and anxious to mediate a peace between the two sides. "As to my part, I am but a fakir, and it is the custom of my sect, with rosary in our hands, to pray for the welfare of mankind, and for the peace and happiness of the inhabitants of this country," he began, "and I do now, with my head uncovered, entreat that you may cease all hostilities against the Deb in the future." The Panchen Lama conceded that the Bhutanese had started the fighting. "I have been repeatedly informed," he frankly confessed to Hastings,

that you have been engaged in hostilities against the Deb Judhur, to which, it is said, the Deb's own criminal conduct in committing ravages and other outrages on your frontier, has given rise. As he is of a rude and ignorant race (past times are not destitute of instances of the like misconduct, which his own avarice tempted him to commit), it is not unlikely that he has now renewed the instances; and the ravages and plunder which he may have committed on the skirts of Bengal and [Cooch] Behar provinces has given you provocation to send your vindictive army against him.[25]

The only Tibetan sources we have for the British mission in 1774 – the official biographies of the Eighth Dalai Lama and the Fourth Panchen Lama, and the 'autobiography' of the Third Panchen Lama – all show that at this time the Tibetans viewed Hastings as "the lord of Bhangala [Bengal]" or "the lord of Kal-la-ka-dha [Calcutta]."[26] They knew of the British takeover in Bengal and the military capability of the Company's

---

[23] Note on the Panchen (or Tashi) Lama, Lamb, *Bhutan and Tibet*, pp. 38, 39.

[24] Lieutenant Colonel Ravenshaw (Resident in Nepal) to Secretary of the Foreign Department, Government of India, February 7, 1904, India Office Records, L/PS/7/162, Tibet Mission Correspondence, BL.

[25] Letter from the Tashi (Panchen) Lama to Warren Hastings, Lamb, *Bhutan and Tibet*, p. 37.

[26] Luciano Petech, "The Missions of Bogle and Turner according to the Tibetan Texts," *T'oung pao* 39 (1950), pp. 340, 344.

army from pilgrim-merchants like Purangir, and from diplomatic representatives sent to Tashilhunpo by other rulers in north India, such as the Raja of Benares, Chait Singh. The Panchen Lama took care to mollify this new power with flattery at the same time as he tried to educate this new player on the Indian scene about the Buddhist values he represented:

Having been informed by travellers from your quarter of your exalted fame and reputation, my heart, like the blossom of spring, abounds with gaiety, gladness and joy; praise that the star of your fortune is in ascension; praise that happiness and ease are the surrounding attendants of myself and family. Neither to molest or persecute is my aim; it is even the characteristic of my sect to deprive ourselves of the necessary refreshment of sleep, should an injury be done to a single individual. But in justice and humanity I am informed you far surpass us. May you ever adorn the seat of justice and power, that mankind may, under the shadow of your bosom, enjoy the blessings of happiness and ease.[27]

At this stage, as we have noted, Hastings thought that the Panchen Lama was the ruler of Tibet. It was on that basis that Hastings developed his policy. He had three objectives. One was simply to consolidate Company authority along Bengal's northern borderlands. A second consideration was that the Gurkha conquests in Nepal were closing off the trade routes from the Ganges valley to Tibet through Kathmandu and the Nepalese passes. The Gurkha takeover in Nepal prompted the Company to see if it could expand the trans-Himalayan trade through Bhutanese routes. The third and grander prospect beyond these regional benefits was access to China. The Tibet route might prove to be an avenue into China at a time when the Company was restricted to the port of Canton and prohibited from making direct diplomatic contact with the court in Peking.

For Hastings, improving trade with Tibet was also part of a strategy to recover the Company's trading and financial position which was being undermined by the new administrative costs in Bengal, and the substantial military expenditures it was now incurring across India. His long service in Madras and in Bengal had given him a deep understanding of the underlying economic factors. The Company's predicament by the 1770s involved two commodities – tea and silver. The Company needed tea from China; the Chinese required payment in silver. The first tea imports had reached Britain in the 1660s, marked by a special presentation of a few pounds of the rare commodity to Charles II in 1664. By the early 1700s, the Company was importing about £100,000 each year into Britain; by the 1760s, the total had risen to about £10,000,000. Britain,

---

[27] Letter from the Tashi (Panchen) Lama to Warren Hastings, Lamb, *Bhutan and Tibet*, p. 37.

like other western European states, had been able to obtain silver by various mechanisms from the Spanish silver mines in Central and South America, but this system had been thrown out of kilter by the Seven Years' War (1756–1763). During that war the British had briefly held Manila in the Philippines, which had also been a destination for some of the South American silver. If the Company could more effectively tap into the trading networks of south-east Asia that trade might provide additional sources of silver. Alexander Dalrymple, a Company servant who had traveled widely in south-east Asia and along the Chinese coast between 1758 and 1762, was one of the first to advocate the expansion of Company trade in the region east of India to gain access to non-British sources of silver.

Related to this general approach to the Company's economic predicament was the attempt to gain access to markets in China by some other route than the port of Canton with its severe restrictions on foreign traders. So the Bogle mission was the beginning part of this grand plan to ease the Company's position in India by expanding trade with neighboring economies, and, in the case of Tibet, hoping that it would provide an open door into China.[28]

In the course of his journey through Bhutan and into Tibet Bogle wrote to many different people, from Governor Hastings, to his sisters and his father at Daldowie, to friends in the Company service in Bengal. It is possible to piece together all these different voiced accounts and present a composite travel narrative of his Tibet mission. There was no publication of his correspondence in Bogle's lifetime. It was not until 1876 that Clements Markham, then Head of the Geographical Section at the India Office in London, and later President of the Royal Geographical Society, put together some East India Company records and family correspondence to which he had been given access, and published a version of Bogle's travels to Tibet.[29]

Notwithstanding the absence of any publication during Bogle's own lifetime, there was some public awareness in England of the Tibet mission. When Bogle's friend John Stewart returned to London he delivered a lecture to the Royal Society in 1777 which was based on some of the manuscript journals.[30] Hastings also corresponded with contacts in

---

[28] Kate Teltscher, *The High Road to China. George Bogle, the Panchen Lama and the First British Expedition to Tibet* (London: Bloomsbury, 2006), pp. 1–6; Lamb, *Bhutan and Tibet*, pp. 19–27.

[29] Clements Markham, ed., *Narratives of the Mission of George Bogle to Tibet and of the Journey of Thomas Manning to Lhasa* (New Delhi: Manjusri, 1970 [London, 1876]).

[30] John Stewart, "An Account of the Kingdom of Thibet," Royal Society, *Philosophical Transactions* (1777), reprinted in Lamb, *Bhutan and Tibet*, pp. 372–382.

London about the possible publication of Bogle's travels. Hastings was so impressed by Bogle's journals and letters that he approached no less a figure than Samuel Johnson about the prospect of publishing a volume on the mission to Tibet. He sent a copy of Bogle's journals to Johnson. "The accompanying sheets," Hastings explained,

contain the journal of a friend of mine into the country of Tibet, which, though bordering on this, has till lately been little known to the inhabitants of it as if it were at a distance of many degrees. The people, their form of government, their manners, and even their climate differ as much from Bengal as Bengal does from England. When I read your account of your visit to the Hebrides, I could not help wishing that a patron of that spirit which could draw so much entertainment and instruction from a region so little befriended by nature, or improved by the arts of society, could have animated Mr. Bogle, the author of this journal, but I flatter myself that you will find it not unworthy of your perusal.

Hastings also included in the packet sent to Johnson copies of some of the letters from the Panchen Lama, who appeared as such an appealing character in Bogle's account. "I confess I received great pleasure from it [Bogle's journal]," Hastings continued,

and I assure myself that whatever originality you may discover in the description of the countries and inhabitants of which it treats, you will at least be pleased with the amiable character of the Lama, which has been confirmed to me by the testimonies of other travelers who have visited his capital. I have added to the journal two letters from him, one of which furnished me with the first hint of deputing Mr. Bogle to his presence, and the other contains the issue of his negotiations.[31]

Hastings saw this as an opportunity to make a name for himself as the patron of this remarkable narrative. As Bogle's first reports came in from Bhutan, Hastings was captivated and urged Bogle to persist in his efforts to gain permission to enter Tibet. "Having engaged in this Business, I do not like to give it up," Hastings wrote, "we shall both acquire reputation from its success."[32] Travel narratives were popular in eighteenth-century Britain. John Hawkesworth's *Voyages* (1773), which followed Captain Cook's explorations in the Pacific, were enjoying great success. The story of idyllic Pacific islands, navigational triumphs, and "freely available women" had made the book a bestseller and "helped to establish Cook as a national hero."[33] Hastings opened up his hopes for a similar publishing success in a letter to Bogle. "I feel myself more

[31] Extract from Warren Hastings to Dr. Samuel Johnson, Fort William, August 7, 1775, Lamb, *Bhutan and Tibet*, pp. 346–347.
[32] Warren Hastings to George Bogle, Fort William, August 10, 1774, Warren Hastings Papers, Add. 29117, f. 61, BL.
[33] Teltscher, *The High Road to China*, p. 50.

interested in the success of your Commission than in Reason perhaps I ought to be . . . Go on and prosper – Your Journal has travelled as much as you, and is confessed to contain more matter than Hawkesworth's three Volumes."[34]

It is interesting to note too that Hastings had no difficulty in placing this Tibet journey alongside Johnson's own journey to the remote Highlands and islands of Scotland ("your account of your visit to the Hebrides"). This was a piece of flattery designed to persuade Johnson to take an interest but it also shows that notions of the exotic were not confined to "oriental" subject matter. The remote western Highlands and islands of Scotland, the mountains of Tibet, and the Pacific islands were all strange locations. They could easily be included within the same frame of reference.

Reflecting its varied audiences – Hastings, the Council members, his family, and his friends – Bogle's account of his journey is diverse in content and style. At its core was a utilitarian travel narrative. Bogle was despatched to negotiate trade matters with the Bhutanese and Tibetans. He was on Company business and was being paid by Company money. Much of the narrative discusses trade and currency issues of immediate concern to the Company's activities in Bengal. The language and topics become more personal in the letters to his friends and family. For Hastings and Bogle there was also that potential public audience to write for. From very early in the enterprise, Hastings encouraged Bogle to write in a style that might appeal to a public in England keen to read about travels in parts of the world unknown to Europeans. Bogle concentrated on commercial matters for the Company, but Hastings urged him to approach his travels with a broader vision than the commercial concerns of the Company. "Be not an economist," Hastings advised his young protégé in September 1774, "if you can bring home splendid vouchers of the land which you have visited."[35]

Bogle was characteristically open about his own motives for accepting the chance to go to Tibet:

The Governor having occasion to send a person with some despatches to the Lama of Tibet, thought proper to pitch upon me, and I readily accepted of the commission. I was glad of the opportunity which this journey through a country hitherto unfrequented by Europeans would give me of showing my zeal for the Governor's service, at the same time that it gratified a fondness I always had for travelling, and would afford me some respite from that close and sedentary business in which I had for some years been engaged.

---

[34] *Ibid.*, p. 51.
[35] Hastings to Bogle, Fort William, September 8, 1774, Lamb, *Bhutan and Tibet*, p. 122.

The terms were generous. Bogle would be allowed to keep the posts he held in Bengal, and the continuing closeness between him and Hastings augured well for his future career in Bengal. "I was to be continued in my offices at the Presidency, and allowed to act by deputy during my absence," Bogle proudly announced to his sister, "and Mr. Hastings was also pleased to assure me that whatever might be the issue of this commission, I might depend upon the continuance of his favour."[36]

Bogle headed for Tibet to indulge his pleasure in traveling to new places, but also to forward his career in the Company. He was a dedicated Company servant; he had taken pains to learn the necessary languages to conduct business and diplomacy in Bengal and north India; and he was determined to get ahead up the Company's ladder of promotion. He had been appointed as a Writer in the normal way – through family connections and business patronage. He mixed well with all the other young employees, and he worked assiduously in his various offices in Calcutta. As he set out for Tibet he was by all outward signs a typical East India Company man – a representative example of the British presence in India at the time. Let us follow him on his journey from the plains of Bengal through the Bhutanese mountains and up through the high passes into Tibet.

Bogle wrote one of his early letters just as he crossed over Buxaduar – the first mountain pass that led into Bhutan. The letter was to his friend David Anderson, another Scot in the Company who at this time held the post of Persian translator at Murshidabad. Bogle and Anderson enjoyed a warm, jocular relationship. Bogle was pleased to have already received a letter from his friend. He was struck by how efficient the postal system was, even in this apparently remote and inaccessible country. "Your Hooghly letter," he delightedly told Anderson,

reached me at the first Stage within the Hills. I am pleased to find your Ideas about Dawks [the postal system] as mistaken as my own; for there is a Vast Satisfaction in having Companions in Error. We may laugh at the Italians for calling every man born beyond their Mountains Barbarian; but we are certainly bred up with the same arrogant Principles. We are taught to think there can be no Police without a Quorum or a Sir John Fielding... no Justice without [Sir Edward] Coke upon Littleton, and no regular conveyance of letters without a Post Office General and alphabetical Pigeon Holes.[37]

[36] Bogle's Journals, The Journey to Tashichodzong, May–August 1774, *ibid.*, p. 59.
[37] George Bogle to David Anderson, Lamboolong, June 20, 1774, David Anderson Papers, Add. 45421, f. 11, BL.

This letter offers a strong hint that Bogle was eager for new experiences. He was already anticipating that the journey would provide him with the pleasure of looking at things from fresh perspectives, and his travels might well jolt him out of some of the "arrogant Principles" that all people assume when they judge others by their own standards.

He was forced to stay in Bhutan for almost three months because of the reluctance of the Tibetan authorities to allow him cross their border. He spent most of that time at the palace-fortress of Tashichodzong, the residence of the Deb Rajah. Built of timber in 1642, the palace had been destroyed by fire in 1772 and was newly reconstructed when Bogle arrived.[38] Bogle was held up in Bhutan because the Tibetans refused to allow him to proceed. The Panchen Lama later explained to Bogle what had happened. The regent for the Dalai Lama at Lhasa, and the Chinese Ambans stationed there, had tried to block Bogle's entry. "The obstacles to my journey arose chiefly from Gesub Rimpoche," Bogle reported. This "Gesub" in Bogle's narrative was Demo Tulku Jampel Delek, who was acting as the regent for the infant Dalai Lama. (The Eighth Dalai Lama, Jampal Gyatso, was born in 1758, recognized in 1763, formally acknowledged by the Panchen Lama in 1765, and came fully of age in 1781.) "Soon after my arrival at Dechenrubji [one of the Panchen Lama's monasteries]," Bogle reported to Hastings, "the Tashi Lama gave me one of his [the Regent's] letters in which he advised Tashi Lama . . . to find some method of sending me back, either on account of the violence of the smallpox, or on any other pretence. It was upon this letter that the Tashi Lama wrote to me to return to Calcutta."[39]

This was one of the many occasions on which Purangir Gosain proved invaluable, for he agreed to go on to Tashilhunpo, carrying letters from Bogle pleading his case. As Bogle noted, "My hopes of success are founded on the Gosain."[40] In his plea to the Panchen Lama, Bogle explained the purpose of his mission – that the Company deeply appreciated his mediation efforts, that the Company had already stopped fighting and had restored Bhutanese territory to the Bhutanese, and that now the Governor of Bengal wished to send this embassy to thank him. The letter, claimed Bogle, "procured me admittance." But in the meantime, these negotiations kept Bogle at Tashichodzong.

While Bogle was waiting for a reply from the Panchen Lama a civil war broke out in Bhutan between supporters of the deposed Deb Rajah,

---

[38] Lamb, *Bhutan and Tibet*, p. 58.

[39] Extract from Bogle's letter to Hastings, Paro, Bhutan, April 27, 1775, Lamb, *Bhutan and Tibet*, pp. 204–205.

[40] Bogle's Report on the Negotiations, Tashichodzong, July 5–14, 1774, Lamb, *Bhutan and Tibet*, p. 90.

who had fought against the Company, and the Dharma Rajah, normally head of the clerical establishment, who had taken over both religious and secular power. In these circumstances, which threatened to end his mission even before it got started, it would have been easy for Bogle to rail against Tibetan intransigence and Bhutanese intrigue and violence. But as he talked to officials and rode about the valley he developed some understanding of Bhutanese society. He sent many of his servants back to Bengal and was able to mix more directly with the local people. "If I am to acquire knowledge I must lay aside the Governor's deputy [role] and mix with the people on a more equal footing."[41]

The overall picture he painted of Bhutan was a sympathetic one. He tried to make sense of the political and administrative structures, and as his knowledge of them improved he came to admire these structures. The Bhutanese state had been created in the 1600s by Ngawang Namgyal (1594?–1651) who took the title of Shabdrung. After his death, a doctrine of multiple incarnations was adopted – with "mental" aspects being carried on by successive Dharma Rajahs, who represented spiritual authority, and the "verbal" incarnations, the Deb Rajahs, representing secular leadership (as, for example, in military campaigns). As Michael Aris helpfully explains, "the system bears a close comparison to that of Tibet under the Dalai Lamas. Bhutan's religious potentate is commonly known as the Shabdrung but sometimes as the Dharma Raja or 'King of Religion'. In theory he delegated his secular powers to a regent called the Druk Desi who ruled in his name; this regent is sometimes referred to as the Deb Raja."[42] The Deb Rajah and the Dharma Rajah were normally identified and then elected by a council of high monastic officials. The system thus contained an attempt to separate religious and secular authority, and involved some elective mechanisms.[43] Bogle noticed all these features:

So far from being barbarian, which with transalpine arrogance is too often considered as the lot of every native unknown to Europeans I found a little state governed by a regular and strict police, independent by the situation of the country, and subject to an elective government which though absolute was checked by the free spirit of the people, unawed by mercenary troops, and apt to rebel when treated with oppression. The inhabitants, living in a country where a subsistence is with difficulty obtained, with little money, with less ambition, and bartering

[41] *Ibid.*, p. 87.
[42] Michael Aris, *The Raven Crown. The Origins of Buddhist Monarchy in Bhutan* (London: Serindia Publications, 1994), p. 11.
[43] Bogle's Journals, May–August 1774, entries on Tashichodzong the Capital of Bhutan; Bogle's Journals, History and Government of Bhutan, May–August 1774, Lamb, *Bhutan and Tibet*, pp. 67, 70, 96.

the different necessaries of life by trade, or an intercourse with strangers, and under a very strong sense of religion, are industrious, faithful, hospitable, honest, grateful and brave.[44]

An appealing example of Bogle's growing ability to move outside his own cultural reference points, and to see how the world looked from other perspectives, came as he crossed the border into Tibet. The first halting place was Phari. He described an incident that took place as he and his party left the village to continue on the trail to Gyantse. As they headed out over the plateau the great snow peak of Chomolhari (almost 22,000 feet high) dominated the landscape. Here is Bogle's account of what happened next:

One of Padma's servants carried a branch of a tree with a white handkerchief tied to it. Imagining it to be a mark of respect to me and my embassy, I set myself upright in my saddle; but was soon undeceived . . . We rode over the plain till we came to a heap of stones opposite to a high rock covered with snow . . . When the fire was well kindled . . . they began their rites. Paima acted as chaplain. He chanted his prayers in a loud voice, the others accompanying him, and every now and then the little cup was emptied toward the rock. About eight or ten of these libations being poured forth, the ceremony was finished by placing upon the heap of stones the little ensign, which in my fond imagination had before offered up to my own vanity. The mountain to which this sacrifice was made is named Chumalhari. It stands between Tibet and Bhutan and is generally white with snow. It rises almost perpendicular like a wall, and is attended with a string of smaller rocks which obtain the name of Chumalhari's sons and daughters.[45]

Bogle's companions – Hindus and Buddhists alike – had been doing a *puja* to the mountain goddess who was believed to inhabit this striking peak. This was Bogle's first exposure to the Tibetan view that landscape was suffused by spirit presences. As Alex McKay points out, while this "understanding of the landscape as empowered" appeared in Indian and other Asian settings too, it was "emphasized within the Tibetan cultural world to a greater degree."[46]

The incident is telling as it shows Bogle making more adjustments to the new world he had been moving into since he had left Bengal. He began his journey with an assumption of his own centrality as an important British emissary in this remote part of the world. As he watched the ceremony below Chomolhari he understood how mistaken that assumption

---

[44] Bogle's Journals, History and Government of Bhutan, May–August 1774, Lamb, *Bhutan and Tibet*, p. 95.

[45] Markham, *Bogle*, p. 5; Bogle's Journals, The Journey to Tibet, Pharidzong to Dechenrubje, October–November 1774, Lamb, *Bhutan and Tibet*, p. 139.

[46] McKay, *History of Tibet*, vol. II, p. 10.

was. He noticed that he and the cultural values he carried with him were not necessarily at the center of things.

This revelation set the stage for many of Bogle's subsequent observations and commentaries during the rest of his journey and his five-month sojourn with the Panchen Lama. The jocular open-mindedness of that early letter to David Anderson was also manifest in Bogle's sympathetic exchanges with many Tibetan people. In the course of these exchanges he was often forced to question his own cultural assumptions. Another sign of this open attitude came shortly after the incident at Chomolhari. This time the issue was hunting. There were plenty of game animals -- antelopes, kyangs, and hares – and Bogle wanted to shoot them. The Panchen Lama's representative, Padma, objected. Bogle described the debate that took place:

We should have had excellent sport, but for my friend Padma's scruples. He strongly opposed our shooting, insisting that it was a great crime, would give much scandal to the inhabitants, and was particularly unlawful within the liberties of Chumalhari. We had many long debates on the subject, which were supported on his side by plain commonsense reasons drawn from his religion and customs; on mine by those fine-spun European arguments, which serve rather to perplex than convince. I gained nothing by them, and at length we compromised the matter. I engaged not to shoot till we were fairly out of sight of the holy mountain, and Padma agreed to suspend the authority of the game laws in solitary and sequestered places.[47]

Bogle was displaying a certain cockiness here but he was at the same time entering into dialogue with Padma. He took Padma's explanations seriously, and he recognized the self-serving nature of his own defense of European views on hunting.

As the party moved into more settled agricultural areas of Tibet once they were beyond Gyantse, Bogle was impressed by the neatness and efficiency of the villages and farms. "The valley to the north of Penam-dzong," he noted, "was by far the most populous I had yet seen. The villages stand very thick. A small town called Ghadong is built on the side of one of the hills, and the houses being all whitened make a good appearance." The previous day he had noted how the Tibetan farmers prepared feed for their stock.

I met here also a machine for cutting straw for cattle, but it is not worthy of description. As I remember what a great discovery the cutting of straw was considered in England, I mention it only to show that nations undervalued by

[47] Bogle's Journals, The Journey to Tibet, Pharidzong to Dechenrubje, October–November 1774, Lamb, *Bhutan and Tibet*, p. 141.

Europeans can, without the assistance of Royal Societies, find out the useful arts of life, and for the rest, whether they be of advantage to mankind or otherwise is a question above my reach.[48]

Bogle is poking fun here at the contemporary British scene during the intense period of agricultural transformation when animal breeding and crop management were regarded as matters of national importance – when "Farmer George" was on the throne and methods for improving practices in the field or farmyard were the topic of learned papers at Royal Society meetings. By drawing attention to the Tibetan farming practices he is, even through the heavy irony, recognizing that Tibetan farmers had skills and talent similar to their British counterparts. Tibetan farmers were equally adept in these "useful arts of life."

By this stage in his journey Bogle thought he had seen enough to make some tentative comparisons between Bhutanese and Tibetan societies. In developing these comparisons Bogle seems to have been influenced by Montesquieu's *Spirit of the Laws* (1748) which argued that differences in populations could be explained in terms of varying geographical conditions. When Bogle had stood on the first hills beyond Bengal and looked back over the Indian plains, he had briefly ruminated on all the different changes that "volcanoes, inundations, and earthquakes have produced on the face of the globe" which seems to be a reference to Buffon's seven epochs of the earth's history.[49] He then turned from "these antediluvian reveries" to the more immediate theme of how nature "fits the inhabitants for their respective [geographical] situations." So this concept of human societies being shaped by geography was certainly Bogle's starting point.

He was struck by how "robust and well-built" the Bhutanese were compared to Tibetans. "One might seek for the cause of this in the difference of soil and climate. I will endeavour to account for it on another principle, because it may throw some light on the way of life among each people." Bogle's new principle emerged from the contrasting nature of labor in each society. "Labour certainly renders a man strong," he reasoned,

caeteris paribus, a blacksmith or a carpenter will be stronger than a tailor or a barber. I have already mentioned the toilsome life of the Deb Rajah's subjects. The nature of this country [Tibet] exposes its inhabitants to no such hardships. The hills, although in many places abundantly steep and high, are so bare and sterile that they are left in a state of nature. The valleys only are cultivated, and

[48] *Ibid.*, pp. 145, 146.
[49] Bogle's Journals, From Cooch Behar to Tashichodzong, May–August 1774, Lamb, *Bhutan and Tibet*, p. 63.

the roads lead through them which cuts off all climbing of mountains. Goods are chiefly carried on bullocks and asses; the corn is trod by cattle, and ground by water-mills, and the country producing no forests, the inhabitants are free from the hard labour of hewing down trees, and transporting them from the tops of mountains.[50]

Bogle's claim to have discovered "another principle" here is weak, but the fact that he made such a claim at all reveals that he viewed himself as engaged in an emblematic discussion of his time on explanations of cultural differences. Bogle's opening statement referring to climatic factors is derived from Montesquieu's and Buffon's theories, and his own argument that differing labor demands held the key is simply a derivative proposition related to the general geographical conditions in Tibet and Bhutan. Such reasoning shows Bogle, in a characteristic Enlightenment mode, trying to make sense of variations between societies in terms of natural conditions rather than any inherent qualities which made one society superior or inferior to another. Bogle's conclusion was that humans adapt to their environments and that those adaptations explain why there are so many differences among human societies.

Bogle's commentaries on the postal service in Bhutan, the Bhutanese political system, agricultural practices in Tibet, and differences between Bhutanese and Tibetans were all made from an outside perspective. Bogle saw things as he traveled, he talked to his companions on the mission – to Padma, who was Tibetan, and to Purangir, who was a Bengali with years of experience in these regions – and he had held many conversations with Bhutanese officials during his enforced stay at Tashichodzong. But the next stage of his journey was to be a substantially different kind of experience. Once he reached the small monastery of Desheripgay, where the Panchen Lama was staying because of a smallpox epidemic in Shigatse, Bogle entered into a remarkable personal relationship with the Panchen Lama. They held many conversations across a wide range of subjects. In these conversations we can see again how Bogle was open to other perspectives, and how attuned he became to non-European ways of looking at the world.

Bogle had his first meeting with the Panchen Lama on the afternoon of November 9, 1774. As the Panchen Lama sat cross-legged on his cushioned throne Bogle "laid the Governor's presents before him, delivering the letter and pearl necklace into his own hands, together with a white pelong handkerchief on my own part, according to the custom of the

---

[50] Bogle's Journals, The Journey to Tibet, Pharidzong to Dechenrubje, October–November 1774, Lamb, *Bhutan and Tibet*, pp. 143, 144.

country."[51] Bogle took an immediate liking to the Panchen Lama. His descriptions of these first meetings are full of respect and admiration. Over the course of the next four months, a deep affection developed between the two men. At their first ceremonial meeting, Bogle reported that the Panchen Lama "received me in a most engaging manner." Thereafter, the Panchen Lama met with Bogle frequently "without any ceremony." The two men were able to talk together in Hindustani without translators. They covered a wide range of topics from current events in Tibet, India, and China to philosophy, religion, cosmology, and history. Bogle described how the Panchen Lama

would walk with me about the room, explain to me the pictures, make remarks on the colour of my eyes etc. For although venerated as God's Viceregent through all the eastern countries of Asia, endowed with a portion of omniscience, and with many other divine attributes, he throws aside, in conversation, all the awful part of his character, accommodates himself to the weakness of mortals, endeavours to make himself loved rather than feared, and behaves with the greatest affability to everybody, particularly to strangers.[52]

During his stay at Desheripgay Bogle elaborated on the character of this revered figure whose hospitality he now enjoyed. "The Tashi Lama is about forty years of age, of low stature, and though not corpulent, rather inclining to be fat." Bogle was taken by his benign disposition and the way in which he established easy and pleasant relations with all his visitors. "The impression of his countenance is smiling and good humoured," Bogle reported.

His father was Tibetan; his mother a near relation of the Rajahs of Ladakh. From her he learned the Hindustani language, of which he has a moderate knowledge, and is fond of speaking it. His disposition is open, candid, and generous. He is extremely merry and entertaining in conversation, and tells a pleasant story with a great deal of humour and action.

Bogle could find no one who had anything bad to say about the Panchen Lama. "I endeavoured to find out in his character those defects which are inseparable from humanity, but he is so universally beloved that I had no success, and not a man could find it in his heart to speak ill of him."[53]

On one occasion, as he witnessed the Panchen Lama's reception by the people of Shigatse, when the Lama's entourage made its way back to Shigatse, Bogle contrasted this occasion with public demonstrations of

---

[51] Bogle's Journals, Dechenrubje and the Return to Tashilhunpo, November–December 1774, Lamb, *Bhutan and Tibet*, p. 150.
[52] *Ibid.*, p. 151.   [53] *Ibid.*, p. 151.

loyalty in contemporary England. At such ceremonies in London cannons would be fired from the Tower and laudatory verses written by the Poet Laureate to stimulate expressions of loyalty. Bogle was impressed by the more profound expressions of veneration that the Panchen Lama evoked without any such prompts. As the entourage approached Tashilhunpo monastery Bogle described the scene:

From the resting place till we arrived at Tashi Lama's palace the road was lined on both sides with ranks of spectators. They were all dressed in their holiday clothes. The peasants were singing and dancing. Almost three thousand gylongs [monks], some with large pieces of chequered cloth hung upon their breasts, others with their cymbals and tabors, were ranked next to the palace. As Tashi Lama passed they bent half forwards and followed him with their eyes. But there was a look of veneration mixed with joy in their countenances which pleased me beyond anything, and was a surer testimony of satisfaction than all the guns in the Tower, and all the odes of Whitehead [William Whitehead, Poet Laureate, 1757–1785] would have given. One catches affection by sympathy; and I could not help, in some measure, feeling the same emotions as the Tashi Lama's votaries.[54]

In this description Bogle puts Tibetan and British public rituals on equal footing, and suggests there was a more genuine and profound display of affection in the Tibetan case. The distinction between secular and religious rule was a significant difference to be sure, but the King of England was also head of the Church of England, and the Panchen Lama had some civil administration responsibilities as well as his religious role. The comparison is a rough one; the interest lies in the fact that Bogle was open to making such a comparison. Whatever qualifications are made, it is evident that Bogle was prepared to give Tibetan public rituals just as much credit as British ones.

The placing of Tibetan and European customs on a footing of equality was a sustained posture of Bogle's during his time in Tibet. His experiences at Tibetan ceremonies, along with the informative conversations with the Panchen Lama, helped him gain some distance from his own familiar cultural bearings. He began to understand the universal human tendency to make crude formulations about others who are unknown or strange. This awareness was apparent during an exchange with the Panchen Lama on the subject of religion. The conversation began with the Panchen Lama inquiring about Bogle's religion as he "desired to know the name of my great priest or guru." Bogle replied that "as the language of my country was entirely different from his, he could not

---

[54] Bogle's Journal from Dechenrubje to Tashilhunpo, December 1774, Lamb, *Bhutan and Tibet*, p. 173.

understand our names." The Panchen Lama pressed the issue, asking if Bogle and the British "worshipped the Criss; making a cross with his fingers, and adding that there were formerly [at Lhasa] some Fringy [European] padres who worshipped the Criss, but they bred disturbances, and were turned out of the country."

This turn in the conversation, with its reference to the Capuchin missionaries who had been expelled from Lhasa in 1745, forced Bogle to think how the Panchen Lama was viewing Christian Europe. The Jesuits had reached eastern Tibet in the 1600s, and in 1661 two Jesuits, J. Grueber and A. d'Orville, had stayed in Lhasa on their overland journey from Peking to India. The Jesuits had been followed by the Capuchins who set up their mission in Lhasa in the 1720s. The Panchen Lama's knowledge of Christianity came from what he knew of these Roman Catholic orders and their teachings. He was also seeing it from the outside, from the perspective of his own religion – just as Bogle struggled to understand the religion of the lamas from his Christian perspective. For Bogle, the difference between a Capuchin monk and a Scottish Presbyterian was an important piece of cultural knowledge, but for the Panchen Lama the difference mattered little, for they were all Christians.

As they conversed about such matters, Bogle suddenly thought he understood the core problem in these attempts at cross-cultural understanding. He tried to convey his insight in what for him was clearly a noteworthy moment in the conversation.

I replied that the Chinese and the people of Hindustan, and of his country, gave the name Fringistan to all the lands on the west side of the world, which are divided into fifteen or twenty separate kingdoms, of different languages and religions, governed by their respective princes, and independent of one another. In the same manner the people of my country comprehended under the name of Asia, China, Bengal, Surat, Tibet and many other states, with which he was unacquainted; but he well knew that China and Bengal were at an immense distance, unconnected and almost opposite to one another in almost every particular.[55]

Bogle had been taken aback by the Panchen Lama's uniform view of Europe. As he listened he was jolted into an awareness that Europeans had similarly simplified views of Asian countries. This conversation with the Panchen Lama enabled Bogle to see how both East and West, Asia and Europe, viewed each other in over-simplified ways. The fact that

[55] Bogle's Memorandum on Negotiations with the Tashi Lama, November 1774, Lamb, *Bhutan and Tibet*, p. 215. The word "Fringies" for Europeans (and hence "Fringistan" for Europe) had come through Arabic and Persian words for "Franks," an omnibus term for the French and other Europeans who had come to the Middle East as soldiers and traders during the Crusades.

Bogle was able, in the course of an informal conversation, to tentatively identify what we now describe as Orientalism (stereotypes of the East) and Occidentalism (stereotypes of the West) was a remarkable instance of the relative objectivity he possessed as the result of his education and reading.

To help the Panchen Lama improve his knowledge of Christianity and of Europe (and to distance himself from those troublesome Capuchin monks), Bogle embarked on an explanation of the differences amongst Christians. "I said I had heard of the priests who had been at Lhasa," Bogle began,

that they were not of my country, spoke another language, and that their religion differed from mine; that the clergy of England remained at home, and travelled not into other countries; that we allowed everyone to worship God in his own way, to which the Gosain or any of his people who had been in Bengal could bear witness; and that we esteemed a good and pious man, of whatever religion he might be. He changed the subject, and I was not sorry for it.[56]

Bogle got himself into deep water here. His Presbyterian instincts encouraged him to launch into a critique of Catholic missionary orders, but he knew he was drawing too defined a contrast which ignored intolerance within Protestantism. He had to avoid mentioning the common Christian view – among Protestants and Catholics alike – of benighted heathens in the Americas and elsewhere. He was glad the Panchen Lama shifted to other topics. The Panchen Lama, as Bogle noted with palpable relief, "changed the subject, and I was not sorry for it."[57] These conversations were forcing Bogle to think hard about his own part of the world.

Shortly after his arrival at Tashilhunpo, Bogle described an amusing example of how easy it was to leap to mistaken conclusions about strangers. This time it was not different religions but the different clothes that people wore. The incident took place as the winter cold set in. The Panchen Lama gave Bogle some Tibetan and Mongolian clothes to keep warm. "Some days after my arrival," explained Bogle, "the Tashi Lama had given me a Tibetan dress, consisting of a purple satin tunic, lined with Siberian fox skins; a yellow satin cap, faced round with sable and crowned with a red silk tassel, and a pair of red silk Bulgar hide boots." (Some of these clothes are featured in Tilly Kettle's portrait of Bogle painted on his return to Calcutta, and now in the Royal Collection.) These local clothes had the advantage of keeping Bogle warmer than his European ones as the temperature plunged (water by now was freezing

---

[56] *Ibid.*, p. 215.   [57] *Ibid.*, p. 215.

solid in his room even in daytime). They also enabled him to move about without being stared at. "In this [the clothes supplied by the Panchen Lama] I equipped myself, glad to abandon my European habit, which was both uncomfortable and exposed me to abundance of that troublesome curiosity which the Tibetans possess to a degree inferior to no other people."[58] The wearing of these clothes was in a way symbolic of Bogle setting aside some of his European assumptions – "abandoning my Europe habit" in more than one sense.

The change of clothes led to an unexpected lesson in cross-cultural mis-perceptions. In addition to the clothes described above, the Panchen Lama had also given Bogle a tunic and a cap which he had received as a gift from some Turki Tartars who had come on a pilgrimage to Tashilhunpo. As Bogle walked about in his Tartar clothes, he was visited by Depon Dinji who was "the governor of a castle belonging to the Tashi Lama" about six days' journey higher up the Tsangpo valley. Depon Dinji paid Bogle "frequent and unceremonious visits in my tents upon the road." Bogle thought him an odd character – "his looks and manners are exactly those of an overgrown country farmer, and smelling plentifully of tobacco. I could not help sometimes thinking him a little crack brained." When he saw Bogle wearing his Tartar clothes, "he discovered that the dress of the English was exactly that of the Russians."[59] This case of mistaken identity was for Bogle a comical example of how easy it was to make ill-informed judgments about others.

This issue of perception across cultures arose again when the Panchen Lama returned to the subject of religion and posed challenging questions about Christianity. This time the Panchen Lama briefly commented on the relationship between religion in Tibet and India, and "then asked me how many gods there were in my religion." Bogle soon got into difficulties. "I told him one. He replied that he had heard that in my religion God was born three times. I had no mind to attempt an explanation of the mysteries of the Trinity. I felt unequal to it." Bogle side-stepped that complex aspect of Christian theology by replying that "according to my faith God had always existed." The Panchen Lama, responding to the cue,

observed charitably that we all worshipped the same God, but under different names, and all aimed at the same object, though we pursued different ways. The answer I gave him was in the same tolerant spirit; for I am not sent as a missionary, and after so many able and ingenious Jesuits, dressed up in the habits of apostles

[58] Bogle's Journals, Dechenrubje and the Return to Tashilhunpo, November–December 1774, Lamb, *Bhutan and Tibet*, p. 155.

[59] Bogle's Journals, Tashilhunpo, December 1774–April 1775, Lamb, *Bhutan and Tibet*, p. 179.

and armed with beads and crucifixes, have tried in vain to convert unbelieving nations, I am not so arrogant as to believe that my labours would be successful. Tashi Lama observed that his religion and that of China were the same. What a tract of country does it extend over![60]

That exclamation mark registers Bogle's new appreciation of the vast impact of Tibetan Buddhism across central Asia and western China. It also hints at his reservations about Christianity. The discussion had led him to reflect on the controversies about the nature of Jesus that had caused so much division in the early Christian Church until the authorized version of the Trinity emerged. Faced with the Panchen Lama as audience, Bogle appreciated how hard it was for people from other religions to follow the tortuous solution to the problem of Jesus' divinity. He was forced to see Christianity from an outside perspective. He never gave up his Christian beliefs, but his presentation of this exchange conveys that he did not think the Christian religion was obviously superior to the Panchen Lama's religion, or that Christianity had any right to spread its particular views of God round the world. He was glad he was not "sent as a missionary."

Bogle's determination to understand other cultures in their own terms rather than judge them by his own values was evident in his commentary on marriage customs in Bhutan, Tibet, and Bengal. He was prompted to think in comparative terms about this topic because of the different practices he had seen on his journey and during his time in Bengal. He already knew about the practice of *sati* – Hindu widows immolating themselves on their husband's funeral pyre – which had made him think about marriage in Bengal. Now in Tibet he came across the system of polyandry in which one woman married several husbands. During his stay at Tashichodzong in Bhutan Bogle had taken an interest in local social customs and how they compared to those he knew in Bengal. "The Bhutanese, like their neighbours in Bengal, burn their dead," but they did not practice *sati*. He noted in his journal that "The barbarous Gentoo [Hindu] custom of women burning themselves is unknown in this country . . . the Bhutanese women never give such heroic proofs of their fortitude and affection." This led him to ruminate about why such customs appeared in one place but not another. His answer was that "this difference in their conduct naturally arises from the manners peculiar to each country."[61]

---

[60] Bogle's Memorandum on Negotiations with the Tashi Lama at Dechenrubje, November 1774, Lamb, *Bhutan and Tibet*, pp. 221, 222.
[61] Bogle's Journals, Tashichodzong, July 1774, Lamb, *Bhutan and Tibet*, pp. 72, 73.

Bogle tried to reason his way through to an understanding of this complex and controverted subject:

The practice of burning has been condemned by some as a political institution to deter women from poisoning their husbands, and by others as proceeding solely from excessive love. The first opinion seems as groundless as it is ungenerous, and the last is, perhaps, too refined for this iron age. Mankind are neither so good nor so bad as they are generally represented. Human life is a stream formed and impelled by a variety of passions, and its actions seldom flow from single and unmixed sources.

He thought the divergent status of women in Bhutan and Bengal held the key to understanding the different customs:

A Hindu woman, married at an early age, and immured within the walls of a zenana, is unacquainted with all the pleasures and avocations to which a liberal education or the free intercourse of society gives birth. A fondness for dress and the management of her family occupy her whole attention, and the solaces of conjugal and maternal affection are the only sources of her enjoyments. She lives but for her husband and her children, and every passion of her soul, heightened by the force of the climate, is centred on them. On the death of her husband, by devoting herself to the flames she performs an action meritorious in the highest degree, and which reflects the greatest honour on herself and her family. If she survives him she is confined to her room, condemned to perpetual widow-hood, obliged to lay aside all gaudy apparel, and to feed on the most abstemious diet. "Alas!" says she, "a life so gloomy and joyless is not worth preserving – is not to be supported!" Her breast sinks in despair, and it is overwhelmed with grief and affection for her husband. Now zeal for the honour of her children and the desire of distinguishing herself combine with this indifference to life. She forms the fatal resolution while under the first impression of those different passions, and mounts the funeral pile before they have had time to spend their force.[62]

Bogle contrasted this picture of the Bengal widow with circumstances in Bhutan where women and men were closer in status, and where women of all ranks worked outside the family household. He had already noted that Bhutanese women worked in the fields and the forest; he passed many women carrying heavy loads on the mountain trails. He also noted that there did not appear to be the same elaborate social and religious caste divisions as in Bengal. As a member of the landed class himself, and familiar with the social hierarchy in eighteenth-century Britain, he believed that social distinctions gave rise to a more refined range of feelings – presumably stimulated by twin pressures of example and emulation:

[62] *Ibid.*, p. 73.

But the institution of castes and every other hereditary distinction being unknown in Bhutan, the elevated sentiments which spring from a consciousness of superiority are never felt. As the Rajah, the priests, and all the officers of government lead a life of celibacy, they [women] are married only to landholders and husbandmen. They are employed in the most laborious offices, they are dirty in their persons, they use strong liquors, they are bred up with the greatest liberty, and they mix with the lowest class of people. They are allowed to enter into a second marriage; and the death of a husband opens up to them no such dismal prospect.[63]

These are interesting commentaries. They are a peculiar mixture of what Bogle thought he understood of customs in Bengal and Bhutan, and of the lessons he thought were displayed from eighteenth-century British society. He is writing as an outsider with respect to Bhutan and Bengal. His knowledge was still limited. He had been in Bengal for just over three years, working in the Company buildings at Fort William, he had been only a few weeks in Bhutan, and he had just arrived in Tibet. He was also an outsider because he was male – for example, assuming that because women liked "gaudy" clothes their reasoning powers were somehow weakened. He sees women as driven by passion – noble though it may be. He assumes a hot climate will somehow impel people to behave in odd ways. He is also revealing the assumptions of his own social class in Britain – a family with a country estate and servants – by declaring that only societies with social hierarchies can produce refined behavior (and that only in the upper ranks). But in spite of all these caveats about Bogle's thinking on this matter, the point remains that he was trying to understand *sati* from inside its own culture. He could have stopped with his first statement – that *sati* was "barbarous" – and elaborated on that for a presumably receptive British audience. But he pushed himself to try and reason out why humans behaved in such ways, and why such customs could possibly be accepted as a legitimate, even a noble, expression of cultural and religious values.

By the 1820s and 1830s many British officials in Bengal would use widow burning to characterize Hindu society as a whole as backward and barbaric. There were already signs of these less tolerant attitudes amongst Company servants who were shaped by the new force of evangelical Christianity. Charles Grant, a fellow Scot, had been born in the same year as Bogle and went out to Bengal as a Writer in 1772. He became a leading figure in the evangelical movement and advocated missionary work in Bengal. For Grant there were no two ways of looking at *sati*. This practice was but one example of "the cruel genius which pervades the Hindoo

---

[63] *Ibid.*, p. 73.

code... [that] sanctions this inhuman and astonishing custom."[64] He compared *sati* to human sacrifice the Spaniards had found in Mexico as another example of the degenerate state of non-Christian societies:

For near thirty years we have with perfect unconcern seen rites, in reality more cruel and atrocious [than those in Mexico] practiced in our Indian territories [by which] mothers of families are taken from the midst of their children who have just lost their father and by a most diabolical combination of force and fraud are driven into the flames.[65]

We shall deal with Grant later in a broader discussion of the impact of the evangelical movement on the empire, but meanwhile it is the contrast between Grant's and Bogle's responses to *sati* that is worth noting. Grant used *sati* to make a comprehensive condemnation of Hindu culture. There is none of that attitude in Bogle's thinking. Even though he got some things wrong, he was trying to understand from the other cultural perspective; he even tried to see it from a pious Hindu woman's point of view. He did not use his comments on *sati* as an occasion to condemn Hinduism as a whole. On the contrary, later in his journey, while noting Tibetan respect for all life forms, he commented that "the humane maxims of the Hindu faith are taught in Tibet."[66]

A similar attentiveness to other cultural perspectives was evident in Bogle's comments on polyandry, which was common in the region of Tibet he traveled through. As with *sati*, his outsider's understanding was limited, yet Bogle's references to the practice of one wife with several husbands were invariably sympathetic. In October and November 1774, two days outside Gyantse, Bogle arrived at Dudukpai, a village under the jurisdiction of the Panchen Lama. Bogle lodged at a household where a woman was married to two men.

The people were all busy building and stacking their straw, and were singing at their work. Our landlord's family seemed to be one of the happiest in Tibet. The house belongs to two brothers, who are married to a very handsome wife, and have three of the prettiest children I ever saw. They all came to drink tea and eat sugar-candy. After night came on, the whole family assembled in a room to dance to their own singing, and spent two hours in this manner with abundance of mirth and glee.[67]

---

[64] Charles Grant, *Observations on the State of Society among the Asiatic Subjects of Great Britain particularly with respect to Morals and the Means of Improving It. Written Chiefly in the Year 1792*, pp. 104, 108, BL.

[65] *Ibid.*, pp. 145n, 146.

[66] Bogle's Journals, The Journey to Tibet, Pharidzong to Dechenrubje, November 1774, Lamb, *Bhutan and Tibet*, p. 141.

[67] *Ibid.*, p. 143.

About one month later, when he was settled at the Panchen Lama's country residence at Dechenrubje with more time on his hands to think about the new customs he was encountering, he still gave a warm endorsement of polyandry. In a memorandum for his superiors in Calcutta, entitled "An Account of Tibet," he drew attention to "the two customs [in Tibet] that appear most singular" to Europeans. The first was the practice of air burial by which the dead body is carried to a high spot, dismembered, and "left to be devoured by wild beasts." Bogle noted that "as there is little wood in the country, they cannot afford to burn their dead; but they take an equally effectual way of destroying them."[68] Far from being bizarre, the practice was a perfectly reasonable method of dealing with corpses in high, treeless terrain.

The Tibetan marriage practices he encountered on his journey were more challenging to comprehend but they too could be seen to have a reasonable basis. Bogle wrote that he was "at a loss to name the other custom, unless I call it polyandry." He was struck by how well the custom seemed to work in the part of Tibet he traveled through. His own observations, and his reading of Montesquieu on a related subject, convinced him that the system was beneficial to women, especially when contrasted to polygamic systems of marriage:

In most Eastern countries polygamy is allowed. The advocates for it compare mankind to the deer; its enemies liken them to turtle doves. Montesquieu and other political writers insist that it is destructive of population; and the women cry that it is unjust and unreasonable that so many of their sex should be subjected to the pleasures of one man. But in this country they have their revenge. The elder brother marries a woman, and she becomes the wife of the whole family. They club together in matrimony as merchants do in trade. Nor is this joint concern often productive of jealousy among the partners. They are little addicted to jealousy. Disputes do indeed sometimes arise about the children of the marriage; but they are settled either by a comparison of the features of the child with those of its several fathers, or left to the determination of the mother.[69]

Here again Bogle places polyandry in a favorable light, even going so far as to compare its benefits to those gained by astute merchants in the commercial society of England who pooled their combined resources together in joint-stock companies.

An interesting encounter with polyandry took place in February 1775 when Bogle was spending time in the country with the Pung Cushos – two

---

[68] Bogle's Journals, An Account of Tibet, Dechenrubje, December 1774, Lamb, *Bhutan and Tibet*, p. 167.
[69] *Ibid.*, p. 167.

nephews of the Panchen Lama. Bogle became fast friends with these two young men. Bogle described the fun they had together one day:

We spent the day with the Pung Cushos, at some tents prepared for us on the side of a hill, a few miles from Tashilhunpo. Shooting at a mark, running races, and seeing some of the peasants dance and sing, formed our entertainment, for there is no hunting or killing animals so near the palace. Our friends had prepared a great feast for us. Not knowing what we would like, [they] took care to have every kind of flesh, fish, and fowl they could think of. After dinner, tables covered with fruits were brought in, and they insisted on presenting us with dresses and horses. Having drunk plenty of tea and chang, we returned to the palace. I rode the horse the Pung Cushos gave me, which was a Kalmuk, but I did not find it so tractable as those horses are said to be. I had enough ado to keep it from running away with me.[70]

The solicitude the Pung Cushos extended to him, and the deep pleasure Bogle took in this friendship, is palpable in this description. Bogle wished to reciprocate by offering gifts of his own. The response of the Pung Cushos to these efforts deepened Bogle's respect and affection for his new friends. "I may be excused," Bogle could not resist noting in his official report,

in mentioning a circumstance, which although it does not properly belong in these memoranda, I cannot, in justice to my Tibetan friends, omit. From the civilities which the Tashi Lama and everybody about him had shown me, as well as from my desire of conciliating the good-will of the Tibetans, whose country I believe no Englishman had ever visited before, I resolved to make some presents to the Tashi Lama's relations; and accordingly purchased coral beads, which are much valued in this part of the world . . . I believe I spent an hour in their [Pung Cushos'] tent before I could get them to agree to take my beads. "You" said they, "are come from a far country; it is our business to render your stay agreeable; why should you make us presents?"[71]

The polyandry issue intruded into this friendship. While staying at Tashilhunpo Bogle had also met the Tashitzay Depon who had presented Bogle with fruits and sweetmeats. Bogle wished to return the compliment but hesitated because there was bad blood between the Depon and the Pung Cushos. "I did not wish to appear over zealous in cultivating his [the Depon's] friendship, as it would have hurt my connection with the Pung Cushos, who are on but indifferent terms with him on account of his wife, who belongs also to them. It is a strange story and exhibits manners very different from our own; but I forbear to lay open the family disputes of my two young friends."[72]

[70] Bogle's Journals, Tashilhunpo, December 1774–April 1775, Lamb, *Bhutan and Tibet*, p. 185.
[71] *Ibid.*, p. 186.   [72] *Ibid.*, pp. 184, 185.

This is a revealing moment. The subject matter here – tensions between three Tibetan males over a common wife – could have served as a seductive anecdote in Bogle's journal, especially so if Bogle had some hopes of publishing his journal and making an impact on the reading public in Britain. It was an alluring topic with possibilities of enticing potential readers with tales of strange conjugal, or even sexual, jealousies and tensions. Yet Bogle firmly chose silence.[73] As he drew this veil over the marital troubles of his Tibetan friends, Bogle refused to indulge any prurient interest in the strange ways of foreigners on matters of sex and marriage. He chose to exclude his English readers because of his respect for his friends' privacy, giving his Tibetan friends the same respect he would have extended to his intimate friends in Britain.

In this incident, and throughout his journals and letters, Bogle took the position that human beings were similar wherever they lived. When customs and beliefs varied, it was because of the different conditions that people lived in rather than the result of any unchanging ethnic traits. Each culture had its own integrity. Every custom could be explained reasonably in its own context. There are numerous passages where this mentality informs Bogle's responses to Bhutan and Tibet. When he noticed that Tibetans employed a lower class of people to butcher their animals for meat in spite of their religious scruples about the taking of life, he chose not to draw attention to Tibetan hypocrisy but instead drew a universal lesson about human behavior. "But mankind in every part of the world," he remarked, "accommodate their consciences to their passions."[74] In March 1775 when engaged in a discussion with the Gurkha representative at Tashilhunpo, who told Bogle that the Gurkhas had completed their takeover of Nepal easily because of internecine bickering amongst the Nepalese, thus inviting Bogle to condemn the Nepalese as a quarrelsome people, Bogle simply replied that "every nation thought their own customs best."[75] When faced with an unfamiliar array of dishes at a meal, including raw beef beaten into a jelly, Bogle commented "it is far from unsavoury, when one can get the better of European prejudices."[76] On another occasion, when he was gazed at by crowds of onlookers while going through the town of Gyantse, he tried to construct a universal

---

[73] Amrita Sen, "Bogle's Travels and the Limits of Colonial Discourse," unpub. paper, AL 892, March 2006, Michigan State University.

[74] Bogle's Journals, The Journey to Tibet, Decehenrubje, December 1774, Lamb, *Bhutan and Tibet*, p. 141.

[75] Bogle's Journals, Negotiations with the Tashi Lama, Tashilhunpo, December 1774– April 1775, Lamb, *Bhutan and Tibet*, p. 252.

[76] *Ibid.*, p. 188.

rule about urban and rural responses to strangers. He was struck by the fact that town dwellers showed more interest in him than country folk, and speculated that this was because they had more frequent interactions with foreign travelers and had thus developed a wider range of responses. "Curiosity, perhaps, although natural to mankind," he reasoned, "and however the seeds of it may be implanted in them, requires, like music, to be cultivated. It gathers strength from being exercised; it languishes and lies asleep when there are no objects to encourage its attention."[77] Early in his stay at Tashilhunpo monastery he witnessed a public dispute between the monks much "embellished with great powers of action, such as clapping hands, shaking the head etc." which seemed exaggerated and inappropriate to outsiders. Instead of leaving the impression that this behavior was bizarre, Bogle told his readers that "these gestures seem very ridiculous to an European; perhaps our orators would appear equally ridiculous to them."[78] At every opportunity, Bogle resisted a posture of European superiority and tried to position himself as a neutral observer.

Because of the novelty and difficulty of his journey, it would have been easy for Bogle to have presented himself as the heroic European traveler overcoming all obstacles as he made his way from the Bengal plains up through the Bhutan hills and across the high Himalayan passes into Tibet. But once again Bogle was at pains to place his achievement in a context which gave acknowledgment to others, and recognized his essentially dependent position. He was always aware of how much the success of his mission depended on the status and the skills of Purangir who was well connected in the Bhutanese court and at Tashilhunpo. What for Bogle was a remarkable and strenuous trip – a life-changing experience – was familiar ground for Purangir. He had made the journey from Calcutta to Shigatse many times. He was part pilgrim, part merchant, a member of the Gosain sect that played a major role in conducting trade through the Himalayan routes into Tibet. As an illustration of the significance of their role in communications between the Ganges valley and Tibet, Bogle reckoned there were about 150 Gosains at Tashilhunpo while he was there.[79]

Purangir's help was vital for Bogle and Hastings. He carried the first letter from the Panchen Lama to Hastings, he knew the Bhutanese

---

[77] Bogle's Journals, Pharidzong to Dechenrubje, November 1774, Lamb, *Bhutan and Tibet*, p. 145.

[78] Bogle's Journals, Tashilhunpo, December 1774–April 1775, Lamb, *Bhutan and Tibet*, p. 177.

[79] Bogle's Journals, Dechenrubje and the Return to Tashilhunpo, November–December 1774, Lamb, *Bhutan and Tibet*, p. 153.

merchants and the routes through Bhutan, and he spoke the necessary languages. When Bogle was held up in Bhutan and the Panchen Lama, pressed by the Chinese Ambans and the Tibetan regent at Lhasa, urged him to return to Calcutta, Bogle reported to Hastings that all his hopes now rested on Purangir. "My hopes of success," he told Hastings, "are founded on the Gosain." He repeated this key point in July 1774: "in this situation my hopes of seeing the Tashi Lama were chiefly founded on the Gosain."[80] Eventually Purangir's intervention succeeded. The Panchen Lama wrote to inform the Deb Rajah of Bhutan and Bogle that "he [the Panchen Lama] had written to Lhasa, the residence of the Dalai Lama, on the subject of passports, and had obtained their consent to my proceeding on the journey, provided I came only with a few attendants; and that he had therefore sent back the Gosain, who had been down in Calcutta, to wait for me on the borders of his country."[81]

In his pioneering study of these early British attempts to open trade across the Himalayas, the American scholar Schuyler Cammann noted that Purangir had played a critical role but that British writers had not given him any recognition. "He [Purangir] has been so completely forgotten," Cammann complained, "that Graham Sandberg, in his much quoted book on foreign travelers in Tibet was able to confuse him with the Panchen Lama who wrote to Hastings."[82] Cammann's book is now old (1951), and since that time British scholars have fully recognized Purangir's role but it was a telling example of colonial assumptions still prevalent at the time of the publication of Cammann's book, that the role of Purangir had not yet been noticed.

Bogle, however, did not exhibit such colonialist mentalities in this matter. He understood fully that his success rested on Purangir's skills, and he did not hesitate to praise Purangir to his English readers. Beyond Purangir's contribution to the success of his own mission, Bogle recognized the breadth of Purangir's achievements. In January 1778, Bogle introduced Purangir to his friend David Anderson with a hearty endorsement. "The Bearer of this is Purangir, just from Tibet, and recommended by the Teshho Lama," he wrote, and then added that "he is a great Traveller and can talk to you about Ceylon or about St. Petersburg."[83] Purangir

---

[80] Bogle's Report on Negotiations, Tashichodzong, July 5–14, 1774; Bogle to Hastings, Tashichodzong, July 17, 1774, Lamb, *Bhutan and Tibet*, pp. 90, 115.

[81] Bogle to Hastings, Tashichodzong, August 25, 1774, Lamb, *Bhutan and Tibet*, pp. 121, 122.

[82] Schuyler Cammann, *Trade through the Himalayas. The Early British Attempts to Open Tibet* (Princeton University Press, 1951), p. 30.

[83] Bogle to Anderson, [Calcutta], January 7, 1778, David Anderson Papers, Add. 45421, f. 67, BL.

continued a close friendship with Bogle. Just before his own death Bogle wrote again to Anderson about "My friend Purangir [who] has set out for the Lama and I expect soon to hear from him."[84] In all this writings from 1774 until his death in 1781 Bogle never failed to give due acknowledgment to Purangir. He pointed out to his British friends what a cosmopolitan figure and a great traveler Purangir was. Bogle hoped his own journey might one day be published as an example of European achievement in travel, but he knew that the same journey for Purangir was a routine affair.

Bogle's engagement with his Tibetan friends, his sustained efforts to enter into Bhutanese and Tibetan perspectives about the world, show how far he had traveled from his own home background in Scotland. When his father wrote to him about the Tibet journey from the family estate at Daldowie he expressed mild interest in his son's travels but he tended to be dismissive of the entire enterprise. He was blinkered to the possibility of learning anything from other cultures. He complained that the trip had prevented Bogle writing home often enough. "Your long Journey to, and abode with the Grand Lama of Tibet, is one sufficient reason for the Irregularity of your correspondence for some time past. But I flatter myself that that Irksome Journey, tho' otherwise Honourable Embassy, is now at an end."[85]

His father's approach to non-British cultures was already evident in a letter he had written to Bogle shortly after his son had arrived in Bengal. He was convinced that

the original natives in that part of the Country where you reside have only the light of the religion of nature, corrupted by gross superstition and blind Idolatry in a degree entirely ignorant of the Sublime Apprehensions of the infinite Perfections of the Deity whom the Christians worship and adore, and I suppose they are still more Ignorant of the method of Grace and Salvation published and made known to us here in the Scriptures of Truth, and of that life and immortality brought to light by the Gospel of Jesus Christ who is the way, the truth and the Life.[86]

Bogle's father was entirely confined within his own culture and saw no possibility that there could be any merit in non-Christian societies.

Bogle's father was by no means ignorant. As we noted at the beginning of the chapter, he had been an eminent member of the merchant community in Glasgow and like many such merchants had taken an active

---

[84] Bogle to Anderson, [Rangpur], January 28, 1780, David Anderson Papers, Add. 45421, f. 91, BL.

[85] George Bogle (father) to Bogle, Daldowie, February 19, 1776, Bogle Papers, Box: 1770–1781 and Estate Lists [marked 48], Folder 3, Mitchell Library.

[86] George Bogle (father) to Bogle, Daldowie, January 21, 1771, Bogle Papers, Box: India and Tibet [marked 37], Folder 3, Mitchell Library.

role in the intellectual and cultural life of the city, even serving as Lord Rector of Glasgow University. When young George was studying at Edinburgh his father had expressed the hope that his son would pay "close attention [to] Montesquieu whose Spirit of the Laws you are probably reading."[87] When George went out to Bengal his father thought that his reading in history and philosophy made him stand out from the other young Company servants who had only a commercial training. "You, my dear George," he wrote, "have gone out in the East India Company's service with many superior advantages to numbers employed in the same manner of Business, blessed with a good natural disposition, with a fine liberal Education."[88] As Bogle's letters from Bhutan and Tibet began reaching Daldowie Bogle's father became very proud of his son's accomplishments:

Your letters Containing an Accurate Account of your Journey to Thibet Together with ample descriptions you give of the manners, police, Religion, dress etc. of the Different Countrys and dominions you went through, together with the strength of reason and arguments you was oblidged to make use of to Oppose their entering into any trade with Bengal or even allowing free Access to and thro their respective Countrys and Dominions, All those and other Difficultys you had to Encounter and to Subdue Show, my Dear George when I consider your Success, Show I affirm, the Strength of genius, Address and Penetration which few, very few, of your age and Experience are capable of.[89]

The emphatic repetition of words and phrases reveal the depth of pride in the son's achievements. But as the quotation on religion in Bengal suggests, Bogle's father could never escape his own Presbyterian framing of the world. Bogle had come a long distance from the circumscribed parochial views of his father. The journey from Calcutta to Tashilhunpo was remarkable, but so too was the intellectual distance Bogle had traveled from the family estate at Daldowie.

Bogle's stoic demeanor after he returned to Calcutta in 1775 confirms the favorable impression that emerges from his letters and journals. He arrived back in Calcutta in circumstances that were stacked against him. Warren Hastings, the sponsor of his Tibet mission, and the patron from whom he expected so much, was in deep trouble. Any Company servant who was close to Hastings was in danger of losing all prospects for

[87] George Bogle (father) to Bogle, Daldowie, September 19, 1761, Bogle Papers, Box: India and Tibet, Folder: George Bogle 1762–1769 [marked 45], Mitchell Library.

[88] George Bogle (father) to Bogle, Daldowie, April 16, 1771, Bogle Papers, Folder: Bogle 1771 [marked 120], Mitchell Library.

[89] George Bogle (father) to Bogle, Daldowie, November 23, 1776, Bogle Papers, Folder: George Bogle 1776 [marked 48], Mitchell Library.

advancement. The Government of India Act of 1773 had set up a new system for Company rule which went into effect shortly after Bogle had departed for Tibet. The Governor of Bengal now became the Governor General of India with supervisory power over the Company Councils and their Presidents at Madras and Bombay. That provision appeared to strengthen the position of Bogle's patron. However, the Act also provided for a new Supreme Council in Bengal, appointed by the ministry in London. The new Council members General George Clavering, George Monson, and Philip Francis were determined to root out the corruption and exploitation that critics complained had characterized Company rule in Bengal. The new Council members viewed Hastings as a holdover from the corrupt system they had been sent to reform.

They were led by the sharp-tongued Francis, who, most scholars now agree, was probably the author of the letters of "Junius," written to the *Public Advertiser* between 1769 and 1772, which had used brilliant invective to castigate the government in London. Francis was now on the hunt for political targets in Calcutta. Parliamentary enquiries had already exposed many of the Company's misdeeds in Bengal. As soon as the new Council members landed in Calcutta they bent all their efforts to opposing Hastings' policies, and his general authority and standing. Hastings could be outvoted on the Council and was so again and again by the new majority. Anyone connected with Hastings faced daunting challenges to his career in Bengal.

Bogle sketched out the unpropitious circumstances on his return from Tibet in a letter to his brother Robin in August 1775. "The late Revolution in the Government of this Country," he explained,

is a serious Check to my Views at present. I have sacrificed a great Deal to get myself some Credit, and by entering a path which nobody had trod, bring myself forward in the Service . . . but my attachment to Mr. Hastings against whom they have taken a direct line of Opposition naturally renders me obnoxious to them.[90]

He wrote to his father in the same vein, lamenting that he would now receive no benefit from the Tibet mission. The late changes had been "particularly severe upon me," he sadly noted. "I had sacrificed a great deal to get myself sound Credit, and it was now I expected to have reaped the Fruits of it."[91]

It is testimony to the quality of Bogle's conduct and reporting on his Tibet mission that the new Council caused no difficulties when it came

---

[90] George Bogle to Robert (Robin) Bogle, Calcutta, August 4, 1775, Bogle Papers, Folder: George Bogle 1775 [marked 61], Mitchell Library.
[91] George Bogle to George Bogle (father), Calcutta, August 5, 1775, Bogle Papers, *ibid.*

to rewarding him for his efforts. He was given money for his expenses, and a generous monthly allowance for the duration of the trip. He told Robin in January 1776 that "the Board, however, were so well pleased with My Expedition, and put in a good Humour I believe with reading my Journal, that they have given me 15000 Rupees besides my expenses which I assure you I hardly expected."[92] The full Council reported to India House in London in January 1776 that they were "well satisfied with the manner in which Mr. Bogle has executed the Hazardous and extraordinary Service on which he was deputed."[93]

While he had been well paid for his mission Bogle's prospects were now dim. He no longer held any office under the Company because those he did hold had been abolished by the new Council. There was no prospect of another Company appointment as long as the Council opposed Hastings and viewed Bogle as one of his protégés. As Bogle told Robin, "My fate, however, is closely tied with Mr. Hastings." Bogle could have chosen to abandon his ill-starred patron and curry favor with the new members of the Council but he refused to do so:

I have no Line but one to take in these Times, and although it may not square very well with my Interests, it is perfectly conformable to my Principles. If Mr. Hastings succeeds there is nothing but I may expect. If he falls I have no favour to expect from his opponents.

Bogle was so despondent about his prospects in Bengal that he even contemplated returning on his own to Bhutan or Tibet. "If I find Bengal without Prospects you may perhaps hear that I have returned to my Mountains on the Borders of Tartary."[94]

Hastings did what he could to help Bogle. He renewed the appointment as his private secretary which enabled Bogle to continue on in Calcutta. Bogle's loyalty to Hastings, at some cost it seemed at the time to his career in the Company, earned him the admiration of many in the British community as a man of principle who did not trim his sails to the political winds. He took some pride in his standing. "I'll tell you Robin," he wrote to his brother, "if I don't get Profit by my present Conduct I get popularity – for our Side is the favoured one, and fidelity is liked on all sides."[95] In a heartfelt letter to his father, Bogle opened up his state of mind in these trying circumstances. The choice he faced was to distance

---

[92] George Bogle to Robert (Robin) Bogle, Calcutta, January 20, 1776, Bogle Papers, Folder: George Bogle 1776 [marked 48], Mitchell Library.

[93] Amba Prasad, ed., *Fort William-India House Correspondence*, vol. XIV, p. 380.

[94] George Bogle to Robert (Robin) Bogle, Calcutta, January 20, 1776, Bogle Papers, Folder: George Bogle 1776 [marked 48], Mitchell Library.

[95] George Bogle to Robert (Robin) Bogle, Calcutta, January 20, 1776, Bogle Papers, *ibid.*

himself from Hastings in order to gain favor with the Council majority (and hence win a Company office again), or stick to Hastings and face apparently dim prospects for his entire future in Bengal. In a detailed letter of explanation he revealed his admiration for Hastings, and his own determination to show himself as a man of principle:

> While I was about the Mountains of Tartary, the Government of this Country underwent a total Change. My Patron, Mr. Hastings although honoured with superior Titles [i.e. Governor General in India], and continued in the Chair [of the Council] was deprived of all Influence and Authority but what his superior Abilities and Knowledge give him. His colleagues lately sent out by Parliament aim at nothing but to blacken his Character and either to drive him from the Government or by raising Enemies against him in England, endeavour to get him removed. I found things in this Situation on my return to Bengal and they have continued so ever since. Mr. Hastings bears this Attack with Character in the Eyes of everybody.[96]

Bogle confided to his father that he "was too much connected with Mr. Hastings not to suffer from this revolution in the Government." But Bogle was determined to stick to the high road. He chose loyalty over expediency. "Fidelity is in my Opinion a virtue of all others the most indispensable and the only one beau chemin to take."[97] In his own estimation, Bogle was demonstrating his probity and integrity in circumstances that would tempt other men to insinuate themselves into the good opinion of the new Council members. "I have been following for some Years Credit and Character more than Profit."[98]

It was not an easy choice. In a letter to his friend David Anderson written towards the end of 1775, Bogle summed up his position: "I have no Public Business or publick Office. The Select Committee you know was swallowed up in the Council. The Sudder Dewanee Adwalat has, I am told, been abolished within these few days, and I suppose I shall not get another post when I ask it. For indeed Anderson in these times I hug myself in unimportance."[99] On one occasion when Company officials were casting aspersions on some of Bogle's friends who still held posts in the Company "Bogle almost cried of talking of it."[100] There was private anguish behind the public face of loyalty and principled behavior.

---

[96] George Bogle to George Bogle (father), Calcutta, February 21, 1776, Bogle Papers, *ibid.*

[97] George Bogle to George Bogle (father), Calcutta, March 26, 1776, Bogle Papers, *ibid.*

[98] George Bogle to George Bogle (father), Calcutta, March 27, 1776, Bogle Papers, *ibid.*

[99] George Bogle to David Anderson, Calcutta, October 26, 1775, David Anderson Papers, Add. 45421, f. 45, BL.

[100] Samuel Charters to David Anderson, Calcutta, August 17, 1775, David Anderson Papers, Add. 45425, f. 109, BL.

Bogle's behavior back in Calcutta was in keeping with the character-istics he had displayed while on his Tibet mission. His determination to stand by Hastings in spite of the blight this put on his own prospects for advancement, his ability to analyze a predicament from various points of view, his quiet and decent attitude were consistent with the charac-ter that was on display in his letters and journal. He was sensitive to other perspectives, he was broad-minded, he remained stoic in the face of adversity, he was curious and rational, and he tried to act honorably. These were characteristics that were supposed to shape the conduct of an Enlightenment-era gentleman.

This brings us back to the issue of Bogle's representativeness. As we take stock of all that we know of him can we say he was an example of Enlightenment-era thinking in Britain? He had studied one year at Edin-burgh. He had become thoroughly familiar with the new commercial knowledge of the age at Enfield, and as the result of his business experi-ences in London and Calcutta. In Calcutta he had given serious attention to learning Persian and the languages of north India. By the mid-1770s he had acquired a substantial collection of books. When he died, his library was inventoried prior to being sold off under the supervision of Claud Alexander and David Anderson, the administrators of Bogle's estate. The list begins with "Bacon's works, 5 vols. Compleat" and includes such entries as "Vatell's *Law of Nations* (two volumes)," "William Robertson's *History of Scotland* and *History of the Reign of Charles V*, four volumes," "Machiavelli's works," "Herodotus' *History of the Persian Wars* in four volumes," and "*Spectator* Complt 8 vols."[101]

We do not know the extent to which Bogle read the books in his library. He may have picked them up in a sale in the same way as other servants of the Company bought his books after he died. There is no sustained engagement with the major philosophers of the Enlightenment in Bogle's journals or the letters. He cannot be presented as a major thinker but his letters and journals do show him to be a minor example of Enlighten-ment views in action. He mentioned, at apposite moments in his travels, Montesquieu, Buffon, Grotius, Pufendorf, and Robertson. His approach to understanding variation in human societies, and to topics like *sati* and polyandry, was informed by the writings of Montesquieu and Buf-fon. Perhaps the very limitations of his reading and understanding make

---

[101] Account Sales of the following Effects belonging to the Estate of the late George Bogle Esq. deceased, sold at public auction the 18th. 19th. and 20th September last by orders of Claud Alexander and David Anderson Esq. The Administrators, Bogle Papers, Folder: George Bogle [marked 9], Mitchell Library.

him more typical of the age than the great intellectual figures whose works now define the Enlightenment in encyclopedias and scholarly debates.

We can at the very least say that he represented an outward-looking Scottish Enlightenment way of thinking about the world rather than the Scottish narrowness evident in his father's bleak Calvinist voice. These Enlightenment orientations were reflected throughout the letters, reports, and journals that described his journey to Tibet. He viewed human nature as being similar around the world. Differences between customs and beliefs were explicable in terms of climatic or geographical circumstances to which all human societies had to adapt. He thought it worthwhile and informative to try to understand those other cultures from their own perspectives rather than judging by the standards of his own culture. He accepted the integrity and reasonableness of other cultures. He was puzzled at times, and critical too, but he was never derogatory in his judgments, and rarely condescending. He saw himself as bringing this new understanding and new knowledge to the attention of his family, his friends, and, he hoped, eventually to a wider reading public in Britain. He positioned himself as an enlightened and sensitive observer in a part of the world hitherto unknown to the British. He thought he could learn lessons about the human condition, and he thought others could too if he wrote interestingly and entertainingly about his experiences.

At the very beginning of his journey to Tibet Bogle had received a private commission from Hastings in which Hastings urged him

> to keep a diary, inserting whatever passes before your observation which shall be characteristic of the people, the country, the climate, or the road, their manners, customs, building, cookery etc., or interesting to the trade of this country, carrying with you a pencil and a pocket-book for the purpose of minuting short notes of every fact or remark as it occurs, and putting them in order at your leisure while they are fresh in your memory.[102]

Bogle, as we have seen, was assiduous in following these injunctions, and went beyond them by making numerous observations in letters to friends and family. At the end of it all, he was intellectually stimulated by what he had witnessed and experienced in Bhutan and Tibet. He confided in David Anderson when he got back to Calcutta, "the Governor wants me to publish something on my Pilgrimage. It is a tremendous Affair, and

---

[102] Private Commission to Mr. Bogle, Fort William, May 16, 1774, Lamb, *Bhutan and Tibet*, p. 48.

yet I have promised to attempt it."[103] For both Hastings and Bogle there was a declared intention to learn something of lasting value from these new encounters.

Hastings, moreover, believed that there was a large audience in England more interested in reading about this kind of new geographical and cultural knowledge than they were in reading about the exploits of the East India Company as it made money and acquired territory in India. "There are thousands of Men in England whose good will is worth seeking," Hastings assured Bogle, "and who will listen to the story of such enterprises in search of knowledge with ten times more avidity than they would read Accounts that brought Crores [the Indian term for 100,000] to the National Credit, or descriptions of Victories that slaughtered thousands of the National Enemies."[104]

Before Bogle set out, Hastings reminded him that "every nation excels others in some particular art or science."[105] Many of the letters and journals on his journey to Tibet were informed by this open-minded approach which readily acknowledged the excellence in other cultures. Hastings had also urged his emissary to "remember that everything you see is of Importance" and Bogle had followed that advice by paying earnest and respectful attention to all aspects of Tibetan and Bhutanese society, economy, politics, and culture.[106] He never simplified Tibet or Bhutan by reducing their cultures to one essential characteristic. For Bogle both places were as complex and as interesting as the European countries he knew. On several occasions Bogle was even able to stand outside his own culture and appreciate how odd British ways might look to Tibetans and Bhutanese.

Hastings hoped that Bogle's journal, if published, might rival the narratives of eighteenth-century European explorers in the Pacific. Many scholars who have studied those narratives have argued that the act of narration was but one aspect of the destructive impact of Europeans on Pacific islanders. "Whatever the intentions of captains, missionaries, and scientists," explains Stuart Schwartz, "knowing and 'collecting' the 'other' invariably led to the advantage of the knower and the massive

---

[103] Bogle to Anderson, Calcutta, October 26, 1775, David Anderson Papers, Add. 45421, f. 46, BL.

[104] Warren Hastings to George Bogle, Fort William, September 8, 1774, Warren Hastings Papers, Add. 29117, f. 63, BL.

[105] Private Commission to Mr. Bogle, Fort William, May 16, 1774, Lamb, *Bhutan and Tibet*, p. 48.

[106] Warren Hastings to George Bogle, Fort William, September 8, 1774, Warren Hastings Papers, Add. 29117, f. 63, BL.

dispossession and transformation of the 'native'."[107] This was certainly not the outcome with Bogle and Hastings in Bhutan and Tibet. On the contrary, they felt somewhat chastened by the encounter. They had been well and truly outmaneuvered by Tibetan and Bhutanese officials. Yet they were not disheartened by their failure. They also thought they had learned a great deal of useful information from these (for the British) hitherto unknown places. Hastings even suggested to Bogle that such knowledge about humanity would be of more lasting value than knowledge about wars and territorial acquisitions. Nor were there any signs of Bogle thinking in terms of the oft-cited binaries of imperial mentalities in the Victorian and Edwardian eras – savage/civilized, inferior/superior, primitive/advanced – that were to be so amply demonstrated during the 1904 British mission to Tibet. He even noticed, during that revealing moment in his conversations with the Panchen Lama, that Europeans and Asians were just the same in holding over-simplified views of each other.

Bogle gave full recognition to the integrity of the cultures he met on his travels. He noted that the Panchen Lama, as he welcomed Moslem and Hindu as well as Buddhist pilgrims at Shigatse, was "free from those narrow prejudices which, next to ambition and avarice, have opened the most copious source of human misery."[108] Intolerance in any religion was repugnant to Bogle. He was quite willing to acknowledge that the religious toleration he valued was not an exclusively European invention but was perfectly well exhibited as an intrinsic feature of the Himalayan cultures he encountered during his mission. He witnessed this tolerant attitude not only at the court of the Panchen Lama but in the ecumenical religious ceremony to the mountain gods at the foot of Chomolhari where Tibet, Sikkim, and Bhutan met. He also noted the same tolerant outlook during his discussions with Tibetan and Bengali companions like Padma and Purangir Gosain who accompanied him on his journey through the mountains. Bogle preferred open minds to closed minds and he recognized and respected similar outlooks in other cultures. His commentaries on his journey to Bhutan and Tibet appear to be an exemplary Enlightenment narrative.

[107] Greg Dening, "The Theatricality of Observing and Being Observed. Eighteenth-Century Europe Discovers the Pacific," in Stuart Schwartz, ed., *Implicit Understandings. Observing, Reporting and Reflecting on the Encounters between Europeans and Other Peoples in the Early Modern Era* (Cambridge University Press, 1994), pp. 451–483 and Schwartz's comments (*ibid.*, p. 17) summarizing the arguments of Dening and other scholars.

[108] Bogle's Journal, At Dechenrubje and the Return to Tashilhunpo, November–December 1774, Lamb, *Bhutan and Tibet*, p. 154.

2   Wives, concubines, and "domestic arrangements"

Bogle's curiosity about the marriage practices of Tibetans may have moved beyond a detached intellectual interest to a more personal level of engagement with that topic. He may well have married a Tibetan woman. When Hugh Richardson returned to Britain, after the end of his service as the British and Indian representative at Lhasa, he undertook a genealogical study of Bogle's family. He had already questioned his Tibetan friends in Shigatse about Bogle; now he set to work in the family archives in Scotland. Richardson was shown a genealogical tree by Nora Heathcote, one of Bogle's descendants, which unambiguously stated that Bogle had married "Tichan, sister of the Teshoo Lama."[1] Could this claim be true? If it is true, Bogle had even closer ties with the Panchen Lama than his narrative revealed. If such a marriage did indeed take place, it seems additional confirmation that Bogle viewed Tibetan society in a positive light, and adds another attractive dimension to the story of his sympathetic engagement with Tibet. But there is an intriguing mystery about this Tibetan wife.

We know that Bogle was the father of two girls who were sent back to the family estate at Daldowie after his death.[2] We also know that he left a pension of twenty rupees per month for "Bibi Bogle" in his will. The term "Bibi," used in Bengal as a general term for a married Muslim woman, was taken over by British men to describe the Indian women with whom they lived, or with whom they had sexual relations on a long-term basis. There is considerable confusion, as we shall see, about the identity of this "Bibi Bogle" – whether she was Tibetan, Bhutanese, or Bengali. We do not even know her name. There is no doubt that Bogle did "marry" in Bengal, that he had children, and that he provided for his widow and children in the event of his death. When the family solicitors in Glasgow made their enquiries in 1820, they were told by the Calcutta lawyers that

---

[1] Hugh Richardson, "George Bogle and His Children," *Scottish Genealogist* 29 (September 1982), pp. 74, 76.
[2] *Ibid.*, p. 79.

there remained a balance of about 6,000 rupees in Bogle's estate "but as nearly the whole of it is required to provide for the pension we do not at present make any further remittance. The Pensioner is still an active healthy woman likely to live for many years to come."[3] Bibi Bogle died in 1838 having survived her husband by fifty-seven years.

This willingness to marry a local woman, to openly acknowledge and assume responsibility for the children, and to take care of the widow through a monthly pension disbursed by a Calcutta law firm, is in marked contrast to later British behavior in India. Bogle's conduct in these matters was not unusual for the time however. All colonial regimes, as Suresh Ghosh reminds us, "whether Spanish or Portuguese, Mughal or British, have created mixed communities in their country of settlement. But the manner of creation, the social range involved, the attitudes displayed – from positive encouragement to vigorous disapproval – have been specific."[4] We need to explore the specific circumstances of these cross-racial liaisons in Bengal in the 1770s and 1780s so we can better understand what Bogle and his friends referred to as their "domestic arrangements."

The topic of interracial marriage in India in the late 1700s has fascinated scholars and general readers alike. That world has been brought to vivid life in William Dalrymple's *The White Mughals*, which presents an engaging picture of intermarriage between Indian women and British men. Dalrymple's starting point was the marriage in 1800 of Lieutenant Colonel James Achilles Kirkpatrick, the British Resident at the Court of the Nizam of Hyderabad, to Khair un-Nissa (Most Excellent Among Women), the grand-niece of the *diwan* or Prime Minister.[5] Outside the Asian and African Reading Room of the British Library there is a large oil painting which captures the world Dalrymple describes so well. It is a 1785 canvas by Johan Zoffany depicting "General William Palmer and His Family." In addition to Palmer, the figures represented in the painting are "Faiz Baksh, a Begum of the Oudh royal family, their two sons and daughter, two Indian female attendants and the Begum's sister."[6]

---

[3] Colvin Bennett and Company to Robert Brown (c/o Brown and Watson, Glasgow), Calcutta, September 18, 1820, Bogle Papers, Folder: George Bogle [marked 9], Mitchell Library.

[4] Suresh Chandra Ghosh, *The Social Condition of the British Community in Bengal 1757–1800* (Leiden: E. J. Brill, 1970), p. 57.

[5] William Dalrymple, *The White Mughals. Love and Betrayal in Eighteenth-Century India* (London: HarperCollins, 2002).

[6] Suresh Ghosh, *British Community in Bengal*, p. 78. For many decades the picture was hung on the walls of the room of the Parliamentary Secretary of State for India. It was subsequently displayed (until recently) on the wall to the right of the entrance to the

The painting presents a happy domestic scene of complete intimacy and mutual respect between British men and Indian women.

Both the Zoffany painting and Dalrymple's book deal with the top ranks of society on the Indian and British sides. A broader study of male–female relationships in this period has been made by Durba Ghosh in her comprehensive account of "bibis, begums, and concubines" in north India between 1760 and 1830.[7] Ghosh discovered that in the five-year period from 1780 to 1785, which includes the year of Bogle's death, one out of every three wills filed in the Calcutta High Court made reference to a native woman or a concubine. Basing her estimates on wills and baptismal records, she calculates that "anywhere from 20%–50%" of Company men were involved in some sort of relationship with local women.[8] The challenge facing the Company men who sought female company or wished to marry and have children was that there were very few English women in Bengal. It was also prohibitively expensive to maintain the European-style household expected of a British couple. "The situation of the large majority who did not marry was only rendered tolerable," Suresh Ghosh notes in a matter-of-fact manner, "because concubinage with women of the country was possible financially, and was socially tolerated. Concubinage was indeed the rule rather than the exception."[9]

These interracial relationships began to decline over the next fifty years. Anxieties about them took hold as early as the 1790s. During the Governor-Generalship of Lord Cornwallis (1786–1793), for example, regulations were issued prohibiting the admission of mixed race individuals to the civil service or military branches of the Company. Suresh Ghosh

Asian and African Reading Room in the British Library. There is a question of attribution about this painting. It has sometimes been put down as one of Francesco Renaldi's works. See, for example, Beth F. Tobin, *Picturing Imperial Power. Colonial Subjects in Eighteenth Century British Painting* (Durham, NC: Duke University Press, 1999), pp. 112–113. William Dalrymple in *White Mughals*, pp. 206–207, describes it as "the famous Zoffany picture." The National Portrait Gallery catalogue for its exhibition of many of Zoffany's paintings and drawings does not list this picture. See Mary Webster, *Johan Zoffany 1733–1810* (London: National Portrait Gallery, 1976). For our purposes, the attribution issue is not significant. Both Zoffany and Renaldi painted pictures of families – often with both Indian and British members – in eighteenth-century India.

[7] Durba Ghosh, *Colonial Companions: Bibis, Begums, and Concubines of the British in North India, 1760–1830*, Ph.D. dissertation, University of California, Berkeley (2000). This has now been revised and published in book form as *Sex and the Family in Colonial India. The Making of Empire* (Cambridge University Press, 2006). I took my notes from Ghosh when her work was still in dissertation form so all my references are to that source. The argument in the book has been refined and developed but the data she discovered is largely the same and that is what I have used here.

[8] Durba Ghosh, *Bibis, Begums, and Concubines*, p. 41.

[9] Suresh Ghosh, *British Community in Bengal*, p. 70.

proposes that there was a practical reason for this exclusion. Because of their familiarity with the languages and customs of north India, many of the Eurasian young men from these mixed marriages would have been ideal candidates for posts in the Company service, but if they received Company positions there would be fewer jobs for candidates from Britain. This would have threatened the patronage valued by Company Directors and large shareholders in Britain.[10] Durba Ghosh argues that there were broader motivations at work. Such mixed race individuals were beginning to be viewed as signs of the widespread corruption and degeneracy which had infected the Company and which the reformers were trying to root out.[11]

These observations by Suresh Ghosh and Durba Ghosh are contributions to an interesting discussion, going back to Percival Spear's pioneering work in the 1950s, about why British attitudes on these matters began to change from the 1790s onwards. Spear proposed that the arrival in India of more British women in the 1840s closed off opportunities for interracial marriages and shaped opinion against them. Margaret Strobel counters that this explanation allowed too much power to the English women who came to India, and argues that the reaction against interracial marriage was connected to the emergence of a more fully developed imperial ideology. This emerging ideology tried to "make empire respectable" by "frowning upon miscegenation" and distancing the colonial administrators from those who were being ruled. The impact of evangelical Protestantism, the appearance of quasi-scientific theories about "race," the segregating of communities after the bloody events of 1857, and the increasing numbers of British women who traveled to India on P&O steamships following the opening of the Suez canal in 1869 are the developments usually cited to explain the widening gulf between British men and Indian women. All these factors worked gradually to end the cultural and sexual reciprocity of the 1700s.[12]

---

[10] *Ibid.*, p. 83.

[11] Durba Ghosh, *Bibis, Begums, and Concubines*, p. 7.

[12] The literature on this topic, and the conceptual issues at stake, are neatly summarized by Durba Ghosh, *Bibis, Begums, and Concubines*, pp. 8–12. See too Ann Stoler, "Making Empire Respectable. The Politics of Race and Sexual Morality in Twentieth-Century Colonial Cultures," *American Ethnologist* 16 (1989), pp. 634–660, and Margaret Strobel, *European Women and the Second British Empire* (Bloomington: Indiana University Press, 1991), pp. 1–5, 7–8, 10–13. The key works which mark the evolution of scholarly thinking on the subject are T. C. P. Spear, *The Nabobs. English Social Life in Eighteenth Century India* (Oxford University Press, 1963 [1951]), Kenneth Ballhatchet, *Race, Sex and Class under the Raj. Imperial Attitudes and Policies and their Critics 1793–1905* (London: Weidenfeld and Nicolson, 1980), Ronald Hyam, *Empire and Sexuality. The British Experience* (Manchester University Press, 1990), Christopher Hawes, *Poor*

At the height of the British *Raj*, between 1857 and 1914, the small British communities throughout India separated themselves from the local population. Most of the British lived in cantonments outside Indian towns which enabled them to maintain a physical and cultural distance from local communities in India. By 1900 there were legal prohibitions against concubinage and cohabitation.[13] Although sexual liaisons continued to take place, children of those illicit liaisons were no longer sent back to families in Britain, and a British official could not have lived openly with an Indian woman without risking his career and social ostracism from the British club and the British community. Francis Younghusband, as we shall see later, never thought for an instant that he might marry an Indian woman. So in this realm too – family life and sexual relationships – the behavior of Bogle appears to be free from later prejudices, and an example of relatively enlightened eighteenth-century attitudes. However, a closer study of Bogle's case, and of similar examples from amongst his circle of friends in Bengal, casts some doubt on this common distinction between a tolerant 1700s and a racist 1800s in British India.

Many of the Company men had "wives" in Bengal. The men talked to each other about the women in their "zenanas," borrowing another Muslim term for the women's quarters of the household. Apart from the pension provision in Bogle's will there is no other reference in any of his letters or in his journals to a wife. When his journals, and some letters, were finally published in 1876, Clements Markham, who edited the volume, drew a discreet veil over this aspect of Bogle's career in Bengal. Markham referred to the two daughters who had been sent home to Daldowie but no mother was mentioned. By the time Markham saw the Bogle family papers they had been "judiciously sorted and arranged" by a trusted friend of the family.[14] It may well be that letters referring to Bogle's wife were removed from the collection.

It is also possible that Bogle omitted any reference to a wife or wives he had in Bengal for fear of offending his father's religious and moral rigidities. His father's view that "the original natives of that part of the Country where you reside [were] corrupted by gross superstition and blind Idolatory" would not have made him well-disposed to Bogle marrying

---

Relations. The Making of a Eurasian Community in British India 1773–1833 (Richmond, Surrey: Curzon Press, 1996), and Ann Stoler, *Race and the Education of Desire* (Durham, NC: Duke University Press, 1995).

[13] Hyam, *Empire and Sexuality*, pp. 152–159.
[14] Richardson, "George Bogle and His Children," p. 74.

a "heathen" woman.[15] Bogle's father was a traditional patriarch. He described the rebellion in the American colonies, for example, in terms of ungrateful children rising up against a caring father. "We are at present Engaged in an unnatural War with our Children Colonys in America," he wrote to his son in February 1776. "God only knows what may be the Event of this Rebellious Paricide."[16] Bogle always treated his father with formal respect, apologizing for his irregular correspondence, and for not sending enough money back in the difficult two years of 1775 and 1776 to help with the debt on the Daldowie estate. It is hard to imagine Bogle writing to his father to tell him of a Tibetan or Bengali wife. On the other hand, he may have felt able to broach such a topic with his sisters, hoping that they might mediate on his behalf with his father – if so, those letters no longer exist. For whatever reason, there is a frustrating silence in the Bogle papers on this marriage.

The scholarly detective who has done the most work to clear up this mystery is Hugh Richardson. As well as being one of the most respected Tibetologists of the twentieth century, Richardson was a significant figure in terms of Anglo-Tibetan relations. He joined the Indian Civil Service in 1930 and was posted to Bengal. He visited Sikkim during his leaves, crossed into Tibet from there, and began to learn Tibetan and build up a knowledge of Tibetan religion and culture. This was "the start of a long love affair with the country and its peoples."[17] In 1934 he transferred to the Foreign and Political Service of the Government of India, which dealt with the Indian princely states and with neighboring countries. In 1936 he was appointed Trade Agent at Gyantse in Tibet, an office created by the 1904 negotiations at the end of the Younghusband mission. In his first year at Gyantse he went to Lhasa as a member of the British Commission led by Sir Basil Gould to open a relationship with the new Dalai Lama (Tenzin Gyatso [1935–], the Fourteenth, and current, Incarnation) and his officials. As one outcome of these negotiations, Richardson was allowed to remain in Lhasa as a representative of the British Indian government – "the first white representative to function in the capital."[18] He served at Lhasa from 1936 to 1940 and returned after the war in 1946. When Britain left India in 1947 he stayed on as

---

[15] George Bogle (father) to Bogle, Daldowie, January 21, 1771, Bogle Papers, Box: India and Tibet [marked 37], Mitchell Library.

[16] George Bogle (father) to Bogle, Daldowie, February 19, 1776, Bogle Papers, George Bogle, 1770–1781/ Folder 3 [marked 48], Mitchell Library.

[17] "Obituary. Hugh Edward Richardson," *Tibet Foundation Newsletter* 31 (February 2001), p. 23.

[18] *The Scotsman*, December 7, 2000, "Obituary of Dr. Hugh Edward Richardson, Civil Servant and Scholar."

the officer in charge of the Indian mission to Lhasa, finally relinquishing this post in 1950 when the Chinese invaded Tibet. He spent eight years working in Tibet, traveling widely, and becoming intimately acquainted with Tibetans of all social classes beyond the important people he mixed with in Lhasa.

After his retirement from the diplomatic service, Richardson became a formidable scholar of Tibetan history. He also became an advocate of the Tibetan cause on the international stage. His publications included *A Cultural History of Tibet* (1968), *Ceremonies of the Lhasa Year* (1993), and the collection of essays *High Peaks, Pure Earth* (1998) – this last reprinting an earlier investigation of Bogle's possibly Tibetan wife. In 2003 Alex McKay noted in his survey of modern scholarship on Tibet that Richardson's "modestly titled" *Short History of Tibet* first published in 1962 "has long remained the standard text on the subject."[19] Richardson was often a sharp critic of the British government for what he viewed as the British failure to speak out against Chinese policies in Tibet, and for its abandonment of Tibet after it had seemed to support Tibetan autonomy in the 1913–1950 years. "The British Government, the only Government among Western countries to have had treaty relations with Tibet," he bluntly stated, "sold the Tibetans down the river, and since have constantly cold-shouldered the Tibetans so that in 1959 they could not even support a resolution in the United Nations condemning the violation of human rights in Tibet by the Chinese."[20]

When Richardson died in 2000 at the age of ninety-four, the Dalai Lama, who had been a friend of Richardson since the 1930s and 1940s, provided a moving tribute to Richardson's efforts on behalf of Tibet.

In the fifty years since he left Tibet he never once forgot the plight of Tibet . . . In the interest of justice for Tibet he was even prepared to criticise his own government. And because he had lived in Tibet and known Tibet and the Tibetans intimately he was truly precious to us. We feel he is irreplaceable. With his death Tibet has lost one of its foremost champions.[21]

Richardson's prominent role as a critic of Chinese policies in Tibet is not our concern here. Equally knowledgeable Tibetologists in the West, such as the American scholar Melvyn Goldstein, have made a general case that openly anti-Chinese rhetoric and activist support of the exiled Dalai Lama by Westerners have not helped the Tibetan cause.[22] The point here

---

[19] McKay, ed., *History of Tibet*, vol. I, p. 1.
[20] *The Scotsman*, December 7, 2000, "Richardson Obituary."
[21] *Tibet Foundation Newsletter* 31 (February 2001), p. 23.
[22] Melvyn C. Goldstein, *The Snow Lion and the Dragon. China, Tibet and the Dalai Lama* (Berkeley: University of California Press, 1997), p. 123, argues that the Chinese have some basis for their claim that pro-Tibetan lobbyists in the US are "stirring up" Tibetans

is simply to establish Richardson's credentials as someone who deserves to be taken seriously on George Bogle and Tibet.

Richardson first became aware of the mystery of Bogle's wife and family in Bengal when reading some issues of the *Sunday Times* in 1948. In its "Do You Know?" section on February 15 *The Times* had asked "Who was the first Englishman to enter Tibet?" The answer was given on page 6: "George Bogle, a Writer in the East India Company." A week later, a Mrs. Nora Heathcote, indignant that Bogle had been described as English rather than Scottish, wrote a letter to the editor. She identified herself as the great-great-granddaughter of Bogle, and described how Bogle had been "an intimate friend of the Tashi Lama who gave him a sacred necklace (still in possession of one of his descendants in Scotland)."[23] This exchange was apparently read by Richardson and led him, while he was still in Tibet, to make some inquiries about Bogle's marriage. After his return to Britain he launched a thorough investigation of the family claims of a distinguished Tibetan ancestor. Between 1959 and 1962, he conducted what he called "a delightful correspondence" with Nora Heathcote. From that correspondence he developed a full picture of what the family tradition had to say about Bogle's Tibetan wife. Richardson's enquiries before he left Tibet, however, had led to a dead end. He reported, with apparent regret, that "before leaving Tibet in 1950 I questioned many friends, especially those in Shigatse, about that intriguing story, but none had heard of it: no one had even heard of George Bogle."[24]

The absence of any Tibetan sources on this matter, along with the silence in Bogle's own papers, make the question of Bogle's wife an apparently insoluble problem. But with Richardson's able guidance some light can be shed on the mystery. Looking for evidence of a special relationship with a Tibetan woman, Richardson searched for clues in Bogle's account of his activities in Tibet. Bogle described his five-month sojourn at Dechenrubje and Tashilhunpo as the happiest period in his life. As he prepared to leave Shigatse in April 1775, he tried to find words, in a letter to his sister Elizabeth (Bess), to express this happiness. Above all, he wished to convey his affection for the Panchen Lama but there was also a broader sense of pleasure that extended beyond that friendship:

and threatening China's strategic interests in their frontier regions. Goldstein made the same case in his paper "Tibet and the People's Republic of China. Is there Light at the End of the Tunnel?" Lecture, October 13, 2003, Asian Studies Center, Michigan State University.

[23] *Sunday Times*, February 15, 1948, pp. 2, 6; February 22, 1948, p. 6.
[24] Richardson, "George Bogle and His Children," p. 75.

As the time of my departure drew near, I found that I should not be able to bid adieu to the Lama without a heavy heart. The kind and hospitable reception he had given me, and the amiable disposition he possesses, I must confess had attached me to him, and I shall feel a hearty regret at parting. In spite of all my journeyings and wanderings over the face of the earth, I have not yet learnt to take leave, and I cannot reconcile myself to the thoughts of that last farewell. When I look at the time I have spent among these hills it appears like a fairy dream. The novelty of the scene, and the people I have met with, and the novelty of the life I have led, seem a perfect illusion. Although my days have been spent without business or amusement, they have passed without care or uneasiness, and I may set this down as the most peaceful period of my life. It is now almost over, and I am about to return to the hurry and bustle of Calcutta.[25]

To convey the depth of his feelings Bogle turned to the archaic "ye": "Farewell, ye honest and simple people! May ye long enjoy the happiness which is denied to more polished nations; and while they are engaged in the endless pursuit of avarice and ambition, defended by your barren mountains, may ye continue to live in peace and contentment, and know no limits but those of nature."[26]

Such passages reveal Bogle's attachment to the Panchen Lama, and a general affection for the Tibetans he had befriended, but there is not even a suggestion of a close relationship with a Tibetan woman. He even told his sisters that he lived like a monk – which was a plausible tale since he spent most of his time in guest quarters at the two monasteries at Dechenrubje and Tashilhunpo. In a letter to his friend David Anderson he explained that "the life of a Monk is the most tiresome of all lives unless seasoned with a larger Portion of Devotion than I, alas!, am possessed of."[27] In the passage quoted above he states that his days were spent without amusement but on the way back to Calcutta, Dr. Alexander Hamilton, the assistant surgeon in the Company service who was assigned to accompany Bogle, treated him for a venereal infection, advising him to apply poultices "in which a small quantity of mercurial ointment is dissolved."[28] We do not know where he picked up such symptoms – it could have been in Bhutan, or the sores may have been a recurrence from even earlier sexual contacts in Calcutta – but it is at least possible that he became infected as the result of a sexual relationship during his stay in Tibet. Kate Teltscher has discovered one reference

[25] Markham, *Bogle*, p. 177; Lamb, *Bhutan and Tibet*, p. 276.

[26] Markham, *Bogle*, p. 177; Lamb, *Bhutan and Tibet*, p. 276; Teltscher, *High Road to China*, pp. 158, 159.

[27] George Bogle to David Anderson [Tibet, 1775], David Anderson Papers, Add. 45421, f. 33, BL.

[28] Alexander Hamilton to George Bogle, Cooch Behar, May 17, 1775, Lamb, *Bhutan and Tibet*, p. 387.

that might be revealing. Bogle claimed that "Tibetan women are kind, tender-hearted, and easily won" but Teltscher cautiously adds that "it is not clear whether Bogle was writing from experience or hearsay."[29] Such brief snatches of evidence as these, however, are not very satisfactory. Even when he is telling his friends and family how happy he was in Tibet, there are simply no direct references to a Tibetan woman whom he may have taken as a wife or lover.

Richardson dismisses outright the possibility that Bogle married a sister of the Panchen Lama, which was the story insisted upon by the family memory in Scotland. Richardson's cogent objections to this possibility rest primarily on political and diplomatic grounds. The Panchen Lama was at that time, during the minority of the Dalai Lama, perhaps the most powerful figure in Tibet, and a hugely significant figure in Mongolia and all the other regions in the western borderlands of China influenced by Tibetan Buddhism. He was shortly to be invited to Peking by the Chinese emperor. Bogle's mission was to persuade the Panchen Lama to help increase trade between Bengal and Tibet, and beyond that to help in opening up trade with China itself. To have entered into an intimate relationship with a sister of the Panchen Lama would have threatened to bring an abrupt and unseemly end to the mission. For his part, the Panchen Lama well knew that the Regent and the Chinese Ambans at Lhasa had not wanted to allow Bogle entry into Tibet in the first place. They had reluctantly agreed to allow Bogle to proceed as far as Shigatse but had refused permission for him to go to Lhasa. For the Panchen Lama to have permitted this English interloper to marry one of his sisters would have seemed far too friendly and accommodating to the officials in Lhasa. On top of all that, Richardson points out that the Panchen Lama probably did not even have a sister.[30]

In Bogle's narrative, however, there is reference to a woman who was, in Richardson's view, a much more likely candidate for Bogle's Tibetan wife. In addition to his warm friendship with the Panchen Lama, Bogle established, as we noted in the previous chapter, a close relationship with two of his nephews, the Pung Cushos. The Pung Cusho brothers were sons of the Chanzo Cusho (Chungpa Hutuktu) who was the Panchen Lama's half brother, having the same mother but a different father. (Chanzo Cusho became Regent at Tashilhunpo in 1780 upon the death of his half brother.) There were also two nieces – sisters of the Pung Cushos – and Bogle spent time in the company of these young women. Bogle first met the nephews and their sisters when the Panchen Lama's

---

[29] Teltscher, *High Road to China*, p. 150.
[30] Richardson, "George Bogle and His Children," p. 77.

entourage returned from Dechenrubje to Tashilhunpo. The party had reached Tashitzay where there was a monastery and a small garrison in the local dzong or fort. Tashitzay was also the Panchen Lama's birthplace and a welcoming celebration was to be held. Bogle was lodged

in a good room in the castle, which looked into a small court, where the dancers were to exhibit. Tashi Lama's nephews came and passed the whole day with me, and here I began an acquaintance and connection with them, which turned out to be the most pleasurable of any I made in the country. I also had a visit from his nieces, the nuns, and the Tasitzay Depon or Killadar [a Bengal term for the commander of a fort or garrison].[31]

Here is the first hint of special personal friendship amidst the official and semi-official contacts that Bogle was making during his stay.

The contacts with the nephews and the two nieces, who were described as nuns, were resumed when Bogle reached Tashilhunpo. Bogle spent a lot of time in their company during the celebrations marking the Tibetan new year:

The holidays at the New Year drew nigh, and the Tashi Lama's relations came from different parts of the country to pay their respects to him. His cousin, the Tashitzay Depon, with his wife and family; his nieces, the two annis (nuns) whom I saw at Tashitzay; their mother Chum Cusho; their two brothers, the Pung Cushos, and a half sister named Dorje Phakmo [Thunderbolt Sow], a female Lama, who is abbess of a monastery [Samding] near the Palti Lake, and according to the belief of the people is animated by the spirit of a holy lady who died many hundred years ago. All the ladies, together with the Depon, were lodged in a house situated in a grove of old trees under the palace, and the Pung Cushos in a Kalmuk tent adjoining to it. Mr. Hamilton cured Dorje Phakmo and Chum Cusho of complaints they had been subject to, and I improved my connection with the Pung Cushos.[32]

Bogle described how the two Pung Cushos, who were about the same age as him, "used often to come and pass two or three hours with me. I sometimes went down to their tent, where we spent time in singing, smoking, drinking chang, and playing upon the flute or guitar, at which the elder brother is a great adept. We made little excursions into the country; and I afterwards accompanied them to their estate at Rinjaitzay, and spent five or six cheery days at their castle."[33]

---

[31] Bogle's Journal from Dechenrubje to Tashilhunpo, Lamb, *Bhutan and Tibet*, p. 170.
[32] Bogle's Journal, Tashilhunpo, December 1774–April 1775, Lamb, *Bhutan and Tibet*, p. 183.
[33] *Ibid.*, p. 183.

On February 15, 1775 Bogle and Hamilton made another extended visit with the young Tibetans. They spent time shooting at a mark, running horse races, and feasting at an encampment in the countryside a few miles from Tashilhunpo. Three days later, when the entire party was back at Tashilhunpo, Bogle told his sister that he "waited upon the ladies." He described the mother, "the Chum Cusho," as "a cheerful widow of about five and forty, with a ruddy complexion, and the remains of having once been handsome." Her sister, her sons, and her daughters were also present. "We had plenty of tea, mutton, broth, fruits etc.," reported Bogle, "and the old woman was as merry as a cricket." After describing a blessing he received from the Dorje Phakmo, who "laid her hand upon my head" as he knelt before her, Bogle mentioned the two young women again. The two nuns, he wrote, "are as merry and good-humoured as their mother. The eldest who is about seven or eight and twenty, is dark complexioned and hard featured. The youngest is about nineteen; remarkably fair and ruddy."[34]

Hugh Richardson suggests that one of these two women could have been Bogle's Tibetan wife. These are the only likely candidates hinted at in his letters. The female incarnation can be easily ruled out as a marriage partner, and so too can Chum Cusho, the widow in her forties with a grown family. "But there are her two merry, good humoured daughters of about 27 and 18 years old, the last of whom Bogle singled out as remarkably fair and ruddy, and who is specially mentioned in a letter to his favourite sister Mary."[35] The fact that the two young women were nuns was not, in Richardson's view, an insuperable obstacle to a relationship with Bogle. "In practice a great deal of licence was allowed to nuns in Tibet," he points out, "especially those of noble family whose vows were often a matter of convenience or convention."[36] Bogle himself noted the sometimes lax standards (when measured against conventional European views of these matters). He informed his sister Mary that

there are a good many Nunneries in the Kingdom. The vows taken in them are much the same as in Roman Catholic Countries; but the Discipline is not so strict. The nuns are allowed to go abroad where they sometimes form such Connections as puts an End to their monastick character, and to their Life of Celibacy.[37]

This arch commentary to his sister hints tantalizingly at the possibility that Bogle was speaking from experience.

[34] *Ibid.*, pp. 185, 186.
[35] Richardson, "George Bogle and His Children," p. 77.   [36] *Ibid.*, p. 77.
[37] George Bogle to Mary Bogle, n.d. [at Tashilhunpo], India Office Records, MSS. EUR. E226/77j, BL.

Richardson concedes there is a great deal of speculation involved in this hypothesis but he thinks it the most likely possibility from the fleeting clues left in the Bogle letters and journals. A possibly supportive piece of evidence is Bogle's determined silence on a quarrel involving the girls' brothers. We noted in the preceding chapter that Bogle drew a veil of silence over a dispute between the two Pung Cusho brothers and the Tashitzay Depon. They were on "but indifferent terms with him on account of his wife who belongs also to them."[38] If it is true, as Richardson suggests, that Bogle had formed a relationship with one of the sisters, then Bogle's refusal to indulge his readers' curiosity on this matter becomes more understandable. It may be that he was writing about a family with whom he was now in a relationship more intimate than friendship.

In his pursuit of the identity of Bogle's wife, Richardson also deals with the troubling matter of the pension. The amount of twenty rupees a month seems small for a Tibetan woman closely related to the Panchen Lama. When George Woodcock took up this Bogle marriage mystery in his book *Into Tibet* (1971) he argued that this monthly pension was so miserly it could not possibly have been intended for a high-status Tibetan woman. Woodcock therefore dismissed the possibility that Bogle had a Tibetan wife at all. Richardson rejects this view, arguing that

Dr. Woodcock, who regards Rs 20 per month as an incredibly cheap rate for a relative of the Panchen Lama, exaggerates the difficulty by describing Bogle's supposed wife as a "Tibetan Princess" – a grossly inflated title even for a sister of a high lama; and if lesser relatives were concerned, Rs 20, which in the early decades of the present century [the twentieth] went quite a long way in an Indian family, would not have been an insignificant sum, to which would be added the jewellery and such things which would have been given to a Bebee.[39]

Woodcock's proposed solution to the puzzle was that Bogle might have married a Tibetan woman after he returned to Calcutta in 1775. Richardson counters that Bogle had no Company position after he returned and little income at the time, surviving precariously, as we have seen, as Hastings' private secretary. Moreover, Richardson points out that it was highly unlikely there were any Tibetan women living in Calcutta. It could be argued that Bogle married after he was posted to Rangpur in northern Bengal – where it was slightly more likely there were Tibetan women. Richardson does not think that rings true either. Bogle arrived in Rangpur in 1779 and died in April 1781. If the children had been

---

[38] Bogle's Journal, Tashilhunpo, December 1774–April 1775, Lamb, *Bhutan and Tibet*, pp. 184, 185.
[39] Richardson, "George Bogle and His Children," p. 78.

born in that period they would not have been old enough to be sent to Scotland in the winter of 1783–1784.[40]

Richardson surely has the better case than Woodcock in this wrangle over Bogle's marriage. Richardson had more knowledge of Tibetan history and culture, and Woodcock took some untenable positions. For example, Woodcock expressed doubts that Bogle had any daughters who were sent from India to Scotland but all the sources are clear on that basic fact. Richardson also doubts Woodcock's judgment because Woodcock "perhaps unreceptive to the language of manners of the eighteenth century takes a strangely sour view of the personality of George Bogle, whom he sees as self-centered, callous and hypocritical."[41] Richardson easily disposes of Woodcock's reasoning and defends his own suggestion that Bogle probably had daughters by one of the two nieces of the Panchen Lama. As we have seen, he thinks the fact that the women were nuns was no obstacle.

He also reads significance into the words used when Nora Heathcote spoke to him about the traditional family tale. He is wary of the fanciful story of "a Tibetan lady wading a river to follow George as he left Tibet." But there are features of the family lore that Richardson thought were authentic. When Richardson was writing back and forth to Nora Heathcote she showed him a family tree with the notation that George married "Tichan, sister of the Teshoo Lama." While Richardson rejected the sister of the Panchen Lama part of the story he was struck by the use of the name "Tichan." For Richardson this was significant. "There is a further point which inclines me strongly to believe it [the family tradition]," he writes. "The name 'Tichan, sister of the Teshoo Lama' is not Indian but can readily be identified with the Tibetan name Dechan (bde-can)." Richardson makes the point that "a lady born in the middle of the nineteenth century and living at a time when little was known or written about Tibet, could not have invented such a name."[42]

Richardson's meticulous research, his judicious approach, and his profound familiarity with Tibet all add weight to his case. He does concede that "there is no documentary proof that George did have a Tibetan wife [but] it is difficult to dismiss a story which has survived with such strength and persistence." It is clear that Richardson, in spite of his painstaking scholarly approach, wanted the Tibetan wife story to be true. He ended his investigation with an admission: "I would like to think that the redoubtable Bebee Bogle, who withstood the climate of Calcutta for so long, was a Tibetan."[43] Richardson's love of Tibet – and the part played by his own career in connecting Britain and Tibet, just as Bogle had done – may have swayed his judgment a little.

[40] *Ibid.*, p. 78.   [41] *Ibid.*, p. 76.   [42] *Ibid.*, pp. 76, 80.   [43] *Ibid.*, p. 80.

The perplexing question of Bogle's Tibetan wife is just the beginning of the story. Focusing on the truth or falsehood of this family tradition obscures other possibilities, and does not fully take into account the broader context of relations between European men and Indian women in this era. The images created in the Bogle family tradition, with a Tibetan girl wading across a mountain stream to follow Bogle, and the authoritative arguments for a Tibetan wife made by Hugh Richardson, leave an enchanting impression of a cross-cultural romance. Bogle's own lyrical description of his time in Tibet, ending with his rapturous leave-taking of "ye honest and simple people," adds to the sense that we are dealing with an entirely innocent story. All the commentary so far seems to suggest that Bogle married a young Tibetan woman with whom he had spent many happy times during his sojourn at Tashilhunpo enjoying country festivities with her and her brothers. Because the story is told from Bogle's perspective, the impression we are left with is one of mutuality – an appealing example of cultural exchange and sharing across gender and national boundaries. The provision of a pension for what turned out to be a very long life for the widow adds to the sense that something honorable was going on.

Yet there are features of Bogle's own case that point to a more exploitative dynamic. One clue that leads into this more complex story is that the two girls who were sent to Daldowie in 1783–1784 were not Bogle's only children. This raises the possibility that Bogle had more than one "wife" while he was in Bengal. Richardson himself was well aware of the other children. In the course of his genealogical investigation he referred to a letter written from London to Bogle in 1780 by a Mrs. Stewart. This Mrs. Stewart was the widow of John Stewart who had read the paper on Bogle's Tibet mission to the Royal Society in 1777. Stewart and Bogle had been friends in Bengal. Presumably Bogle had provided Stewart with copies of some journals and other information that enabled Stewart to give the lecture to the Royal Society. The 1780 letter from Mrs. Stewart thanks Bogle for helping settle her husband's affairs in Calcutta. Having done that, she continues:

The present you sent me home is a fine creature. I shall regret my inability if I cannot educate her in the manner I should wish. What is in my power I will do for her with the most heartfelt satisfaction for the sake of him she belongs to. She often mentions you and whenever anything is not quite to her wishes, she says she will go back to Bengal and her Papa Bogle.[44]

This letter is endorsed, but in another hand, "Mary Bogle from Bengal." Richardson notes that this Bogle daughter was sent to London rather

___
[44] *Ibid.*, p. 78.

than Daldowie – perhaps because of fear of Bogle's father's disapproval. Reckoning the girl must have been about six years old (the usual age for sending children back to Britain) Richardson argues that "it seems probable that she was born or at least conceived before he went there [to Tibet]."[45]

There are enigmatic snippets in the correspondence between Bogle's friends from that period which may add weight to this possibility. In September 1772, for example, Samuel Charters, who was Collector at Jessore, complained to David Anderson that "Bogle wrote me he would call here but he is in leading strings."[46] This is the kind of language young Company men might have used to each other when a friend was being preoccupied by a woman. The existence of this child sent to London in the mid-1770s suggests, in Richardson's view, "that Bogle maintained two separate families."[47]

Bogle's extant letters remain silent on this matter of female companionship in Calcutta just as they are silent on the Tibetan wife possibility. This silence is frustrating but we can explore the issues by looking at Bogle's circle of friends in Bengal. This is second best to direct evidence but it will help place Bogle in the context of his own time and place, and open up the attitudes of Company men with respect to liaisons, marriages, and children with Indian women. The more one reads about the behavior of the Company men in Bengal at this time the more likely it appears that Richardson's suggestion of "two separate families" may be far too conservative.

We can enter this world through the letters of Bogle's friends and contemporaries in the Company service in Bengal. The evidence, even with this broader canvas, is, alas, still meagre. In *The White Mughals* Dalrymple deals with the elite levels of British and Indian society where the records are plentiful for both British and Indians. In the lower and middle levels of the Company, where Bogle and his friends were operating in the 1770s, the evidence is much thinner. Although Durba Ghosh discovered many examples of sexual relationships in the course of her research, she confesses that the task of following a clear trail became harder the lower down the men were in the Company ranks. The men worked in various offices in Calcutta, or were posted to stations scattered in the interior of the province where they were isolated from friends. They were collectors, merchants, translators, clerks, accountants, attorneys, and magistrates rather than distinguished Residents appointed to

[45] *Ibid.*, p. 79.
[46] Samuel Charters to David Anderson, Jessore, February 12, 1772, David Anderson Papers, Add. 45425, f. 51, BL.
[47] Richardson, "George Bogle and His Children," p. 79.

princely courts. The letters they wrote to each other – the letters that have survived – are not always forthcoming about key details. At times the letters are difficult to decipher because of the cryptic language used.

It is also frustratingly difficult to hear the voices of the Indian women involved in these relationships. In the letters that survive in the India Office Records held in the British Library and in the West Bengal archives, most of the Indian women are nameless or identified by nicknames or by puzzlingly corrupt versions of Indian names. Durba Ghosh discovered in the course of her research that "the recording of women by name is largely incomplete." The Company men frequently used impenetrable nicknames such as "Bunnoo." They also used phrases such as "my housekeeper," "my girl," or "a woman under my protection." Even when Indian-looking names were attempted they were often corrupted by garbled usage and transliteration across several languages. As Durba Ghosh regretfully notes, all this is a great pity for accurate surnames in this Indian setting would have provided information about the regional origins and the religious and caste status of the women. What we see in this Bengal context is part of the general phenomenon of nameless indigenous subjects in colonial records – a typical example of "the olympian violation of women's names" in colonial records, as Gayatri Spivak puts it.[48]

On the men's side, as we shall see, there is a mixture of tenderness and cruelty in their words and actions. They were intimately involved with the women but they often remained detached outsiders. They generally took responsibility for the children, and frequently expressed deep feelings of affection for them. The men even spoke of their "families." Many of the Company men kept several "wives" in their zenanas, and, as their letters will reveal, they sometimes shared the same woman. The general context for their relations with the Indian women was informed by the patriarchal values that shaped marriage and male–female relations in Britain at the time. The men always believed they had the right to be the decision makers. In Bengal, however, many of the constraints on courting and marriage conventions and sexual behavior which would have restrained the men in Britain were loosened.

David Anderson is an interesting example of all these dimensions of gender relations between British men and Indian women in the 1770s. He had arrived in Bengal three years before Bogle. The two Scotsmen developed a close friendship. They both became favorites of

---

[48] Gayatri Spivak, "The Rani of Sirmur. An Essay in Reading the Archives," *History and Theory* 24 (October 1985), p. 267; Durba Ghosh, *Bibis, Begums, and Concubines*, pp. 18–20, 28, 169.

Hastings – part of the loyal, hard-working Scottish circle that Hastings relied upon. In 1776, for example, Hastings used his casting vote on the Council (an act for which he was subsequently censured by the Company Directors in London) to appoint Bogle and Anderson to a three-person commission to prepare a comprehensive study of the Bengal revenues. In spite of the censure, the "usefulness of the report could not be challenged. It provided the basis for the subsequent settlement and determined to some extent the character of the permanent plan for the revenue established in February 1781 [sic]."[49] The importance of the report is not the issue here but is worth noting to illustrate the close relationship that was developing between these two Company servants (and between those two and Hastings). Anderson wrote to thank Bogle for bringing his name to Hastings' attention for this post: "I ought to offer you many Thanks for the part you must have had in bringing this Matter about and I ought to tell you how much Satisfaction I enjoy in the Prospect of being united with you in Business as well as in Friendship."[50]

Anderson ended his career with considerable *éclat* when he was selected by Hastings and the Council to negotiate a peace treaty with Mahadji Scindia and other Maratha leaders in 1782. The Salbai treaty was viewed at the time as a great achievement. The British position throughout India had become precarious with the pressure from Hyder Ali of Mysore in the south and from the dangerous Maratha raids in central India and the Ganges valley. In his excellent study of the Marathas, Stewart Gordon has summed up the position by 1781: there was "a grand alliance to drive out the British [which] included the Nizam [of Hyderabad], Haidar Ali of Mysore, the Bhonsle family, and the Peshwa [at Pune]."[51] All this was against the background of French intervention in the American war for independence and French help for British foes in India. The Company leaders in London warned Hastings and the Bengal Council in February 1780 of "the designs formed by France and Spain to send a strong Squadron of Ships and a considerable number of Troops to attempt the reduction of our Settlements in India."[52] All these dangers loomed as funds for the Company troops were badly depleted. It was during these desperate years from 1778 to 1782 that Hastings resorted to the

---

[49] B. B. Misra, *The Central Administration of the East India Company 1773–1834* (Manchester University Press, 1959), p. 122.

[50] David Anderson to George Bogle, Plassey, November 8, 1776, David Anderson Papers, Add. 45421, f. 65. The letters was signed "Yr. ever affectionate friend."

[51] Stewart Gordon, *The Marathas 1600–1818* (Cambridge University Press, 1993), p. 167.

[52] To Our Governor-General at Fort William in Bengal, London, February 28, 1780, Warren Hastings Papers, Add. 29144, f. 378, BL.

aggressive methods of revenue raising for the Company armies that were to lead to his impeachment.

At the time, most of the Company servants in India admired Hastings' energy and resourcefulness. They viewed making peace with the Marathas as part of a necessary strategy for rescuing the Company position in India. Thomas Graham, a mutual friend of Anderson and Bogle, conveyed the sense of relief in the British community at the signing of the peace treaty. "I congratulate you, my friend, most cordially," he wrote to Anderson, "on the very Honourable, and in my Opinion very Advantageous Issue to which you have brought your negotiations with Scindia." Graham's effusive language shows how significant the peace with the Marathas was regarded as being by the British community in India:

The Conclusion of your laborious Industry has happened at so interesting a Period, as will raise your Reputation far beyond any Idea you can at present form of it. Never did the Mother Country stand in need of so wholesome a comforter for the numberless Misfortunes which in these last Twelve Months have arisen in her European Contests. The News, my friend, of what you have ably accomplished for the good of your Nation will prove the most acceptable Intelligence it has at any time received from India.[53]

While he was in the midst of these critical negotiations, with the entire British position in India at stake, Anderson was also dealing with the affairs of his friend George Bogle.

Bogle died in April 1781. He had named his two friends – David Anderson and Claud Alexander – to settle his estate. In 1782, Alexander, who was then Paymaster General to the Army, wrote to Anderson, who was up at Salbai conducting the Maratha diplomacy, about one of Bogle's last requests. Since Anderson was in regular communication with Hastings about the Maratha peace terms, Alexander thought that he could slip in a note about Bogle's affairs. While Bogle was gravely ill he had requested reimbursement to his estate for presents exchanged (through Purangir Gosain's help) between him and the Panchen Lama. Alexander urged Anderson to write to Hastings

asking him to comply with the last request of our mutual Friend Geo: B. I believe I wrote you some time ago that among Bogle's papers I found a letter addressed to you . . . The following paragraph of it is what I want you to communicate to the Governor. Purangir is returned, but, as Bogle is Dead, he delivered to the

---

[53] Thomas Graham to David Anderson, Chouthy Plain, June 27, 1782, David Anderson Papers, Add. 45423, f. 98, BL.

Governor all the presents which were meant for George and therefore his Estate does not benefit a Sixpence.[54]

Anderson, busy as he was with the Scindia negotiations, took up the issue with Hastings who readily agreed that the money should be transferred to Bogle's estate. "I am happy to inform you," Alexander reported from Calcutta, "that the Governor signed and passed Bogle's Bill."[55]

Anderson and Alexander also discussed what to do with Bogle's children. Alexander sent the sad news that one child had died. "With respect to Bogle's Children," he explained to Anderson on May 3, 1782,

I have now received 36,000 Sicca Rupees on their Account but I am sorry to tell you that the Eldest boy, Master George Bogle Esquire, died suddenly on the last day of April. The acct. I have of his Death is that he was seized with a violent Headache in the Evening and afterwards a vomitting. He expired during the Night . . . I had his Corps buried next to his Father but, not being a Christian, the Funeral Service was not read over him.[56]

Alexander was now concerned about the well-being of the other children and wished to make some contingency plans. "I wish you was come Down that we might take some Steps towards being apptd. the Court Guardians to the Children, and consider what we are to do with the Money in case they should all die."[57]

In these letters Bogle's family business was intertwined with high matters of state. While Anderson was engaged in crucial treaty negotiations with the Marathas he was also spending time on Bogle's affairs – arranging for the value of the Panchen Lama's presents to be added to the Bogle estate, worrying about Bogle's children, and asking the Governor General to become involved. The two men shifted easily from the personal to the political. Anderson's success in the Maratha negotiations had been such a triumph that Alexander believed Anderson would be rewarded with a plum post by the Company – the Resident to the Court of the Nawab-Vizier of Oudh at Lucknow. In the same letter in which he reported the death of Bogle's son, and opened up the guardianship issue, he discussed what would happen to Anderson's career. "I am exceedingly happy to find that your Business is at last finished. It will do you immortal Honor, I hope you will be rewarded with Lucknow, nothing else is good enough for you."[58] When Anderson suggested that the guardianship matter be

[54] Claud Alexander to David Anderson, Calcutta, April 13, 1782, David Anderson Papers, Add. 45424, f. 74, BL.
[55] Claud Alexander to David Anderson, Calcutta, May 31, 1782, *ibid.*, f. 83, BL.
[56] Claud Alexander to David Anderson, Calcutta, May 3, 1782, *ibid.*, f. 77, BL.
[57] *Ibid.*   [58] *Ibid.*

put off until he could get back to Calcutta from Gwalior, Alexander once more mixed personal and political matters. "Yes my Friend, I agree with you that it would be better to let the Guardianship alone until you return but I hope that will not be soon for I shall be very much disappointed if you do not get Lucknow as a reward for your good services."[59]

In this Anderson–Alexander–Bogle triangle of friends we begin to get glimpses into the family world of these Company men. There is close attention paid to money matters. There is concern for the children – the dead boy and the well-being of the remaining youngsters. The dead child is respectfully referred to as "Master George Bogle Esq." and was buried alongside his father in the European cemetery. On the other hand, he was not given a funeral service. This could simply have been because the boy had not been baptized, or it may be the boy had been left to be brought up by the mother in her own religion. The phrase "not being a Christian" suggests something more substantial than not being baptized. Alexander could simply have noted that the boy had not yet been baptized if that had been the problem. The boy was also well beyond the usual age for baptism in the Anglican church. By using the phrase "not being a Christian" Alexander appears to be putting some distance between Christians like himself and Master Bogle. The brief account of the boy's death and burial raises questions about the status of such children within the British community – they were of it but not quite in it. And amidst all the detailed discussion of the money in the estate, the death of the boy, and the guardianship of the surviving children, there is no mention whatsoever of the mother.

The death of another child takes us deeper into this world. This time it was one of David Anderson's. In August 1775, Samuel Charters, a friend of both Bogle and Anderson, agreed to visit one of Anderson's children born while Anderson was away from Calcutta. "I had fixed this day to go to see your Child 7 days old when, after dinner, news of its death was brought me," Charters explained.

I was alarmed a little at the suddenness of it and sent people to examine it and the Circumstances attending it – it appears to have been something in its throat for it has never been able to suck or take any nutriment – all suspicions of the Mother are removed by the grief she discovers very violently – I had it buried tonight, and as it has happened I do not regret it much for your sake.[60]

59 Claud Alexander to David Anderson, Calcutta, June 20, 1782, David Anderson Papers, Add. 45424, f. 87, BL.
60 Samuel Charters to David Anderson, Calcutta, August 10, 1775, David Anderson Papers, Add. 45425, f. 106, BL.

One week later, Charters reported the results of further enquiries he had made into the child's death. Apparently he was not quite sure of the genuineness of the grief expressed by the mother – he also wanted to make sure, as far as was possible, that the child was Anderson's. "I am perfectly satisfied as to the death of the Child and that it had fair play," he assured Anderson. "My people who saw the Child say it was very fair and of a white man; she treated it tenderly and expressed great grief by crying etc. at the time." The question now was what to do about the mother.

I cannot advise you with respect to provision for her – if you continue a small allowance to her till she gets a Master it would do well; but all the time she will take herself to her old trade of basket making and I see no necessity for you to assist other than in this amount. I will see her, and sound her own inclinations, and then we may hit on some expedient to rid you of her without hurting your humanity.[61]

There is a finely calibrated sense of responsibility at work here. In having these liaisons the men seemed to reject any radical taboos against miscegenation. Such relationships therefore might possibly be cited as signs of mutual cultural respect between British men and Indian women. Yet the men were only prepared to fully acknowledge the children who were white enough to pass muster in the English community. The deliberations seemed to follow a series of necessary steps in such matters. First, there is an effort to determine if the child was white enough to be Anderson's. This particular scrutiny of skin color satisfied Charters that the father was English; the general features of the child confirmed Anderson's paternity. But the way in which Charters described his investigation also suggests that he thought there was a possibility that the child was not by a Company man – that is, that the mother might have been in a relationship with a Bengali man or men. Second, the two British men anticipate the woman might move on to another "Master," presumably a European man who would pay her a regular allowance as Anderson had been doing. Third, Anderson and Charters acknowledge, somewhat perfunctorily, the woman's grief, and accept that Anderson should continue to support her – but only until he can get rid of her.

The two men, by their lights, think they are acting humanely but they also know perfectly well (and tell each other) that they are looking for an expedient way out. Charters thought it a good thing the child had died – "I do not regret it much for your sake" – because the death presumably lessened Anderson's financial liability. Through all this discussion, the

[61] Samuel Charters to David Anderson, Calcutta, August 17, 1775, *ibid.*, f. 109, BL.

mother, initially suspected of infanticide, remains nameless although we do learn she was a basket maker by trade, a low-status woman who had little leverage over these men. The impact on her of her child's death is completely discounted by these two gentlemen.

As this incident shows, the Company men shared stories about their women and thought nothing of mixing discussion of these matters with discussion of their work in the Company. This was evident when Thomas Graham, another friend in Bogle's circle, wrote about Anderson's job of translating some Muslim laws. Graham noted that Anderson had made a good impression on Hastings. He wrote to Anderson in September 1774 to "congratulate you most heartily my friend on your having acquired so considerable a Share of His Honor's good Opinion. I assure you I look upon it as one of the luckiest Circumstances cd. have befallen you in these Times and seriously hope you will one Day benefit from it."[62] One of the tasks Hastings had given Anderson was the translation of Muslim law for use in the Company-supervised courts. Graham joked with Anderson about the possibility of mixing up his official business with thoughts about a woman he was interested in. "You are a sly fellow," he mockingly continued.

In Raptures with a young lady forsooth, and will not vouchsafe to let me into the Secret. I hope as punishment that you will one of these Days insensibly introduce a description of her perfections into your Translation of the Mussulman Laws, and still occupied with the same absence of thought, lay it before His Excellency for his Approval... Oh how I should laugh to see you overcome with that *je ne sais quoi*.[63]

Anderson was on the receiving end of such ribbing because it was apparently not unusual for him to have an interest in more than one woman. In August 1775 his friend Charters, who had helped him over the dead baby, jokingly (and somewhat admiringly) reprimanded Anderson: "You are a Devil of a Fellow at getting Children – You will have a legion by and by."[64]

The letters exchanged between Charters and Anderson in 1774 and 1775 suggest that the men sometimes shared women, which is consistent with Durba Ghosh's findings that the Company men often had several sexual partners in one household.[65] For example, in May 1775 Charters

[62] Thomas Graham to David Anderson, September 13, 1774, David Anderson Papers, Add. 45422, f. 38, BL.
[63] Thomas Graham to David Anderson, Burdwan, August 9, 1774, *ibid.*, f. 28, BL. Graham then added: "But to proceed to Business..."
[64] Samuel Charters to David Anderson, Calcutta, August 17, 1775, David Anderson Papers, Add. 45425, f. 109, BL.
[65] Durba Ghosh, *Bibis, Begums, and Concubines*, p. 189.

wrote to Anderson: "Your Lady timed a visit to me about 12 o'clock last night – the consequence was a joint Concern which she engaged in without ceremony."[66] This reads like coy language for engaging in sex. Charters added that "she is clamorous for some Clothes – what say you to 30 Rupees or so on that account."[67] That last comment from Charters inadvertently shows the woman asking to get something extra in return for her extra work, but it also shows the two men are agreeing on what they will jointly pay for shared service.

A similar situation existed between Anderson and Thomas Graham. In June 1775 a woman the men called "Boulaky" [Golaub (Rose) or perhaps Chembayly/Chameli (Jasmine)?] turned up at Graham's house. She had come from Anderson's household. Graham sent a messenger to Anderson informing him of this development.

The Bearer who is the person that accompanied Boulaky to Patna has brought me the news to this place of her arrival. Not only of her arrival, but of her having taken up her lodging in my Zenana. As she is inclined to be Familiar I have no Objection to her amusing herself there until my return when she shall be kindly entertained for a few Nights and receive her Dismission with the Sum you have desired.[68]

Graham updated Anderson on the situation two months later. "I believe I forgot to tell you what has become of Boulaky," he began.

She is still in my Zenana. She and the other spar a little but they are not yet come to daggers drawing. I hope in this I have not transgressed your Inclinations. She would not let me be familiar with her until I paid her the 100 Rupees you ordered, and wherewith I believe she treated her relations and sent them to their Home, and after that she came and offered her Services to me.[69]

Graham ended his report by telling Anderson that he would soon be letting one of his women go. "I must however dismiss one of my family – and I am afraid it will fall to her lot to go . . . for she is not so handsome

[66] Samuel Charters to David Anderson, Calcutta, May 4, 1775, David Anderson Papers, Add. 45425, f. 78, BL.

[67] Ibid.

[68] Thomas Graham to David Anderson, June 11, 1775, David Anderson Papers, Add. 45422, f. 81, BL. As Durba Ghosh tells us, names for the women are a major problem when investigating this topic. In his guidebook for men going out to India in the service of the Company, Captain Thomas Williamson listed some names he claimed were used by the British men: "Golaub (rose water), Chembayly (jasmine), Gool-begum (queen of roses), Meevah-Jahan (fruit of life), Soorooj (the sun)." See *The East India Vade-Mecum or Complete Guide to Gentlemen intended for the Civil, Military or Naval Service of the East India Company* (London, 1810), vol. I, p. 451. What looks like "Boulaky" in these letters may be "Golauby."

[69] Thomas Graham to David Anderson, September 1, 1775, David Anderson Papers, Add. 45422, f. 102, BL.

as the other, which is a great Eye Sore and cause of Jealousy."[70] It is not clear which woman Graham is referring to here but if it was "Boulaky" she apparently outmaneuvered Graham and stayed. On September 21, 1775 Graham informed Anderson that "Boulaky has by her [wanton?] management gained the Day, and is Sola in my Rabbit Warren."[71]

This interchange between Graham and Anderson apparently shows that the women were in dependent positions. The men made decisions about who should go or stay, and they determined how much they were going to pay. The men treated the women as sexual beings who could be shipped round between households. But reading between the lines even in the men's letters it is evident that there was some room for the women to exercise agency, albeit in constraining circumstances. In this case it looks like "Boulaky" was able to maintain her position in spite of Graham's initial plans. The women also made sure that they were paid for their sexual work. According to the evidence in these letters, the pay was substantial enough to allow one woman to help her extended family return to their own home. So even as they appear as ciphers in the letters of the men who kept them, the women did have limited opportunities to advance their own interests. They got money, they got clothes, and they were sometimes able to manage the men to their own advantage. But their position was always shaped by the men who paid them.

This was true even in matters of early child care. For example, when a baby girl was born to Boyd Alexander, one of his friends explained to Anderson what arrangements were to be made for the baby while the father was away on business. "As the child is much better with the Mother than with any other Person, I think it had best remain with her til it is weaned, as he may depend on the greatest care being taken of it in my House."[72] While the nursing mother was allowed to keep the child for the time being, the letter-writer, William Maxwell, assumed he and the father had the right to decide where the baby would go. In this case too, we seem to have another multiple-person household, with two men having some kind of relationship with one woman. Boyd Alexander was the father but the mother and baby were part of Maxwell's household (they were "in my House"). Perhaps Maxwell had simply taken the mother and child in as a helpful gesture while Alexander was absent, but again all this suggests that the decision-making power always rested with the men.

[70] *Ibid.*
[71] Thomas Graham to David Anderson, Patna, September 21, 1775, David Anderson Papers, Add. 45422, f. 106, BL.
[72] William Maxwell to David Anderson, Patna, February 9, 1778, David Anderson Papers, Add. 45427, f. 41, BL.

Anderson, Graham, Charters, and the other men in Bogle's circle of friends, in spite of their cavalier language towards their women, referred, with apparent tenderness, to their "families." Graham wrote to Anderson in October 1775 and made a point of telling him that "the family here are well and always Desire to be remembered to you."[73] Again in 1780 he wrote, asking Anderson to "make my Comp[liment]s. to all your Family, Male as well as Female."[74] The attitudes towards the children were a mixed bag. The men took responsibility for their children, displayed tenderness, and gave them respect – as in "Master George Bogle Esq." But there was also considerable callousness alongside the concern. When a child of Anderson's died soon after birth, Graham wrote to "congratulate you on such a speedy Annihilation of your prospects of a numerous Family. But you will, I am afraid, soon revive them if you continue to plough the same fertile Soil."[75]

The men were always concerned about skin color. They scrutinized the children carefully from the moment the babies were born. In August 1775 Samuel Charters wrote to Anderson about another woman whom they called "Mrs. Mack" who had just given birth.

I cannot say I do it with pleasure, but I must acquaint you that Mrs. Mack was delivered of a daughter on Thursday night the 3rd. I have not yet seen it but mean to go tomorrow attended by someone also to judge the colour etc. which at its present Age is not to be done with certainty, nor will I take it upon me to pronounce who is the father, or who is not, till its features are more discernible than they can at present be.[76]

In this case the British men were unsure which one of them was the father – or whether there was possibly a Bengali father – but if it turned out to be one of theirs they wanted the child to be fair complexioned. This was a constant preoccupation. In February 1778 when William Maxwell wrote to Anderson to tell him about the new child of Boyd Alexander's (by "the Macage Girl"), this crucial matter was again addressed. "I have therefore to tell you," reported Maxwell, "she was safely delivered of a Daughter to him about the end of October. The Child is very well

---

[73] Thomas Graham to David Anderson, Patna, October 26, 1775, David Anderson Papers, Add. 45422, f. 112, BL; Graham to Anderson, Patna, September 11, 1775, *ibid.*, f. 103, BL.

[74] Thomas Graham to David Anderson, October 17, 1780, David Anderson Papers, Add. 45423, f. 92, BL.

[75] Thomas Graham to David Anderson, September 21, 1775, David Anderson Papers, Add. 45422, f. 116, BL.

[76] Samuel Charters to David Anderson, August 2, 1775 [?], David Anderson Papers, Add. 45425, f. 104, BL.

and of a Colour which will not shame him."[77] Two years later, Graham, after a visit to Anderson's household in Calcutta, told Anderson that "I went twice and saw your Family who were well, but the little female does not get white. It is darker than the Mother who is grown tall."[78] Here is another anonymous mother, apparently immature enough to still be growing after she had been impregnated by Anderson. Graham paused long enough to notice that even as he was checking the baby's skin color.

Even if the child was fair enough to be taken part way into the English community the language used often kept the child at a distance. For example, Graham wrote to Anderson in 1778 to describe a christening ceremony for a child of one of his friends. Graham had agreed to be the godfather of the child but he could not make it to the ceremony. He wanted Anderson to stand in for him since he was at Benares and could not get down to Calcutta. "The purpose of this is to beg the favor of you shd. you be in Calcutta at the time of the ceremony of Christening Hampton's little Infidel to stand Proxy for me as God Father."[79] Yet there is also evidence of serious attention given to the well-being of the children. This sense of long-term responsibility is nicely conveyed in a letter Graham sent to Anderson in 1780 about the daughter of a mutual friend. "This will be delivered to you by William Berrie's eldest daughter by Name Betsey and who I hereby consign to your Fatherly Care – and I do entreat you will put Her in school and that she be in all respects taken care of as if one of your own. I mean by this that she be upon the same footing in point of Education and Expense."[80]

The peculiar combination of concern and callousness can also be seen when it came to sending some of these children back "home" to Britain. The decision to send a child back to Britain can be viewed as an example of generosity, and a sign of the relative openness of racial values before the rigidities and prejudices of the Victorian era took hold. On the other hand, only some of the children were sent to Britain. The fathers selected from amongst their Indian offspring, and only chose a few who were deemed to be white enough – and these were usually girls. The mothers' wishes were rarely taken into consideration. For the children, of course, Bengal was their home, as was poignantly demonstrated when the Bogle daughter who was sent to London would say, when she was thwarted, that she "will go back to Bengal and her Papa Bogle."

[77] William Maxwell to David Anderson, Patna, February 9, 1778, David Anderson Papers, Add. 45427, f. 41, BL.

[78] Thomas Graham to David Anderson, March 31, 1782, David Anderson Papers, Add. 45423, f. 97, BL.

[79] Thomas Graham to David Anderson, Benares, March 10, 1778, *ibid.*, f. 7, BL.

[80] Thomas Graham to David Anderson, Benares, February 13, 1780, *ibid.*, f. 76, BL.

All of these aspects can be seen playing out in the homecoming of David Anderson and one of his children. Anderson, as we have seen, was probably Bogle's closest friend, a guardian of the Bogle children, and an executor of Bogle's will. The friendship was well known back at Daldowie. In a letter written a few months before his death, Bogle assured Anderson that "you cannot imagine what a favourite you are in my Father's family."[81] In contrast to Bogle, whose untimely death in 1781 prevented him from achieving fame or fortune, Anderson left Bengal with both. He came home in 1785 a rich and highly esteemed servant of the East India Company. After his reputation had been made by his role as the chief British negotiator in the peace treaty with the Marathas during the winter months of 1781–1782 he stayed on at Gwalior as Resident to Scindia's Court until 1785. Anderson had been in Bengal since 1767 – three years before Bogle arrived in Calcutta – which had given him eighteen years to make money. When he left Bengal in February 1785 he sailed back to Britain with a bevy of top officials including Warren Hastings. Sitting in his cabin on board the East Indiaman the *Barrington*, Anderson described the ship-board accommodations for this group of distinguished voyagers home: "[Sir John] Shore and I have 4 Windows of the great Cabbin with a Curtain to let fall betwixt us if we should find it convenient to make a Separation . . . The Govr. will have the Round House, and Dr. Francis will have a division of the Cuddy."[82]

As the *Barrington* rode at anchor off Sagar Island, waiting for the Hooghly pilot to be taken off, Anderson, in a revealing letter to his brother, summed up his thoughts on leaving Bengal. He began by counting his money:

I have added to it [his total earnings] an Estimate of my Estate in India which leaves a surplus of Rs. 54,000. Including this [his estate in India], and making Allowance for failures in my Remittances, I reckon that my whole Fortune is about £50,000. This is very handsome. And if my Name had not been raised so high by the Maratha Business, it is more than ever I could have Occasion for.[83]

This amount did not put Anderson in the very top group of Company men who came home to Britain as rich nabobs. Peter Marshall has calculated that Company men "at the leading commercial and revenue stations," such as John Graham from Burdwan in 1774 or George Vansittart

[81] George Bogle to David Anderson, Rangpur, November 11, 1780, David Anderson Papers, Add. 45421, f. 116, BL.
[82] David Anderson to James Anderson, *Barrington* off Sagar Island, February 4, 1785, David Anderson Papers, Add. 45437, f. 13, BL.
[83] *Ibid.*

from Patna in 1776, could come home with fortunes from £70,000 to £100,000. Hastings himself came back in 1785 with £75,000, although Marshall thinks his fortune had been much larger but had lost value through mismanagement.[84] Still, Anderson had done very well indeed. Back in 1778 he had written about his hopes to his father. He wanted to return from Bengal with enough money "for a small estate in a pleasant part of Scotland and situated in a good neighbourhood with a house upon it fit for one who wishes to live like a gentleman of five or six hundred pound a year."[85] By 1785 he had made it.

Anderson was leaving behind several women and children who had constituted his "family" during his eighteen years in Bengal. As we have seen, his friends had joked about his "ploughing fertile soil" and having "a legion" of children. Some of his Bengali family sailed down the Hooghly to the anchored *Barrington* to take their leave of Anderson. His description of the leave-taking reveals that he cast no backward glances of regret. There is acknowledgment of a momentary sadness, but Anderson makes it abundantly clear that he was glad to be going:

I have suffered much in leaving my Friends, and my old Servants and Dependents, Some of whom followed me with imminent peril down to the Ship. But now that the scene of parting is over I find myself in the midst of some of my best Friends; and the severest Stroke that could possibly happen to me would be to be obliged from any Accident to return to Bengal.[86]

Two months later, as the *Barrington* made a remarkably speedy passage home – it was now at "4 Degrees South of the Line" and well beyond St. Helena – Anderson repeated this sentiment. "Much as I like Bengal, and much as my Affections are attached to the people in it, I have never once felt the least Desire in my mind to return to it."[87]

When the *Barrington* reached the gray waters of the English Channel, Anderson and the other passengers were taken off by a small boat and landed at Plymouth. They made their way to London by coach. In keeping with his new-found status, Anderson made the journey in the company of Hastings. On the same day they landed at Plymouth he "set off for London in a post chaise with Mr. Hastings."[88] When he arrived

[84] Peter Marshall, *East Indian Fortunes. The British in Bengal in the Eighteenth Century* (Oxford University Press, 1976), p. 243.

[85] *Ibid.*, p. 216.

[86] David Anderson to James Anderson, *Barrington* off Sagar Island, February 4, 1785, David Anderson Papers, Add. 45437, f. 13, BL.

[87] David Anderson to James Anderson, *Barrington* 4 Degrees South of the Line, April 27, 1785, *ibid.*, f. 20, BL.

[88] David Anderson, Daily Diary Aboard the *Barrington*, June 13, 1785, *ibid.*, f. 33–f. 38, BL.

in London he met the Chairman of the East India Company and some of the Directors. He then proceeded on to Scotland where he may have called on Bogle's family at Daldowie. He apparently expected to do that because Claud Alexander, his fellow guardian of Bogle's children, had written to Anderson before he left Bengal asking him to "Give my Complts. to Mr. Bogle."[89] By July 10, 1785 Anderson was back in London where he met formally with the Company Directors. "I visited all the Directors," Anderson noted with pride. "I dined with them in a Body one Day at the London Tavern by Invitation of the Deputy Chairman and Mr. Sullivan."[90] David Anderson arrived back in Britain in high spirits – and a rich and well-esteemed man.

Anderson's career in Bengal had been a great success in personal terms, and in the estimation of the East India Company. The reputation he had gained from the Maratha peace negotiations made him an honored figure in London. The fortune he had made in India enabled him to acquire an estate in the countryside outside Edinburgh, sixty or so miles east of the Bogle estate at Daldowie. Shortly after his return, Anderson married and by 1792 had three children. In July 1789 a friend in Lucknow wrote to offer congratulations:

I cannot help congratulating you most sincerely upon your marriage. I have learned from other quarters such accounts of the object of your choice as convinces me you must be happy – and as I have also learned that your family was in the way of being increased, I trust that nothing is wanting to complete your domestic arrangements: which I begin to think are, after all, the most rational, the most precious, and the best thing that we have to look to.[91]

In 1792 Thomas Graham, who was still in Calcutta, replied to a letter he had received from Anderson reporting on his marriage and the birth of the children. "I have much pleasure in acknowledging receipt of your favor of 3 Feby last and of offering my most sincere Congratulations on the increasing State of your family, and in particular upon one of the three little ones being a Son and Heir."[92]

Anderson still had a "family" back in Bengal but the family in Britain was the real thing. It was the male child born in Britain who would become the heir to the Anderson fortune and estate. The Indian children did not count in that respect (which explains why the men preferred to

---

[89] Claud Alexander to David Anderson, March 21, 1785, *ibid.*, f. 22, BL.

[90] David Anderson, Daily Diary Aboard the *Barrington*, July 10, 1785, *ibid.*, f. 33–f. 38, BL.

[91] W. Blane to David Anderson, Lucknow, July 29, 1789, *ibid.*, f. 75, BL.

[92] Thomas Graham to David Anderson, Calcutta, September 3, 1792, David Anderson Papers, Add. 45423, f. 159, BL.

send girls home rather than boys). Anderson still thought of his Indian children, however. In 1791 he even decided to bring one of the girls from Patna to Britain, presumably a child born just before he left Bengal and now about six or seven years of age. We have an account of how this was managed. His friend Blane wrote to Anderson from Lucknow in January 1791 about the girl. "I hope Charters will have executed your wishes in regard to your little girl. My distance from Patna has long precluded my learning anything of her. The Separation will be a bitter cup to the Mother but what can be done when necessity calls."[93] What indeed? This is a poignant anecdote. It encapsulates the asymmetric relationships between British men and Bengali women who bore their children. Here was another nameless Indian mother whose child is taken "home" by the father who now had a wife and three children back in Britain. Although the mother's feelings of bitter sadness are noted, the decision was seen to be one the man had the right to make.

This was the world of wives, concubines, and children that David Anderson, George Bogle, and their friends lived in during their time in Bengal. With this general context in mind it is evident that Bogle's circumstances with respect to wives and children were probably more complicated than the family in Daldowie realized. Hugh Richardson suggests that Bogle may have had two households – a Bengal wife as well as his Tibetan wife. But amongst Bogle's friends it was possible to have children by women who were not permanent residents in their households but were paid concubines – and then have the child taken into the household occupied by a principal "wife," or have it looked after by a woman attached to another Company friend. The men may also have had children by the same woman since they occasionally shared sexual partners.

We know that Bogle had at least three daughters – the two sent to Daldowie after his death, and the one sent to Mrs. Stewart in London in the 1770s. We also know he had at least two sons. If Claud Alexander was paying attention to his grammar when he wrote to Anderson in 1782, describing Bogle's dead child as "the Eldest boy," then there were perhaps three boys in Bogle's household, which, along with the two girls sent to Daldowie and the girl sent to London, makes for a total of at least six Bogle children. If we assume the term "eldest boy" was used loosely because of the total number in Bogle's Bengal family, that still leaves five known Bogle children. A possible third Bogle boy does appear in the Calcutta records in 1784. The entry reads: "Bogle, George. *Baptism*

---

[93] W. Blane to David Anderson, Lucknow, January 22, 1791, David Anderson Papers, Add. 45437, f. 99, BL.

10 February 1784 *Burial* 4 September 1784 *Birth* (illeg.) *Place* Calcutta. *Parents* George (dec[eased].)."[94] This is a puzzling entry for, as we have seen, a boy called George died in April 1782. Assuming this second George was conceived shortly before his father died in April 1781 he would have still been a baby when "Master George Bogle Esq." died in April 1782, and was possibly given his father's name once that child was no longer around. Perhaps he was named George because there was a different mother involved. We simply do not know. Here is another child noted in the records of the British community – and another nameless mother.

It is still possible there was only one Tibetan wife, the Bibi Bogle to whom Bogle left a pension. But it is also possible that Bogle's children came from relationships with various women in a like manner as his friends Anderson, Graham, and Charters. The Bengal context of the 1770s that we can partially reconstruct by looking at Bogle's similarly situated contemporaries suggests that sexual behavior, "marriage," and children were extremely complicated matters. The usual arrangements were rarely monogamous. The framework presented in *The White Mughals*, populated by British men and Indian women engaged in "efforts at promoting tolerance and understanding," is not broad enough to capture all that was taking place between British men and Indian women in Bengal in the 1770s.[95]

A darker picture of relations between British men and Indian women emerges from this investigation of Bogle's network of friends. The world of Anderson, Charters, and Graham, serving at the mid-levels of the Company in the 1770s, was not the same as the world of General William Palmer who held appointments as Resident at the princely courts at Lucknow, Gwalior, and Poona between 1782 and 1801. Palmer was so proud of his Indian family that he commissioned the painting from Zoffany. Charters discussed with Anderson how they could "hit on some expedient" to get rid of one "wife" who was becoming too much trouble. In contrast to the benign image of Anglo-Indian harmony in Zoffany's painting of the Palmer family, the men we have been following often treated their Indian wives and families with callous indifference.

The dismissive approach that was exhibited at times towards Indian women by Bogle's friends can be seen in other sources from the period. Thomas Williamson, an officer in the army who arrived in India when

---

[94] Biographical Index N/1/4/f. 8, 10 [from card catalogue], Asian and African Reading Room, BL.
[95] Dalrymple, *White Mughals*, p. 345.

Bogle was still alive (1778), and spent twenty years in Bengal, wrote a two-volume advice manual for men going out to India in the Company service. *The East India Vade-Mecum; or Complete Guide to Gentlemen intended for the Civil, Military or Naval Service of the East India Company* was full of humorous asides for his intended audience of young males. Williamson retailed the story "of an elderly military officer who kept an Indian harem of sixteen in Bengal [who] could say easily when interrogated by a friend as to what he had done with such a number: 'Oh, I gave them a little rice and let them run about.'"[96]

Even such a high-status (though not aristocratic) British personage as Philip Francis, Hastings' arch-enemy, and confidant of Edmund Burke and others at the top level of British politics at the time, used this kind of off-hand language. Describing life in Bengal to his London friend, John Bourke, in March 1776, Francis wrote: "Here I live, Master of the finest House in Bengal, with a hundred Servants, a country House and spacious Garden, Horses, Carriages, and Black Ladies without End."[97] In this case, we have testimony from a member of the governing Council, who spent much of his time sending off a stream of missives to Lord North, the Prime Minister, about the state of affairs in Bengal. Francis enjoyed his numerous "Black Ladies" and he placed these Indian women in the same category as horses and carriages.

The men in Bogle's networks within the Company service had multiple sexual contacts with Indian women; they had many children to whom they gave varying degrees of acknowledgment; the mothers were often anonymous even when the men wrote about them; the men made the decisions about what would happen to the children; the mother's wishes were often not taken into account; and the skin color of the children had a major impact on how they would be treated. Bogle's friends and contemporaries modified the rules of British patriarchy to suit their desires in the "freer" world of Bengal. We do not hear the women's voices directly, but implicitly in the letters between the men, we can try to imagine a world of constrained pleasure and complex negotiations between them and the men with whom they were involved. Durba Ghosh shows that some of the women had a sense of possessing enforceable rights in terms of support for them and their children after their "husbands" had died.[98] At the end of it all, if we can take Anderson as typical, there was not

---

[96] Thomas Williamson, *The East India Vade-Mecum; or Complete Guide to Gentlemen intended for the Civil, Military or Naval Service of the East India Company* (London, 1810), vol. I, p. 412, BL.

[97] Philip Francis to John Bourke, Calcutta, March 20, 1776, MSS. EUR. E15, f. 283, BL.

[98] Durba Ghosh, *Bibis, Begums, and Concubines*, pp. 237–238.

much looking back with warm affection on Indian wives and children. As the *Barrington* slipped its moorings off Sagar Island and headed into the Bay of Bengal, Anderson was pleased to think that he would never set foot in India again. He was not much interested in bringing East and West together.

How can we ever know that we have recovered a full understanding about sex, marriage, and concubinage in Bengal during this era? This question is prompted by frustrating gaps in the evidence, and by the clashes between those who have written on this tangled topic. Gyan Prakash, for example, has used the publication of Dalrymple's book *The Last Mughal* to criticize Dalrymple's entire approach to British India. Dalrymple's books and articles, complains Prakash, have promoted too gentle a view of the empire in India in which "a human story of interest and immersion in other cultures, languages and artifacts – not mastery – underpinned British imperial expansion." He chides Dalrymple for being too "impatient with Edward Said and postcolonial critics." As a counterweight to Dalrymple, he cites the recent work of Nicholas Dirks whose *Scandal of Empire* shows "greed, duplicity, corruption, exploitation and violence were present at the birth of Company rule in India."[99] The charge here is that Dalrymple's anecdotal description of refined British and Indian encounters misses out the exploitation that characterized most relationships between British men and Indian women. Dalrymple, in short, ignores the "mastery" that the British colonizers had in India.[100]

But when, if ever, did the British achieve such mastery? As we shall see in following chapters, Younghusband and Curzon imagined that they had a mastery over India but Bogle and Hastings were more skeptical and realistic on this score. The letters of Bogle and his contemporaries show that they had grave doubts about their position in India. They had a precarious bridgehead in Bengal but they were faced with powerful threats from Mysore and from the Marathas. They needed Indian bankers and traders and intermediaries to be able to function – as Purangir Gosain's role in facilitating the missions to Tibet clearly demonstrated. Christopher Bayly's account of this period in *The New Cambridge History of India* series is significantly titled *Indian Society and the Making of the British Empire*. He notes that "much of the amazing dynamism of early British penetration and conquest of the subcontinent was due to the underlying

---

[99] Gyan Prakash, "Inevitable Revolutions," *The Nation*, April 30, 2007, pp. 26, 29, 30.
[100] William Dalrymple, "Plain Tales from British India," *New York Review of Books*, April 26, 2007, pp. 47–50; Prakash, "Inevitable Revolutions," pp. 25–30.

tides of petty commodity production, marketing and financial speculation within Indian society."[101] As a result of these conditions in the
eighteenth century, there was much more necessary mutuality and much
more cross-cultural exchange in Hastings' era than was the case by the
time Curzon became Viceroy of India.

Dalrymple's counter-charge against his critics is that their formulaic
approach to empire history puts blinkers on their reading of the evidence. They remain enmeshed in a binary view of empire which deter-
minedly ignores cultural exchanges and interactions in the eighteenth
century which were quite different from conditions by the later decades
of the nineteenth century when racial distancing and separation had
taken hold. He protests that academic criticism of his work "completely
ignores [the] interplay of cultures in the early colonial period." Scholars such as Dirks, he insists, paint "a somewhat reductionist picture
of simple binary oppositions." Dalrymple cites approvingly the work of
Durba Ghosh, some of whose insights we have used in this chapter, as
an example of a new generation of South Asia scholars who "break genuinely new ground in the study of the relationships between colonizer and
colonized."[102]

This subject of wives and concubines is now mired in claims and
counter-claims about gender and colonial culture in eighteenth-century
Bengal. As in many debates of this kind about a complex topic on which
there is not complete evidence, there is merit on both sides. Dalrymple's
beautifully reconstructed world of cultural sharing is so richly embedded in evidence that it is hard to see how his version can be dismissed
as untrue to the lived historical experiences of the Indian and British
women and men he has brought to life in his writings. On the other hand,
the conceptual propositions of Prakash and others, based on aggregate
assessments of the impact of colonialism on male–female relationships,
warn us to take account of the imbalance of power typical in all such settings. To understand the full range of interactions between British men
and Indian women we need to apply all the approaches and perspectives
that can be mustered. Pieces of evidence we have looked at from Bogle
and his contemporaries can be marshaled in ways that could support
either side in the debate. There are examples of tenderness and genuine
respect for the Indian women and the families they created and shared
with the Company men. There are also examples of cruel treatment of
women and children by men whose source of power was the Company's

---

[101] C. A. Bayly, *Indian Society and the Making of the British Empire* (Cambridge University
Press, 1988), p. 204.
[102] Dalrymple, "Plain Tales from British India," p. 49.

position in Bengal. And Philip Francis can be used to suggest that all was not sweetness and light even when the men involved were members of the ruling council of British India.

While many of the women were subject to the power of the Company men, some were able to hold their own at times, and earn status in the community. Even unpleasant witnesses like the callow Captain Thomas Williamson of the Bengal Army, who was not sensitive to female points of view either in Britain or India, noticed that the women in some of these relationships had a certain standing. In the midst of his condescending attitude towards Indian "natives," he was struck by the respect many of the women were given:

In India a woman "under the protection" of an European gentleman is accounted, not only among the natives, but even by his countrymen, to be equally sacred as though she were married to him; and the woman herself values her reputation exactly in proportion as she may have refrained from indulging in variety; some are said to have passed twenty years or more without the possibility of scandal to attach to their conduct.[103]

Suresh Ghosh makes the interesting point in his analysis of this topic that "it is notable that the unofficial wives or mistresses, whether Muslim, Hindus or Portuguese rarely gave up their own religion, customs and way of life. They had their own separate establishments provided by their European protector and seldom went out of their residence."[104] This may explain why "Master George Bogle Esquire" could not be buried as a Christian – perhaps he had been brought up in his mother's religion and culture.

The fragmentary evidence that survives suggests that all of the attitudes and behaviors described by writers who have argued about this subject were present at different times and places. Insights from all sides of the debate have some validity and help shine light into the historical obscurity of the lives of the men and women who cohabited and produced children in eighteenth-century Bengal. It is hard to render definitive and final judgments about male–female relationships in our own society even when we have a cornucopia of evidence from modern social science studies and statistics from government agencies. With incomplete evidence the task is well nigh impossible for eighteenth-century Bengal unless historians simply choose to force their preferred interpretation on the past. The past is rarely as tidy as historians make it. For some couples in Company-ruled Bengal there was true reciprocity; for many women there was poorly paid

---

[103] Williamson, *The East India Vade-Mecum*, vol. I, p. 451.
[104] Suresh Ghosh, *British Community in Bengal*, p. 76.

sexual drudgery; and for others engaged in these relationships, a range of human interactions between these two ends of the spectrum.

Anderson's calculated farewell to Bengal was utterly at odds with Bogle's regretful departure from Tibet. Was Bogle different from Anderson and the other men in the service of the East India Company? Did he remain steadfast to one woman he had met during his happy days in Tibet? Was he as respectful in his treatment of women as he seemed to be in his responses to Tibetan society? There are nagging doubts after reading the letters of his friends. We know that the records from Daldowie were culled in the 1800s which may explain why there is no reference whatsoever to a Tibetan wife in the extant Bogle letters. It is also possible that Bogle was as attentive to the privacy of the wife or wives in his zenana as the most strict Bengali patriarch might have been, and chose not to write about such matters. He was certainly reluctant to write about the marriages of his Tibetan friends. Yet it is hard to accept that there is no mention of a Tibetan wife – or even a hint of such an unusual wife – in any of the correspondence within his extensive network of friends when they wrote to each other about their "domestic arrangements" in Bengal. The men did not restrain themselves from making casual remarks about the women in their lives. Having a Tibetan wife at all, and even more so if she was connected in any way with the Panchen Lama, would surely have prompted some comment amongst his friends over the six years between Bogle's return from Tibet in 1775 and his death at Rangpur in 1781.

There is even some direct evidence that Bogle was not an exception in Anderson's world of multiple sexual liaisons and children by several women. Throughout the 1770s Bogle and Anderson were close friends. Bogle knew some of Anderson's female companions. At the end of a letter written in October 1772, for example, he requested that Anderson "remember me kindly to [Cotta?] and your Betty."[105] After both men had been appointed by Hastings to the new revenue commission in November 1776, Bogle encouraged Anderson to stay with him when he came down to Calcutta to take up the appointment. He held out an enticing prospect waiting in store for his friend:

I have a Room at your Service. Alexander and I live together. We shall go every night to visit the Ladies – in the mornings to visit Mr. Francis and other great men. We shall try to carry the Punch about your Brother's and I don't know what all.[106]

[105] George Bogle to David Anderson, Calcutta, October 17, 1772, David Anderson Papers, Add. 45421, f. 22, BL.

[106] George Bogle to David Anderson, Calcutta, November 4, 1776, David Anderson Papers, Add. 45421, f. 59, BL.

Here we are almost two years after Bogle's visit to Tibet and all the signs are that Bogle is still sharing quarters with other Company men rather than living in his own household. He and Anderson plan to "go every night to visit the Ladies." The light-hearted language in the letter, with its happy anticipation of sexual adventures by a group of bachelor friends, suggests that in late 1776 at any rate Bogle was not in an exclusive relationship with a Tibetan or any other woman.

The pension allowance of twenty rupees per month also remains a problematic issue. Suresh Ghosh reckoned that a minimum stipend for a kept woman was twenty-five rupees per month. According to Durba Ghosh, the stipend for female companions ranged from twelve to one hundred rupees per month. She cites several cases of men leaving monthly allowances in their wills from 100 to 250 rupees for their companions. In his forthright advice manual Thomas Williamson estimated that "taking a broad outline we may put down the whole at about forty rupees monthly [for] the expenses attendant on concubinage."[107] The twenty rupees per month left for Bibi Bogle is at the low end of this scale of estimated costs. Bogle had not been able to make the fortune he and his family had hoped for before he died. He had been in Bengal for just over ten years and three of those, between 1775 and 1778, had been lean years without a Company post which he could use to bring in extra money. Throughout his time in Bengal Bogle had also sent home many remittances to help with the Daldowie debt. Beyond that, his estate also had to help fund the education and upbringing of the three daughters sent to Britain. In this overall financial context, the twenty rupees a month for the widow may have been all that Bogle's estate could afford. The amount, however, is modest and makes one wonder whether Bogle's wife was as exceptional as his descendants believed.

The possession of some Tibetan "jewelry" in the Bogle family cannot be offered as proof of a Tibetan wife. As Richardson noted, if Bogle's wife had jewels when Bogle died she would have kept them – this was the usual custom (and a sign of some decency in these Bengal relationships). The Panchen Lama himself was the source for these Tibetan pieces that fetched up in Scotland. The family papers in the Mitchell Library describe one such gift as the "Rosary and Amulets presented by the Grand Lama to Mr. George Bogle 1775."[108] As we have seen, Bogle continued to exchange gifts with the Panchen Lama right down until his

---

[107] Suresh Ghosh, *The British Community in Bengal*, p. 70; Durba Ghosh, *Bibis, Begums, and Concubines*, pp. 204, 208, 211; Williamson, *The East India Vade-Mecum*, vol. I, p. 414.
[108] Bogle Papers, Box: India and Tibet [3 cards], Mitchell Library.

death in 1781. It is possible to imagine that the Panchen Lama exchanged presents not simply out of his own friendship with Bogle, and as acts of diplomatic courtesy, but because Bogle had become part of his extended family as a result of the special relationship Bogle had formed with one of his nieces back in 1775. Within a year of the mission, Alexander Hamilton (now back in Bhutan), after complaining to Bogle that he had received no news from Tibet, supposed that "the Lama has been more particular in his letters to you."[109] This phrasing could be read to suggest a family tie, but can be read more plausibly as simply a reflection of the close friendship that had developed between Bogle and the Panchen Lama.

If we accept Richardson's reasoning that Bogle had a romantic and sexual relationship with one of the Panchen Lama's nieces during his happy time in Tibet, we can also speculate that after Bogle left Tibet he might have kept in touch by his own letters to her, or through her uncle, or through Purangir who made several trips back to Shigatse. When Bogle wrote to his sisters at Daldowie it would have been easier for him to imply that he had a Tibetan wife (complete with the name "Tichan") rather than admit that the children he was sending home were the consequence of "nights visiting the Ladies" in Calcutta. That is one possible explanation for the family tradition. So the solution to the mystery might be that Bogle, while having multiple female partners like Anderson and the other Company men, made use of his remarkable trip to Tibet to leave the impression with his family that he was married to a Tibetan woman related to his important friend the Panchen Lama. All of this is conjectural but it is in keeping with much of the evidence left to us. It is a scenario that ties together many of the loose ends in the puzzle.

It seems, however, that we shall never recover the complete truth about Bogle's wife or wives while he lived in Bengal. The world of male–female relations that we can catch glimpses of in the letters between Bogle's friends, and between Bogle himself and Anderson, casts considerable doubt on the romantic story of a Tibetan wife. At the end of historical detective work such as this, with its fragmentary evidence, we can never pin down the motivations of the men and women in these colonial encounters. But the issues opened up in these letters reveal some of the social, cultural, and sexual codes and conventions which shaped the behavior of the Company men. Their proprietorial attitude towards their Indian women and children was broadly in keeping with the prevailing patriarchal culture in eighteenth-century Britain. The distancing

---

[109] Alexander Hamilton to George Bogle, Buxa Duar, March 25, 1776, India Office Records, E226/86(a)–(w), BL.

language used towards many of the women, and the numerous incidents of off-hand treatment, suggest that the men, because of the license they assumed in a colonial setting, behaved in a cruder manner than they would have done towards women they might have courted, married, and created families with in Britain. There is certainly a dramatic contrast between the idyllic encounters Bogle described in the Tibetan countryside with the merry nieces of the Panchen Lama, and this world of his British peers in Bengal – with its multiple-female households, money payments for sex, anxious scrutiny of skin color, and examinations to figure out who had fathered a particular child.

1   Tilly Kettle's painting of Warren Hastings, *c.* 1772. Hastings (1732–1818) was the first Governor General of British India. After receiving a letter from the Panchen Lama he sent George Bogle on a mission to open trade and diplomatic relations with Tibet and, he hoped, find a back door into the Chinese empire. An admirer of Indian cultures, he was also a founder of the Asiatic Society of Bengal, one of the goals of which was to bring the richness of Indian civilization to the attention of European audiences.

2 View of Phari. This was the first Tibetan town on the road once the pass at the head of the Chumbi valley had been crossed. During his stay in Phari Bogle witnessed a debate on whether some Bhutanese rebels should be sent back to Bhutan for punishment. He thought the debate displayed examples of the legal maxims found in the books of Hugo Grotius and Samuel Pufendorf, sophisticated European writers on natural and international law. During the 1904 mission British troops occupied the Phari Dzong in their ongoing effort to over-awe Tibetans.

3 and 4 (*opposite*)   Chomolhari mountain from Phari and from Tuna.
It was below this imposing peak lying on the Tibet–Bhutan border
that Bogle witnessed the ecumenical religious service as Buddhists and
Hindus in his party made their *pujas* to the mountain gods. Bogle at
first thought there was going to be a ceremony to mark his entry into
Tibet. He began to understand that he was not at the center of things.

4

5   Tilly Kettle's painting of the Panchen Lama and George Bogle. The
Third Panchen Lama (Lobsang Palden Yeshes, 1738–1780) is seated,
receiving a ceremonial white scarf, while Bogle, dressed in Bhutanese
clothes, is framed by the open window and mountains in the distance.
Bogle's willingness to be painted with local clothes is in marked contrast to Younghusband's insistence during the 1904 Tibet mission that
English dress must be worn to convey messages of British power and
prestige.

LOSSAÑ PALDAN YEŚE

6   This is an inconographic representation of Lobsang Palden Yeshes
(1738–1780), the Third Panchen Lama. The Panchen Lamas were
Incarnations of Amitabha, one of the Five Supreme Buddhas, representing Infinite Light or Wisdom. There were differences between the Lhasa
and Tashilhunpo accounts of the origins of this Incarnation (which led
to rival numbering systems for the Panchen Lamas), and the relationship between Panchen Lamas and Dalai Lamas was complex and often
controverted. This Panchen Lama developed a warm friendship with
Bogle and incorporated Bogle's commentary on India (the "holy land"
for Buddhists) into his guidebook *An Explanation of Shambala together
with a Narrative of the Holy Land* (1775).

7 Shigatse Dzong and Tashilhunpo monastery. Tashilhunpo monastery, just outside Shigatse (pictured here in the 1920s), was the seat of the Panchen Lamas. George Bogle stayed here in the winter and spring months of 1774–1775. It was from this base that he made many of his excursions into the Tibetan countryside where he may have met the Tibetan woman who is believed to have become his wife.

8   Johan Zoffany's painting of William Palmer and his family, 1785.
This painting is used by William Dalrymple and others to show the
mutual respect and tolerance that existed between British men and
Indian women by the middle decades of the eighteenth century. The
family is painted just as an English family would have been presented at
the time with no hint that there was anything questionable about such
cultural and racial mixing.

9   Daldowie House. This was the Bogle country house, built sometime in the 1730s and 1740s (completed by 1745). In this picture it has been considerably altered and its Georgian lines spoiled by nineteenth-century additions. Throughout his time in Bengal from 1770 until his death in 1781 George Bogle sent money back to help pay off the family debts which threatened to force the sale of the house. Shortly before he died, his father sent a letter to Calcutta to thank Bogle for keeping the house in the family by his Bengal remittances. The house was saved at that time by Bogle's Indian career but was sold in 1825 after a little over 100 years in the Bogle family.

10 Hugh Richardson on horseback in Tibet. Hugh Richardson (1905–2000) served as the British and Indian representative in Lhasa in the 1930s and 1940s, the first European diplomat to be posted in Lhasa. After he returned to Britain in 1950, he became a world-renowned expert on Tibetan history and culture, and an advocate for Tibet in its struggle with China. During his time in Tibet he began his detective work to discover the identity of Bogle's supposed Tibetan wife by questioning his friends living in Shigatse. He continued his researches after he retired to Scotland and tentatively concluded that Bogle married a niece of the Third Panchen Lama.

3   Imperial eyes in "the Golden Territories"

George Bogle went to India to get rich. In that respect he was just like all the other men who gained posts in the East India Company's Bengal establishment. The salaries were low but the Writers expected to use their positions in the Company to engage in some private trade within Bengal and, as they rose to more senior ranks, to participate in the trade from Calcutta to ports throughout Asia. David Anderson's satisfaction with his career, on returning to Britain with a fortune of £50,000, is apparent. Others were not so successful. The death rate was high – Bogle's demise at the age of thirty-five was not in the least noteworthy. The early deaths of many Company men are still mutely recorded on the memorial stones in the European cemeteries, and along the walls of the nave in St. John's Church, in modern Kolkata. As Peter Marshall has bluntly pointed out, "above all, success depended on the simple fact of survival." Of all the men appointed to the civil side of the Company between 1707 and 1775 (most of whom were in their late teens and twenties when they first went out) almost 57 percent died in India.[1]

But the enticing prospect of "shaking the Pagoda tree" and making lots of money was a powerful incentive to risk a life in India. That was the irrepressible hope of the men and their families. The high death rate only added a sense of urgency to the enterprise of making money in Bengal. In the opening chapter we presented Bogle as a tolerant, curious, open-minded traveler – an admirable case study of enlightened thinking in action. In the second chapter our admiration was tempered somewhat because of his and his friends' ambiguous treatment of Indian women. In this chapter we shall directly confront his role as an agent of empire. His career reveals all the connections between commerce, military power, and empire in eighteenth-century British India.

---

[1] P. J. Marshall, *East Indian Fortunes. The British in Bengal in the Eighteenth Century* (Oxford University Press, 1976), p. 217.

Great expectations of making money in Bengal were commonplace. In a letter Anderson received shortly after his arrival in Calcutta in 1767, a friend who remained behind in Scotland sketched out the prospects that lay in store for Anderson:

It is now a considerable time since you sett out from this [country], bound on a voyage to the Golden Territories of the East, a Nabob hunting, or in other terms, to procure a fortune, which the Miserable situation of Trade in our Country deny us; wherein I hope you will succeed to the utmost of your wishes.[2]

This reference to poor economic conditions in Scotland is a reminder that many Scots turned to India as a way of making or repairing their family fortunes, as young George tried to do by helping with the Daldowie debt. Anderson himself, as we saw in the last chapter, wrote of his hopes of making enough money to set himself up as gentleman "on a small estate in a pleasant part of Scotland."[3] Claud Alexander, who helped Anderson settle Bogle's estate in 1781–1782, left Bengal in 1785 with enough of a competence to build a cotton mill and found a new manufacturing town at Catrine in Ayrshire – although, as Peter Marshall notes, he too hoped that he would be able to set himself up on a country estate.[4]

In 1750 three out of every eight Writers employed by the Company were Scots, marking the beginning of a significant Scottish connection with India.[5] As political influence on the Company increased after the passage of the Regulating Act of 1773 and the establishment of a Board of Control in London to oversee appointments, Scottish participation intensified. From the 1760s onwards the Scottish interest at Westminster – forty-five Members of Parliament and sixteen peers – was always in support of the government. The politicians who managed these Scottish votes, such as Henry Dundas during the Pitt administrations, were rewarded with access to Indian patronage. "One result of the increase of political influence in appointments to Bengal was to further accelerate the growth of the Scottish element in the service," notes Suresh Ghosh in his study of the British community in Bengal during the 1757–1800 years. "By the end of the period the Scottish interest in Bengal was firmly entrenched."[6] Warren Hastings was so partial to the Scottish servants in the Company that he could be viewed as

---

[2] John Brown to David Anderson, Edinburgh, July 6, 1769, David Anderson Papers, Add. 45429, f. 18, BL.

[3] Marshall, *East Indian Fortunes*, p. 216.

[4] *Ibid.*, p. 215.   [5] *Ibid.*, p. 12.

[6] Suresh Ghosh, *British Community in Bengal*, pp. 18, 50; Michael Fry, *The Scottish Empire* (Edinburgh: Birlinn Ltd., 2001), pp. 84–87.

"Scotland's benefactor."[7] There were so many Scots making money in India by the turn of the century that Walter Scott referred to the country as "the cornchest for Scotland."[8]

But it was not only his Scottish friends who expected Anderson to make money in Bengal. A business acquaintance in London wrote to Anderson that "all your friends here rejoice to hear you keep your health so well and that you are in so fair a way of soon being in a Situation to return to your native Country with a fortune."[9] Lest Scots be unfairly singled out as inordinately fond of making money it is worth noting other examples of these kinds of expectations about service in Bengal. In 1765 Richard Barwell, who eventually attained enough seniority to be made a member of the Council (where he became an ally of Hastings), wrote confidently to his father that "India is a sure road to competency." With an honesty that does not appear in many of the letters of those who survived and became rich, Barwell added that "a moderate amount of attention, and your being not quite an idiot are . . . ample qualities for the attainment of riches."[10]

The extraordinarily favorable circumstances of the 1760s when the Company first gained access to the Bengal revenues, and pressured compliant Nawabs into making special payments, did not last. "In the early 1770s," Peter Marshall observes, "the period of easy fortune making which had lasted since 1757 was being brought to an end."[11] During the debate in the House of Commons on Pitt's India Bill in July 1784, Major John Scott, who acted as Hastings' agent and did his duty by stoutly defending the Company's record, argued at length that "the time for making large fortunes had passed." Scott claimed that "from a total of 508 civil servants appointed from 1762 to 1784 only 37 had returned to England, 150 were dead, and 321 were still in Bengal and had been unable to return with fortunes. Out of the 37 who had returned only two were members of Parliament, none had an immense fortune and some not a shilling." Scott declared that "nineteen out of twenty servants in India would be exceedingly happy at the prospect of being worth £10,000 after ten years."[12] When he produced these figures Scott was engaged in

[7] John Riddy, "Warren Hastings: Scotland's Benefactor?" in Geoffrey Carnall and Colin Nicholson, eds., *The Impeachment of Warren Hastings: Papers from a Bicentenary Commemoration* (Edinburgh University Press, 1989), pp. 30–57.

[8] Alex M. Cain, *The Cornchest for Scotland: Scots in India* (Edinburgh: National Library of Scotland, 1986).

[9] John Henderson to David Anderson, London, February 15, 1770, David Anderson Papers, Add. 45429, f. 31, BL.

[10] Suresh Ghosh, *British Community in Bengal*, p. 12.

[11] Marshall, *East Indian Fortunes*, p. 243.

[12] Suresh Ghosh, *British Community in Bengal*, p. 65.

special pleading on behalf of the Company servants against the popular allegations that they were all making large fortunes in Bengal and returning to buy their way into Parliament, but his figures are a reminder that by the time Bogle arrived in Bengal making a fortune was by no means assured.

Yet although money making in Bengal became more difficult by the 1770s, expectations remained undaunted. Even someone like Philip Francis, who already had a political reputation in England and who came to Calcutta with high-minded plans of rooting out corruption, did not allow his reform agenda to detract from that other enticement of service in India. He told his friend John Bourke in 1776 that "I will not return without an Independence. You know the spirit that is in me."[13] The hope of financial success was general throughout all levels of the Company – and such hopes were not viewed as unworthy. As Peter Marshall pointed out in his study of East Indian fortunes, "they were in India to get rich and, so long as they dealt fairly with the Company and did not infringe its monopoly, contemporaries regarded success in making fortunes as highly praiseworthy."[14]

The constant attention given to the matter of getting a fortune (and related worries about health) is well illustrated in a heartfelt letter Anderson received after his own career in Bengal had come to its successful end. The writer was F. Redfearn who was still at a Company post in Bengal. Redfearn was worried about the impact of the impeachment of Hastings on the ability of Company servants to continue trading in Bengal. He was also concerned about the new regime of Lord Cornwallis, the aristocratic Governor General who already possessed title and land in England (and was therefore deemed to be above temptation), who had been sent out to reform the Company's ways in India. Redfearn opened by defending Hastings and, by implication, the old ways of doing things. "It must, I am sure, throw a Gloom upon all the Comforts and Pleasures you would otherwise be enjoying," he commiserated with Anderson (correctly assuming Anderson would be sympathetic), "to see with what Rancour and Malice our Friend Mr. Hastings is pursued by a Set of desperate and disappointed Men who have been able to communicate their Inveteracy to a great Part of the English Nation, and whose only Object was to seize the Treasures which they now accuse him of squandering away."[15]

---

[13] Philip Francis to John Bourke, Calcutta, March 20, 1776, India Office Records, MSS. EUR. E15, f. 283, BL.

[14] Marshall, *East Indian Fortunes*, p. 3.

[15] F. Redfearn to David Anderson, Kishnagar, September 7, 1787, David Anderson Papers, Add. 45437, f. 60, BL.

With the coming of the Cornwallis regime, salaries had been increased in an attempt to reduce the practice of private trading by the Company's servants. But Redfearn complained that salaries were still too low and that private trading was essential if any accumulation of wealth was to be made. He acknowledged that the larger salary "has put us on a much better footing, but the Salary is too small, and you know what length of Time it will require to make a Fortune in this country out of them alone." Redfearn calculated it would take him three more years to make enough to take home:

From oeconomical Management and my not being liable to much Expence at this Station [he was collector at Kishnagar], my Acquisitions for the last two years have been very handsome, and with a tolerable State of Health I should hope that in about 3 Years more, and perhaps less, my Object will be accomplished. I am very anxious to revisit my native Country as soon as Possible, as upon my speedy return depends so much the Re-establishment of my Health, and if no material Change takes place in my Situation, as soon as I have realized 2 lacks [200,000] of Rupees I shall without Loss of Time turn my Thoughts to old England.[16]

Redfearn understood that this was only "a modest fortune" but in his case he had modest goals when he returned to England. This amount "will scarce provide a man with Board and Lodging but I still think that if not in London, at least in some parts of England or Scotland or Wales, a Bachelor may continue to live tolerably well upon it."[17] Redfearn had reconciled himself to not returning with a fortune as large as Anderson's or of other men who had worked at the prime revenue and commercial posts in Bengal. He had adjusted his sights in view of his money-making potential in the wake of the Cornwallis reforms. But he had not changed his plans for making some level of fortune in India. The goal was the same for all of them – to keep their health and make enough money for a comfortable life in Britain.

How did George Bogle fit into this world? He certainly thought about making money even before he set foot in India. His commercial education at Enfield and the training he had received in his brother's London company had been designed to make him a productive contributor to the family's wealth. Going to India in the service of the Company offered attractive opportunities. While still in London he and his brothers had considered the prospects in Canton, the Company's base in China. Bengal was preferred because it offered better commercial opportunities for

[16] *Ibid.*
[17] F. Redfearn to David Anderson, Kishnagar, March 6, 1788, David Anderson Papers, Add. 45437, f. 69, BL.

the family. This was a joint decision based on the brothers' assessment of the potential business and patronage connections they had in Calcutta compared to Canton. In December 1769 Bogle wrote to his father from London informing him of the decision:

we have now fixed on Bengal where I shall have a great many Advantages which I could not expect in China. I shall be able to procure Letters, and very strong ones, to many of the Principal People in the Settlement, and as the field is much larger I hope the Business I have seen in London, and the Experience I have had, may be more Service to me there than it could possibly be in China.[18]

He assured his father that "the Chance or rather Prospect of gaining an Independence is great, and I go out with every Advantage I could wish for."[19]

After his landfall in Calcutta Bogle's letters were full of ideas on how he might get ahead. As a newly arrived Writer he knew he would have to bide his time, and that he would struggle initially even to meet his own living expenses, but he expected he would eventually make money out of trading. Writers were promoted on a strict basis of seniority, usually spending three years in a post before becoming a Factor, then Junior Merchant, and after six years a Senior Merchant.[20] Bogle knew he would have to work diligently in his Company posts but he anticipated that as he advanced in seniority opportunities well beyond salary earnings would open up. "The Great Advantage derived from the Service of the Company," he explained to his brother Robin in September 1771, "is the Security it affords of one Day rising to that Rank as to entitle us to Plans of Profits and Consequence, and under that Hope we Submit to any immediate Disadvantages. One of the greatest of these is the Expensiveness of living in Calcutta."[21] He asked Robin's help in improving his store of commercial knowledge in preparation for this next stage. "Send me a Letter," he asked, "with the prices and rates of everything that concerns India." He also requested specific information on what kind of merchandise was being sent out from London for the Indian markets – "the kind and quantities of Goods Company ships are bringing out to India."[22]

Bogle was pleased with his first appointment as one of four assistants to the Select Committee, chaired by the Governor, which dealt with the

---

[18] George Bogle to his Father, London, December 1, 1769, Bogle Papers, Folder George Bogle 1762–1769 [marked 45], Mitchell Library.
[19] *Ibid.*   [20] Marshall, *East Indian Fortunes*, p. 10.
[21] George Bogle to Robin Bogle, Calcutta, September 1, 1771, Bogle Papers, Box: India and Tibet [marked 37], Mitchell Library.
[22] *Ibid.*

internal administration of Bengal, and relations with the Mughal emperor in Delhi as well as the neighboring provinces such as Oudh. The position would enable Bogle to become personally known to the most powerful Company officials in Bengal and would help him build up his knowledge of the country. He explained to Robin in October 1770 that

I consider myself as very lucky in this, for it is preferable in my Opinion to any other [post], in point of affording me the Means of becoming acquainted with the Company's Affairs, and the Nature and Government of the Country, as this department has the Sole Regulation and Management of the Government of this Country, and in the Negotiations with the Country Powers. Besides, I will not possibly have got any Information without being an Assistant, as every person is bound to Secrecy . . . I consider it also an Advantage to be immediately under the Governor and these first [members] in Council.[23]

Bogle was taking other deliberate steps to prepare the ground for his own trading ventures by studying local markets and currency exchange issues. He reassured Robin that he was following his wise advice "not to engage in trade until I know more about its conditions." While cautious, Bogle expressed confidence about his prospects. "I hope, however, when I have got some more Experience that I shall find some good Opening in this extensive Field." He promised Robin he would only seek "moderate Advantage" rather than "enter into some tempting projects that are attended with some Risque."[24] He explained to his sister that at this early stage "I am only examining and reconnoitering it [trade prospects] yet I hope afterwards to be able to meet with some Game, and discover which is the Path I should follow, and what is the most likely ground to go upon."[25]

He understood that the best opportunities lay outside Calcutta. Appointment in the interior provided opportunities for engaging in the country trade by using the privileged position of the Company to move goods without paying for local permits and other charges. He explained to Robin that he entertained

great hopes of getting up the Country as an Assistant to Mr. Higginson . . . but the Governor refused me, at the same time assured me that he wished to serve me, but that I must remain longer in Calcutta. I hope I won't be kept too long, and if I am it shall not be my fault. If I was in the interior Parts of the Country

---

[23] George Bogle to Robin Bogle, Calcutta, October 25, 1770, Bogle Papers, Folder George Bogle [marked 9], Mitchell Library.
[24] *Ibid.*
[25] George Bogle to Mrs. Brown, Calcutta, November 1, 1770, Bogle Papers, Folder: Bogle October–December 1770 [marked 70], Mitchell Library.

I should be able to live very cheap and perhaps carry on some Trade at a secure and certain Advantage.[26]

By 1772, two years after his arrival, Bogle began to trade on his own behalf. Although he was still in Calcutta, he had made contacts with Company men posted up country.

It was trade that first brought Bogle and David Anderson together. Anderson was at Murshidabad and Bogle approached him with a proposal for trading in cooking oil. There was a price difference between the Patna and Calcutta markets which the two men hoped to use to make a profit.

Have you a mind to purchase some Oyl in order to make money [Bogle asked Anderson]. If you have, I will go halfs. The price is now at 6 or 7 I am told with you, or at least at Cossimbazar, and here it is 10 to 11 p. Maund; besides I believe your Maund is larger than ours, so that we should make handsomely by it . . . If you chuse to engage in this tell me to whom I am to pay money here for my proportion and let no time be lost in sending it down.[27]

Anderson agreed to the proposal. "I am favoured with yours," Bogle replied on March 9, "and am glad to observe you have despatched some Oyl. The price keeps up and I hope will till ours arrives."[28] Bogle then scouted the possibility of making a similar business deal with rice. "Would you be so good," he asked Anderson, "as to let me know the price of Rice at Murshidabad."[29] He appealed to Anderson to introduce him to other Company men such as Redfearn to develop a network of potential trading contacts.[30] Bogle also enlisted Anderson's help in an attempt to gain redress when some of the boats Bogle had hired to bring goods to Calcutta had been stopped and the goods seized, apparently by officials still trying to enforce local regulations on the movement of goods. In March 1772 Bogle thanked Anderson for "your friendship in putting me in the way of obtaining Redress from the Son of a Gun who stopped my Boats."[31]

These first forays into trade, as the last incident suggests, were not an immediate triumph for Bogle. He was still in a junior position, he had no experience in the country trade, he was unsure of the rights of the Company servants with respect to local regulations, and he had not yet

[26] George Bogle to Robin Bogle, Calcutta, December 26, 1770, *ibid.*
[27] George Bogle to David Anderson, Calcutta, February 22, 1772, David Anderson Papers, Add. 45421, f. 3, BL.
[28] George Bogle to David Anderson, Calcutta, March 9, 1772, *ibid.*, f. 6, BL.
[29] George Bogle to David Anderson, Calcutta, December 5, 1772, *ibid.*, f. 25, BL.
[30] George Bogle to David Anderson, Calcutta, March 22, 1772, *ibid.*, f. 9, BL.
[31] *Ibid.*

built up a network of partners. Moreover, he was spending most of his time on the duties of his offices in Calcutta and on learning Persian. He still viewed the salaried posts he held in Calcutta as the foundation of his income. Accumulating serious money by salary alone, however, was very difficult – the average salary for servants on the civilian side of the Company by the mid-1770s was £455 a year.[32] Several months after the oil business he told Robin, somewhat defensively, that he had "not had time to turn my Mind to different Articles of Trade – but I don't regret it as I would much rather be employed about the Company's Business than my own."[33]

It is by no means clear that Bogle had much choice in the matter at this stage in his career. The trade ventures were still new and uncertain whereas the contacts he was making with the Governor and Council members were promising different kinds of dividends. It was Bogle's language skills, and the confidence Hastings had in him from seeing Bogle work at his side in Calcutta, that led to his selection for the Tibet mission in 1774. Bogle made money from the mission and was clearly delighted to have done so for this was the first substantial boost to his earnings since his arrival in Bengal. As we have seen, in spite of the bitter divisions within the Council, Bogle's mission was judged a success and he was well rewarded. The Company's general letter from London stated that the Court was

glad to find that effectual methods have been adopted to open a communication with the Government of Tibet, by the Agency of Mr. Bogle, who appears to have been a person well qualified for the employment, and to have acquitted himself to your satisfaction. We are pleased that he has punctually accounted for such Presents as were received by him from his Embassy; We fully approve of the salary of Rups. 1200 Per Month allowed him during his absence.[34]

Bogle wrote, with evident relief, to his brother in January 1776 that "the Board were so well pleased with my Expedition and put in good Humour, I believe, with reading my Journal that they have given me 15,000 Rs. besides my Expenses which I assure you I hardly expected." In spite of losing his Company offices because of the general house-cleaning of Hastings' appointees done by the new Council, including the general restructuring of the administration which eliminated the Select Committee, Bogle remained hopeful about his future. "Upon the whole,"

---

[32] Marshall, *East Indian Fortunes*, p. 181.

[33] George Bogle to Robin Bogle, Calcutta, February 20, 1773, Bogle Papers, Folder George Bogle 1773 [marked 76], Mitchell Library.

[34] Hira Lal Gupta, ed., *Fort William-India House Correspondence*, vol. VIII (New Delhi: National Archives of India, 1981), p. 85.

he reflected, "I am perfectly satisfied with the Issue of this Strange Trip from which I derived Reputation which may afterwards be of use to me."[35]

He remained philosophical, as we noted in the last chapter, even when he realized that the deep enmity between the Council majority and Hastings threatened to bar him from any future Company appointment. He believed he was now the most senior Company servant without a position. Bogle was determined to be loyal to his patron rather than curry favor with the new wielders of power and patronage. Towards the end of 1776, six years after his arrival in Calcutta, he took stock of his circumstances. "I expect no office although I am now the highest Servant unprovided for because I want to get it without asking; and I can ask nothing of Men who are so hostile to my Patron . . . I am now worth very little and I almost despair of ever getting a Fortune." In a moment of self-doubt, he wondered whether he had any capacity for making money – "I have no turn for it," he wrote dejectedly.[36] Yet at this low ebb in his business dealings Bogle still had income enough, from his position as Hastings' private secretary and from small trades, to send some money home to help with the debt payments on the Daldowie estate. He apologized for being able to send only £110 in 1776 but he insisted to Robin that he had not given up: "You may be assured that I shall exert myself for that Cause we are so much interested in [saving Daldowie]."[37]

When Hastings regained control of the Council in 1778 upon the death of General Clavering, Bogle's prospects improved. His loyalty was about to pay dividends. In October 1779 he was appointed Collector at Rangpur. This made eminent sense in terms of the ongoing efforts to open trade between Bengal, Bhutan, and Tibet – Bogle had played a major role in that endeavor and he might be able to advance the cause from Rangpur. The posting also enabled Bogle, at last, to engage fully in trade. In addition to its strategic siting for cross-border trade into Bhutan and Tibet, the district itself had a population of about 720,000.[38] The impact on his earning power was immediate. His letters were full of renewed energy, and the remittances to Scotland rose substantially. There is an unsigned note in the Bogle papers in the Mitchell Library dated "Bengal 21 Novr. 1779" which marked the new possibilities: "Mr. George Bogle is appointed Resident and Collector of the Province of Rangpoor, about 6 or 700 Miles from this Near the borders of Bhoutan

[35] George Bogle to Robin Bogle, Calcutta, January 20, 1776, Bogle Papers, Folder George Bogle 1776 [marked 48], Mitchell Library.
[36] *Ibid.*   [37] *Ibid.*
[38] E. G. Glazier, Officiating Magistrate and Collector Rungpore, *Further Notes on the Rungpore Records* (Calcutta, 1876), vol. II, p. 41, BL.

and Thibet. His Appointment is a very good one and it is thought he may make a fortune in a few years."[39] His predecessor in the post, Charles Purling, had gone on to become the Resident in Oudh which augured well for a move to even higher level positions.[40]

In January 1780 Bogle reported the good news to his father. "I was appointed to this Province which is bounded on the north by the Bootan Mountains, and is not less agreeable to me on that Account."[41] Two weeks later he explained to Robin that he was not sorry to have quitted Calcutta. He was delighted to be back in the north, near the Bhutanese hills "which you know is my Hobby Horse . . . I have Schemes and Projects for introducing new Articles of Commerce through their Country, and of Perfecting what has already cost me so much Trouble."[42] In March 1780 he summed up his promising new circumstances: "The situation that I have at present is as good as I had any Reason to expect."[43]

As early as August 1780 Bogle was able to send a remittance of £1,000 back to Scotland. He told Robin that he would send another £1,500 before the year was out, and, in a turn of phrase that revealed his deep commitment to this family project, he added that "the money that I have sent home to save Daldowie is sacred to that Purpose."[44] These large amounts eventually met the debt burden on the family estate. Bogle's father wrote gratefully from Daldowie thanking his son for the "substantial favour you lay me under in your Clearing off the debt affecting my Estate of Daldowie by which it may be continued in the family."[45] His father anticipated that such rapid money-making at Rangpur would enable Bogle to return home sooner than expected. He was pleased, he told his son,

to find you satisfied with your residentship at Ranpoor and hope the Climate will agree with your Constitution, and answer in its being a Lucrative Situation which may shorten your remaining at so great a Distance from your friends and many worthy relations.[46]

[39] "Mr George Bogle is Appointed Resident and Collector of the Province of Rangpoor about 6 or 700 Miles from this Near the borders of Bhoutan and Thibet," Bengal, November 21, 1779, Bogle Papers, Folder George Bogle 1779 [marked 30], Mitchell Library.

[40] W. K. Firminger, ed., *Bengal District Records. Rangpur* (Calcutta, 1914), vol. II *1779–1782*, p. ii, BL.

[41] George Bogle to his Father, Rungpoor, January 2, 1780, Bogle Papers, Folder George Bogle 1780–1781 [marked 54], Mitchell Library.

[42] George Bogle to Robin Bogle, Rungpoor, January 17, 1780, *ibid.*

[43] George Bogle to Robin Bogle, Rungpoor, March 1, 1780, *ibid.*

[44] George Bogle to Robin Bogle, Rungpoor, August 4, 1780, *ibid.*

[45] George Bogle (Father) to George Bogle, Daldowie, September 5, 1780, *ibid.*

[46] George Bogle (Father) to George Bogle, Daldowie, September 8, 1780, *ibid.*

If Bogle had remained in this "Lucrative Situation" another seven years he might have returned home as rich as David Anderson after his seventeen years in Bengal.

Bogle's business activities and his letters show that he was typical of the Company men in treating Bengal as a place to make money. He was also ready to use the knowledge he had gained during his 1774 diplomatic mission to develop his own "Schemes and Projects" in the Bhutan trade.[47] But Bogle lost out in the lottery of life, as so many of the Company servants did. An ominous harbinger had occurred in May 1780 when he wrote to Anderson that he had suffered a "severe fit of the Bile." He died suddenly early in 1781.[48] Even with this shortened span in Bengal, and the difficult patch he had from 1775 to 1778 because of his attachment to Hastings, Bogle had done reasonably well. After his death his estate was valued at 46,000 current rupees. In a list of all the estates registered in the Calcutta court for that year (1781) Bogle's came in ninth out of forty – the largest estate was valued at 80,000 rupees and the lowest came in at 4,000 rupees. The previous year twenty-six estates had come in below 46,000 with fourteen above that level.[49] So Bogle's was coming in the top third of estates registered in 1780–1781 and his two executors were prominent members of the British community – the signer of the peace treaty with Scindia and the Paymaster General of the Army. This was not the fortune he and his family had hoped for but the record was a respectable one given the problematic ten years he had been in Bengal and his early death.

As might be expected from the likeable and sensitive individual we met on the Tibet journey, Bogle did not engage in this fortune hunting without, at times, questioning the morality of it all. Bogle's ability to see matters from a variety of perspectives led him to have qualms of conscience as soon as he set foot in Bengal. The famine conditions that were ravaging the province in 1770, and the generally depressed economic conditions of the early 1770s, forced some immediate uneasy thinking about the impact of the Company's rule. He was already aware of the tawdry history of exploitation since 1757. The huge fortunes quickly made by dubious means, and the controversial role of the Indian nabobs in British politics and society, had led to extensive public criticism in

---

[47] George Bogle to Robin Bogle, Rungpore, January 17, 1780, *ibid*.

[48] George Bogle to David Anderson, Rungpore, May 4, 1780, and June 27, 1780, David Anderson Papers, Add. 45421, fos. 106, 112, BL.

[49] Bengal Administrations 1774–1779, Administrations Granted in the Year 1780, 1781, L/AG/34/29/1, BL.

Britain of the Company's activities. The criticism made headway in Parliament when investigative committees were set up to study what had been going on in Bengal.[50] The Regulating Act of 1773, by placing a government-appointed Board of Control in London to oversee the Company, was an attempt to better supervise Company operations and rein in the more extreme exploitation. Bogle's early observations on the general situation in Bengal show that he shared some of the negative views held by critics of the Company in Britain.

Shortly after arriving in Calcutta, in December 1770, he described the parlous situation in Bengal, and the ways in which the Company had made things worse. Bogle was clearly concerned about the financial health of the Company on which he had staked his future, but he was also prepared to recognize that the Company itself bore considerable responsibility for the terrible conditions he was now witnessing with his own eyes. The famine had contributed to a plunge in revenues, which in turn had depressed Company stock prices in London. "I fear it will be some time before it [the fall in stock prices] is reversed," he told Robin. He then began to analyze the roots of the crisis:

This Country is, to be sure, a very singular one, and the English Company is placed in it with every Advantage – but still it [Bengal] has suffered so much from the late Dearth as well as from the Ruinous Schemes that were formerly pursued, and the Consequences of which are now severely felt ... I don't know whether the India Company have not followed a good deal the Example of the Boy who had a Hen that laid a Gold Egg every day, and, impatient to get rich as soon as possible, killed the Hen, in order to get all the Eggs at once. You remember the Fable, I dare say, among Aesops, and the Moral is a very Striking one.[51]

Bogle followed other critics of the Company by pointing to the abuses of the revenue collectors and, more broadly, to the punishing consequences of imposing an English-supervised revenue collecting operation on top of the existing system. As an example, Bogle pointed to the practice in place when he arrived in Bengal of the Indian tax gatherers, in order to keep their privileges, paying bribes to members of the Council-appointed Supervisors assigned to collect the revenues from the six revenue divisions. That extra cost was passed on to the villagers.

There is one thing indeed that might be urged for recalling all the Councillors from the Subordinate Settlements – that many of them formerly behaved very ill, oppressed the People to extort Money from them, so that they have sometimes

[50] H. V. Bowen, *Revenue and Reform. The Indian Problem in British Politics 1757–1773* (Cambridge University Press, 1991).

[51] George Bogle to Robin Bogle, Calcutta, December 26, 1770, Bogle Papers, Folder George Bogle October–December 1770 [marked 70], Mitchell Library.

been in a worse Situation than under the Moor's Government [the Mughals], for they had to satisfy the Collectors of the Revenue not only for himself but also for the large Sum which he had given to the English Chief by way of Douceur or Permit to squeeze the People.[52]

He was also struck by the aggressive methods used by Company officials when they engaged in private trade. "Besides making money by Presents, there is another very good secure way which is attended with the Advantage of being less open to Detection – and this is by Trade." The Company chiefs in each district of the province allowed no one to trade without first paying him for permits. "The late chief at Patna," Bogle learned, "made a fortune in a few years by this method."[53]

Bogle tried to understand the behavior of his fellow countrymen. He came to the conclusion that they did things in Bengal that they would not have dared to do back in Britain:

One of the greatest Checks upon a Man that wants to increase his Fortune by unfair Means in Europe is the Odium that he is liable to draw upon himself, and be despised, and shunned by all his Acquaintances, but that is not the case here, and several People keep the best Company, and are exceedingly well-regarded, who are great Rogues, not only from Suspicion, but by their own Confession, and have even been obliged to refund Money that they had unjustly taken away, either by extortion or in cheating People that employed them. Indeed, the Court of Directors sometimes give Encouragement for this by reinstating People in the Service who were turned out for faults of a very black Kind.[54]

He was troubled during these first months in Calcutta as he discovered that the conventional guidelines on business behavior in the British setting were utterly disregarded in Bengal.

Bogle made a marked effort to be honest in assessing his and the Company's actions in Bengal. While he was forthright in his condemnation of the "rogues" and some of the iniquities of Company rule, he also expressed some regret that he had arrived too late to collect the golden eggs available in the 1760s (when young Richard Barwell was relishing his prospects). This made his observations a contradictory mixture of condemnation and disappointment over his own missed opportunities. The letters he wrote to Robin brought out the ambiguity of his early responses to what he saw happening in Bengal. "I cannot help sometimes regretting the Gilded Days that are past and gone, where a Man was almost absolutely certain of a Fortune by Trade, and at the same Time could command Money and Credit to enable him to carry it on to

[52] *Ibid.*   [53] *Ibid.*   [54] *Ibid.*

any Extent he Chose." That was the frankly expressed regret; then came the condemnation:

Even at that time we formed too favourable an Idea of India from the large Sums of Money that were brought from it by private Persons into England. It was good fishing in muddy Waters. And afterwards when everything was settled, and these Provinces were to all Intents and Purposes our own, and the People already under our Government and Protection, they have been squeezed and oppressed in spite of every Order from home or every Regulation that was made here, and Individuals have carried home Princely Fortunes. O my dear Robin, how amazed you would be to learn the way in which Money has been made in this Country and how different people's Characters are here from what they are in England.[55]

Again, Bogle was forcibly struck by the way in which the conduct of Englishmen in Bengal evaded the moral and business conventions which shaped life in Britain. He hoped that the reforms being contemplated in the early 1770s – imposing tighter central control and setting up revenue councils at Murshidabad and Patna – might help improve matters.[56] He explained to Robin that "They [the Council members] have lately fallen on a method which will, I hope, effectively prevent any of these immense Fortunes being torn from the Bowels of the People."[57]

While he spoke in apparently unequivocal terms of abuses, and the need for reform, he also accepted much of what was going on. A pose of jocular cynicism helped him overcome his scruples. He noted how moral constraints seemed to disappear among the English in Bengal, he thought that profits in the past had been "torn from the Bowels of the People," but in the end he participated. After all, he had come to make money too. He explained tongue in cheek to Robin that "we are all very honest here, we don't turn Rogues till we get out of Calcutta." And then he added, in a more serious voice, that he was "convinced in spite of all that I have said, that the Indian Company were never better served upon the whole than they are by the present Servants, and there are many of their principal Servants People of great Ability and of an Excellent Character."[58] He proceeded to defend the Company against the parliamentary busybodies at home who kept on interfering when they knew nothing about conditions in Bengal.[59]

---

[55] George Bogle to Robin Bogle, Calcutta, December 20, 1770, *ibid.*

[56] P. J. Marshall, *Bengal. The British Bridgehead* (Cambridge University Press, 1987), p. 118.

[57] George Bogle to Robin Bogle, Calcutta, December 20, 1770, Bogle Papers, Folder George Bogle October–December 1770 [marked 70], Mitchell Library.

[58] George Bogle to Robin Bogle, Calcutta, December 26, 1770, *ibid.*

[59] *Ibid.*

So in spite of his misgivings, Bogle threw his lot in with the Company. He acknowledged its faults, and the historical ones he condemned quite fiercely, but he ended by hoping that the Company would be left to its own devices in India. He cannily bided his time. He was trading in oil and rice by 1772, he made money from the Tibet mission in 1775, and he launched into private trade and deployed the usual revenue-collection methods when he worked at Rangpur in 1780. One of the first tasks at Rangpur was to enforce an order from the Council which directed him "to carry into Execution our general Orders of 14 October 1777 for the Confinement of Zamindars as shall fail to pay their monthly kists after the Expiration of 15 days of the ensuing Month; and if after that Term they shall still remain in arrears, you will keep them in Confinement until they shall have paid the Arrears."[60]

Perhaps, like all the Company servants, he knew time was not on his side. Back in 1771 he had explained to his sister that "there is not one of us that has not his Heart fixed on his native Land, and buoy ourselves with the Hopes of returning to it." He acknowledged that this outlook had its dark side for "it tempts a man to make use of any Means to get a Fortune, and he hopes by the Time he arrives in old England all his faults will be forgot."[61] Bogle was tempted but he was also temperate. He noted the bad behavior amongst his compatriots in Bengal. He had a sense of the historical wrong done by the Company. He tried to act honorably. But he became part of the system.

In doing so, Bogle looked at the world around him with imperial eyes. This underlying commitment to the Company's position in India was evident throughout Bogle's mission to Tibet. The purpose of the mission, as we have noted, was to improve trade with Bhutan and Tibet. In the report of his mission, dated September 30, 1775, Bogle meticulously evaluated all the items in the existing trade with Tibet and suggested new goods that he thought might find markets. "I will now beg leave to submit to you my ideas on the nature of trade between Bengal and Tibet," he informed the Council, "and on the measures most likely to revive and extend it."

He began with a discussion of broadcloth, that ubiquitous item in British colonial commerce in the seventeenth and eighteenth centuries. "The most important commodity in this traffic is broadcloth: all the Tibetans of a station elevated above the populace are fond of wearing it, and it forms also an article of their commerce with the neighbouring

---

[60] Firminger, *Bengal District Records. Rangpur*, vol. II, p. 12, BL.

[61] George Bogle to Mrs. Brown, Calcutta, April 10, 1771, Bogle Papers, Folder George Bogle 1771 [marked 120], Mitchell Library.

tribes of Tartars." Bogle warned that France, the great imperial rival, was making headway with this product in the Tibet market. Of the broadcloth he saw in Tibet "a large proportion is of French manufacture. I had occasion to buy several pieces in Tibet to give away in presents, and except once, I could never meet with any English cloth." Bogle then turned to coral beads, "great quantities [of which] are used in Tibet, and from thence also sent into Tartary." He wrote out a detailed list of "the prices and articles" in the Tibet trade, and concluded by proposing some new goods that he thought would sell.

But besides the articles hitherto employed in this trade with Tibet, there appears to be room to introduce or extend the sale of many new ones. The inhabitants are fond of everything that comes from a strange country, and even the lowest class of people possess a curiosity seldom to be met with. This promises a good opening for the sale of cutlery, glassware and many other European manufactures.[62]

Throughout his entire career in Bengal – his oil and rice transactions in the early 1770s, evaluating trade prospects in Bhutan and Tibet in 1775, engaging in "Schemes and Projects" at Rangpur between 1779 and 1781 – Bogle was always thinking about trade and money-making.

Because of his interest in the Company's success in India Bogle also paid attention to military matters. When he entered the first pass at Buxa Duar that led from the Bengal plains into the Bhutan hill country, he cast an appraising eye over the Bhutanese defense works at this strategic point. He knew about the victories of the Company armies at Plassey in 1757 and Buxar in 1764 which had led to the takeover in Bengal. He was a member of the Calcutta militia and took part in military drills on the *maidan* in front of Fort William. He also knew that his mission to Tibet had been prompted in part by the closing of the Nepal trade routes to Tibet because of the Gurkha conquest of the Kathmandu valley. And of course the immediate cause of the mission had been the Bhutanese incursion into Cooch Behar. Bogle understood that armies and wars shaped the Company's fortunes in India. During his enforced stay at Tashichodzong he set down a series of observations on military options available to the Company.

Such military considerations had entered his mind as soon as he crossed the northern border of Bengal. Toiling up the mountain trail, with a Bhutanese fort at the height of the pass, he began to notice features from a soldier's perspective. "The Ascent was at first easy, the way

---

[62] Bogle's General Report on his Return from Tibet, Calcutta, September 30, 1775, Lamb, *Bhutan and Tibet*, pp. 359, 360.

through a wood with some fine groves of first-rate trees," he noted in his journal. "It grew steep, a narrow path zigzagging up the hill. What a road for troops!"[63] Bogle actually thought that he was being led by his Bhutanese guides on a high-level circuitous route as a deliberate attempt to conceal from him an easier valley road and so make him think (and report) that the Company could not possibly send troops into Bhutan. If this was the case, the Bhutanese were correct in anticipating that Bogle would indeed be interested in scouting out potential invasion routes.

In his journals he described the difficult terrain at the foot of the hills that the Company troops had operated in as they forced the Bhutanese out of Cooch Behar. "The scene of our military operations against the Bhutanese," he reminded his superiors, "[was] almost impenetrable jungles" which led to debilitating disease for the troops in such "low and unhealthy country." In view of these conditions, Bogle advised that if the Bhutanese were to be engaged again, the Company army should go on the offensive and take the campaign into the hills.

For these reasons, acting offensively is to be preferred. There are two ways this may be done; either by penetrating into their country at once, or else by seizing and garrisoning the passes at Chichakotta, Buxaduar and Repuduar; for although they reckon eighteen passes, these are the principal ones.[64]

Bogle had already noted that the frontier post at Buxa Duar was picturesque, but in poor condition for defending the pass – "a 3 feet wall of loose stones about it; a fine old banyan tree; that's all."[65]

In the final analysis, however, Bogle argued that such an "expedition into Bhutan" would not serve the Company's interests. He reasoned that the present strategic situation – "possession of [Cooch] Behar and quiet from the Bhutanese" – was the best the Company could hope for. An attempted conquest of Bhutan would drag the Company into a long series of costly campaigns in tortuous mountain terrain. "Attempting it [the takeover of Bhutan] by force will never answer. The difficulties are insurmountable, at least without a force and expense much greater than the object is worth." He hastened to add that it was not the military capacity of the Bhutanese that was the issue but the nature of the country. "This does not arise from the power of the Bhutanese. Two battalions, I think, would reduce their country, but two brigades would not keep the

---

[63] Bogle's Journals, From Cooch Behar to Tashichodzong, May–August 1774, Lamb, *Bhutan and Tibet*, p. 61.

[64] Bogle's Suggestions Respecting Bhutan and Assam (written before his arrival in Tibet), Lamb, *Bhutan and Tibet*, p. 106.

[65] Bogle's Journals, From Cooch Behar to Tashichodzong, May–August 1774, Lamb, *Bhutan and Tibet*, p. 61.

communications open, and if that is cut off the conquest could be of no use."[66]

Bogle broadened his commentary on Company military options in these northern borderlands to include Nepal and Tibet. "The objections I have made against an expedition into Bhutan hold good with respect to Nepal and Lhasa," he continued, "for this sole reason, that communication cannot be kept open, and should our troops march into these countries, they must consider all communication with the low country out of the question until they return." The Company strategy should be to mount quick, punitive strikes to force treaty negotiations. "I am no advocate for an expedition into these countries unless the people should commence hostilities, and then it should be done only with a view to reduce them to peace on such terms as should appear reasonable and advantageous to the Company; and this would be easily effected by acting vigorously for one season."[67]

His thinking on the relationship between trade and military power was even more explicit in his commentary on Bengal's neighbor to the north-east. The state of Assam with a population of about 2,500,000 people also bordered Bhutan, and ran along the Brahmaputra valley to the east of Cooch Behar up to the hills of Burma (Myanmar). The crucial contrast with Bhutan was that in the case of Assam river communications could be kept open. Bogle proceeded to describe this tempting case for expansion. "Assam itself is an open country of great extent, and by all accounts well-cultivated and inhabited; the road into it either by land or the Brahmaputra lies open. The communication can always be preserved." Assam was also a worthwhile economic target. The country "yields many valuable articles for exportation – including gold, and teak timber of great size." The potential value of the trade involved, and the agricultural richness of the main river valley, would ensure that "in a few months after our entering Assam, the troops might be paid and provisioned without making any demands on the Company's treasury." Bogle advocated conquest in this case:

The advantages of a river navigable the whole year, whether considered with regard to commerce or war, are obvious, as the great objection to our entering Nepal etc. arises from the difficulty of keeping open the communications; so, on the other hand, the easy access to Assam, whether by land or water, invites us to the attempt.[68]

These "Suggestions Respecting Bhutan and Assam" reveal Bogle in full imperial mode. In spite of his misgivings about the behavior of some

[66] Bogle's Suggestions Respecting Bhutan and Assam, Lamb, *Bhutan and Tibet*, p. 107.
[67] *Ibid.*, p. 107.   [68] *Ibid.*, pp. 108–109.

Company servants, and his privately expressed disapproval of the Company's earlier record in Bengal, he was quite prepared to see its troops invade Assam in order to extend its trade – and territorial control – in that part of India. Even though he argued against the same treatment for Bhutan, it was only because of the difficulty of the terrain. Our Enlightenment man Bogle had no objection to military conquest if it could be easily accomplished.

As he sat in the Bhutanese capital of Tashichodzong, writing up these suggestions, which he knew would be read by the Council in Calcutta, he understood that he was now a front-line agent for the Company. He did not let the moment go by without offering his views on how the Company could expand and prosper. Throughout his journey to Tibet he paid careful attention to all the military and economic issues involved in extending the Company's reach. Since Bogle was on Company business it is hardly surprising that he would offer his superiors an extended commentary on how the Company could improve its prospects in these neighboring regions. The thoughtful detail with which he laid out the military possibilities suggests a comprehensive commitment to the Company's interests in spite of his occasional scruples about the morality of the British enterprise in India.

During his stay in Tibet he mounted a vigorous defense of the Company on several occasions when confronted by its critics. On November 11, 1774, just three days after he arrived at Dechenrubje, Bogle held a long conversation with the Panchen Lama on the Company's position in India and, in contrast to the doubts he had revealed in his private letters, he offered an entirely benign picture of the Company's record. The conversation turned in this direction when the Panchen Lama explained to Bogle that many people had urged him to refuse permission for Bogle to enter Tibet on the grounds that he was the agent of a Company that used force to expand its territories. The Panchen Lama admitted that he himself had shared these views. He told Bogle he "had learned also much of the power of the Fringies [Europeans]; that the Company was like a great king, and fond of war and conquest; and, as my business, and that of my people is to pray to God, I was afraid to admit any Fringies into the Country." Bogle immediately launched into a vigorous justification of the Company's actions. "I begged his patience while I laid before him an account of the Company."[69]

Bogle, now in historian mode, went right back to the first English contacts with India. Although this is well-known material it is worth

---

[69] Bogle's Memorandum on Negotiations with the Tashi Lama, Lamb, *Bhutan and Tibet*, p. 212.

summarizing Bogle's little history lesson not only because it reveals Bogle's imperial mind-set, but because (as we shall see in the chapter on "Tibet Lessons") the Panchen Lama incorporated some of Bogle's information about India into a major text in Tibetan Buddhism. Bogle told the Panchen Lama that the English had heard of

the fame of the [Mughal] Emperor and sent an Embassy to his Court. After a long and dangerous journey he arrived at Delhi; delivered the King of England's letter and presents, and was very graciously received by the Emperor [who] then issued his firman [edict] to the nawab of Bengal, that the English should be allowed to settle and trade in his kingdom, and be protected by his Government.

As long as the nawabs of Bengal continued to view themselves as subject to the emperor, and abided by his edicts, things proceeded peacefully. But the weakening of the Mughal empire, marked by such events as the plundering of Delhi by Nadir Shah of Persia in 1739, led Bengal to break away from Mughal rule. In the 1740s, Aliverdi Khan, the reigning Nawab, "seizing the opportunity of these commotions, and by the murder of his brother, and by many other crimes I omit to mention in your presence, usurped the Government of Bengal and threw off all allegiance to the Emperor." Aliverdi Khan was "cruel and oppressive" but he "encouraged trade and protected the English who continued to live in tranquility under his Government, and to enrich his country."

The situation deteriorated when his grandson, Siraj-ud-daula, took over. In 1756 he "attacked the English, plundered Calcutta where they resided, and which was granted to them by the Emperor's firman, and having hundreds of them prisoner, he put them to death in a dungeon." These actions by Siraj-ud-daula forced the English to defend their position in Bengal.

The English thus being obliged in self-defence to go to war with Siraj-ud-daulah who was defeated and slain [at Plassey in 1757], another Nawab [Mir Jafar] was appointed by the Emperor. Although raised and befriended by the English, he turned his arms against them and murdered a great many of them at Patna, but the English being favoured of the Almighty God, and assisted by Bulwant Singh [the rajah of Benares], the wisest man in Hindustan, and other princes who knew the justice of their cause, the Nawab was driven out of Bengal and the Emperor bestowed upon them [the East India Company] the management of Bengal.

Once in control of the province, the English "kept up a large army for the defence of Bengal [but] have not attempted to extend their possessions, and the limits of Bengal are the same as in ancient times."[70]

---

[70] *Ibid.*, p. 213.

This account of the British in India, with the Panchen Lama as audience, presented the Company's actions in the best possible light. The narrative as it stands has many inaccuracies, and it turns a blind eye to any aggression or manipulation by the British. At the battle of Plassey the Company's forces were assisted to victory by their ally Mir Jafar who held back his troops at a crucial moment. The Company then supported Mir Jafar as a puppet nawab. When even Mir Jafar resisted doing the Company's bidding, he was replaced by his son-in-law Mir Kasim. Mir Kasim refused to be pliant enough and tried to remove the Company's tightening grip by military force, but he and his allies, the Emperor Shah Alam and Nawab Shuja-ud-daula of Oudh, were defeated at the battle of Buxar in 1764, after which the Emperor granted the Company the right to administer Bengal. The Company then brought back the chastened Mir Jafar. After his death in 1765 the succeeding nawabs gradually had their revenue and powers reduced by the Company until in 1772 the Company "stood forth as Diwan" and ran the province with the nawabs as mere pensioners at Murshidabad.

Bogle's selective narrative missed out the fighting, and all the political intriguing by the Company. There was no reference to the exploitation and oppression he had spoken of in his letters home. And there was no mention of the fear in neighboring states of further depredations by the Company. In spite of his advice to the Council that Assam was a likely candidate for invasion by Company troops, Bogle even had the effrontery to hold up that province as an example. He invited the Panchen Lama to speak to "the people of Assam who visit your country [who] can say whether any attempts have been made on their kingdom."[71] It was a tendentious narrative designed to present the Company in a good light.

Bogle, to be fair, was attempting to cover a lot of complicated history in the course of a brief conversation but his account was a partisan one on behalf of the East India Company. In many ways Bogle's historical narrative anticipated the British justifications of their Indian empire that became standard in the 1800s – complete with a wildly exaggerated reference to the putting to death of hundreds of British prisoners in a dungeon (which became known in Victorian Britain as "the Black Hole of Calcutta"). There were not "hundreds" of prisoners put in a dungeon by Siraj-ud-daula and they were not put to death on his orders. The over-arching theme in this version of imperial history was of a declining Mughal empire after the death of Aurangzeb in 1707, leading to anarchy across much of India, and the emergence of aggressive regional rulers like Siraj-ud-daula, against whom the British had to protect themselves. In

[71] *Ibid.*, p. 213.

Bogle's presentation of the history of the British in India, all the violence, iniquity, oppression, and cruelty was on the Indian side.

The tone and content of Bogle's report on this conversation with the Panchen Lama suggests Bogle opted for language that would conform with the Company's self-image. It is hard to imagine Bogle invoking "Almighty God" on the English side when speaking to the Panchen Lama. It was early in his visit, to be sure, and perhaps he did speak like this, not yet having taken the measure of the Panchen Lama, but he never used such expressions in any of the letters to his family and colleagues – not even when writing to his god-fearing father. So while this blameless account of the Company's record in India is no doubt what Bogle did indeed convey at Dechenrubje, Bogle reported the conversation in a way that would make it appealing to the Company officials in Calcutta. He was certainly pleased on his return that his journals put the Council in "a good Humour." This narrative was the Company line on its history in India. It was a partisan account, designed to please his superiors by explaining to the leader of a neighboring state all the justifications for the rise of British power in Bengal. It was part of Bogle's unremitting campaign to reassure the Panchen Lama that the Company had no designs on Tibet.

Bogle was confronted by an alternative narrative about the Company's history in India while he was in Tashilhunpo. He learned that the *vakil*, or representative, of Chait Singh, the Raja of Benares, had warned the Panchen Lama against the Company's penchant for conquest. Bogle reported that he had

been told that Chait Singh's *vakil* had described the English as a people designing and ambitious; who insinuating themselves into a country on pretence of trade, became acquainted with its situation and inhabitants, and afterwards endeavoured to become masters of it.[72]

In Bogle's view it was these insinuations, along with the opposition from Lhasa, that "had contributed to raise up obstacles to my journey."[73] Benares was in an odd relationship with the Company during this period. As Alastair Lamb explains, Chait Singh's father, Bulwant Singh, had "built up the jagir, or zamindari, of Benares from a small cluster of villages into one of the major districts in what in Bogle's day was still the Province (Subah) of Oudh (Awadh)."[74] Bulwant Singh died in 1770, still acknowledging the suzerainty of Oudh. Chait Singh continued to do so until July 1775 when, following the death of Shuja-ud-daula, the Nawab-Vizier of Oudh, he shifted his allegiance to the Company,

[72] *Ibid.*, p. 216.   [73] *Ibid.*, p. 216.   [74] Lamb, *Bhutan and Tibet*, p. 159 n. 8.

acknowledged its overlordship, and agreed to pay an annual tribute of twenty-two and a half *lakhs* of rupees.

When Warren Hastings was desperately trying to raise money for the Maratha and Mysore wars in 1778, he imposed a large revenue request on Chait Singh on the grounds that he was now under Company authority. Chait Singh refused to meet the additional fiscal and military demands, fled to Gwalior, and was deposed by Hastings.[75] This treatment of Chait Singh was one of the items cited in the indictment of Hastings, and was the particular charge that led the Prime Minister, William Pitt, to vote for the impeachment to proceed. Hastings claimed this was a legitimate war-time request from a zamindar within the Company's jurisdiction. Edmund Burke and other critics saw it as an example of the Company mistreating local rulers and mulcting their people. This, of course, was all in the future when Bogle confronted Chait Singh's *vakil* at Tashilhunpo, but the Tibetan encounter hints that at least one of Chait Singh's officials already had some foreboding about how regional rulers like his master, the Raja of Benares, might be treated by the Company.

When Bogle and the *vakil* met at Tashilhunpo, Bogle decided to confront him over these allegations against the Company.

As I think it best and most becoming the character of the English to deal openly with every man, I resolved to mention this [the critical comments about the Company] to him. I accordingly told him what I had heard. I said that the English had always been befriended by Bulwant Singh, his master's father; and if their transactions in Bengal were unjustifiable, Bulwant Singh was equally to blame in assisting them; that, however, it was known to the whole world that the English were obliged by necessity and in self-defence to go to war.[76]

Bogle then gave a similar homily to the one he had recently delivered to the Panchen Lama. "I briefly mentioned their [the Company's] rise in Bengal, enlarged upon the assistance Bulwant Singh had afforded them; the friendship that had always subsisted between him and the Company, which was still continued by Chait Singh." Bogle assumed at this stage that the *vakil* was expressing his own views rather than Chait Singh's who currently had a good relationship with the Company. In mildly threatening language, Bogle raised the prospect of Hastings and Chait Singh finding out that the *vakil* was spreading such tales about the Company. "I added that as I knew how displeased the Governor would be were I to say anything unfavourable of his master, I was convinced

---

[75] *Ibid.*, pp. 176 n. 1, 180.
[76] Bogle's Memorandum on Negotiations with the Tashi Lama, Lamb, *Bhutan and Tibet*, p. 216.

that Chait Singh would disown him in anything he might say to the disadvantage of the Company."[77]

The *vakil* denied he had spread negative reports of the Company's activities in India. He agreed that such tales were circulating, but suggested that the *vakil* of Kashmiri Mull, a banker and trader who operated in Benares, might have been the culprit – he "was lately gone to Lhasa," the *vakil* added meaningfully. He further claimed that when he had spoken to the Panchen Lama "that he only told Tashi Lama what he knew of the affairs of Hindustan." The *vakil* adopted a submissive stance towards Bogle, telling Bogle that "I was his master, a great man etc." Bogle accepted the implied apology:

I replied, that he was sent to Tashi Lama by the Rajah of Benares, I in the same manner was deputed by the Governor on the part of the Company; that it was my duty to attend to the character of my constituents, and it was the custom of the English to deal openly; that I had only reported to him what I had heard, and was glad to find from him that I was misinformed. After this altercation he and I became great friends.[78]

In this exchange, relying on Bogle's own words, which are the only ones we have, we can see Bogle adopting a rather haughty tone. (Such passages perhaps explain why George Woodcock took such a sour view of Bogle.) Bogle contrasted the open, honest character of the English with the servility of the *vakil*. He made no bones about it, using the *vakil*'s behavior to make a generalization about all Indians – the *vakil* "concluded with the rote of all Hindustanis, that I was his master, a great man etc." In dressing down Chait Singh's *vakil* in this manner Bogle unintentionally revealed some of his own views of Indians. It is not entirely clear from Bogle's words whether he believed that the *vakil* was the source of the negative accounts of the Company, but in the interview he conveyed his displeasure. Throughout the exchange Bogle was speaking *de haut en bas*. Only when the *vakil* had been put in his proper place could they become "great friends."

Bogle could challenge these individual cases of criticism of the Company during his stay at Tashilhunpo. He could even apparently convince at least one very important Tibetan – the Panchen Lama himself – that the Company was pursuing an honorable course in India. But Bogle could do little to make any headway against the larger forces arrayed against him in Lhasa and Peking. The terse account Bogle gave of his meeting with two delegates who eventually came from Lhasa shows that the Company

[77] *Ibid.*, p. 217.   [78] *Ibid.*, p. 217.

continued to be viewed with deep suspicion. It was only the entreaties of the Panchen Lama that had persuaded the Gesub Rimpoche, the regent during the Dalai Lama's minority, and the Chinese Ambans in Lhasa, to communicate with Bogle during his stay at Tashilhunpo. In late December 1774, "the Lhasa deputies" – one a monk, the other a layman – turned up, and, with palpable reluctance, agreed to meet with Bogle. They told Bogle bluntly that they had come to Tashilhunpo

to wait upon the [Panchen] Lama, and brought these presents from Gesub to me, of which they desired my acceptance; that, although it was not the custom, Tashi Lama had ordered them to call upon me, as I had come from such a distance, and from the chief of the Fringies.[79]

They made it clear that they were only prepared to repeat the Panchen Lama's message of appreciation to the Company for the signing of generous peace terms with the Bhutanese. "They said that the Fringies had shown great favour to the Tashi Lama and to them, by making peace with the Bhutanese and restoring their country."[80]

Bogle replied with his now standard refrain. "The English," he informed the Lhasa delegation,

were far from that quarrelsome people which some evil minded persons represented them to be, and wished not for extent of territories... that so far from desiring conquest, the boundaries of Bengal remained the same as formerly; and although the English kept up a large army, the war with the Deb Rajah was the first they had been engaged in for many years.

The Lhasa deputies were not impressed – in reply to this fulsome defense of the Company "the layman gave a nod of his head." This perfunctory acknowledgment of Bogle's grand speech was followed by repetition of the position that the Chinese were set against any opening up of trade communications between Bengal and China by way of Tibet. "They answered that the Gesub Rimpoche would do everything in his power but that he and all the country were subject to the Emperor of China... This is the stumbling block which crosses me in all my paths."[81]

Bogle worked hard to overcome this opposition but to no avail. The Lhasa deputies even refused to allow Bogle a second meeting. He wrote in disappointed mood on December 30 that "Gesub Rimpoche's people came to take leave of me. I mentioned to them that I wished to have waited upon them; but they declined my visit." Bogle then asked if he could write a letter for them to deliver to the Regent when they returned

---

[79] Negotiations with the Tashi Lama at Tashilhunpo, December 1774–April 1775, Lamb, *Bhutan and Tibet*, p. 231.
[80] *Ibid.*, p. 231. [81] *Ibid.*, pp. 231, 232.

to Lhasa. "They said if I mentioned simply in my letter the receipt of the Chinese brandy etc., they would carry it, but that if I said anything of business . . . they would not carry it." Bogle was taken aback by this sharp reply. "I confess I was much struck with this answer." He insisted again that he had "come into the country with a pure heart and wished its happiness and the Gesub Rimpoche's happiness." The deputies insisted on reading any letter before it was sealed. They also declined to explain "the ground of the Gesub's suspicions." Bogle tried again to convince them of the Company's good intentions. He told the deputies that "as I knew the uprightness of my constituents' intentions as well as my own, I was ready to give him every satisfaction." The Lhasa envoys remained adamant:

> Their answer was that they were come to take leave of me, that much conversation was not the custom of this country, and so wished me a good journey to Bengal. I endeavoured to get them to listen to me. I wished to introduce the subject of trade, but it was to no purpose; so we parted.[82]

As he became aware of the intensity of these negative views of the British, Bogle monitored his own behavior even more carefully. He was particularly cautious with regard to maps and map-making. He was aware that if he showed an interest in acquiring maps this might well confirm that he was scouting out the land with a military eye. The connection between map-making and territorial takeover in India has been interestingly analyzed in recent scholarship on empire.[83] As Tzvetan Todorov has argued, "the ability to name, describe and portray are in some ways an appropriation that constitutes an essential step towards control and exploitation."[84] Maps were useful for asserting rights to possession, for imposing revenue demands in conquered lands, for scrutinizing trade possibilities, and for identifying invasion routes. On his journey up to Tibet Bogle took care never to be seen making maps of the route, or even making sketches that could be turned into maps. When he arrived at Tashilhunpo he continued with this posture of studied indifference to geographical information that could have any possible military significance. Bogle drew the attention of the Panchen Lama to his good behavior, telling him in January 1775 that "he might judge himself of my indifference on this subject, from my having been so long

---

[82] *Ibid.*, p. 235.
[83] Ian J. Barrow, *Making History, Drawing Territory. British Mapping in India c.1756–1905* (Oxford University Press, 2003); Matthew H. Edney, *Mapping an Empire. The Geographical Construction of British India 1765–1843* (University of Chicago Press, 1997).
[84] Tzvetan Todorov, *The Conquest of America. The Question of the Other*, translated by Richard Howard (New York: Harper & Row, 1984), quoted in Stuart Schwartz, ed., *Implicit Understandings. Observing, Reporting and Reflecting on the Encounters between Europeans and Other Peoples in the Early Modern Era* (Cambridge University Press, 1994), p. 5.

at Tashilhunpo, and having never once visited Shigatse, a town in its neighbourhood."[85]

During his stay at Tashilhunpo Bogle became fully aware that he was suspected as an agent sent to spy out the land – that "Gesub Rimpoche was extremely jealous of me as come to spy 'the nakedness of the land,' and that the English had designs upon his country." In the course of the conversation in which Bogle protested his, and the Company's, innocence by pointing out his lack of interest in the layout of the country round Shigatse, the Panchen Lama surprised Bogle with the offer of a detailed map of Tibet. The Panchen Lama, he remarks, "offered to give me a map of Tibet from Ladakh to the frontier of China, with the names and places and their distances." Bogle was sorely tempted: "This was a splendid object, and to obtain it, I was sensible, would reflect much lustre on my commission."[86] But Bogle prudently declined to accept the map. In his final report he gave a detailed explanation of why he had done so:

I replied, therefore, in the same style of indifference, after thanking Tashi Lama for his kind offer, that the situation of the country, its strength and forces, etc., were of no concern to my constituents; that the Company considered Tibet as at such a distance from Bengal, and separated by such mountains, the difficulty of which I had but too well experienced, that they never dreamt of any danger to Bengal from that quarter, and that the same causes, supposing the Company had even intentions of extending their territories, which their conduct showed they had not, served equally to insure Tibet from any danger from Bengal.[87]

The Panchen Lama, apparently testing Bogle, replied that he need not worry about raising suspicions in Lhasa because if Bogle took the map "Gesub would know nothing of it."

Bogle replied resolutely that he would still not accept the offer. Having a detailed map of Tibet, he repeated, "was not an object with my constituents." Bogle then invoked his innocent traveler persona. He was curious about all things Tibetan so that he could learn new things. Drawing on the language used in Hastings' private commission to him, he declared earnestly that he

would be glad indeed to know the laws and customs of Tibet because, as every country excelled others in some of these particulars, it was the business of the traveller to inform himself of these, and to adopt such as were good; and I would own to him that the Governor had desired me to inquire about their manners, but at the same time to concern myself in no way about the strength or forces of Tibet.[88]

---

[85] Negotiations with the Tashi Lama at Tashilhunpo, December 1774–April 1775, Lamb, *Bhutan and Tibet*, p. 239.
[86] *Ibid.*, p. 239.   [87] *Ibid.*, p. 240.   [88] *Ibid.*, p. 240.

This was a revealing moment in Bogle's meetings at Tashilhunpo. He knew it too, which is why there is such an abundance of self-justification.

He admits that the map was "a splendid object" and obtaining it would be viewed as a significant achievement of his mission. He had to explain to Hastings and the other Council members why he did not accept such an information-packed gift. Bogle reported that he had informed the Panchen Lama

The Company could have no interest in the country but that of commerce, and that to know a number of outlandish names or to correct the geography of Tibet, although a matter of great curiosity and extremely interesting to geographers and map sellers, was of no use to my constituents, or indeed to mankind in general.[89]

If he took the map he would be "exciting that jealousy which had hitherto so cruelly thwarted me in all my negotiations." He knew the map would be highly valued in Calcutta but he concealed that truth from the Panchen Lama for fear of confirming the suspicions that he was spying out the land.

Bogle tells us openly how he was thinking at this time: "To tell the truth I had restrained my curiosity [in connection with his decision not to visit Shigatse] in order to counteract the idea of my having come to examine and pry into the country." In this affair over the map, Bogle believed he was being subjected to further testing of his good faith. At the opening of the conversation, the Panchen Lama had offered to help obtain passports for Bogle's servants so that they could go to Lhasa and provide the Company "an account of it and of anything I needed to know."[90] That proposal was followed by the offer of the map without letting the Gesub Rimpoche know that Bogle had accepted it. Bogle could see the consequences of taking up either of these offers – he would be seen as too keen to uncover details about Tibet.

In his own account Bogle comes out in a favorable light. He declined the map to reassure the Panchen Lama of his innocuous presence in Tibet. This suggests an ability to appreciate the Tibetan perspective. His actions over the map might be cited as yet another example of Bogle's solicitude towards his Tibetan hosts. But the incident is also an example of Bogle's capacity for duplicity in the cause of improving the Company's prospects in business and diplomacy. The elaborate, staged refusal was designed to allay Tibetan suspicions about the Company. Moreover, Bogle clearly took some pride in being able to act in such a fruitfully misleading way. He expected his English readers, beginning with Hastings and the other Council members, to admire his diplomatic adroitness.

[89] *Ibid.*, p. 240.   [90] *Ibid.*, p. 239.

His refusal of the map of Tibet was motivated by a wish to remove suspicions about the Company's proclivity for territorial expansion. So the deception was in a good cause (from the Company viewpoint) but it was deception nevertheless.

Perhaps there is no grave fault in all this, but Bogle was incapable of noticing any similarity between his behavior over the map and the conduct of the Bhutanese when he negotiated with them. Although the case is not exactly parallel with the map incident, the Bhutanese negotiators' choice of words over a proposed trade treaty also involved some diplomatic duplicity. In his general report, written on his return to Calcutta, Bogle alleged that the Bhutanese had played an obstructive role. Quite apart from Chinese and Tibetan objections to opening up the trade routes, Bogle pointed out that there was no hope for the Company to prevail in these negotiations because the Bhutanese were also opposed. He explained to the Council that the

administration at Tashichodzong accordingly made many objections to allowing merchants to pass through Bhutan, insisting that it had never been the custom for strangers to come into their kingdom; that the inhabitants were of a hot and violent temper and the country woody and mountainous; and in the case of a merchant being robbed, it might occasion disputes and misunderstandings between them and the Company's government.[91]

These were specious reasons, according to Bogle. The real motive was to keep the trade in the hands of Bhutanese merchants and officials. "They were apprehensive that the admission of foreign merchants into their country would lessen the profits which they at present derive from their trade with Tibet, and they were still more afraid that by allowing strangers to come into Bhutan they would open the door to the introduction of Europeans."

These were reasonable fears on the part of the Bhutanese. They wished to retain their middle-man role in the trans-Himalayan trade; they feared the consequences of European traders arriving in Bhutan; they had the example of the Company takeover in Bengal right next door. But Bogle judged the Bhutanese reasons to be mere pretexts: "The opposition of the Bhutanese to my proposals proceeded from motives which they industriously concealed."[92] In his own case he too had "industrially concealed" his motives over the map of Tibet. In each instance deceptive words were used in the pursuit of self-interest, but he judged his behavior to have been legitimate – even admirable.

---

[91] Bogle's General Report on his Return from Tibet, September 30, 1775, Lamb, *Bhutan and Tibet*, p. 355.
[92] *Ibid.*, p. 355.

This charge of hypocrisy on Bogle's part cannot be pushed too far without being too naive about the Bhutanese officials who wished to maintain control of the trade routes. The Company had no plans for sending troops to Tibet or Bhutan. In that immediate sense Tibetan and Bhutanese fears were overwrought, and we can understand Bogle's frustration. On the other hand, Cooch Behar was now under the Company (forking over half its annual revenue), and the Company was holding on to districts in northern Bengal which the Bhutanese thought were theirs. Within a span of seventeen years the Company had taken control of the entire province of Bengal. The Company clearly posed a real danger to Indian states and their rulers. Bhutanese and Tibetans alike had every reason to be wary.

Most of the material in this chapter runs counter to the case that George Bogle is an appealing example of the neutral Enlightenment observer, studying other places and peoples with no ulterior motives. He went to Bengal to make a fortune; he knew of Company misdeeds but he was willing to overlook those faults so that he could profit from the system. He engaged in private trade within two years of his arrival; he used Company troops to help enforce tax collections when he was posted to Rangpur; he used his position in Rangpur to accelerate his money-making from trade. He dressed down those Indians who had the temerity to criticize the Company, and he gave the Panchen Lama a calculated, self-serving version of the Company's record in India. He even scouted the possibility of an invasion of Assam. In short, he was complicit in the colonial project. The lure of "the Golden Territories" had infected Bogle too. The open-minded traveler was also the opportunistic and mercenary Company agent. He was the product of a "liberal education" in an enlightened age which made him attentive to cultural differences, but he also looked at the world through imperial eyes.

4   Enter Younghusband

As the small army of 2,500 men forced its way to Lhasa in 1904 the British government attempted to justify the invasion by claiming that Curzon and Younghusband were merely taking up matters where Hastings and Bogle had left them in 1774. The Earl of Hardwicke, the Under-Secretary of State for India, made this case during the Tibet debate in the House of Lords:

It is as long ago as 1774 that Warren Hastings, with this very object, despatched a Mission under Mr. Bogle . . . I can only hope that the historian of the future will be able to write that the desire of Warren Hastings to promote friendly relations and commercial intercourse with the neighbours of our greatest dependency was attained 130 years later under the able administration of Lord Curzon.[1]

In a remote Tibetan village Younghusband made the same linkage. In July 1903, just after he entered Tibet with an armed escort, he told the delegates sent by the Ninth Panchen Lama, Chokyi Nyima, that the 1774 mission "had never been forgotten by the British and Indian governments."[2] The chief representative of the Panchen Lama, Badula, the Abbot of Tashilhunpo monastery, was taken aback by this reference. He told Younghusband that no one at Shigatse had even heard of Bogle and his mission.[3] What are we to make of these extraordinary claims about lively British memories of the 1774 mission made by Younghusband in 1903 – and of the perplexed Tibetan response?

On the British side, the claim of extraordinary continuity of memory and policy was largely a sham. Younghusband and his sponsor, Curzon,

---

[1] *Parliamentary Debates*, House of Lords, vol. CXXX (1904), cols. 1123, 1131.
[2] Younghusband to Louis Dane, Khamba Jong, July 29, 1903, Government of India, Foreign Department. Secret-E. Proceedings, September 1903, nos. 189–235, Tibet Negotiations, National Archives of India [NAI hereafter]; Younghusband to Helen Younghusband, Younghusband Papers, MSS. EUR. F197/173, BL.
[3] Tibet Frontier Commission, Diary of Captain O'Connor, Khamba Jong, July 29, 1903, *ibid.*

liked to invoke the Bogle mission because it had been entirely peaceful. Their more aggressive policy towards Tibet, made palpable by the troops of the 32nd Sikh Pioneers who were camped with Younghusband at Khamba Dzong, could seem to be more innocent if it could be linked to Hastings' tentative trade and diplomatic overtures back in 1774.

By this time too, of course, harking back to the Hastings legacy worked well because of the popularity of imperial ideology in British culture. Hastings had survived impeachment, and the blistering critique by Thomas Babington Macaulay in the famous *Edinburgh Review* article of 1841, to be seen by late Victorian times as the great founding genius of the British *Raj* in India. When yet another biography of Hastings was published in 1890 in *The Rulers of India* series, one reviewer remarked that "this man will not die. Here is the third book about Hastings that we have had to notice in the last few months." The reviewer went on to claim that "there is not one statesman of his day with whom comparison will not be advantageous to Hastings" and proceeded to assert Hastings' superiority over both William Pitt and Napoleon Bonaparte.[4] Even Macaulay's brilliant diatribe back in 1841, occasioned by G. R. Gleig's cloying biography of Hastings, had ended with a positive image of the great man:

While we cannot with truth describe him either as a righteous or as a merciful ruler, we cannot regard without admiration the amplitude and fertility of his intellect – his rare talents for command, for administration, and for controversy – his dauntless courage – his honourable poverty – his fervent zeal for the interests of the state – his noble equanimity, tried by both extremes of fortune, and never disturbed by either.[5]

Curzon and Younghusband invoked this hero of the British empire in India, and the patron of the 1774 mission, as a ploy to make their policy seem more traditional and peaceful rather than novel and aggressive. In pursuing this course, they convinced themselves at times that their actions were indeed directly linked with the eighteenth-century missions. At one point on his march to Lhasa, Younghusband made a risky visit to the Tibetan camp. When he explained his reasons for doing so he invoked the memory of Hastings. "I thought this visit to the Tibetan camp was worth such little risk as there was," he told Curzon, "for never before – from the time of Warren Hastings to your own great Viceroyalty – had a

---

[4] H. G. Keene, "Review of L. J. Trotter's *Warren Hastings*," *The Academy* 968 (November 22, 1890), p. 471.
[5] Thomas Babington Macaulay, "Review of G. R. Gleig's *Memoirs of the Life of Warren Hastings*," *Edinburgh Review* 74:149 (October 1841), p. 255.

British officer met a really representative body of Tibetans in their own surroundings."[6]

To appreciate the full significance of the extraordinary encounter at Khamba Dzong in July 1903 we need to look at how the Bogle mission itself, and general relations with Tibet in this period, were reported and remembered (and mis-remembered) in Britain. When Warren Hastings wrote to Samuel Johnson about Bogle's Tibet journals he was imagining a public success similar to that of Johnson's own *Journey to the Hebrides* or Hawkesworth's *Pacific Voyages*, but Bogle's narrative languished in obscurity for another hundred years. When Clements Markham finally published some of Bogle's journals and letters in 1876, he remarked in his Preface that the memory of the Bogle mission had been lost even in the India Office, which supervised from London the government of British India. Markham observed that

so completely was the policy of opening commercial intercourse between India and the Trans-Himalayan region abandoned, that the very history of the Hastings negotiations was forgotten, and most of the valuable records of the Tibet and Bhutan missions were lost. Thus the knowledge that was then acquired with so much care, the lessons of experience that were taught, instead of being carefully stored up and made available as a point of departure for future efforts, have been totally disregarded.[7]

At the time he edited the Bogle narrative Markham had worked at the India Office for over a decade and knew the records intimately. His unambiguous assessment contradicts Younghusband's claim that the British government had never forgotten the 1774 mission. Markham's avowed purpose in publishing the Bogle narrative was to help policy-makers of the 1870s recover a lost memory.

The Bogle mission began to slip beyond the margins of public memory in Britain within twenty years of his death. While he was still alive he had one more opportunity to make an impact on imperial history and so achieve lasting public notice. In 1779 he was selected for a follow-up mission to Tibet which Hastings hoped would finally enable the Company to break through into China. By this time, the prospects looked very promising indeed for Bogle. His patron was now back in control of the Council and Bogle was the key player in the Company's relations with Tibet. Because of the war expenses between 1778 and 1782, and the

---

[6] Younghusband to Curzon, Tuna, February 3, 1904, Younghusband Collection, MSS. EUR. 197/80.

[7] Clements Markham, ed., *Narratives of the Mission of George Bogle to Tibet . . .* (New Delhi: Manjusri, 1970 [1876]), p. xxii.

ongoing stream of money leaving the province, the Company was even more anxious than it had been in 1774 to increase trade with Bengal's neighbors.

Hastings set out the issues in a memorandum to the Board in April 1779. The root of the problem was that too much money was still flowing out of Bengal. There was an even more urgent need to increase regional trade and bring in fresh money to circulate through, and revitalize, the economy. As Hastings explained,

the constant drain of money from these Provinces is a consequence arising naturally from the relative situation in which this country is placed with respect to Great Britain; and as the sources from which money flows into Bengal are known to be very disproportionate, this evil has been repeatedly pointed out as the most alarming kind.[8]

The 1774 mission had been sent to address this problem. "It was with this in view," Hastings reminded the Board, "that an attempt was made some years ago to form an intercourse with the nations to the northward of Bengal by means of a person deputed into Tibet." Hastings, repeating some of the recommendations made by Bogle, listed the expected benefits that would come from the Tibet trade, including gold dust, cow tails (used for swatting flies in India), and the fine wool that went into "Kashmir" shawls; the Tibet market would take broadcloth, coral, "and other goods either native to these provinces or imported from England." The Gurkha wars in Nepal and the refusal of the Bhutanese to allow open trade through their country had prevented the Company from taking full advantage of these possibilities even though Bogle had managed to establish warm relations with the Panchen Lama.

By 1779 Hastings thought that events had taken such an encouraging turn that it was time once more to pursue the Tibet option. The death of the Deb Rajah, and the assumption of power by Lama Rinpoche (the Dharma Rajah), had led to an improvement in relations with Bhutan. Hastings had "received repeated assurances that he is ready to grant a passage of safe conduct through his country to the merchants." Hastings also argued that developments at Lhasa had moved in a good direction for the Company. The death of the frosty regent, Gesub Rimpoche, and the assumption of power by the Dalai Lama (who had been tutored under the supervision of the Panchen Lama), led Hastings to hope that the Panchen Lama would now be able to influence events more than he had been able to do in 1774. The deputies of the regent had been stiff

---

[8] Extract of Bengal General Consultations, April 19, 1779, Lamb, *Bhutan and Tibet*, pp. 431, 432.

towards Bogle back in 1774, so his death "added much to the influence of the Tashi Lama, both in the administration of Tibet, and at the Court of Peking." In view of these changes in Bhutan and Tibet, Hastings was hopeful "that many of the obstacles which have hitherto obstructed a liberal communication of trade may be removed, and that the expectations which the Company entertain from a commercial intercourse with Tibet will in great measure be fulfilled."[9]

Hastings hoped that he could now exploit the good relationships Bogle had established at Shigatse in 1774. "The connection and friendship which has been formed with the Tashi Lama," Hastings observed, "may eventually produce advantages of a far more extensive nature." Hastings pinned his hopes on the wide-ranging influence of the Panchen Lama throughout the Buddhist regions of Central Asia and in China itself. The current Dalai Lama, "having been discovered and consecrated by Tashi Lama, and educated and instructed by his dependants, is naturally under his influence." The current Grand Lama of Mongolia, still an infant, was presently under the Panchen Lama's care and tutelage at Tashilhunpo. The Panchen Lama also had a close friendship with Changkya Hutukhta, the most senior Lama at the court in Peking, who was "immediately attendant on the person of the Emperor, [and] who from his great age and character is held in much respect at Peking."[10]

With all these possibilities dancing before his eyes, Hastings argued that it was time to make use of the Panchen Lama's friendship towards the Company, begun by Bogle. "By the means of the Tashi Lama, therefore, I am inclined to hope that a communication may be opened with the Court at Peking, either through his mediation or by an agent directly from this Government." Hastings conceded that there was much uncertainty in all this but, in a characteristically optimistic manner, and in enticing language, he made the case that the attempt was worth making.

Like the navigation of unknown seas which are explored not for the attainment of any certain or prescribed object, but for the discovery of what they may contain, in so new and remote a search we can only propose to adventure for possibilities. The attempt may be crowned with the most splendid and substantial success, or it may terminate in the mere gratification of useless curiosity; but the hazard is small, the design worthy of the pursuit of a rising state, the Company have both approved and recommended it, and the means are too promising to be neglected.[11]

It was Bogle's exceptionally friendly relationship with the Panchen Lama that made Hastings' visionary plan possible. Bogle's loyalty to

---

[9] *Ibid.*, p. 433.   [10] *Ibid.*, pp. 433, 434.   [11] *Ibid.*, p. 434.

Hastings was now to be rewarded even more than he could have anticipated as Hastings proposed that Bogle lead this ambitious enterprise.

I beg leave to recommend that Mr. Bogle be appointed to proceed again into
Bhutan and Tibet with instructions to cultivate and improve the good understanding subsisting between the Chiefs of these countries and this Government,
to endeavour to establish a free and lasting intercourse of trade with the kingdom
of Tibet and the other states to the northward of Bengal, to endeavour, by the
means of the Lamas of Tibet, to open a communication with the Court of Peking,
and, if possible, procure leave to proceed thither, and that objects of this last destination be left to his own discretion in the application of such opportunities and
advantages as may be presented to him.[12]

The free rein given to Bogle to improvise shows the extent to which
Hastings respected his expertise and trusted his judgment. The four
other Council members agreed to Bogle's appointment. He was given
a generous stipend – the pay of a Lieutenant Colonel, full travel and
subsistence allowances, money for servants, and a salary.

Bogle's opportunity to make his mark on British empire history seemed
to have arrived. He would have gained great renown, well beyond even
what Anderson was to achieve three years later at the treaty of Salbai, if
he could have reached Peking. Even Lord Macartney's failed mission to
Peking in 1793–1794 still makes a regular appearance in British and world
history textbooks. Bogle was confident he could pull it off. "The Emperor
of China is now seventy years of age. He is of the Tartar religion, of which
the Lamas are the head," he told the Council members. "When I was in
Tibet the Lama promised to endeavour to procure for me passports to go
to Peking."[13] Now that conditions had improved, Bogle was convinced
he could make a success of this second mission and finally achieve a
wider public reputation. But just as it seemed Bogle's career in Bengal
would be crowned with success and lasting fame, fate intervened. The
mission was postponed when it was learned, in the summer of 1779, that
the Panchen Lama, at the invitation of the Emperor, had already left
Tashilhunpo to visit Peking. During that visit the Panchen Lama died,
which brought Hastings' grand plans crashing down to earth. Bogle was
left with the Collectorship at Rangpur where he could only engage in
the decidedly less glamorous task of encouraging small steps in opening
up trans-Himalayan trade. Early in 1781 Bogle was promoted, again at
Hastings' instigation, to membership of a new Committee of Revenue at
Calcutta. He left Rangpur to take up this new position but died, probably

[12] *Ibid.*, p. 435.
[13] Bogle Memorandum on the possibility of visiting Peking, July 1779, Lamb, *Bhutan and
Tibet*, p. 439.

of cholera, on April 3, 1781. Bogle's luck had run out. The collapse of the mission to China, his failure to prepare his 1774 journals for publication, and his early death meant that he faded from historical memory.

It was in any case the end of an era in terms of Company relations with Tibet. As Alastair Lamb has pointed out, the hopes of opening up markets in Tibet and China disappeared in the late 1780s and early 1790s because of events along India's northern borderlands. The expansionist policies of the new Gurkha state of Nepal had widespread repercussions. On the grounds that neither the Tibetans nor the Chinese had replied to his notes about a Tibeto-Nepalese border dispute, Bahadur Shah, the Gurkha king of Nepal, attacked Sikkim, occupied Darjeeling, and blocked the trade routes to Shigatse. The Tibetans bought peace in 1789 by promising to provide an annual tribute to Nepal, but when they declined to pay this in 1790 the Gurkhas responded by invading Tibet and plundering the monastery at Tashilhunpo. The Chinese responded in their turn by sending a large imperial army which drove the Gurkhas out of Tibet, and pursued them through the steep Himalayan valleys to within fifty miles of Kathmandu. A significant consequence of these developments was the weakening of the local autonomy enjoyed at Tashilhunpo, which now prevented the Panchen Lamas from entering into any kind of negotiations with the states of northern India – including Bengal:

In Lhasa the structure of Chinese authority was overhauled and revised so as to emphasize the dominant position of the Ambans (the two Chinese Residents), and behind them the Chinese Emperor. In 1794 Sung-yan, a very important Manchu official, was appointed senior Amban in Tibet, as a symbol of the new Chinese policy.[14]

The Chinese believed that the British in Bengal had supported the Gurkha invasion of Tibet. This was not the case, but Lord Cornwallis' refusal to intervene when asked to do so by the Tibetans prompted suspicions about British policy in Lhasa and Peking. These suspicions had some plausibility in spite of Cornwallis' official assurances of non-intervention. As Samuel Turner noted in a private letter to Hastings, written in November 1792, "Nepal has long been a Resort to our disbanded Sepoys, particularly Rajpoots." He added that "they have not wanted for firearms." An observer from Tibet could not be blamed for thinking there was some British complicity in the "formidable invasion" of their country.[15] These developments had an interesting impact on

---

[14] The End of an Era 1784–1793, Lamb, *Bhutan and Tibet*, pp. 470, 472, 476.
[15] Samuel Turner to Warren Hastings, Lucknow, November 25, 1792, Warren Hastings Papers, Add. 39871, f. 51, BL.

Macartney's mission to Peking. The secretary to that mission, Sir George Stanton, thought the Chinese perception that the British had aided the Gurkhas in their incursions into Tibet was one factor that made the Chinese respond so coldly to Macartney's overtures.[16] In any event, the Chinese were now determined "to prevent, if at all possible, any direct diplomatic contact between the Tibetans and the Government of British India to the south."[17] The door which Bogle edged ajar for a moment in 1774, and which he and Hastings hoped to push wide open in 1779, had closed.

There had been one more Tibet mission before the closing of the border to the British in the 1790s. It too began with the intermediary efforts of Purangir Gosain. In February 1782 Purangir arrived in Calcutta to explain what had happened during the Panchen Lama's ill-fated journey to Peking.[18] Purangir brought with him letters from Tashilhunpo, including some from officials Bogle had met in 1774–1775. The ever-hopeful Hastings took this as a hint that the Tibetans were interested in resuming trade talks. When news also reached Calcutta that an infant successor to the Panchen Lama had been identified, Hastings decided to send a representative to mark the occasion. Samuel Turner was appointed in January 1783. In contrast to Bogle, Turner did publish an account of his Tibet mission in his own lifetime. *An Account of an Embassy to the Court of the Teshoo Lama*, which appeared in 1800, was a great success. It went into a second edition, and was translated into French and German. A high point of the narrative was a description of Turner's meeting with the infant Incarnation. When Turner entered the presence and made some formal remarks,

The little creature turned, looking steadfastly towards me, with the appearance of much attention while I spoke, and nodded with repeated but slow movements of the head, as though he understood and approved every word, but could not utter a reply . . . and with whatever pains his manners may have been so correctly formed, I must own that his behaviour, on this occasion, appeared perfectly natural and spontaneous, and not directed by any external actions or signs of authority.[19]

It was this kind of anecdote, so fascinating to European readers, that helped make Turner's book such a success.

In his narrative Turner paid a generous compliment to Bogle's character, and acknowledged the significance of the 1774 mission for its seminal

---

[16] The End of an Era 1784–1793, Lamb, *Bhutan and Tibet*, p. 478.   [17] *Ibid.*, p. 478.
[18] The Turner Mission to Bhutan and Tibet, Lamb, *Bhutan and Tibet*, p. 450.
[19] Samuel Turner, *An Account of an Embassy to the Court of the Teshoo Lama* (London: W. Bulmer & Co., 1800), p. 335.

role in giving the English a good reputation at Shigatse. On one occasion during his embassy Turner was

visited by two officers of the Lama's household immediately attendant on his person. They sat and conversed with me some time, inquiring after Mr. Bogle, whom both of them had seen, and then remarking how extremely fortunate it was that the young Lama had regarded us with so very particular notice; they observed a strong partiality of the former Teshoo Lama for our nation, and said that the present Lama often tried already to utter the name of the English.[20]

The officials assured Turner that when the infant Lama "began to speak... they would early teach him to repeat the name Hastings." Turner generously attributed the warmth of his reception at Tashilhunpo to the impact of Bogle.

That the effect produced on the mind of the Lama, by a disposition of manners perfectly congenial with his own, was so great and powerful, cannot excite our surprise. Indeed, toward whatever object it was directed, the patient and laborious exercise of the powers of a strong mind in my predecessor Mr. Bogle was also accompanied by a most engaging mildness and benevolence which marked every part of his character. I am thoroughly aware of the very favourable impression which these amicable qualities left behind them in the court of the Teshoo Lama.[21]

So Bogle's 1774 mission was recollected in Turner's book but that was all that was left in the British public memory by 1800.

Bogle had only himself to blame for not having written his own book. He talked about preparing his notes for publication but he never followed through. It may be that bouts of what seemed to be depression made it difficult for him to complete such a major project. After his initial ebullience upon his return to Calcutta, especially when he learned of his ample reward from the Council, Bogle fell into a gloomy mood. He told Anderson that "in these times I hug myself in unimportance."[22] His companion on the Tibet journey, Alexander Hamilton, tried to prod Bogle into action. Bogle had taken a house near the cemetery, which Hamilton thought deepened Bogle's gloom. "I can't help lamenting your situation at Melancholy Hall," wrote Hamilton, "not only on your own account but from the loss that the world is likely to sustain by it. Who the deuce would ever think of sitting down to compose anything but homilies and elegies by the walls of a churchyard?"[23] Hamilton's letter

---

[20] *Ibid.*, p. 337.   [21] *Ibid.*, p. 339.

[22] George Bogle to David Anderson, Calcutta, October 26, 1775, David Anderson Papers, Add. 45421, f. 45, BL.

[23] Alexander Hamilton to George Bogle, Kiranty, December 26, 1775, Lamb, *Bhutan and Tibet*, p. 391; Teltscher, *High Road to China*, pp. 165–177.

tells us something of Bogle's mood at this time. It was not a frame of mind conducive to buckling down and bringing his notes to a state ready for publication.

There was another chance for publication shortly after Bogle died. Some of Bogle's papers including those which described his friendly private discussions with the Panchen Lama at Dechenrubje and Tashilhunpo had come into the possession of Bogle's brother Robert. Alastair Lamb suggests they may have been given to the Bogle family by David Anderson and Claud Alexander after they helped settle Bogle's estate in Calcutta. In 1792 Robert Bogle handed these papers over to Alexander Dalrymple who was then (1779–1795) serving as the Hydrographer to the East India Company. This made sense because of Dalrymple's role in promoting the Company's trade with China's neighbors, of which Hastings' Tibet policy was but one aspect. In a letter written from Daldowie in 1792, Robert explained to Dalrymple what he had in mind for the papers. "With regard to my brother's Tibet papers," he told Dalrymple,

I have always had it in view to publish them, and the Company gave me permission, but many circumstances have occurred, which have hitherto prevented me from executing my design, but the principal cause of delay has been a difficulty in meeting with any person qualified to correct and arrange them properly for the press; but as you have been so good as to offer me voluntarily your assistance, I propose to bring them with me, & on my arrival I shall have the pleasure of conferring with you on this point.[24]

The papers were duly handed over, and Dalrymple did begin some editorial work, but he was transferred to the Admiralty in 1795 and, as Lamb notes, "he apparently put the work to one side and never resumed it."[25] This particular set of papers passed through private hands before they found their way into the British Museum's additional manuscript collections in the 1850s.

It was therefore left to Clements Markham to finally bring Bogle to public attention in 1876. Markham's career reflected in interesting ways many of the links between geography, exploration, and empire in the Victorian and Edwardian eras. Markham had been a member of the expedition that had searched for traces of the Franklin ships lost in the Arctic seas north of Canada during yet another valiant attempt to find the Northwest passage. He later became President of the Royal Geographical Society from 1893 to 1905, when that institution was closely involved in imperial

---

[24] Robert Bogle to Alexander Dalrymple, Daldowie, January 28, 1792, Lamb, *Bhutan and Tibet*, p. 12.
[25] Lamb, *Bhutan and Tibet*, p. 13.

matters.[26] At the time he edited the Bogle volume, he was in charge of the geographical section of the India Office. His lifelong engagement in travel and exploration is an obvious reason for his interest in the Bogle mission, but there was a specific political and commercial context in the 1870s that helps explain the timing of the first publication of Bogle's Tibet journals.

In the 1700s the Company had to buy its tea from China but by the mid-1800s there were extensive tea plantations in India, including those near Darjeeling in northern Bengal, as well as those in Assam. Bogle himself had been involved in the very beginning of the tea industry in northern Bengal. When he was posted to Rangpur in 1779 he and Hastings had experimented with tea plants. Bogle wrote to Hastings in March 1780 describing how he had showed the "tea seeds . . . to the Buxa Subah [who] got up and danced round them like David [because] he says they are worth to his country a lakh of rupees, considering how much money goes annually out of it for tea brought overland from China."[27] Since tea was a staple of the Tibetan diet, there was a growing anticipation by this time that tea from British India could replace the vast quantities of China tea consumed in the Tibetan market. This was combined with the hope that Tibet would prove to be a valuable additional source of fine Kashmiri-style wool for use in the textile mills of cities such as Manchester and Paisley. Hastings and Bogle had discussed this possibility too back in the 1770s, and one of Bogle's charges had been to send shawl-wool goats back to Bengal to see if they could be bred there.

The Chefoo Convention signed between Britain and China in 1876 allowed the British to send a commercial mission to Tibet. Markham dedicated the Bogle book to Lord Northbrook, the current Governor General of India, to signal formally the volume's relevance to this new trade opportunity. The publication of Bogle's account was designed to link the commercial strategies of the 1870s with those of Hastings a hundred years before. The Bogle book, wrote Markham, would,

without doubt, have been dedicated to Warren Hastings . . . if untoward circumstances had not intervened to prevent its publication. A century has since elapsed,
and now that the intention of Warren Hastings that it should be given to the world
is fulfilled, it is appropriate that the book should be dedicated to his successor,
the present Governor-General and Viceroy of India.[28]

[26] Ian Cameron, *To the Farthest Ends of the Earth. 150 Years of World Exploration by the Royal Geographical Society* (New York: E. P. Dutton, 1980).

[27] Bogle to Hastings, Rangpur, March 2, 1780, Lamb, *Bhutan and Tibet*, p. 443.

[28] Clements Markham to Lord Northbrook, Geographical Department, India Office, December 1875, in Markham, *Bogle*, pp. iii–iv; Lamb, *Bhutan and Tibet*, p. 15.

Markham's careful contextualization of the Bogle narrative in 1876 shows that he was attempting to bring back into British public memory an episode that had long been forgotten.

On the Tibetan side there are only three sources which provide information on the Bogle and Turner missions – the official biographies of the Third and Fourth Tashi Lamas, and a slightly less formal life history of the Third Panchen Lama. Unfortunately, the information in these sources is meager. That is a great pity. It would have been deeply satisfying if historians of Tibet could have found extensive commentaries on these eighteenth-century British missions. "What we can find in the biographies of the Tashi-Lamas," explains the Italian scholar Luciano Petech, who has investigated all the possible sources on the Tibetan side, "is a bare record of formal audiences."[29] Because the biographies served as a kind of court diary, the descriptions of the missions are brief and businesslike, noting when the Panchen Lamas met Bogle and Turner, and the ceremonies that took place at those meetings. The "autobiography" of the Third Panchen Lama described how his diplomatic efforts had led to peace between Bhutan and the Company: "the lord of Bhangala listened with respect to my word. He gave back the districts of Bhutan, and on both sides they remained without fighting." Bogle's first meeting with the Panchen Lama at Dechenrubje is mentioned in brief, formal terms: "Acarya Bho-gol with his attendants offered presents of glass bottles etc. and took their appointed places for the distribution of ceremonial tea; they made conversation in the Nagara language (Hindustani)."

Since many of Bogle's meetings with the Panchen Lama were private affairs there is no reference to them in the official biography, but there are some hints that Bogle's characterization of the relationship was accurate. For example, there is an entry for the meeting on December 23 which reads: "On this day [the Panchen Lama] gave to Bho-gol Sa-heb and his attendants a joyful midday feast (gun-ston) at his side; his order was exactly carried out."[30] In these Tibetan texts Hastings is referred to as "the Bha-ra Saheb (Bara Saheb, the Great Lord, governor general) ruler of Bhan-gha-la in India" and "the Bha-ra Sa-heb of the Inka-ral-ce (English), lord of Ka-la-ka-dha (Calcutta)."[31] The British envoys to Shigatse were mentioned in the same way as the other envoys to the Panchen Lamas from various states in north India and Central Asia. The two Englishmen were simply another set of diplomatic visitors, and their presence was not marked by unusual or extensive entries in the official

---

[29] Luciano Petech, "The Missions of Bogle and Turner according to the Tibetan Texts," *T'oung pao* 39 (1950), p. 331.
[30] *Ibid.*, pp. 340, 341, 342.   [31] *Ibid.*, p. 344.

records. Petech could find no later references. So the missions were spar-
ingly noted in Tibet and soon forgotten. All this helps to explain the
Tibetan side of the encounter at Khamba Dzong in 1903 – Younghusband brandishing Markham's *Bogle* and Badula, the representative of the
current Panchen Lama, wondering what on earth Younghusband was
making such a fuss about.

Developments within Tibet, and in relations between Tibet and British
India, from the 1870s onwards led to the "crisis" that Curzon claimed to
exist during his viceroyalty – and brought about the uncomprehending
encounter at Khamba Dzong. The Chinese-imposed policy (willingly
accepted by Tibetan officials) of closing off Tibetan contacts with India,
initiated in the 1790s because of the Gurkha invasion and the suspicion
that the British had been involved, was continued for the next eighty years
or so. But the Chinese empire – which had been at the height of its power
when it pushed the Gurkhas out of Tibet, closed down communication
with British India, and spurned the Macartney mission – entered a long
period of decline in the course of the 1800s. The defeat in the Opium
war of 1839–1842, Britain's acquisition of Hong Kong, the setting up of
treaty ports by Britain and other foreign powers, the disruption caused by
the Taiping rebellion in the 1850s and 1860s, and the "Boxer" uprising
in 1900 were all signs of instability and decline. By the 1880s and 1890s
the general diminution of Chinese power had led to a weakening of its
position internationally.

This general weakness also eroded China's position in Lhasa. The
Ambans appointed by this time were often second-rate functionaries who
detested being assigned to such a remote outpost. Melvyn Goldstein
states categorically that "by the mid-nineteenth century, if not earlier,
Manchu Chinese influence was minuscule."[32] When Thubten Gyatso,
the Thirteenth Dalai Lama (1876–1933), reached his majority and took
power in Lhasa in 1895, he intensified efforts to assert more autonomy
from the Chinese empire. The Ninth, Tenth, Eleventh, and Twelfth Dalai
Lamas in the 1800s had all died at a young age – perhaps "encouraged"
to leave their human form early. The Eighth had survived longer but
allowed a lay minister to control political affairs.[33] So the Thirteenth
Dalai Lama was the first strong Tibetan leader since Bogle's time.

Such a powerful and politically astute Dalai Lama was able to articulate
fully the Tibetan interpretation of the Sino-Tibetan relationship. This

---

[32] Melvyn C. Goldstein, *A History of Modern Tibet 1913–1951. The Demise of the Lamaist
State* (Berkeley: University of California Press, 1989), p. 44.
[33] *Ibid.*, pp. 41, 44.

view held that the Dalai Lama was the spiritual teacher and the Manchu emperor a lay patron – rather than one being a subject and the other the sovereign. One example of the weakening Chinese position in Tibet was the refusal of the Tibetans to implement treaties made between China and British India that dealt with boundary disputes between Sikkim (by now a client state in British India) and arrangements for trans-Himalayan commerce. The Tibetans claimed they had not been consulted, and, moreover, that China could not make treaties such as these on their behalf.

On the British side, Tibet became a factor in the Great Game – the struggle between Britain and Russia for influence throughout Central Asia. The relentless Russian expansion into the khanates of south-central Asia, across Siberia to the Pacific, and the growing Russian influence in Persia and Afghanistan, worried British policy-makers. By the time he became Viceroy of India Curzon was the most prominent British commentator on the Great Game.[34] He had made his reputation as an intrepid traveler in Central Asia, and burnished it by major contributions to the literature on the topic in his books *Russia in Central Asia* (1889), *Persia and the Persian Question* (1892), and *Problems of the Far East* (1894). Although Curzon was viewed as an expert in Persian and Central Asian matters he was also accused by his critics of being an alarmist about the Russian threat to India. After he took up his post as Viceroy of India in 1899, Curzon became acutely worried when he read reports of Russian influence at Lhasa. A Russian monk Agvan Dorjieff, who was a Buriat Mongol, had established a close relationship with the Thirteenth Dalai Lama. Dorjieff led delegations to meet the Czar at St. Petersburg in 1898 and again in 1901. Curzon convinced himself that these were a prelude to a Russian presence in Lhasa which would place Russia, already creeping into western Afghanistan, on the northern glacis of India.

Curzon tried to deal with the threat by opening negotiations with Tibet through China. This was the very time however when the Thirteenth Dalai Lama was trying to distance Tibet from Chinese political authority. The Lhasa regime ignored treaties negotiated between British India and China officials. The Dalai Lama and his officials even refused to open the messages Curzon sent directly to them. They did so because they wished to keep the British out of Tibet. While China's power had declined throughout the 1800s British power in the world was reaching its apogee. The British had taken India over completely. Nepal was defeated in 1815. Assam was conquered in the 1820s. Sikkim was

---

[34] Karl E. Meyer and Shareen Blair Brysac, *Tournament of Shadows. The Great Game and the Race for Empire in Central Asia* (Washington DC: Counterpoint, 1999), pp. 283–309.

annexed as a client state in the 1830s. Bhutan had also become dependent on British India. During hostilities in 1864 Britain annexed all the *duars* or passes leading into Bhutan. The following year Bhutan signed a treaty with British India and agreed to pay an annual tribute. Bhutan was deeply influenced by Tibetan culture (as Bogle discovered in 1774), and Tibetans viewed this northward expansion of British India with grave concern. They responded by trying to keep in force the policy of closed communications.

The situation had developed into a crisis by 1903 – at least in Curzon's view. His case was that Tibet was disrespecting the British *Raj* by refusing to open diplomatic despatches from him; that the Tibetans were ignoring treaties about borders and trade; and that Dorjieff's presence in Lhasa, and Tibetan contacts with the Czar, showed a clear and present danger of the Russians establishing their influence in Lhasa. His critics claimed he was exaggerating the Russian menace to India – pouring scorn on the idea that there was an invasion threat from across the highest mountain range in the world (not to mention the forbidding high-desert terrain north and west of Lhasa). Because of Curzon's well-known reputation for magnifying the Russian danger, he had considerable difficulty convincing even the Tory government in London that urgent action was needed. The Prime Minister, Arthur Balfour, and the Foreign Secretary, Lord Lansdowne, much preferred to deal with the issue by the more cautious method of diplomatic discussions with Russia. As Charles Hardinge, who attended the first informal Cabinet meeting at the India Office to read Curzon's urgent plea for action, acidly observed: "there was a strong feeling against Curzon's proposal."[35]

Through persistent pestering of the India Office, Curzon eventually persuaded a reluctant Tory Cabinet to allow him to send a mission to Tibet in 1903. Following the failure of the Khamba Dzong negotiations in the summer and autumn of 1903, the Younghusband expedition, officially called "The Tibet Frontier Commission," was beefed up with additional military support in the form of six companies of Sikhs from the Indian Army, and a mountain artillery detachment from the Norfolk regiment. It was this small army that fought its way to Lhasa in 1904. Because of the unease in the Cabinet about stirring up trouble with Russia, Curzon always had to downplay the Russian-threat justification for moving into Tibet. The public reason for the mission had to focus on alleged Tibetan violations of the trade and border issues with India that had simmered since the 1890s. He tried to get Younghusband

---

[35] Charles Hardinge to Sir Charles Scott, London, February 25, 1903, Add. 61867, f. 211, BL.

to understand this and urged him to be careful when speaking of the purpose of the mission. As Curzon patiently explained to Younghusband after the Cabinet had given reluctant permission to advance as far as Gyantse, "we are advancing not because of Dorjieff, or the missions to the Czar, or the Russian rifles in Lhasa but because of our Convention shamelessly violated, our frontier trespassed upon, our subjects arrested, our missions flouted, our representations ignored."[36] Curzon was hoping that the Tibetans would offer some resistance so the diplomatic expedition could be transformed into an armed incursion as far as Lhasa which both he and Younghusband wanted from the beginning of the business. As Curzon knowingly wrote to Younghusband, "The Mission remains a pacific one (however much the Lhasa monks may frown and scowl) until it is converted by hostile acts into a military expedition."[37]

Younghusband met the representatives from the Sixth Panchen Lama, Chokyi Nyima (1883–1937), in July 1903 – before the British government had given permission for him to proceed to Gyantse and Lhasa, and when there was still some hope that local border negotiations might settle matters. The Tibetans viewed the fortified camp Younghusband had established at Khamba Dzong as an aggressive entry into their country, and insisted that if talks were to take place they should be held at Yatung (the trade mart in the Chumbi valley established by the 1893 agreement), or back over the frontier in the first Sikkimese settlement. This particular section of the Tibetan border, marching along the frontiers of Nepal and Sikkim, was subject to the local jurisdiction of the authorities at Shigatse. The Panchen Lama, at the behest of the Dalai Lama, sent official representatives to the British camp "to demand the reason for our armed presence within the country of his August master and to request our immediate withdrawal." This was the first encounter between a British envoy and representatives of the Panchen Lama since 1774 and 1783 and it led to the remarkable exchanges between Younghusband and Badula, the chief delegate from Tashilhunpo.

On July 29, 1903, Younghusband reported to Simla what happened at that first contact:

I would have been within my rights in refusing to receive him, as he was not deputed either by the Chinese or the Lhasa authorities; but these Tibetans are so ignorant that I do not like to lose any opportunity which presents itself of educating them in the elements of their foreign policy. I therefore consented to

[36] Curzon to Younghusband, Government House, Calcutta, January 23, 1904, Younghusband Collection, MSS. EUR. F197/80, BL.
[37] Ibid.

receive him; and, on his arrival, said I understood he was a Deputy from the Tashi Lama of Tashi Lampo: and, he assenting, I went on to say His Holiness had been exceedingly kind to two Englishmen who had visited him. The Deputy looked surprised: and I added that I dared say the Tashi Lama did not remember this, as it happened 130 years ago in one of his former existences: but the British Government had not forgotten it, and I desired on their behalf to offer thanks to His Holiness for his great kindness to these two countrymen of mine, by name, Bogle and Turner.[38]

Captain Frederick O'Connor, who was Younghusband's Intelligence Officer, and who did the translating for the mission, kept a weekly diary in which this meeting was also recorded. According to O'Connor, Younghusband referred to Bogle and Turner as soon as the discussions began:

at 12:30PM the Tashi-Chenpo delegate, Ba-du-la, came into camp bringing presents for the Commissioners. Colonel Younghusband began by informing him of the visits of Bogle and Turner to Shigatse at the close of the eighteenth century, and requested him to inform the Penchen Rinpoche that their hospitable reception had never been forgotten by the Indian Government . . . Neither he nor any of the Tibetans present seemed to have any knowledge regarding the visits to Tashi-Chenpo of Bogle and Turner.[39]

O'Connor added that "Ba-du-la is an elderly man of fine presence, who has been for more than twenty years in the service of the Tashi Chenpo Government"[40] – the implication being that such an experienced official surely would have known if the eighteenth-century missions were part of the official memory at Shigatse.

Four days later, O'Connor held another, less formal, meeting with the Shigatse delegates. This time the history lesson was supplemented with written materials, and was accompanied by a demonstration of modern firepower. O'Connor's diary entry for August 3 described the scene:

The Shigatse officer, Ba-du-la, with the old and new Jongpens [of Khamba Dzong] came into camp about noon and were entertained by the Kumar who showed them pictures and photographs. While they were in camp, Captain Bethune worked the Maxim gun which excited their utmost astonishment and evidently gave them an increased respect for the power of modern armaments. I also showed them the books on Turner's and Bogle's Missions to Tashi-Chenpo, which contained pictures of places with which they were well-acquainted, and

---

[38] Younghusband to Louis W. Dane, Khamba Jong, July 29, 1903, Government of India, Foreign Department. Secret-E. Proceedings, September 1903, Nos. 189–235, Tibet Negotiations, NAI.

[39] Diary Kept by Captain O'Connor during the Tibet Frontier Mission, Khamba Jong, July 29, 1903, *ibid.*

[40] *Ibid.*

a copy of a Tibetan letter from the Panchen Rinpoche of that time addressed to Turner. After this the Kumar and I entertained them at tiffin, and we parted on very friendly terms. Ba-du-la, I found, has a good acquaintance with the history of Tibet, more especially where it deals with the Gurkha and other campaigns.[41]

None of the delegates from the Panchen Lama who spoke to the British at Khamba Dzong apparently had any knowledge of the earlier missions – nor did they seem particularly interested. In reply to Younghusband's speech, Badula explained simply that

although unused to earthly affairs, he had been deputed by the Penchen Rinpoche to visit the British Commissioners and to request them, as a favour, to return from Tibet either to Giaogong [in Sikkim] or to Yatung in the Chumbi valley. He said His Holiness had been influenced in the matter by the strong representations made to him from Lhasa that the British were trespassing on soil under his jurisdiction, and that he was responsible for their withdrawal.[42]

The private letters of Younghusband are even more revealing of what was happening during these meetings. Writing to his wife, Helen, Younghusband explained his strategy:

We are going on very pleasantly here, getting fitter every day and also acquiring a lot of knowledge of Tibet. Yesterday a gentleman came from a very great Lama who resides four marches from here with a request from the Lama that I should remove across the frontier. I told him I was sorry I could not comply with his request. I told his Deputy to thank the Lama for the very great kindness he had shown the two Englishmen who had visited. The Deputy looked very surprised: I said that possibly His Holiness might have forgotten these Englishmen as he did it 130 years ago in one of his former existences: but the British Government had not forgotten his kindness and I desired on their behalf to thank him for it. This is a great piece of diplomacy on my part! You know theoretically these great Lamas never die and it is supposed to be the same person merely in different bodies. And as two Englishmen had been sent on an Embassy to the Lama by Warren Hastings and been well-received by him I thought this was an appropriate way of reminding these Tibetans that an English Mission was no new thing.[43]

Writing to his father three days later, Younghusband repeated the story and added, by way of explanation: "I made much of this idea of

[41] Diary Kept by Captain O'Connor during the Tibet Frontier Mission, Khamba Jong, August 3, 1903, *ibid.*

[42] Diary of Captain O'Connor, Khamba Jong, August 23, 1903, Government of India, Foreign Department. Secret-E. Proceedings, November 1903, Nos. 118–158, NAI.

[43] Younghusband to Helen Younghusband, Khamba Jong, July 30, 1903, MSS. EUR. F197/173, BL.

theirs [reincarnation] to assume that the present man had been kind to Englishmen."[44]

The letters to his wife and his father, as well as his official despatches to Simla, provide a deeply revealing account of Younghusband's attitude and motives in this encounter. He was using this piece of history as a weapon of diplomacy. There were written records in Tibet about the Bogle and Turner missions, as we have seen, but some had been destroyed (perhaps when the Gurkhas looted Tashilhunpo in 1792), and those that did survive were kept in monastic libraries. There was no equivalent to the publicly available volumes on the Bogle and Turner missions that Younghusband could buy in Calcutta bookshops. Younghusband took the Bogle and Turner books along with him to Khamba Dzong. He conjured up these historical records to surprise and (he hoped) outwit the representatives of the Panchen Lama and so score a diplomatic *coup*. Younghusband's tone is triumphant, and his language reveals how superior he felt as he used "this idea of theirs" of reincarnation to add weight to his argument, all the while contrasting Tibetan ignorance of the historical record with his own expert knowledge.

Younghusband staged these revelations of former contact and friendship to encourage the Panchen Lama, and other regional officials involved, including some from Bhutan, to be accommodating to the current British mission. He noted with satisfaction that Bhutanese officials who visited his camp made friendly overtures: "the Thimpuk Jongpen [head of the district just across the Bhutan border] has shown himself decidedly friendly . . . If the Tongsa Penlop [the current ruler of Bhutan] proves equally friendly I hope to be able to increase the intimacy of our relations with Bhutan and lay a foundation for our future intercourse."[45] As the Panchen Lama's representative took leave of Younghusband at Khamba Dzong, he told Younghusband that "he would give my message of thanks to the Tashi Lama, and he asked that we would be friendly towards him."[46] It was precisely this kind of friendly response, already evident in one of the Bhutanese officials, that Younghusband hoped to force from the Tibetans.

Several months after Younghusband had used Bogle at Khamba Dzong, another British official deployed a similar piece of stagecraft to

---

[44] Younghusband to Father, Khamba Jong, August 2, 1903, MSS. EUR. F197/145, BL.

[45] Younghusband to Dane, Camp Tuna, March 13, 1904, Government of India, Foreign Department. Secret-E. Proceedings, July 1904, Nos. 7–105, Tibet Negotiations, in MSS. EUR. F111/344, BL.

[46] Younghusband to Dane, Khamba Jong, July 29, 1903, Government of India, Foreign Department. Secret-E. Proceedings, September 1903, Nos. 189–235, Tibet Negotiations, NAI.

keep up the pressure. In this instance the British officer was E. H. C. Walsh, Deputy Commissioner at Darjeeling, who was also appointed as Assistant to Younghusband.

By March 1904 the British force was well into Tibet. Having wintered over in the Chumbi valley it was now advancing towards Gyantse. Walsh was stationed at Phari, the small, wind-wracked village perched on an exposed but strategic spot as the trail climbed from the Chumbi valley onto the Tibetan plateau (where Bogle had made his comments about Grotius and Pufendorf). The British occupied the crumbling fort to protect their lines of communication and to symbolize their seriousness of purpose. From the beginning of the mission the British had been anxious to bring the Bhutanese over to their side and every opportunity was taken to meet Bhutanese officials. On March 6, 1904, Walsh reported on another meeting with the Jongpen of Thimpuk. The history lesson was again administered, complete with sharing of illustrations contained in the Bogle and Turner books:

I then told him that in the past the intercourse between India and Bhutan had been much closer than it had been in recent times and showed him Markham's account of the Mission of Bogle in 1774, of Dr. Hamilton in 1775 and again in 1777, and of Turner in 1783, giving the equivalent dates in the Tibetan era, and also showed him the passage (on p. 28 of Markham) in which Bogle records how he was invited to play quoits with him. He was very interested, and said that he had never heard of these Missions or the persons named, and that the Tongsa and Paro Forts were the only two in which there were any old records, as those of all the other forts had been destroyed by fires in more recent years.

During this meeting Walsh added another choice morsel of information that put all this history of British contact with Bhutan and Tibet in a good light:

I also told him that Bogle had introduced potatoes into Bhutan, and had planted some at every one of his halting places, as the then Governor General of India, Warren Hastings, had wanted to give Bhutan the advantage of this valuable vegetable. He had not heard this either, but was much interested, and said that this explained the name for potatoes in Bhutanese which is "Pi-long ke'o" (viz., "English brought").[47]

The Bogle and Turner missions were again deployed in this manner several months later when Younghusband was camped at Gyantse, waiting hopefully for permission from London for the final push to Lhasa.

---

[47] E. H. Walsh to Younghusband, Camp Phari Fort, March 6, 1904, Government of India, Foreign Department. Secret-E. Proceedings, July 1904, Tibet Negotiations, in MSS. EUR. F111/344, BL.

Younghusband had levied a fine on the local monasteries because of the alleged participation of monks in the fighting against the British at Guru. Some of the accused monks fell under the jurisdiction of the Panchen Lama and he had intervened to request clemency on their behalf. In his reply, Younghusband once more invoked the memory of Bogle and Turner. On April 25 he reported his actions to Dane:

> Tashi Lama has sent me an Abbot with a small present and credentials sealed with Lama's private seal, to make representation in behalf of monastery here. Tashi Lama says monks only fought against us under pressure from Lhasa, and those that did fight have now been well beaten by his orders, and he hopes I will remit the fine on the monastery. I replied that we had always borne friendly feelings to Tashi Lama on account of hospitality shown to Bogle and Turner. At Khamba Jong I had also done my best to show friendship to his representatives, was all the more disappointed therefore, when I found not only Shigatse soldiers, but even monks fighting against us. The latter thus forfeited claims to respect and privileges we had been ready to give them. I was not prepared to let the matter pass entirely unnoticed, but out of respect for Tashi Lama's representation would remit half the fine.[48]

Throughout these months Younghusband was using the record of Bogle and Turner to manipulate good relations with the Panchen Lama. The Shigatse officials responded by showing some friendship, beginning at the Khamba Dzong meetings in July and August 1903. Those accommodating responses had been noticed with dismay in Lhasa. As the Panchen Lama's delegate explained, when pleading for leniency eight months later at Gyantse, Lhasa had punished Shigatse for being too friendly towards the British. "Abbot states," Younghusband reported, "that in consequence of friendship which grew up at Khamba Jong between us and Abbot then sent, Khamba Jong district has been taken out of jurisdiction of Shigatse and placed under Lhasa."[49] Younghusband's strategy had succeeded in widening the tensions between Shigatse and Lhasa.

As the exchange between the Shigatse Abbot and Younghusband at Gyantse suggests, there was no equality to the relationship. Younghusband's inveigling reference to Bogle and Turner was accompanied by a punitive fine. Younghusband was always operating from a position of superior power. He invariably adopted a condescending attitude, using his knowledge of history as a rhetorical device for placing the Tibetans in a subordinate position. As he explained haughtily to Dane, he took

---

[48] Younghusband to Dane, April 27, 1904, Government of India, Foreign Department. Secret-E. Proceedings, July 1904, Nos. 258–387, Tibet Negotiations, NAI.
[49] *Ibid.*

the opportunity "of educating them in the elements of their foreign policy."[50]

This insistent pressure was embedded in a generally threatening context. We have already seen that the Panchen Lama's representatives at Khamba Dzong were treated to a display of the Maxim gun. When Ugyen Kazi, acting as a representative of the Tongsa Penlop of Bhutan, made one of his visits to the British camp eight months later this aspect was not neglected:

That old Bhutanese Envoy has been going round the camp today and is delighted and impressed with everything. He is what you call "a good sort." I let him fire the Maxim and he was delighted and said to me "What can the Tibetans do when you have guns like this. They had much better seek a settlement" . . . I hope to make a great ally of him.[51]

Younghusband anticipated that showing off his knowledge of the Bogle and Turner missions, along with exhibitions of the killing capabilities of the machine gun, would work together to provide overwhelming proof of British mastery of the situation. Dramatic shows of deadly firepower were formidable enough, but Younghusband and his fellow officers also thought they were demonstrating the superior power of their culture by displaying that they had more knowledge of Tibetan and Bhutanese history than the Bhutanese and Tibetans themselves.

Younghusband and O'Connor evinced surprise at the absence of Tibetan memories of the Bogle mission, but there was a similar frailty of memory on the British side. Younghusband misled the Tibetans when he claimed that "the British Government had not forgotten" the eighteenth-century missions, and that they had "never been forgotten by the Indian Government." As we sketched out earlier in this chapter, these were most dubious claims. Even after the publication of Markham's *Bogle*, British memories remained shaky. It is even doubtful that Younghusband himself knew about Bogle and Turner before he took up the leadership of the 1903 mission. Although it is hard to credit, it seems that Younghusband had no knowledge whatsoever of Bogle and Turner before he set out for Tibet. Looking at British recollections of the Bogle mission shows that memory (both private and public) is a problematic business.

The lengthy despatch of January 8, 1903, in which Curzon and his Council mustered all their arguments for an expedition to Tibet, was

---

[50] Younghusband to Dane, Khamba Jong, July 29, 1903, Government of India, Foreign Department. Secret-E. Proceedings, September 1903, Nos. 189–235, Tibet Negotiations, NAI.

[51] Younghusband to Wife, Tuna, February 20, 1904, MSS. EUR. F197/175, OIOC, BL.

composed in the heady atmosphere of the great imperial durbar at Delhi to inaugurate the reign of Edward VII, the new King-Emperor. This was a moment when sentimental references to Hastings' empire-building role in India seemed to be appropriate. Curzon and his Council accordingly referred to the eighteenth-century missions, but they got some of the basic facts wrong. "We need not carry back the history of missions from the Government of India to Lhasa to the attempts, partly successful, partly unsuccessful, that were made to open relations with the Tibetan Government in the latter part of the eighteenth-century, but we may refer to the first revival of a similar proposal in modern times."[52] The despatch then proceeded to discuss the trade and border controversies that had developed since the 1870s. The fact that this important despatch mistakenly referred to "missions from the Government of India to Lhasa" suggests considerable uncertainty of knowledge since neither Bogle nor Turner got as far as Lhasa. For Curzon and his Council, the Bogle and Turner missions were barely – and inaccurately – remembered.

Other high officials who claimed to have some knowledge of these missions had a similar hazy understanding. For example, Lord Roberts, Commander-in-Chief of the British Army, noted in the margins of a "War Office Note on the Situation in Tibet, 1 October 1902" that "we know all about the road to Lhasa, as two civilians were sent there by Warren Hastings and they published very complete accounts of their journey."[53] Since neither Bogle nor Turner got anywhere near Lhasa, both being denied permission to proceed further than Shigatse, and both having traveled circuitously by way of Bhutan, the army could not use their accounts to learn "the road to Lhasa" (although of course their descriptions of the terrain could be helpful for selecting routes through the mountains for the first stages of an invasion). Roberts' knowledge too was decidedly shaky. The phrasing of the Government of India despatch, taken with Roberts' confusion on this point, suggests that this mis-memory of the eighteenth-century missions was widespread, even among people in key positions who claimed to know about them. Markham had remarked on lost memories in 1876 and had tried to improve them, but in 1903 British memories were not much better.

[52] Curzon, Kitchener, T. Ralegh, E. F. G. Law, E. R. Elles, A. T. Arundel, Denzil Ibbetson to the Rt. Hon. Lord George Hamilton, Camp Delhi, January 8, 1903, Government of India, Foreign Department. Secret-E. Proceedings, July 1903, Nos. 38–95, Revision of British Trade and Frontier Relations with Tibet, NAI.

[53] War Office Note on the Situation in Tibet, October 1, 1902, Government of India, Foreign Department. Secret-E. Proceedings, February 1903, Nos. 1–88, Negotiations with Tibet regarding Trade and Frontier Matters, Alleged Secret Treaty between China and Russia regarding Tibet, in MSS. EUR. F111/344, BL.

The extent to which the Bogle and Turner missions had slipped from British memory is even more remarkably revealed in the case of Younghusband himself. Younghusband was a prolific correspondent and kept diaries and notebooks. He frequently listed his reading, and mentioned books he thought he ought to read. Yet in the mountain of personal and official records left by Younghusband there is no reference to Bogle and Turner before 1903.[54] He told his wife that on his way through Calcutta, in June 1903, he had "bought a lot of books on Buddhism and Tibet."[55] While he was bogged down for five months at Khamba Dzong, Younghusband had time to read these books. He told his wife on July 24: "I have been busy all day reading up all former travels in Tibet to know everything I can about the country."[56]

It was only in the course of this reading that he became aware of the Bogle and Turner missions. We can even pin down the very day when he "remembered" this piece of history. He described his activities for July 27:

I had a pretty busy day today getting off a letter and a cipher telegram to Foreign Office about the Tibetans and Russians... I have the feeling I am doing something really big. I have been working up today all about Warren Hastings' attempts to send an envoy up here in 1774 and I am the next since then to come on an official Mission. It is a great thing.[57]

The phrasing in these letters to his wife suggests that this material was new to him. For example, by stating that he was the first envoy since Bogle, he makes it evident that he had not yet read Turner's volume. He was just now swotting up on this history. It was only on this July day in 1903 that he began to create this story about following in Bogle's footsteps.

This admission by Younghusband is very revealing. He only became acquainted with the eighteenth-century missions a few days before he paraded his historical knowledge so confidently before the Panchen Lama's representatives. Presumably he had bought editions of Markham's *Bogle* and Turner's *Account* in the Calcutta bookshops. Having read up on the history, he seized the opportunity to impress (and intimidate) the Tibetans. In doing so, he deliberately misled the Tibetans

---

[54] There is no reference to Bogle or Turner in Patrick French's comprehensive biography; neither are there any references in Anthony Verrier, *Francis Younghusband and the Great Game* (London: Jonathan Cape, 1991). I found none in the Younghusband papers in the Oriental and India Office collections.

[55] Younghusband to Wife, Darjeeling, June 13, 1903, MSS. EUR. F197/173, BL. In this same letter he told his wife that he had also purchased a revolver in Calcutta.

[56] Younghusband to Wife, Khamba Jong, July 24, 1903, MSS. EUR. F197/173, BL.

[57] Younghusband to Wife, Khamba Jong, July 27, 1903, MSS. EUR. F197/173, BL.

into thinking that this history had been a sustained memory on the British side, and that it shaped current British policy. This nicely illustrates the way in which the existence of publicly available printed books gave a powerful advantage in encounters with other cultures with different modes of maintaining historical memory.

Once memory of Bogle and Turner had been recovered in this way, and introduced by Younghusband into his correspondence with Simla and London, the eighteenth-century missions came back to life in British public debates about Tibet. These precedents were especially serviceable for those who had to defend Curzon's conduct. Even within his own party, Curzon was regarded by many as too forward in his Tibetan policy, and the Balfour Cabinet tried hard to keep him on a leash. Once the mission was launched, accusations of adventurism were made by the Liberal and Radical opposition members in Parliament. To counter these, Government spokesmen in parliamentary debates, as we saw at the opening of this chapter, referred to the eighteenth-century history to imply that the 1903 mission was part of a venerable tradition of policy-making rather than a rash innovation. The Earl of Rosebery, replying in the Lords debate for the Liberals, understood what was happening with the deployment of this dubious historical parallel. He complained that Lord Hardwicke "takes two isolated dates separated by a century and imagines that there was a continuity of policy with regard to Tibet between these two dates."[58] Rosebery, sitting on the plush velvet benches at Westminster, was almost as perplexed as the Panchen Lama's representatives had been when they too were confronted, at Younghusband's Himalayan camp, with this linkage between 1774 and 1904. Rosebery's incredulity suggests that British memory of this history was pretty much the same as Tibetan memory.

On the Tibetan side, once the Panchen Lama and his officials had been reminded by Younghusband of the Bogle mission, the "memory" of that 1774 affair took a strange turn as the young Panchen Lama decided to make use of it in his subsequent diplomatic dealings with the British. One clause in the treaty forced on the Tibetans by Younghusband permitted the British to station a Trade Agent at Gyantse – this was the post later held by Hugh Richardson. Before O'Connor officially took over as the first incumbent, he visited the region on his way back to India. His purpose in returning by way of Tashilhunpo was to begin cultivating a relationship with the Panchen Lama. Younghusband had told all his correspondents back in July 1903 that the Panchen Lama's delegate

---

[58] *Parliamentary Debates*, House of Lords, vol. CXXX (1904), col. 1139.

at Khamba Dzong knew nothing of Bogle, but when O'Connor went to Tashilhunpo in October 1904 the Panchen Lama immediately told O'Connor that he knew all about Bogle.

According to O'Connor the Panchen Lama made a welcoming speech in which he stated that he remembered the Bogle and Turner missions. Here is O'Connor's account of that meeting:

> "I am pleased [said the Panchen Lama] to see British officers again at Shigatse. I have always entertained feelings of friendship for the British, and I had very pleasant relations with the other British Officers who have visited me on previous occasions." For a moment I was at a loss to know to what he referred, as I knew, of course, that no British Officers had ever visited this part of Tibet during his lifetime. And then I understood that in speaking of his friendship with other British Officers he was referring to the visits paid to two of his predecessors in the time of Warren Hastings, when Mr. Bogle came on a mission to Shigatse in 1774 and Captain Turner in 1783. Full accounts of these two Missions have been published and I had studied both of them carefully, and the Lama had of course read of them in the monastic records. Being, as he and all Tibetans believed, the same person as his predecessors only in a different bodily shape, he felt that in welcoming us he was merely carrying on his own policy after a lapse of some one hundred and thirty years. It was a rather startling, but quite logical demonstration of the creed of reincarnation accepted by Tibetan Buddhists.[59]

This account of the Panchen Lama's welcoming speech comes from O'Connor's autobiography published in 1940, thirty-six years after the meeting described. It is commonplace for memoirs to be embellished or simply inaccurately remembered – even when the author has expertise and good intentions. Can O'Connor's compelling account in his memoirs be confirmed by evidence directly from the time of his first meeting at Shigatse in 1904?

In the aftermath of the signing of the Lhasa agreement in September 1904, Younghusband was anxious to prod the Indian Government into setting up the Gyantse Agency. Back in Simla by October 1904, he wrote to the Foreign Department about the next stage. "I propose allowing Captain O'Connor to proceed to Gyantse," he informed Dane, "to seek opportunity of making acquaintance of the Tashi Lama."[60] He was initially accompanied by a small party, also detached from the Mission, that was to explore the upper reaches of the Tsangpo valley, move on to Gartok in western Tibet, and return to India by way of Kashmir. On October 18 O'Connor reported his first meeting with the Panchen Lama. Here

---

[59] Frederick O'Connor, *Things Mortal* (London: Hodder, 1940), pp. 79–80.
[60] Francis Younghusband to Louis Dane, Simla, October 2, 1904, Foreign Office [hereafter FO] 17/1753, p. 300, Public Record Office [hereafter PRO – now the National Archives].

is his description, this time written in his official diary shortly after the meeting:

Arrived Shigatse with Gartok party, 13th. Received in most kindly manner and lodged in a house, property of Tashi Lama's parents . . . Received by Tashi Lama 15th. Lama most cordial in his manner, and referred to former friendly relations between his predecessors and the Indian Government . . . We noted in the evening that the big monastery was all lighted up, and found this was on account of its being the anniversary of the death of the Tashi Lama, who had entertained Bogle on his visit here. Our arrival coinciding with this auspicious date is regarded as a very fortunate omen.[61]

These references to the eighteenth-century missions were passed on by O'Connor to the Government of India in a despatch discussing the advisability of providing gifts to the Panchen Lama as an earnest of British friendship. It would, advised O'Connor, be "quite legitimate to introduce the name of the Viceroy in a more personal manner owing to the friendly relations which formerly existed between a former Tashi Lama and a former Viceroy."[62]

These exchanges were duly noted by the Acting Viceroy, Lord Ampthill (Curzon had gone back to England on leave in December 1903), who reported encouragingly to the Secretary of State for India in London that the Panchen Lama "referred to the former friendly relations between the Government of India and his predecessor."[63] O'Connor added more details of this first meeting at Shigatse, confirming the Panchen Lama's references to Bogle and Turner:

After an interchange of compliments, I referred briefly to recent events and to our former friendship with Tashilhunpo, which I hoped would now be renewed. The Lama replied that he had seen with much regret the difficulties between us and the Lhasa Government, that he was rejoiced at the satisfactory termination of the quarrel; and that for his part he felt sure that friendly relations would now be firmly cemented. He also referred to the visits of Bogle and Turner to Tashilhunpo, and remarked on the auspicious day of our arrival.[64]

The Panchen Lama was evidently pulling out all the stops in his effort to show his familiarity with the eighteenth-century missions.

---

[61] O'Connor to Younghusband, Gyantse, October 18, 1904, FO 535/5, p. 77, PRO; O'Connor to Younghusband, Shigatse, October 17, 1904, FO 17/1753, p. 510, PRO.

[62] O'Connor to Secretary of the Government of India in the Foreign Department, Gyantse, November 20, 1904, Government of India, Foreign Department. Secret-E. Proceedings, February 1905, Nos. 1219–1245, Tibet Negotiations, MSS. EUR. F111/345, OIOC, BL.

[63] Viceroy to Secretary of State, Simla, October 21, 1904, FO 17.1753, p. 109, PRO.

[64] O'Connor to Younghusband, Shigatse, October 17, 1904, FO 17/1753, p. 510, PRO.

O'Connor's diary and despatches from 1904 both tell the same story as his autobiography in 1940 – that the Panchen Lama initiated remarks on the Bogle and Turner missions. In his autobiography, O'Connor acknowledges that there were monastic records which the Panchen Lama had presumably read. In that sense, the Panchen Lama could learn about the past by reading up on it just as Younghusband had done. But in both O'Connor's accounts there seemed to be something more to the Panchen Lama's memory than that. The picture that emerges is of a Panchen Lama who was already fully aware of the Bogle and Turner missions before the British turned up at Shigatse in 1904, who introduced that eighteenth-century subject matter to the British, who used language suggesting personal recollections of the visits, and who viewed the 1904 events as simply a resumption of his actions in previous incarnations.

It is easy to understand why O'Connor, vividly recalling these meetings, chose to use this encounter at Shigatse in the title of his autobiography. He remembered the conversations with deep affection:

It was during one of these sessions that the Lama told me that the officers who had previously visited "him" (during the time of Warren Hastings) had made "him" a number of presents, most of which had been carefully preserved. He had had these objects collected, and he instructed one of his Chamberlains to bring them in. Two servants then appeared, carrying a large box, and when this was opened we proceeded to examine the contents together...It was a queer little glimpse into the past, and was given an atmosphere of reality by the Lama's firm belief that these things had actually been presented to him personally by my predecessors of over a century before...I do cherish the memory of those days, and now in my old age, can picture the young Lama in his dark robes, smiling, gentle and short, and myself, sitting on our cushions with our buttered tea in jade and golden bowls before us on carved and brightly painted wooden stools, chatting away to our hearts content of things both mortal and immortal.[65]

O'Connor's fascinating comments on the Panchen Lama's fond recollections of the eighteenth-century missions have been widely incorporated into writings on Tibet. Hugh Richardson, for example, could not resist citing O'Connor's memoirs in his article on "Tibetan Lamas in Western Eyes." Richardson began by reminding us of the extraordinary nature of Bogle's extended visit in 1774:

No foreigner has lived on terms of closer confidence and intimacy with a great lama; and Bogle parted from the Panchen, his family, Tibet and its people, with genuine sadness. Later, writing to his sister, he regrets the absence of his friend

---

[65] O'Connor, *Things Mortal*, p. 85.

the "Teshu [Panchen] Lama for whom I have a hearty liking and could be happy again to have his fat hand on my head."[66]

He then contrasted this happy encounter with "the rough wooing of the Younghusband Expedition," comparing Younghusband's march to Lhasa to Henry VIII's punitive expedition to Scotland in the 1540s which had slashed and burned its way to Edinburgh in an attempt to force an English marriage on the infant Mary, Queen of Scots. By means of this rather surprising historical parallel Richardson diplomatically conveyed to a modern British readership the brutal intimidation involved in the 1904 foray into Tibet.

Richardson finally turned to the significance of O'Connor's visit to Shigatse in 1904 which linked Younghusband back to Bogle. It was the first opportunity for a British official since Bogle of coming to know the Panchen Lama in person:

Sir Frederick O'Connor, who was fluent in Tibetan, enjoyed a warm friendship with him beginning with visits to Tashilunpo in 1904 and 1905; he later accompanied the lama on his visit to India. O'Connor tells a pleasant story that on their first meeting, the Panchen Lama, referring, without need of explanation, to the visits of Bogle and Turner to two of his predecessors, expressed his pleasure at meeting British officers "again" and recalling the happy relations he had with them. He also showed O'Connor a number of presents – watches, china, silver and so on – received on those earlier occasions.[67]

The impression is once more conveyed to Western readers that the Panchen Lama needed no prompting by the 1904 mission to remember the Bogle visit because he had always known about it throughout his successive Incarnations.

O'Connor's accounts about the Panchen Lama's memory of Bogle unintentionally show that the Tibetans gave as good as they got in these contests over memory and history. Younghusband had started things off at Khamba Dzong by brazenly using the Bogle material to gain some diplomatic leverage. The Shigatse delegates had been startled. They did remember some history from that time. As O'Connor noted in his diary, Badula had a perfectly good knowledge of the Gurkha incursions into Tibet in the late 1780s and early 1790s. Those had been big, important historical events of that era so far as Tibetans were concerned. But the envoys from the Company territories in Bengal in 1774 and 1782 were just two among many representatives who made their way to Tashilhunpo from all over north India and Central Asia. Moreover, the

[66] Hugh Richardson, *High Peaks, Pure Earth. Collected Writings on Tibetan History and Culture* (London: Serindia, 1998), p. 491.
[67] *Ibid.*, pp. 494–495.

closing down of communications from the 1790s meant that such contacts became irrelevant to what was going on in Tibet for most of the
next hundred years. The subject matter was simply too unimportant to
remain in circulation.

When Younghusband reminded Tibetans about it all in 1903 they
could recover their memories too. Younghusband stocked his memory by
reading books he found in the bookshops of Calcutta; the Panchen Lama
and his officials could refresh their memory from the official biographies
of the Third and Fourth Panchen Lamas. So when O'Connor turned
up at Shigatse in 1904, the Panchen Lama, anxious to cultivate good
relations, and taking the cue given at Khamba Dzong, made a point of
recalling "his" memories of the Bogle mission in his opening conversation. This was simply courteous and diplomatic historical memory in a
Tibetan idiom. In both Tibet and Britain historical memory was pliable.

The Bogle mission was forgotten again at Shigatse after the Sixth
Panchen Lama and a few of his close officials fled to China in 1924.
Two years after the last Manchu emperor was overthrown in the 1911
revolution, the Thirteenth Dalai Lama, Thubten Gyatso, took advantage
of the instability in China to assert an ambiguous "independence." This
status gained some precarious viability in the 1914 Simla Convention
signed by Britain, China, and the Dalai Lama by which the Chinese
agreed to "respect the territorial integrity of the country, and to abstain
from interference in the administration of Outer Tibet (including the
selection and installation of the Dalai Lama)."[68] Inside Tibet the growth
in the Dalai Lama's power led to fresh tensions between Lhasa and Shigatse. The Panchen Lama complained of the tax and labor demands
imposed upon him, and viewed these as unwarranted extensions of the
authority of the Lhasa government. (Since he was now at odds with
Lhasa, perhaps we should be using Tashilhunpo's system here and refer
to Lobsang Chokyi Nyima as the Ninth Panchen Lama.) There was
also some support for the Panchen Lama because of the perceived secular outlook and pro-Western policies of the Dalai Lama.[69] The first
British attempts to climb Everest in the 1920s, initially approved by the
Dalai Lama, were caught up in these internal Tibetan cross-currents
as they were cited as an example of his willingness to let in Western
influences.

In terms of the Bogle story, the flight of the Panchen Lama to China,
and his death at Jyekundo in 1937, meant that, by the 1930s, no one at

---

[68] The Simla Agreements of 1914, Article 2, Goldstein, *A History of Modern Tibet*,
p. 833.
[69] *Ibid.*, pp. 110–120.

Shigatse now remembered the 1774 mission. It had never been part of general public knowledge even in Shigatse. It had only been recovered for diplomatic purposes in the few years after the Younghusband mission when there was a possibility of some kind of diplomatic accommodation between Simla and Shigatse. So when Hugh Richardson made inquiries about Bogle's Tibetan wife among his Shigatse friends before he left Tibet in the late 1940s none of them knew anything about Bogle or his mission. On the British side, much had been forgotten too but once Tibet became an issue in British policy-making after the 1870s, the memory of the Bogle mission was revived, beginning with Markham's book, and occasionally made use of. Like other historical events, the Bogle mission, even though it was the first British encounter with Tibet, had slipped in and out of public memory, and was resurrected only when it became useable for current purposes.

In spite of Younghusband's dramatic invocation of Bogle, and the claim that Curzon was following in Hastings' footsteps with respect to Tibet, it is the differences rather than the similarities between these two British encounters with Tibet that are striking. Bogle had been curious and respectful about Tibetan religion and culture. Younghusband was dismissive and supercilious. One small but telling contrast was obvious in their attitudes towards clothing. Bogle had enjoyed wearing local clothes. He and his contemporaries were so pleased with his appearance that Tilly Kettle agreed to paint him in this Tibetan garb. Kettle was one of the first portrait painters to make a career amidst the Company community in India and had many commissions; his painting of Bogle found its way into the royal collection at Windsor. As Kate Teltscher observes, Bogle "is identified with his surroundings through his dress. The painting commemorates a moment of cultural accommodation."[70] There was no such accommodation with Younghusband. He took many boxes of European garments with him to Tibet including sixty-seven shirts, a pair of Norfolk breeches, a white evening waistcoat, and a cocked hat.

He took all this kit because he thought it essential to dress like a European to impress the Tibetans.[71] In his reminiscences Younghusband described an earlier moment in his career in India when he had been sent to remonstrate with the Mir of Hunza about raids on Indian traders going from Kashmir to Yarkand through the Karakorum mountain passes. Younghusband recalled that he had "quite a good idea of my

---

[70] Teltscher, *High Road to China*, p. 176.
[71] Patrick French, *Younghusband. The Last Great Imperial Adventurer* (London: HarperCollins, 1994), pp. 200, 201.

own importance as I sat beside the Chief in my full-dress King's Dragoon Guards uniform. And I spoke to him very straight."[72] Younghusband added, in an almost incredible caricature of imperialist language, that "I knew he was a cur at heart, and I have no doubt he was impressed by my bearing."[73] European clothes and uniforms were now indispensable attributes signifying prestige and power. All this was part of Younghusband's goal of "keeping up a good deal of dignity." At the outset of his mission to Tibet he told Louis Dane, the Head of the Foreign Department in the Indian Government in Simla, that the proper formal dress and due attention to ceremony "go down well with the Oriental."[74]

The contrast between Bogle and Younghusband went well beyond the matter of clothes. One source of that difference was that Younghusband was a professional soldier. Bogle had played at being soldier when he offered advice about the vulnerability of the forts defending the passes into Bhutan, and when he scouted the possibility of an invasion of Assam, but Younghusband was the real thing. He came from a military family. His grandfather had been a Major-General in the Royal Artillery, his father joined the Indian Army, fought in the First Afghan War, and served under Sir Charles Napier during the campaign which conquered the Sind. Younghusband followed in this family tradition. He was born at the hill station of Murree, attended public school in England, entered the Royal Military Academy at Sandhurst, and was commissioned as a Second Lieutenant in the 1st King's Dragoon Guards. When he joined the regiment it was based at Meerut, the barrack-town where the 1857 uprising had begun.[75] In his memoirs he remembered how excited he had been as a young officer when the regiment was posted to Rawalpindi in 1885 in response to a perceived Russian threat. "As a cavalry officer, I had to ride escort to the Duke of Connaught, and gallop for various generals, including the Commander-in-Chief, Sir Donald Stewart."

A keen sense of his love for the military life comes through in this section of his autobiography. "I had all the subaltern's contempt for the civilian as such, and not without reason did I prefer the soldier," he recalled. "Man for man, how could commissioners and secretaries compete with scores and scores of officers on parade who had been tested in the ordeal of war, and known the exaltation of life and death

[72] Younghusband, *The Light of Experience* (London: Constable, 1927), p. 47.
[73] *Ibid.*, p. 48.
[74] Younghusband to Louis W. Dane, Tangu, July 8, 1903, Government of India, Foreign Department. Secret-E. Proceedings, August 1903, Nos. 416–647, Negotiations with Tibet, BL.
[75] French, *Younghusband*, pp. 4, 13, 16.

emergency."[76] Younghusband resigned his army commission in 1890 when he transferred to the Political Department of the Government of India, but this early immersion in the military life gave him a knowledge-able respect for weapons. He liked guns and the power they gave him. As well as buying books on Tibet when he passed through Calcutta on his way up to Darjeeling he also bought a revolver. Younghusband described this shopping expedition to his wife: "The gun maker asked me what I wanted the latter for. I told him to kill people with! I certainly do not want to hang it up as an ornament, for it is the most extraordinary weapon I have ever seen."[77]

This jocular bravado may simply have been a dubious attempt to impress his wife, or he may have been responding to what he thought was a stupid question from the gun seller, but he seems at that moment to be more excited by the potential of the gun than the books. Many of the letters he wrote during the mission reflect this belief in the power of the gun. In November 1903, as plans were being made at Simla for a reinforced mission to cross into the Chumbi valley, he wrote to Louis Dane that "of course if it comes to fighting – as it certainly will – we shall have to shut up our bowels of compassion, and hit hard."[78] He was deeply frustrated that the Tibetans refused to recognize the superior firepower he had brought with him into their country. Even after the massacre at Tuna, when 628 Tibetans were killed and 222 wounded by 50 shrapnel shells, 1,400 machine gun rounds, and 14,351 rounds of rifle ammunition, the Tibetans would not yield.[79] Younghus-band wrote in exasperation to his father, "They <u>will</u> not believe in our power."[80]

His frustration boiled over again at Gyantse as the British easily repelled Tibetan attacks on their camp. He confided to the Viceroy that

there is something very pitiful in seeing these poor peasants who really have no other wish than to be allowed to plough their fields in peace being mown down by our merciless magazine rifles. It makes me all the more determined to smash

[76] Younghusband, *The Light of Experience*, pp. 3, 7.
[77] Younghusband to Helen Younghusband, Darjeeling, June 13, 1903, Younghusband Collection, MSS. EUR. F197/173, BL.
[78] Younghusband to Louis W. Dane, Darjeeling, November 18, 1903, Government of India, Foreign Department. Secret-E. Proceedings, January 1904, Nos. 430–520, Tibet Negotiations. Advance of the Mission to Rinchingong, Chumbi, NAI.
[79] French, *Younghusband*, p. 224.
[80] Younghusband to his Father, Tuna, April 1, 1904, Younghusband Collection, F197/145, BL.

these selfish, filthy, lecherous Lamas who are bringing all this trouble upon their country for their own ends.[81]

Younghusband was garrulous in his letters and may have let his thoughts run away from him, but his views on this subject of firepower were not idiosyncratic. He received explicit praise for his actions at Tuna from an ally at the India Office in London after news of the bloody affair reached the imperial capital:

Today's *Times* gives an account of your fight on the way to Gyantse. Everything appears to have been done at the risk of your life and [General] Macdonald's to avoid a collision so that there should be no foolish talk of having forced an encounter. I am glad you struck hard as the blow had to be to the groin; now that the Tibetans have seen our power, and that business is normal, they are likely to prove amenable.[82]

Younghusband's obsession with this Tibetan refusal to recognize the consequences of his superior weaponry is laced through all his letters at this time. He complained to his wife that "these Tibetans take a lot of teaching. I wonder if they will ever learn that it is useless to fight us."[83]

Younghusband was well aware that such attitudes towards the use of force would be questioned by Liberals and Radicals in Britain, both in Parliament and in the press, but he had his answer ready. In a lengthy exchange with Curzon he set out his thinking. He linked the criticism he anticipated receiving with the debate that had taken place at the time of the Boer War in South Africa (1899–1902). He and Curzon would be attacked at home

for bullying a harmless people and trying to curb their independence . . . We are making use of our power, they will say, and spending the resources of the poor people of India in trampling down the independence of the peaceable and religion loving Tibetans. It was bad enough to coerce the Boers but they had plenty of modern arms to use against us. To employ our overwhelming strength against a people who have no arms, whose religion teaches them not to fight, and who only ask to be left alone, will doubtless be presented as the very acme of high handed abuse of power.[84]

---

[81] Younghusband to Lord Ampthill, Gyantse, May 5, 1904, Younghusband Collection, F197/81, BL.

[82] W. H. Wylie to Younghusband, India Office, London, April 1, 1904, Younghusband Collection, F197/83, BL.

[83] Younghusband to Helen Younghusband, Gyantse, May 5, 1904, Younghusband Collection, F197/176, BL.

[84] Younghusband to Curzon, Camp Chumbi, January 1, 1904, Younghusband Collection, F197/80, BL.

Younghusband's answer to such charges can be summed up in one word – empire. The British empire was a force for good in the world, and even the Tibetans would come to understand that truth. Here is his case:

Yet there is another way of looking at this question which I am sure the high-minded English people would see to be the right one if it were put to them in that light. Whether by peaceable or forcible means we must gain a real, unquestionable influence in Tibet from this time onwards; for the Tibetans are not a people fit to be left to themselves between two Great Empires. They have to look to one or the other – to us or the Russians – for protection. We cannot afford to let the Russian influence prevail, and even if we take up the task of securing an influence over them this need not be for their harm. For look at the state they are in at present. They are nothing but slaves in the power of selfish and ignorant monks who hold the supreme authority in Lhasa.[85]

So for Younghusband, the goal of his mission became nothing less than the liberation of the people of Tibet from "the monks in Lhasa."[86] Curzon heartily agreed with his emissary that the march to Lhasa was not only for the empire but for the benefit of the Tibetans. "Our goal is the good of the Tibetans," Curzon assured Younghusband, "no less than the safeguard of imperial interests."[87]

Both men steeled themselves against criticism by viewing themselves as "two workers for the good of the Empire who look not merely to its purely selfish interests, but who believe that England has a high name to make in the history of the world, and hard duties to perform in fulfilling its destiny of advancing the welfare of the human race."[88] As Curzon parried the mounting criticism after the mission had ended, he dined with E. C. Wilton who had been Younghusband's Chinese translator. Wilton reported to Younghusband that Curzon had told him over dinner "that History at any rate would do justice to his policy and your efforts in Tibet."[89] Both Curzon and Younghusband were convinced that their mission to Tibet was on the right side of history. During his time in Tibet, Younghusband had received similar messages of solidarity from colleagues in the Political Department of the Indian Government. Writing from his post as Political Agent to the Phulkan States, J. R. Dwight assured Younghusband that "you know enough of history, and you have

---

[85] *Ibid.*   [86] *Ibid.*
[87] Curzon to Younghusband, Government House, Calcutta, January 23, 1904, Younghusband Collection, F197/80, BL.
[88] Younghusband to Curzon, Camp Chumbi, January 1, 1904, Younghusband Collection, F197/80, BL.
[89] E. C. Wilton to Younghusband, Calcutta, January 24, 1905, Younghusband Collection, F197/83, BL.

enough experience of tight corners to feel that in a big task like this, where you alone can know, you <u>must</u> go it alone and chance it. God send you fortune old chap, and may you soon come safe back having done, and done well, one of the biggest bits of empire building it ever fell to the lot of man to do."[90]

Invoking empire and its benefits to humanity was not unusual in Edwardian Britain. Curzon and Younghusband may have been towards the extreme end of the spectrum but this kind of imperial ideology was common enough. There were always critics of course – those whom the historian A. J. P. Taylor long ago affectionately and mischievously dubbed to be "the trouble makers" in British history who took pot-shots at British foreign and imperial policies round the world.[91] Curzon and Younghusband can also be distinguished from more prudent imperialists who shared their belief in the necessity and beneficence of the empire but had misgivings about activist imperial adventures. Wilton made the distinction clear when he told Younghusband that "you had the courage of your opinions and acted for the Empire rather than for the interests of those elderly estimable gentlemen in the Cabinet."[92] The views on empire that run so strongly through Younghusband's correspondence are interesting and sometimes rather extreme, but they are within the bounds of what we know of the discourse on empire in Edwardian England. What is surprising, even shocking, to modern readers (apart, perhaps, from many members of the Chinese Communist Party and its government bureaucracy) are his venomous views on Tibetan lamas.

We can trace these views in the same way we did with Bogle, for during their time in Tibet both men undertook extensive private letter writing to family and friends, alongside their official correspondence. As in Bogle's case, the family letters were often revealing of Younghusband's innermost feelings. He was certainly utterly candid. "The Lamas were underbred, rude, common and bigoted to the last degree," he told his wife after he had made a visit to the Tibetan camp at Guru. "But the worst of it is they are so appallingly ignorant of their true position in the Universe and so over-weeningly superior that the more you argue with them the more convinced they are that you are afraid of them."[93]

---

[90] J. R. Dwight to Younghusband, Political Agency, Phulkan States, February 22, 1904, Younghusband Papers, F197/83, BL.

[91] A. J. P. Taylor, *The Trouble Makers. Dissent over Foreign Policy 1792–1939* (London: H. Hamilton, 1957).

[92] E. C. Wilton to Younghusband, Calcutta, January 24, 1905, Younghusband Collection, F197/83, BL.

[93] Younghusband to Helen Younghusband, Tuna, January 14, 1904, Younghusband Collection, MSS. EUR. F197/175, BL.

He sometimes broadened his critique to those who slavishly obeyed the lamas. In April 1904 he informed his father that "as I have always said, the Tibetans are nothing but sheep." And in July 1904, after another military defeat for the Tibetans on the last pass before the Tsangpo valley, he told his father that "I always thought the Tibetans were rather a rotten lot."[94]

His official correspondence is also shot through with similar evaluations. He complained that the Tibetans "are very like big children," and he informed Louis W. Dane that "these Lhasa Lamas...are...not only bigoted and ignorant but filled up with ideas of their own omnipotence."[95] In his *Memorandum on Our Relations with Tibet*, written in July and August 1903 at Khamba Dzong (and later printed at Simla), he argued that no one could doubt "that the people as a whole would benefit by the breaking of the monopoly in the hands of these ignorant and self-seeking monks."[96] When he met the monks at Gyantse monastery he allowed that they were "not fanatical like the Lhasa monks" but they "are a low, sensual, lazy looking lot."[97] One of the goals of his mission had now become "the emancipation of a people most willing to be friendly with us who are held in bondage by a cruel, self-seeking oligarchy of monks."[98]

To be sure, Younghusband was engaged in a military campaign when he made these observations, and when invasions are launched it is common to demonize the enemy. There are signs that Younghusband had some success in shaping opinion back in Britain. An article in the *Edinburgh Review* written shortly after the mission ended, and including commentary on the two-volume book written about Younghusband's campaign by the *Times* correspondent, described Lhasa as

the centre and shrine of a religious system which remains without parallel in the world for its power, its completeness, its harshness. We say "harshness" with regret; for truly one of the most disappointing things which the exploration of

[94] Younghusband to his Father, Gyantse, April 12, 1904, and Younghusband to his Father, Camp Zara, July 19, 1904, Younghusband Collection, MSS. EUR. F197/145, BL.

[95] Younghusband to Louis W. Dane, Khamba Jong, August 24, 1903, Government of India, Foreign Department. Secret-E. Proceedings, November 1903, Nos. 118–158, Tibet Negotiations; Younghusband to Dane, Khamba Jong, July 25, 1903, Government of India, Foreign Department. Secret-E. Proceedings, September 1903, Nos. 189–235, Tibet Negotiations, NAI.

[96] Younghusband, *Memorandum on Our Relations with Tibet both Past and Present* (Simla, 1903), p. 41, Younghusband Collection, MSS. EUR. F197/78, BL.

[97] Younghusband to Louis W. Dane, Gyantse, April 16, 1904, Government of India, Foreign Department. Secret-E. Proceedings, July 1904, Nos. 7–105, Tibet Negotiations, BL.

[98] Younghusband to Lord Curzon, Camp Chumbi, January 1, 1904, Younghusband Collection, MSS. EUR. F197/80, BL.

Tibet has revealed to us is that the religion of lamaism is not the mild and gentle influence that seems to beam from the eyes of Buddha but a dark and rigorous intolerance, a harsh priestly rule, a system peopled with all the bogies and terrors of a childish hell, and appealing to crude and simple fears such as only cruelty can impose and ignorance support.[99]

In similar vein, a piece in *The Spectator* on "the incident at Tuna" declared that "the chiefs of the great monasteries at Lhasa, who practically rule Tibet, are not only profoundly ignorant, but insanely proud ... knowing nothing of the enchanted armour of science with which Europe now protects itself, they reckoned on a victory as completely as a London policeman does when he arrests a footpad."[100] But the warmth of Younghusband's language, appearing in both his private and his official correspondence, suggests more than war-time propaganda. The intensity of expression suggests he really believed what he wrote at the time.

The use of such phrases as "my experience with Asiatics" when justifying some of his audacious actions in Tibet is further evidence of Younghusband's deep-seated cultural arrogance, as he put all Asian peoples in the same category.[101] He explained helpfully to his wife as his mission was about to set out for Tibet that

there are rumours here in the bazaar [Darjeeling] that we are going to fight. That is a good thing for the other side will be frightened and I want to establish a funk. Chinamen and Asiatics generally only do business when they are in a funk. If they are not afraid of you they are insufferably arrogant. I am going to do the arrogance this time.[102]

Curzon showed that he shared this disposition when he assured Younghusband that his success in securing the Lhasa treaty was "a most striking tribute to your knowledge of Asiatics."[103]

Younghusband's commentary on Tibetan lamas is the complete antithesis of Bogle's view that "lamas enlighten this part of the world." He used Bogle's mission in his negotiations to claim that the British government had never forgotten that friendly beginning to Anglo-Tibetan relations, but he did not set much store by Bogle's sympathetic engagement

---

[99] *Edinburgh Review* (April 1905), pp. 338–339.

[100] "The Incident at Tuna," *Spectator*, April 9, 1904, p. 557.

[101] Younghusband to Louis W. Dane, Gyantse, May 16, 1904, Government of India, Foreign Department. Secret-E. Proceedings, July 1904, Nos. 258–387, Tibet Negotiations, NAI.

[102] Younghusband to Helen Younghusband, Darjeeling, June 16, 1903, Younghusband Collection, F197/173.

[103] French, *Younghusband*, p. 255.

with Tibetan society. The encounter in 1904 was brutal and arrogant. It was a crude example of a bundle of Orientalist prejudices and misconceptions in the service of aggressive Western imperialism. The business of using Bogle was part and parcel of all this for it made the Tibetans seem primitive and clueless in the face of superior Western knowledge.

11   George Curzon, painting by John Cooke, after John Singer Sargent, 1914. Lord Curzon (1859–1925) was Viceroy of India from 1899 to 1905 and the driving force behind the British invasion of Tibet in 1904. He was convinced that Russia was about to establish a presence in Lhasa. The Younghusband invasion was designed to check those imagined Russian plans and bring Tibet within the British sphere of influence. Curzon described himself as an imperialist through and through.

12   Thomas Jones Barker's painting "The Secret of England's Greatness," 1863. This painting now hanging in Room 23 in the National
Portrait Gallery in London shows how British imperial ideologies had
been deeply influenced by evangelical Christianity in the time between
Bogle's death in 1781 and the arrival on the scene of figures like
Younghusband. The belief that God was by his side, and on the side
of the British empire, sustained Younghusband throughout his Tibet
mission. Back in 1774 Bogle was glad "he had not been sent as a missionary" to Tibet.

13 Francis Younghusband (second from left, front row) and members of the Tibet Mission Force. Younghusband and his officers are pictured here ready to show force to the Tibetans. Younghusband wrote to Louis Dane, the head of the Foreign Department of the Government of India, that "of course if it comes to fighting – as it certainly will – we shall have to shut up our bowels of compassion and hit hard."

14   Khamba Dzong was a small Tibetan village and administrative center just across the northern border of Sikkim. The Younghusband mission went there in July 1903 in an attempt to force the Tibetans into negotiations over trade and boundary disputes. It was at the British camp in the valley below the dzong that Younghusband used the Bogle mission to intimidate the delegation sent by the Sixth Panchen Lama by claiming that incarnated lamas must surely remember all the historical events that had happened in their previous Incarnations. When these negotiations failed Curzon persuaded the British government to allow the march towards Lhasa to begin.

15   Lobsang Chokyi Nyima (1883–1937), the Sixth Panchen Lama
(the Ninth by Tashilhunpo's count), was the Incarnation during and
after the Younghusband invasion. He sent delegates to Khamba Dzong
in an effort to persuade Younghusband to withdraw across the Sikkim
border. After the invasion, he became friendly with the British, assured
them that he well remembered the 1774 mission, and asked for their
help to counter the growing power of the Thirteenth Dalai Lama. He
fled to China in 1924 after a series of disputes with Lhasa. When he left
Shigatse the memory of the Bogle mission disappeared with him – as
Hugh Richardson discovered when he made his enquiries in the 1930s
and 1940s.

16 British column crossing the Tang La. As the British force crossed the Tang La in January 1904 they paused to raise the Union Jack. It was scenes such as this that convinced Tibetans, and observers in other countries, that the British intended to occupy parts of central Tibet.

17 British bayonets in Lhasa. Younghusband put great faith in guns as well as God during his mission. In his letters he complained again and again that the Tibetans stubbornly refused to recognize his superior military strength. This is a telling picture showing how weapons continued to be displayed even when negotiations were taking place in Lhasa. The Tibetan officials were being reminded that they were negotiating under the direct threat of British power.

18   Thubten Gyatso (1876–1933), the Thirteenth Dalai Lama, was able to use Chinese political and military weakness in the 1880–1930 era to build up autonomy for Tibet within the Chinese empire. In the 1890s he declined to recognize treaties made by China with British India which led to Curzon's aggressive response in 1903–1904; after the Chinese revolution in 1911 he asserted Tibet's claims of independence more forcefully. Once the Communists won power in 1949 the Beijing regime reasserted its claims by invading Tibet in 1950–1951. Tenzin Gyatso (1935–), the Fourteenth Dalai Lama, fled Tibet in 1959 and has remained in exile since that time.

5   From Enlightenment to empire

As we noted in the Introduction, something called "the Enlightenment project" is often cited as the ideological driving force behind European imperialism; the Enlightenment is also often presented as one of the glorious achievements of European culture. As Sankar Muthu puts it, the Enlightenment "is demonized by some and extolled by others."[1] It is asking too much of George Bogle and Francis Younghusband to settle once and for all these contrasting views of the Enlightenment and its role in world history, but it is illuminating to use these two British encounters with Tibet to explore some of the core issues at stake. George Bogle looked at his world, as we have seen, both through Enlightened eyes and through imperial eyes. Younghusband seems to have had nothing but imperial eyes. Bogle was shaped by the Enlightenment culture of the mid-eighteenth century; Younghusband was shaped by the imperial culture of the late Victorian and Edwardian era. If we can understand how empire and Enlightenment were related in this comparison we can identify some conceptual benchmarks, sketch out how things changed from Bogle's time to Younghusband's, and judge whether there was a continuum between the two.

There is a problem of definition that needs to be confronted at the outset. What do we mean when we use the term "the Enlightenment"? In spite of all the caveats of scholars, including those of J. G. A. Pocock quoted in the Introduction, it is still perfectly normal to see the definite article and capital letter at work. The capitalization conveys a strong impression that there was an intellectual movement in Europe, beginning in the late 1600s, that had a consistent outlook on the world. That view remains well entrenched in spite of sustained attempts to undermine it. As far back as 1976, the American scholar Henry May identified several different phases of the Enlightenment with examples of thinkers for each stage. There was the Moderate Enlightenment (John Locke and Isaac Newton);

---

[1] Sankar Muthu, *Enlightenment Against Empire* (Princeton University Press, 2003), p. 258.

the Skeptical Enlightenment (David Hume); the Revolutionary Enlightenment (Jean-Jacques Rousseau and Thomas Paine); and the Didactic Enlightenment (represented by Scottish Common Sense philosophers such as Thomas Reid and Adam Smith).[2] There is still an abundance of capitalization but this was an early effort to show a wide range of thinkers – frequently at odds with each other – who operated under the umbrella of the Enlightenment.

In a more recent attempt to disaggregate the Enlightenment, Jonathan Israel has proposed a grand distinction between a radical Enlightenment and a conservative Enlightenment.[3] Radical thinkers, such as Baruch de Spinoza (1632–1677), were prepared to use reason to the utmost limits and deny that there was any evidence for God as a creator or intervener in the universe. The radicals were materialists and atheists. The moderate Enlightenment thinkers prized reason, but were ready to suspend disbelief when it came to a Christian God. To a considerable extent this reflects the difference between continental and British thinkers in the Enlightenment era. Major British intellectual figures who were near contemporaries of Spinoza, such as John Locke (1632–1704) and Isaac Newton (1642–1727), remained very much at ease in the hierarchical, deeply religious English world of the 1600s and 1700s.

Even if we narrow the focus to a regional variation and speak of "the Scottish Enlightenment," as Alastair Lamb does when he introduces Bogle, there are still problems of definition. In the four-volume *Encyclopedia of the Enlightenment* distinctions are made between the intellectual contexts in Aberdeen, Glasgow, and Edinburgh because of the differing social conditions and histories of those places. The entry on Bogle's home town of Glasgow, for example, refers to "an evangelical enlightenment" in Glasgow that had developed by the 1760s and explains that the stronger mercantile presence there curtailed the broader range of intellectual interests that was characteristic of the more literary orientation of Edinburgh.[4] In his study of eighteenth-century thinkers Sankar Muthu agrees with Pocock that there was a variety of enlightenments rather than the Enlightenment. Muthu insists "that 'the Enlightenment' as such and the notion of an overarching 'Enlightenment project' simply do not exist."[5]

---

[2] Henry F. May, *The Enlightenment in America* (New York: Oxford University Press, 1976).
[3] Jonathan Israel, *Enlightenment Contested. Philosophy, Modernity, and the Emancipation of Man 1670–1752* (Oxford University Press, 2006) and *Radical Enlightenment. Philosophy and the Making of Modernity* (Oxford University Press, 2001).
[4] Alan Charles Kors, ed., *Encyclopedia of the Enlightenment*, 4 vols. (Oxford University Press, 2003), vol. I, pp. 380–382; vol. IV, pp. 47–52.
[5] Muthu, *Enlightenment Against Empire*, p. 264.

There is also a problem of definition on the other side of the equation which links the Enlightenment to empire. The Younghusband mission is often cited as characteristic of the somewhat fevered British imperial ideology in the Edwardian era – with its contemptuous views of another culture, its readiness to deploy a far superior military technology against a pathetically ill-armed foe, its insistence that Tibet be brought into a British sphere of interest, and the jingoistic coverage it received in *The Times* and the *Daily Mail*. Yet the British government in London was palpably reluctant throughout the entire enterprise. The Prime Minister Arthur Balfour, the Foreign Secretary Lord Lansdowne, and the two Secretaries of State for India who dealt with the Tibet mission, Lord George Hamilton and St. John Brodrick, all thought they were pursuing the best policy for the empire by restraining Curzon and Younghusband. They believed that maintaining stability in the international relations of the Great Powers was the best way to secure Britain's manifold imperial interests in a complex world. They complained that Curzon wished to conduct British Indian policy as though India were an independent state. The Tibet escapade for them was an unhelpful distraction because, for example, it would provide an excuse for Russia to be obstinate over current negotiations aimed at strengthening Britain's position in Egypt.

Lord Ampthill, who took over as Viceroy while Curzon was on leave in England, attempted to educate Younghusband on these broader imperial considerations:

Now the principal object which His Majesty's Government have at heart is to complete the great and important Treaty which they have just negotiated with France. To do so, it is necessary to persuade all the great Powers to assent to the arrangements which we proposed with respect to Egypt. Russia makes the condition of assent an understanding on the part of Great Britain not to intervene permanently in Tibetan affairs and she thinks, not unnaturally, though without any real justification, that we are taking advantage of her present troubles to extend our frontiers towards her own dominions. The Russians of course judge us by themselves and we must admit appearances are against us . . . But nothing would be more disastrous to the peace of the world than that Russian dislike and resentment against us should be increased at the present time. It is all important to diminish it, and hence the policy of His Majesty's Government. That policy may result in the failure of the Tibet Mission but even that is better than the certain prospect of a war with Russia, from the point of view of the whole British Empire.[6]

As Curzon pressed for action on Tibet, Lord George Hamilton, the current Secretary of State for India, replied that the empire would

---

[6] Lord Ampthill to Younghusband, Simla, June 13, 1904, MSS. EUR. F197/81, BL.

be damaged if pushful proconsuls like him persisted in making these extraordinary demands. Hamilton compared Curzon to Alfred Milner to drive his point home. Milner's activist local policies in South Africa had brought about the difficult and draining Boer War. In a similar way, Curzon's aggressive measures might well embroil the empire in unwelcome problems. Curzon's forcefulness over Tibet, at a delicate moment in international affairs, threatened to undermine Britain's wider interests. "The truth is, my dear George," Hamilton wrote bluntly, "if there were two more of you in other parts of the British Empire occupying big posts, the machine would not be manageable."[7]

Younghusband for his part complained that Hamilton, Brodrick, and the other Cabinet minsters did not understand what the empire was all about. He castigated all these high officials in London for letting down the empire. In February 1904 when he was still waiting for permission to proceed deeper into Tibet, he accused the India Office and the Cabinet of gross timidity. "It is a rotten way of running an empire like ours," he complained to his father.[8] When the Cabinet and the India Office later repudiated the sections of the Lhasa agreement allowing occupation of the Chumbi valley for seventy-five years (and censured Younghusband for inserting that clause in the agreement), Younghusband described Brodrick as "just one of those pig-headed bunglers who ruin the Empire, and the sooner they get rid of him from English politics the better."[9]

Back in the 1770s Bogle had also criticized the London politicians for their lack of understanding of the Company's position in India, and for their impetuous changes in policy. He complained to his brother about "the Ministry interfering so much" and of the problems caused by "your Gentleman at home changing your Plans so often."[10] He told Anderson in 1772 that he wished the politicians in Parliament "would keep themselves to the next election and let us alone, for I fear they will not do us any Good."[11] So in both cases there were marked differences between British agents of empire in India who led the missions to Tibet and British ministers in London. Which figures in British history can we say more truly represented imperial ideology? As with Jonathan Israel's disaggregation of the Enlightenment, we can at least distinguish ultra imperialists from

[7] George Hamilton to Curzon, India Office, July 9, 1903, MSS. EUR. F123/1, BL.
[8] Younghusband to his Father, Tuna, February 5, 1904, MSS. EUR. F197/145, BL.
[9] Younghusband to his Father, Calcutta, October 12, 1904, MSS. EUR. F197/95, BL.
[10] George Bogle to Robert Bogle, Calcutta, November 2, 1770, Bogle Papers, Folder George Bogle [marked 9], Mitchell Library; Same to Same, Calcutta, December 26, 1770, *ibid.*, Folder Bogle October–December 1770 [marked 70], Mitchell Library.
[11] George Bogle to David Anderson, Calcutta, October 6, 1772, David Anderson Papers, Add. 45421, f. 20, BL.

more cautious types, and men on the spot compared to those in charge in London. It is also important to bear in mind the difference between those who viewed things from a British Indian viewpoint and those who viewed matters from a Britain-in-the-world viewpoint.

In the case of the 1904 mission, there was another very curious development which shows the dangers of treating the British empire too simplistically. We opened this book with Younghusband's triumphant statement about going through the wall just beyond Yatung on his way up to Phari. But when he had first entered Tibet by crossing the Jelep La on the Sikkim border and descended into the Chumbi valley there was already an English official there – inside Tibet. The Englishman was Captain Randall Parr of the Chinese Customs Service. Under the terms of the trade agreements of the 1890s, Yatung had been designated as the official port of entry for goods coming into Tibet from India. Since Tibet was technically under Chinese jurisdiction this post was staffed by Chinese customs officials. At this time the Chinese Customs Service was run by the British (another sign of Chinese weakness) and there were many English customs agents stationed at ports of entry throughout China. This role in supervising the customs service has been aptly described as "Britain's imperial cornerstone in China."[12]

Parr was the customs man in Yatung. Since he could speak Chinese, and since he knew the local Chinese and Tibetan officials, Parr was drawn into the negotiations. Yu-t'ai, the Chinese Amban in Lhasa "charged with the administration of Tibetan affairs," appointed Parr as a Joint Commissioner on the Chinese-Tibetan side.[13] It would be lovely to know whether Yu-t'ai did this to have some fun at the expense of Younghusband and Curzon. It certainly made for a sticky situation. Now there was "the Englishman on the other side" as Younghusband accusingly put it.[14] When the mission reached Yatung, Parr often came over to the tents of the British camp to chat with the officers. Younghusband pumped Parr for information on what was happening in Lhasa, but he had a sneaking suspicion that Parr was pumping him so he could report back to his Chinese masters on British plans.

Younghusband later told Dane that Parr may even have been partly responsible for making the Tibetans so intransigent at Khamba Dzong. "I am pretty sure Parr, at the start at Khamba Jong, told the Chinese and

---

[12] Donna Brunero, *Britain's Imperial Cornerstone in China. The Chinese Maritime Customs Service 1854–1949* (London: Routledge, 2006).

[13] Yu-t'ai, Chinese Imperial Resident at Lhasa, to Curzon, Lhasa, June 24, 1903, Younghusband Collection, MSS. EUR. F111/344, BL.

[14] Younghusband to Helen Younghusband, Khamba Jong, September 3, 1903, Younghusband Collection, F197/174, BL.

Tibetans that the Home Government were never likely to let us advance to Gyantse, and that I was not permitted to use this as a threat," he wrote to Dane in August 1904, "[and so] the Tibetans thought they might treat us as they pleased at Khamba Jong, and let the climate do the work in clearing us out when winter came on."[15] Clearly the treatment he had received at Khamba Dzong still rankled with Younghusband, but now he had to entertain the troubling thought that another Englishman may have been partly responsible for encouraging Tibetan resistance. In addition to his critics at home, Younghusband had to contend with an ambiguous British agent on the Tibetan side. Who was working for the best interests of the British empire here?

The problem of what is meant by "the Enlightenment" and "the British empire" will never be solved to the satisfaction of everyone but some key conceptual issues are brought into sharp focus if we look at them through the prism of these two Tibet missions. In the case of Bogle, we can see from the commentaries in his journals and memoranda about Bhutan and Tibet, and from his direct references to Montesquieu, Buffon, and Robertson, that he was working within certain orientations typical of Enlightenment thinking. There was a distinctive Scottish empiricism which gathered, organized, and analyzed evidence about the human world in order to look for patterns and arrive at "common sense" propositions about how things worked. As Colin Kidd has argued, historians and philosophers from lowland Scotland such as Henry Home, Lord Kames (1696–1782), William Robertson (1721–1793), David Hume (1711–1776), Adam Ferguson (1723–1816), John Millar (1735–1801), and Adam Smith (1723–1790) were attracted to this comparative sociological approach partly because their own home region was "located geographically and historically between the patriarchal social organization of the Highlands and English commercial civilization [which] acted as stimulus to both sociological and comparative perspectives."[16] The stadial theory of history – which posited that human societies moved through four stages: the hunter-gatherer, the pastoral, the agricultural, and the commercial – was another distinctive feature of Enlightenment thinking in Scotland. Observers formed by these ways of thinking were encouraged to pay attention to the impact of environmental factors on social and cultural formations, and to recognize that human differences round the world were shaped by such factors rather than by any innate

[15] Younghusband to Dane, Lhasa, August 27, 1904, Younghusband Collection, F111/345, BL.
[16] Colin Kidd, *Subverting Scotland's Past. Scottish Whig Historians and the Creation of an Anglo-British Identity 1689–1830* (Cambridge University Press, 1993), p. 110.

virtues or defects within a particular society. Such thinking was willing to be open to the virtues in other cultures.

In her study of the relationship between Enlightenment and empire Jennifer Pitts has observed that "in the closing years of the eighteenth century, a critical challenge to European imperial conquest and rule was launched by many of the most innovative thinkers of the day, including Adam Smith, Bentham, Burke, Kant, Diderot and Condorcet." These prominent intellectual figures "were universalists in the sense they adhered to the principles that all humans are naturally equal and that certain moral principles are universally valid." She argues that in this period there were still significant hesitations about claiming a European superiority over the rest of humankind:

While Europeans in the late eighteenth century undoubtedly were becoming increasingly secure in their sense of superiority – intellectual, moral, political, economic, and technological – over the rest of the world, we find among a number of eighteenth century thinkers a continued sense of fragility of their civilization's achievements, persistent doubts about the justice of European political and social orders, and respect for the achievements and rationality of other societies.[17]

If we gather all these Enlightenment strands together we can see how they shaped Bogle's narrative on Bhutan and Tibet that we followed in the first chapter. He looked at the geographical and economic circumstances within which people lived, and he made sympathetic assessments about why they had arrived at their particular social and moral arrangements – in the way they organized religion and politics, farmed, married, and buried their dead. He recognized the achievements of Tibetan society, and expressed occasional doubts about British ways and about Company rule in Bengal.

At the very same time as he displayed this Enlightenment outlook, however, Bogle was deeply implicated in empire. When he came to Bengal he understood that he was part of an exploitative colonial project, as his references to oppression and squeezing the people of Bengal make clear. He made his peace with what was taking place, by trusting his fellow Company servants to act well, and by convincing himself that useful reforms had been made since the bad old days of the 1760s. He then felt free to participate and make money in the Company-shaped system. At some moments too, he saw what was going on in Bengal in a global context of British expansion and colonization.

[17] Jennifer Pitts, *A Turn to Empire. The Rise of Imperial Liberalism in Britain and France* (Princeton University Press, 2005), pp. 1, 3, 14.

Such a linkage surged into his mind in 1776 when news of the rebellion in the American colonies reached Calcutta. Bogle's initial reaction was to congratulate his brother on not having any personal commercial stake in the mainland colonies that would suffer in the fighting. Bogle's thoughts then turned in a revealing direction. "I imagine you in the western world are equally uneasy about us Indians, where to be sure, we have carried things to a great Height, but it is all with the Pen; we are not so bloody minded as your Americans."[18]

Bogle knew of the British settlements in North America and the slave systems in the West Indies from, if nothing else, his own family's history of business dealings in the Atlantic economy. Beyond that, in Bogle's library in Calcutta there were the three volumes of William Robertson's *History of the Reign of Charles V* (1769) with its comments on the Spanish empire in Central and South America that were subsequently expanded in his *History of America* (1777). Perhaps Bogle had both his family's practical experience and book knowledge in mind when he made the contrast between imperialism in India and America. Whether or not Bogle had read Robertson, here he is, in the middle of a family letter, falteringly thinking on the same grand scale as the renowned historian. Bogle contrasted the European territorial takeover and population destruction in the Americas with the administrative and commercial takeover in Bengal. He thought the Bengal case less bloody, presumably because there had not been the same kind of wars involving complete territorial dispossession and reduction of populations. But he placed Bengal in the same frame of reference as the ongoing European subjugation of the Americas. "We have carried things to a great Height" was the elliptical phrasing chosen but the meaning was clear – that the Company takeover in Bengal was but one aspect of a world-wide expansion of British power.

The Bogle family had energetically engaged with empire for three generations. The estate at Daldowie had been purchased by money made in the Chesapeake tobacco trade, the Bogle and Scott company in London had been in the business of colonial trade in the 1760s, and when Bogle was sending remittances home from Bengal in the 1770s his elder brother was running his sugar plantation on Grenada. The Bogles lived by the empire. It is no wonder that Bogle's father became agitated when the rebellion in the mainland colonies in America threatened to break up a significant part of this global commercial nexus and wrote the letter trembling with indignation about the revolting colonies who had paid

[18] George Bogle to Robert Bogle, Calcutta, January 20, 1776, Bogle Papers, Folder George Bogle 1776 [marked 48], Mitchell Library.

no heed to all that the mother country had done to nurture and protect them.

For his part, Bogle did not think twice about the legitimacy of Robin's slave-holding enterprise in the West Indies. In an affectionate letter to his sister Bess, he imagined the brothers at their widely separated locations, each working for the good of the family, and each tenderly thinking of their sisters back in Scotland.

We are scattered over the Face of the earth, and are united only by Hope and tender Remembrance . . . While you are passing chearful evenings at Daldowie; while Robin with his Negroes (and happy are they that are under him) is planting his Sugar Canes, and while I am climbing these rugged Mountains, there is a secret Virtue like a Magnet which attracts us together and chears or solaces us in every situation.[19]

This loving letter reveals the appealing closeness of the Bogle family as they maintained links by letter writing across great geographical distances. But this same letter softens and sentimentalizes the empire with its picture of Robin's happy slaves. In such ways did Bogle complacently connive at the empire and its impact on people at the sharp end of British policies.

Another sign that Bogle was shaped by empire was the language he used when describing Bengalis. The contrast between Bogle's comments on Bhutanese and Tibetans and what he said – and did not say – about Bengalis began as soon as he set out for Tibet. The region of Bengal through which Bogle traveled to reach the Bhutanese passes had suffered almost four years of famine, during which almost one third of the population died. Yet, as Lamb notes, "of all of this . . . Bogle makes no mention at all."[20] Bogle's attitude towards the ravages of famine had hardened since 1770, when he had expressed shock at what he saw on his arrival in Calcutta.

As we have seen, Bogle was inquisitive and open-minded in his responses to the people and scenes he encountered in Bhutan and Tibet. On Indians he had by this time made up his mind. We noticed this when he described the ingratiating (in Bogle's eyes) behavior of Chait Singh's representative at Tashilhunpo – Bogle reported contemptuously that the *vakil*'s speech was "concluded with the rote of Hindustanis, that I was his master, a great man etc." There are other such examples of stereotyping generalizations about Indian people. He even offers an early example of what became in the 1800s the conventional British representation of the

[19] Teltscher, *The High Road to China*, p. 60.
[20] Lamb, *Bhutan and Tibet*, pp. 59, 60 n. 2.

weak Bengali. The flat country of Bengal, cut through with creeks and rivers, combined with the hot weather, meant that "the natives of Bengal, weak and thin-skinned, are ill suited to bear fatigue or cold."[21] While he spoke respectfully of the lamas he met in Bhutan and Tibet, Bogle had no patience with the Hindu holy men he encountered on his travels.

The Gentoo [Hindu] fakirs, as far as I can judge, are in general a very worthless set of people, devoid of principle, and being separated by their profession from all those ties of kindred and family which serve to bind the rest of mankind, they have no object but their own interest, and, covered with the cloak of religion, are regardless of their caste, of their character, and of everything else which is held sacred among the Hindus.[22]

Bogle was not describing priests who tended Hindu temples but the itinerant *sanyassis* who often caused disturbances in the northern Bengal countryside in the aftermath of the famine and the general disruption caused by the Company's presence. Bogle chose language which made a distinction between these wandering bands of *sanyassis* and ordinary Hindu believers, and he was not being as prejudiced as this remark appears to make him. A genuine *sanyassi* is a man who has reached the stage of life when he frees himself from family and other material attachments, to wander the land seeking final liberation for his soul. But in the late 1700s as political and economic instability took hold in parts of north India, the *sanyassi* phenomenon became troublesome. Migrant bands of *sanyassis* often intimidated and robbed villagers and traders.[23] An older generation of Indian scholars, writing in the colonial period and using colonial constructions, have used phrases such as "*sanyassi* raiders" to describe the threatening nature of many of these wandering communities.[24] The *sanyassi* phenomenon was more complex than the British allowed since activities like trade and money-exchange were often involved, as well as resistance to local and imperial authorities, but even if the movement is better understood it remains true that large bands of wandering ascetics did cause disturbances in settled communities at times. So Bogle and his Tibetan friends had some grounds for their fearful views. And we noted earlier that Bogle paid homage to "the humane maxims of the Hindus." Even with this critique in front of us, it is therefore worth observing that Bogle did not condemn Hinduism as a general

---

[21] Bogle's Journal, From Cooch Behar to Tashichodzong, May–August 1774, Lamb, *Bhutan and Tibet*, p. 63.

[22] Bogle's Journal, At Dechenrubje and the Return to Tashilhunpo, November 1774–December 1775, Lamb, *Bhutan and Tibet*, p. 154.

[23] Marshall, *Bengal. The British Bridgehead*, p. 96.

[24] J. M. Ghosh, *Sanyassi and Fakir Raiders in Bengal* (Calcutta, 1930).

category. Still, the intensity of the outburst conveys the impatience of an outsider with some of the excessive manifestations of Hindu religiosity.

His impatience with Bengalis also came through when he and his servants were making their way across inhospitable terrain towards Guru (the site of the massacre during the 1904 invasion).

We arrived at Tuna, our next stage, about three o'clock. Some of my servants who walked were so tired that they were brought home on peasants' backs, as I had not been able to find horses for them all. I next day got cow-tailed bullocks, but the Hindus would not ride on them because if any accident should happen to the beast while they were on him, they would be obliged, they said, according to the tenets of the Shaster [Sastra or Shastra, Hindu sacred books; e.g. laws of Manu], to beg their bread during twelve years as an expiation for the crime. Memo: inconvenient carrying Hindu servants into foreign parts.[25]

These comments, revealing his frustration with what he viewed as Hindu stubbornness and a superstitious commitment to the literal interpretation of their holy texts, contrast with Bogle's depiction of Tibetans as adaptable and willing to be skeptical. Padma, for example, was opposed to hunting on religious grounds but agreed that it would be acceptable if Bogle hunted in areas out of sound and sight of settlements and holy sites. Bogle also noted that the Panchen Lama welcomed pilgrims from all over Central Asia, even Muslim ones, thus demonstrating that he "was free from those narrow prejudices which, next to ambition and avarice, have opened the most copious source of human misery."[26] It is unfair to compare the exhausted Bengali servants (who walked while Bogle rode across the barren Tibetan highlands in the first cold of winter) with a highly trained theologian like the Panchen Lama. But when put alongside Bogle's other observations, this one too shows him in more judgmental mode with respect to Bengalis than he was with Tibetans.

What accounts for this difference in Bogle's attitude towards Indians and Tibetans? It may have had something to do with Bogle's Scottishness. His mercantile, lowland family had no fellow-feeling for the feudal, Highland clans when the clans were disturbing the stability of the kingdom, but after their defeat at Culloden in 1746 attitudes began to change.

[25] Bogle's Journal, Tashichodzong to Dechenrubje, October–November 1774, Lamb, *Bhutan and Tibet*, p. 141.
[26] Bogle's Journal, At Dechenrubje and the Return to Tashilhunpo, November 1774–December 1775, Lamb, *Bhutan and Tibet*, p. 154.

The cruel harrying of the clans by "Butcher" Cumberland, and government legislation to suppress clan culture, created widespread sympathy. As the clans ceased to be a military threat, a nostalgia for a disappearing way of life began to take hold. The romanticizing of the Highland clans was already shaping public views in the 1760s with such popular publications as James Macpherson's *Ossian* (1765), two epic poems imagining a legendary age of Gaelic heroes, accompanied by a learned commentary by Hugh Blair, professor of rhetoric and belles-lettres at the University of Edinburgh. Bogle died before the full force of this sentimentalizing of the Scottish Highlands had taken hold in British culture, propelled by the pro-Jacobite poems of Robert Burns in the late 1780s and early 1790s, and culminating in the lyrical evocation of a dying clan culture in the historical novels of Walter Scott early in the 1800s, but the cultural transformation was underway in the 1760s and 1770s during his time in Edinburgh and London. While he was in Bhutan, he drew a humorous but affectionate parallel between Bhutanese and Scottish Highlanders. In a letter to Anderson, he suggested playfully that the letters he had received from Bhutanese correspondents might well contain "all that Loftiness and Sublimity of Style used by Ossian, or any other hilly Writer."[27] Bogle was clearly more sympathetic with the Bhutanese and Tibetan "highlanders" than he was with the plains-dwelling Bengalis. When he was posted to Rangpur in 1779, he wrote to his sister Anne about his pleasure in being near mountain country again – "although not in the Bootan hills, I am within sight of them."[28]

But there was a more basic force at work than possible sentimentality towards highland peoples. The difference can also be understood in terms of power and empire. Stuart Schwartz has noted that "many of the contacts between Europeans and other peoples were forged in a context of unequal power and subordination, but not all of them."[29] Here we have a perfect illustration of that observation. Bogle's views on Tibet were formed in a situation in which the British had very little power, as his summary dismissal by the Lhasa officials demonstrated. But the Company by this time did have power in Bengal, and was beginning to extend its sway up the Ganges valley. Where power was absent, Europeans could use cultural observation "as a means of self-knowledge" but

---

[27] George Bogle to David Anderson, June 20, 1774, David Anderson Papers, Add. 45421, f. 30, BL.

[28] George Bogle to Anne Bogle, Rungpoor, November 22, 1779, Bogle Papers, Folder George Bogle 1779 [marked 30], Mitchell Library.

[29] Stuart Schwartz, ed., *Implicit Understandings. Observing, Reporting and Reflecting on Encounters between Europeans and Other Peoples in the Early Modern Era* (Cambridge University Press, 1994), p. 6.

where power was present cultural observation could become "an element in imperial strategy."[30]

The growth of British power in India meant that Indians had to respond. If they chose not to contest the British advance across India they had to accommodate themselves to the authority of the Company if they wanted to trade with it, or work for it, or avoid its impositions. It was an awareness of the Company's powerful position that explains why Chait Singh's *vakil* hastened to show deference and respect to Bogle when they encountered each other at Tashilhunpo. Whenever new Writers arrived in Calcutta they were besieged by suppliant Bengalis anxious to be their translators or commercial agents or general factotums.[31] The Company men could do no business without the help of such intermediaries but when they spoke of these essential men it was usually in language that kept them in their subordinate places. For example, Bogle explained to Anderson in April 1772 that he could not get hold of some bonds because his servants were not available. "I shall look out for a Company Bond for you as you mention," Bogle explained to Anderson. "We have the Gentoo festivals at present on our Hands, and none of my Black Geniuses are about."[32]

Bogle and Anderson depended on their Indian *banians* to conduct their business. Indian men with such expertise had to plead for employment. The balance of power in the colonial setting led to this type of relationship. In the daily bilateral exchanges that took place under these conditions, the Company servants interpreted the ingratiating behaviors as an inherent characteristic of Indian people, exemplified by Bogle's comment that Chait Singh's representative behaved with "the rote of Hindustanis." Bogle judged such outwardly servile demeanor to be the product of Indian culture rather than the expedient response to a newly threatening colonial intrusion. The way in which Bogle used the term "Gentoo" for Hindus is also revealing. The word was derived from the Portuguese "gentio" (gentile) meaning "heathen" or "infidel." Bogle did not think twice about such a word because it had become common usage amongst Europeans in India. His language and outlook were shaped by the European imperial presence in India.

Tibet was untouched by British power and Bogle thought it would remain untouched – if for no other reason than its geographical inaccessibility. He also thought Bhutan would be hard to take over. In both

[30] *Ibid.*, p. 7.   [31] Marshall, *Bengal. The British Bridgehead*, pp. 100, 101.
[32] George Bogle to David Anderson, Calcutta, April 11, 1772, David Anderson Papers, Add. 45421, f. 14, BL.

those cases he saw little likelihood of the British exercising power. When he did see such possibilities, as in Assam, he did not hesitate to recommend a military advance. In Bengal the Company was already exercising power. When the Company was in a position of power over local populations, Bogle's attitude was less sympathetic than when power was absent.

Bogle's complicity in empire can be linked to his Enlightenment ways of thinking. The very act of categorizing other peoples implied a European attribute of superior objectivity which entitled advanced Europeans to make comparisons between other cultures. The fact that Bogle relied so much on geographical and environmental circumstances to make his cultural comparisons, an approach widely adopted by Enlightenment-era philosophers, suggests that European thinkers could not avoid this intellectual pitfall. The very act of classification was based on an assumption of superior observer status. European travelers like Bogle assumed that they had the right to do this, and that they had a superior capability to be able to undertake such intellectual exercises. These ways of thinking also tended to remove any agency from the cultures being categorized. It was as though other cultures were only accorded authenticity through the act of European observation. Presumably, all human societies were shaped by environments, but European societies had somehow transcended their geographical conditions whereas Tibetans, Bhutanese, and Bengalis were still molded by geography. To some extent, this way of thinking was the outcome of the Enlightenment's stadial theory of history. Hunting and gathering humans were utterly dependent on the natural resources available to them in the environments in which they lived; the commercial society of 1700s Britain, while still influenced by Britain's island location close to the continent and open to the Atlantic, was no longer subject to limitations imposed by geography. Britain had advanced beyond that stage. Bogle's entire approach assumed that the societies he was encountering, even though they had passed through the early stages of human development, had not yet escaped their geography in the ways that Europeans had done.

This allegation of assumed superiority, evident in the categorizing of others, is often made by critics of Enlightenment ways of thinking. But in Bogle's case there is some evidence that raises doubts about whether things are as cut and dried as this familiar allegation assumes. Rather than seeing the Bhutanese and Tibetans as inert specimens for his European curiosity, Bogle realized that he was a subject for *their* curiosity. As Bogle put it, they viewed him as "a Specimen of my Countrymen" and thought they could make generalizations about England based on their observation of his behavior.[33]

Bogle can be made to look narrow and culture-bound, but perhaps all humans are subject to such limitations when faced with new situations. For example, the Panchen Lama was immensely well informed about Tibet, China, Central Asia, and India, and he even knew something of Russia, yet when querying Bogle about England, a place utterly strange to him, he too showed he could think in crude categories. When asking whether England was near Russia, what religion was practiced, and so on, the Panchen Lama also "enquired if it were near the country of the cannibals" – thus hinting at some of his credulous notions of far-off places.[34] The Panchen Lama also seemed to share some of Bogle's negative views on Indians. After Bogle had reported a conversation that he had held with Chauduri, one of the Indian representatives at Tashilhunpo, the Panchen Lama "made no observation, except that the Hindus were fond of appearing of consequence, and scrupled not to tell falsehoods."[35] In a similar vein, Bogle claimed that the Hindu "fakirs" of whom he had such a low opinion were also "universally disliked by the Tibetans."[36]

The Panchen Lama also used derogatory language about the Bhutanese in his first letter to Hastings which began the British engagement with Tibet. He wrote of "the Deb Rajah's own criminal conduct in committing ravages and other outrages on your frontiers . . . as he is of a rude and ignorant race (past times are not destitute of instances of like misconduct) which his own avarice tempted him to commit."[37] The Panchen Lama no doubt chose such condemnatory phrases to seem friendly to Hastings, "the lord of Bengal," even though he was still giving some support to the Deb Rajah at this time. As we saw in Bogle's anecdote about the legal debate at Phari, Tibetan officials were reluctant to return supporters of the Deb Rajah for punishment in Bhutan.[38] But that such a description of the Bhutanese as "a rude and ignorant race" could appear in this letter shows a context in which other people can

[33] Bogle's Remarks on His Mission to Bhutan and Tibet [Calcutta 1774, made when submitting his accounts to the Council], Warren Hastings Papers, Add. 29233, f. 388, BL.

[34] Bogle's Memorandum on Negotiations with the Tashi Lama, Lamb, *Bhutan and Tibet*, p. 211.

[35] Bogle's Journal, Negotiations with the Tashi Lama at Tashilhunpo, December 1774– April 1775, Lamb, *Bhutan and Tibet*, p. 268.

[36] Bogle's Journal, At Dechenrubje and the Return to Tashilhunpo, November 1774– December 1775, Lamb, *Bhutan and Tibet*, p. 154.

[37] Letter from the Tashi Lama to Warren Hastings (received in Calcutta March 29, 1774), Lamb, *Bhutan and Tibet*, p. 38.

[38] Lamb, *Bhutan and Tibet*, p. 123 n. 13.

be categorized to suit the intended audience. Or perhaps the Panchen Lama actually did think that the Bhutanese in general were a rough lot, not quite up to more civilized Tibetan standards of behavior.

In spite of their shared religious culture Tibet and Bhutan had often been at odds. One of the forts along their border, Drugyel Dzong, means "the fortress of the Drukpa Victory" and it was built "to commemorate one or several Bhutanese victories over the Tibetans" in the late seventeenth and early eighteenth centuries.[39] There had been frequent invasions of Bhutan from Tibet.[40] So Tibetans and Bhutanese did indeed have reasons at times to hold antagonistic views of each other. These Tibetan comments on Bhutan in British sources are but snippets of evidence, but even if they are only an approximation of what the Panchen Lama intended to convey, they suggest we should not be too quick to condemn all of Bogle's critical comments about Indians as symptomatic of inimitable colonialist mentalities on the part of Europeans.

The general issue in play here is how humans view themselves in relationship to others. In William Robertson's last published work, *An Historical Disquisition concerning the Knowledge which the Ancients had of India* (1791), he reflected on the general human tendency to think their own ways best:

Men in every stage of their career are so satisfied with the progress made by the community of which they are members, that it becomes to them a standard of perfection, and they are apt to regard people, whose condition is not similar, with contempt, and even aversion.[41]

Bogle had been dead ten years when Robertson made that observation, but it was an insight that flowed naturally from the comparative thinking so typical of this era. Perhaps there is a common propensity among humans, especially during first encounters, or when justifying a policy, to make simple or partial or dismissive judgments, based on inadequate knowledge, of other cultures. In the final analysis, there is really no way for the Enlightenment to escape the criticism that it put Europeans first among humans because the very act of reporting on others, even when done with good intentions, and in the genuine pursuit of new knowledge, can always be presented by critics as proof of claims to superior rationality. In this case, we can say cautiously that the Panchen

---

[39] Michael Aris, *The Raven Crown. The Origins of Buddhist Monarchy in Bhutan* (London: Serindia Publications, 1994), p. 31.

[40] Nirmala Das, *The Dragon Country. The General History of Bhutan* (Bombay: Orient Longman, 1974), p. 19.

[41] Quoted in Karen O'Brien, *Narratives of Enlightenment. Cosmopolitan History from Voltaire to Gibbon* (Cambridge University Press, 1997), p. 166.

Lama made occasionally sharp cultural comparisons too, and that Bogle thought some of his critical views of some features of Hindu culture were shared by some Tibetans.

A more explicit example of Enlightenment thinking shaping Bogle's imperial mind-set is related to commerce. In his second meeting with the Panchen Lama after he arrived at Dechenrubje, Bogle attempted, as we have seen, to provide an overview of the Company's role in India. After describing how the Company first came into Bengal, Bogle added: "In this manner [i.e. with the approval of Emperor and Nawab], they long continued in Bengal, bringing much wealth into the country, and showering down upon it the blessings of commerce."[42]

It is the phrase "showering down upon it the blessings of commerce" that is telling. The use of such imagery implied that there had been no commerce in India before the Company introduced it. But Bogle surely knew that was not the case. Apart from any historical knowledge he may have acquired in his reading, he had the example of his friend and guide Purangir Gosain, who was an experienced and skillful merchant in the Tibetan and north Indian trade. He also knew that the Bhutanese conducted trade. When Bogle had his first audience in the throne room of Tashichodzong palace, he noticed an English engraving hanging on one of the pillars. The subject was Lady Waldegrave who, as the Dowager Countess Waldegrave, had married, in 1766, the Duke of Gloucester, brother of George III. There were many contemporary engravings of her portrait, and one of these had found its way from the Calcutta bazaars to Tashichodzong. Bhutanese traders could be innovative and inventive apparently.[43]

Bogle and other Company officials also wrote to each other about the breakdown of the pre-existing commercial links between north India and Tibet because of the Gurkha conquest of Nepal. Even without any historical knowledge of commerce elsewhere in the Mughal dominions, or of the Indian ocean trading networks, Bogle and the other Company servants were well aware of the commercial, exchange, and banking systems throughout north India and neighboring states. Indeed, in a "Memorandum on the Money and Merchandise of Tibet" appended to his general report, Bogle made an elaborate analysis of the complex patterns of currency exchange that fueled the trans-Himalayan trade.[44] Bogle knew that Indian, Tibetan, and Bhutanese commerce existed before the British

---

[42] Bogle's Memorandum on Negotiations with the Tashi Lama, Lamb, *Bhutan and Tibet*, p. 212.

[43] Bogle's Journal, Tashichodzong, Lamb, *Bhutan and Tibet*, p. 69.

[44] Bogle's Memorandum on the Money and Merchandise of Tibet appended to his General Report, Lamb, *Bhutan and Tibet*, pp. 362–364.

intrusion, and continued after their arrival in India. Thus when Bogle spoke of "the blessings of commerce" he had something more in mind. It was not all commerce that was being promoted, but commerce that benefited England.

Such a self-serving way of looking at European trade and its extension round the world can be linked quite tightly with Enlightenment thought. William Robertson and David Hume, for example, emphasized "the role of commerce in ushering in more civilised forms of social and international relations." Robertson argued that

Commerce tends to wear off those prejudices which maintain distinctions and animosity between nations. It softens and polishes the manners of men. It unites them, by one of the strongest of all ties, the desire of supplying mutual wants.[45]

As he set out his explanations for the Spanish conquests in America in his *History of Charles V*, Robertson explained why Europe had developed advantages. The European countries, made vigorous by the competitive diversity fostered by the Reformation, and by the forging of new states, had created a unique context for the flowering of human genius. The variety of states and cultural currents within Europe had led to "that wide diversity of character and of genius which . . . hath exalted the Europeans above the inhabitants of the other quarter of the globe." Commerce was one of the key elements in this European strength:

All the civilized nations of Europe may be considered as forming one exclusive community. The intercourse among them is great, and every improvement in science, in arts, in commerce, in government introduced into any one of them is soon known in the others, and in time is adopted and imitated. Hence arises . . . the general resemblance among all the people of Europe, and their great superiority over the rest of mankind.[46]

It was the mis-match between the stages of development reached in Europe and America which had led to the Spanish conquests on that continent. Robertson recognized the terrible consequences for the indigenous peoples in this encounter. The Spanish were "enlightened and ambitious [and had] formed already vast ideas with respect to the advantages which they might derive from those regions" while the local Americans, "simple and undiscerning, had no foresight of the calamities and desolation which were now approaching their country."[47]

The tragic outcome was part of the providential course of history. As Karen O'Brien summarizes Robertson's case, "negative evaluations of the American Natives are reinforced by a civic moralist preference

---

[45] Quoted in O'Brien, *Narratives of Enlightenment*, p. 138.
[46] *Ibid.*, p. 150.   [47] *Ibid.*, p. 156.

for social 'vigour', by the notion of the immaturity or degeneracy of America, and by the Enlightenment historical idea of the superiority of Europe."[48] In the end Robertson concluded that once the conquest had been completed the Americas were now open to the introduction of modern commercial society. The conquest had been brutal but the outcome enabled the Americas to leapfrog through several stages of history, and become connected to the European vanguard. In Robertson's Enlightenment narrative, imperialism could be justified because it introduced the most advanced stage of human progress into other parts of the world.

Robertson proceeded to offer further mitigation of European imperialism by arguing that their empires were relatively benign and constructive as they pushed the stages of history onwards. The European territorial empires grew out of the "encounter between peoples at higher and lower levels of social evolution, but only modern Europeans are equipped to temper the rigour of this encounter with flexible economic, political and cultural responses to other civilizations."[49] Because Bogle was not working as a scholar we do not know what the precise sources for his thinking were, but when he made his "blessings of commerce" pitch to the Panchen Lama he seemed to be representing this Enlightenment case for the improving and civilizing effects of European commerce.

It was problematic, to be sure, to apply this American-derived theory of European imperialism to India. In the conventional wisdom of European thinkers at the time, the polities of the indigenous peoples of America represented a state of "barbarism." If that was the premise, then it was an easier intellectual task for European writers to make the case that bringing such a region of the world up to a more advanced state of historical development was a good thing. In the case of India, however, European observers, even those at a quite modest level of knowledge, knew that there had been an ancient civilization.

When David Anderson went to India, an old family friend in Edinburgh had reminded him of the depth and richness of the cultures he would encounter there. Alexander Mackenzie, responding to Anderson's first reports on his reading in Indian texts after his arrival in Bengal, replied that

the Stupendous Works you mention... may be the remains of Indian skill in Mathematics and Architecture... Be that as it may, as nature moves in a Circle, and all things are subject to Change and Revolution, what has been may be again. Arts therefore and Sciences may yet flourish in India while you fill some important station in Bengal.[50]

---

[48] *Ibid.*, p. 160.   [49] *Ibid.*, p. 236.
[50] Alexander Mackenzie to David Anderson, Edinburgh, June 5, 1773, David Anderson Papers, Add. 45430, f. 282, BL.

Anderson, Bogle, and others understood, at an intellectual level, that they were engaging with a region of the world that had civilizational claims which had out-rivaled those of Europe in the past, and retained the capability of doing so again. But in their minds, modern European-style commerce now represented the highest stage of human civilization, and so taking over in India could be justified if it was done in that cause.

This view of commerce as a civilizing influence was especially associated with Scottish thinkers in the eighteenth century.[51] Both Anderson and Bogle were living examples of this particular outlook on the nature of humans and of the course of history. Indeed, the outlook was directly derived from the four-stages view of history. Proponents of the virtue and commerce argument liked to see the sequence as "commerce, leisure, cultivation" but they had to contend with critics who viewed commerce as leading to luxury, vice, and corruption.[52] As Larry Dickey of Columbia University neatly sums up the positive case, this view of history was nothing less than an attempt "on the part of apologists of commerce to persuade their opponents and/or the uncommitted that commercial activity, if allowed to run its natural course, would moderate, socialize and humanize the behavior of men. In a word, their view was that commerce would 'moralize' men as it civilized them."[53] Thus, the Enlightenment taxonomy of historical stages allowed Bogle to approve fully the Company project in India on the grounds that the invigorating commercial activity introduced by the Company would bring Indians, Assamese, Bhutanese, and Tibetans towards the most advanced stage of human association and civic development. Bogle was not being ironic when he told the Panchen Lama that the East India Company was "showering the blessings of commerce" on India. He believed that to be a true characterization of Britain's role in India because he was following, in rough terms, some of the historical formulations proposed by Enlightenment writers.

But Bogle, in his workaday position in the East India Company, and some of the contemporary European philosophers ruminating in their libraries, had a complete blind-spot on this matter of commerce. While Bogle told the Panchen Lama about the blessings of commerce, and Hume and Robertson wrote of the progressive role of commerce in world history, the East India Company was actually bringing a retrograde version of commerce to India. As Peter Marshall has pointed out, the business practices used by the Company in India were thoroughly

---

[51] J. G. A. Pocock, *Virtue, Commerce and History* (Cambridge University Press, 1985). In this collection of essays Pocock set out the issues with characteristic thoroughness.

[52] *Ibid.*, pp. 49, 111, 119, 195–196.

[53] Larry Dickey, "The Pocockian Moment" [review of Pocock's *Virtue, Commerce and History*], *Journal of British Studies* 26 (January 1987), p. 102.

old-fashioned. The Company "preferred to control labour, fix prices and establish monopolies, rather than trust to its superior efficiency."[54] The Enlightenment did produce new theories of commerce, summed up most notably in Adam Smith's *Wealth of Nations* (1776), but the new concept of free trade was not brought by the English to India in the eighteenth century. In *The Wealth of Nations* itself, Smith had directly criticized "the mercantile company which oppresses and domineers in the East Indies."[55] The Company was not interested in new economic theories; it wanted to make profits by using "the well-tried practices from the past."[56]

The Company held a monopoly on trade between India and Britain. Within India it awarded or continued monopolies for the production and sale of commodities such as salt and opium. It also used its position to allow its merchants to override local trade regulations of the nawabs. One of the tasks Bogle was assigned as Collector at Rangpur was to enforce a new monopoly on the trade between Assam and Bengal awarded to a British trader by the Council in Calcutta. When the Council had first developed policies with respect to the Assam trade back in 1765, it had objected to Robert Clive's scheme for allotting a contract to a group of Europeans on the grounds that it was "an intrusion upon the natural rights of the natives of the country who now more particularly claim our protection." This decision seemed to reflect some openness to the new economic thinking, and to an Enlightenment morality which accorded natural rights to indigenous peoples. But in 1780, the Council appointed David Killican as Resident at Goalpara to regulate trade and receive the associated revenues. Killican was also granted the exclusive privilege of trading to Assam.[57] "The natural rights of the natives" gave way to old-fashioned monopolies when it suited the interests of the Company. In such ways the "blessings of commerce" were manipulated to the advantage of the British. Enlightenment-era thinking about commerce was used disingenuously by the East India Company to legitimize economic exploitation in India. The case that Bogle made in his conversation with the Panchen Lama was a small but typical example of this mind-set.

But the Enlightenment had other sides to it, even on the matter of commerce. Bogle, as we have seen, made some outright criticisms of the Company's revenue-raising practices in Bengal. He was not alone among his contemporaries in looking at the evidence on the ground and

54 Marshall, *Bengal. The British Bridgehead*, p. 115.
55 Adam Smith, *The Wealth of Nations* (London: Pickering, 1995 [1776]), vol. I, p. 115.
56 Marshall, *Bengal. The British Bridgehead*, p. 115.
57 S. K. Bhuyan, *Anglo-Assamese Relations 1771–1826* (Gauhati, Assam, 1949), pp. 67, 123.

making allegations against the Company. Even his money-making friend Anderson noticed in the late 1770s that the Company seemed to be impoverishing Bengal. In response to a request to raise more revenue from his district, Anderson pointed out that sustained high levels of taxation without reference to actual economic conditions was one cause "for the Decline of the Province." From his post in Patna, Anderson wrote to Bogle: "You will ask me what is the reason that this District which once paid about 60 Lakhs is now reduced to a little more than 39. I will answer your Question by asking you another – Is it possible that the Revenue of a Country which annually loses from 15 to 20 Lakhs of its Treasure could continue long at an overstrained Rate?"[58] Anderson thought that the local economy was suffering because too much specie was being taken out of circulation due to the fiscal demands of the Company.

This was exactly the same charge leveled against the Company in the famous Parliamentary Report written by Edmund Burke in 1783. "In all other Countries," Burke thundered,

the Revenue, following the natural Course and Order of Things, arises out of their Commerce. Here [in Bengal], by a mischievous Inversion of that Order, the whole Foreign Maritime Trade, whether English, French, Dutch, or Danish, arises from the Revenues; and these are carried out of the Country, without producing any Thing to compensate so heavy a Loss.[59]

Burke, Anderson, and Bogle, in their different ways, were all expressing doubts about the Company record in Bengal based on contemporary enlightened and rational thinking about how economies functioned.

Moreover, Bogle did not hesitate to recognize Indian capabilities in trade. When it became clear that British merchants would not be allowed to conduct trade through Bhutan, Bogle advised the Company to allow Bengali and other Indian merchants to take the lead in opening these trade arteries on behalf of the Company. In a letter to Hastings he argued that "the channel through which trade is carried on, although of consequence to individuals, is, I humbly apprehend, of very little to the country. If any Englishmen choose to embark in this traffic, I do not see why it may not be conducted by Asiatic agents as well as European ones."[60] In making this proposal Bogle showed that he believed local merchants could be as purposeful and as entrepreneurial as British ones.

---

[58] David Anderson to George Bogle, Patna, September 23, 1778, David Anderson Papers, Add. 45421, f. 72, BL.

[59] Ninth Report from the Select Committee, Appointed to take into Consideration the State of the Administration of Justice in the Provinces of Bengal, Bihar, and Orissa, June 25, 1783, in P. J. Marshall, ed., *The Writings and Speeches of Edmund Burke*, vol. V *India: Madras and Bengal 1774–1785* (Oxford University Press, 1981), p. 227.

[60] Bogle to Hastings, Paro, April 27, 1775, Lamb, *Bhutan and Tibet*, p. 207.

Self-criticism, and some recognition of Indian enterprise, co-existed with fortune-hunting by means of Company-controlled commerce.

Whatever reservations there are about the depth of Bogle's sympathy for other peoples, or the extent to which self-interest was always at work, his words and actions were decidedly more respectful of cultures he encountered than the words and actions of Younghusband in 1903–1904. The harshness of Younghusband appears nowhere in Bogle. Some of Younghusband's comments were introduced at the end of the last chapter. It is easy to come up with more from such a prolific source. In their mutual efforts at justification for what they were doing in Tibet, which Younghusband and Curzon both believed was "for the good of the world," they often returned to the condescending theme of liberation. "Look at the state they are in at present," Younghusband expostulated to Curzon in January 1904, "they are nothing but slaves in the power of selfish and ignorant monks who hold the supreme authority in Lhasa."[61] In Bogle's case, while the Enlightenment may have contributed to his imperial posture, the Enlightenment also acted as a brake on his European assumptions of superiority. In Younghusband's case there seemed to be no brakes at all.

With his luxuriant moustache flourishing under his topee, his religious fervor, and his penchant for shaping up "Asiatics," Younghusband personified many of the imperial values in late-Victorian and Edwardian England. He began his formal education in 1876 when he went to Clifton College, a public school near Bristol which was one of many boarding schools of that period founded to train boys for public service in the empire. In the tradition of Dr. Arnold of Rugby, who had led the reform of such schools in the early nineteenth century, the first headmaster of Clifton spoke of the school being "a nursery or seed-plot for high-minded men, devoted to the highest service of the country, a new Christian chivalry of patriotic service." As Patrick French observed in his evocative biography of Younghusband,

Clifton's ambition was to produce the sort of men who would run the British Empire; it was extraordinarily effective at this task. Over the years thousands of Old Cliftonians sallied forth – soldiers, sailors, political officers, box wallahs and colonial servants – to every country that was coloured red on the map. They were generally not the visionaries or the viceroys, but middle class stalwarts who formed the backbone of imperial administration.[62]

[61] Younghusband to Curzon, Camp Chumbi, January 1, 1904, Younghusband Collection, F197/80, BL.
[62] French, *Younghusband*, pp. 8, 9.

One of Younghusband's contemporaries at Clifton was Henry New-bolt, described by French as "the poet laureate of High Imperialism." Newbolt's best-known poem *Vitai Lampada* captures the philosophy of Clifton and the imperial values it inculcated in its pupils. The poem opens with the captain of the school cricket team urging his players on by appealing to their sense of honor. The captain reappears in the next verse "in the thick of battle in some far-flung outpost of the Empire":

> The sand of the desert is sodden red,–
> Red with the wreck of the square that broke;–
> The Gatling's jammed and the colonel dead
> And the regiment blind with dust and smoke.
> The river of death has brimmed his banks
> And England's far, and Honour a name,
> But the voice of a schoolboy rallies the ranks,
> "Play up! Play up! and play the game!"

Younghusband and Newbolt remained friends throughout their lives. During the invasion of Tibet, the poet wrote "an Epistle honouring their schooldays together and sent it out to Lhasa:

> The victories of our youth we count for gain
> Only because they steeled our hearts for pain,
> And hold no longer even Clifton great
> Save as she schooled our wills to serve the State.
> Nay, England's self, whose thousand-year-old name
> Burns in our blood like ever-smouldering flame."

As French notes, Younghusband's Tibet mission "was itself only an extension of that ultimate manifestation of imperial game playing, the Great Game."[63]

Throughout his travels in Central Asia and his government service in India, Younghusband always posed as the imperial Englishman. We have already mentioned his mission to reprimand the Mir of Hunza for raiding trading caravans from Kashmir. When Younghusband approached the narrow northern entrance to the valley, he was confronted by a group of armed men. Younghusband was not to be intimidated. Backed up by his own small detachment of Gurkhas, he declared that "the Queen of England was naturally very angry at her subjects being raided, and had sent me to see their chief." His bravado won the day and he was allowed to proceed for his meeting with the Mir. When he described this incident later in his book *Wonders of the Himalaya* (1924), he wrote that his success "was mainly due to the fact that I was an Englishman [and] that I stood

---

[63] *Ibid.*, p. 10.

for the British Empire."[64] His writings are replete with this attitude that the British empire should teach lessons to natives. In a private note he declared his life's purpose was "in a quiet way to guide the policy of the nation in its rule of subject races."[65]

Shortly after Curzon became Viceroy, Younghusband extolled the work of John Beattie Crozier in a letter to the new ruler of India. Younghusband was "in constant correspondence" with Crozier and deeply admired his *Civilization and Progress* (1898). He animatedly informed Curzon that

[Crozier] knocks down the theory of the equality of man and shows that all men are not equal and [are] even becoming more and more unequal. And he declares that it is not only our interest but our duty and privilege to take over the government of the inferior races and to administer, discipline and protect them . . . it is our special part in the World's history to rule and guide these Asiatics and Africans who cannot govern themselves.[66]

Younghusband's writings reflected the imperial culture of his time. His words and actions made it easy for the pro-empire newspapers in Britain to promote him as a paragon of chivalric imperial virtues committed to the task of improving a stagnant Asia. A profile in the *Daily Mail*, whose correspondent accompanied the Tibet mission, offered this description:

Colonel Younghusband is just the man who would gladly give years of his life to look once upon Lhasa. Beneath the mask of his genial manner, behind the reserve of his quiet voice, there lies an active, eager brain without a single cobweb or grain of dust upon it . . . There you have the elements that go to make the ideal administrator in the ancient and changeless East.[67]

Younghusband's private and public writings from this period, and the commentaries on him in the press, make him almost a perfect specimen of the Orientalist mentalities which Edward Said saw (and many others now see) as lying at the core of European colonial impositions throughout the Middle East and Asia.

How did we get from Bogle's hesitancies and relative openness to Younghusband's racial certainties and sense of righteousness? Religion seems to be a good starting point. In his private journal, written in 1894, Younghusband took stock of his life: "The way I am to go is towards God, to find out God – His meaning – what He wants – what He wishes us to do – to get nearer and nearer to His meaning."[68] Later in the same year he decided that "the object I will have before me is to 'seek God' to try and understand what the principles upon which He governs the universe are, and to practically conform to them."[69] Younghusband

---

[64] *Ibid.*, p. 72.   [65] *Ibid.*, p. 144.   [66] *Ibid.*, p. 155.   [67] *Ibid.*, p. 214.
[68] Younghusband, Private Journal 1894, Younghusband Collection, F197/257, BL.
[69] *Ibid.*, Chitral, October 1894.

was convinced that God was at his side. He had been brought up in an intensely evangelical family. His Indian Army father had a sense of mission about the British role in India which "was reinforced by his strong Evangelical Christianity."[70] At age four and a half Younghusband was sent to his father's two unmarried sisters who lived near Bath.

The Aunts were stringently religious; any hint of laxity in their young charge was beaten out of him with the aid of a leather strap. "They were of the sternest stuff," wrote Francis a year before his death, "dressed in poke bonnets and living in the greatest simplicity. Strict teetotallers waging a war against drunkenness, and teaching in the Sunday school."[71]

During his Tibet mission Younghusband's cutting observations about monkish rule in Tibet were accompanied by a certainty that Younghusband's own God was at his right arm.

God was not only at his side but on his side. As he prepared for his mission at Darjeeling in June 1903, he expected that there would be armed conflict once the negotiations proved fruitless. He explained his state of mind to his father: "I will sit tight for any length of time, but when my opportunity comes, as come it must, I shall strike hard and sharp: and, of course, it is then that I shall want the support of God."[72] He confided to his wife from Camp Chumbi on Christmas Day 1903 that "we both have this deep religious feeling at bottom," and assured her he was reading the "Christian Year" diary she had given him. In February he wrote from Tuna to tell Helen that he was enjoying the "big bible" she had sent – "I have nearly got through Genesis. It is most fascinating."[73] He was convinced that he was "absolutely in God's hands fulfilling some hidden purpose of His."[74] He told the Tongsa Penlop, the *de facto* ruler of Bhutan, that he "never feared" danger as he rode alone from Gyantse back to the Indian border because "I was engaged in a good cause and I know God will protect me."[75] When the convention was signed in the Potala Palace at the end of the mission, the table at which Younghusband sat (wearing his cocked hat) was covered "with a large Union Jack marked with the maxim: 'Heaven's Light Our Guide.'"[76]

---

[70] French, *Younghusband*, p. 15.   [71] *Ibid.*, p. 7.

[72] Younghusband to his Father, Darjeeling, June 16, 1903, Younghusband Collection, MSS. EUR. F197/145, BL.

[73] Younghusband to Helen Younghusband, Camp Chumbi, December 25, 1903, Younghusband Collection, MSS. EUR. F197/174; Younghusband to Helen Younghusband, Tuna, February 10, 1904, Younghusband Collection, MSS. EUR. F197/175, BL.

[74] Younghusband to Helen Younghusband, Tuna, January 24, 1904, Younghusband Collection, MSS. EUR. F197/175, BL.

[75] Younghusband to his Father, Chumbi, June 12, 1904, Younghusband Collection, MSS. EUR. F197/145, BL.

[76] French, *Younghusband*, p. 247.

Evangelical Christianity was a significant factor in causing this fundamental shift in British attitudes towards Indians and other Asian peoples
by the time Younghusband appeared on the imperial stage. We can trace
the beginning moments of this sea change by looking at a contemporary
of Bogle's and contrasting his views with those of Bogle. We have already
met Charles Grant in the discussion of Bogle's views on *sati* but that was
only one subject on which the two men differed. Grant was born near
Elgin in 1746, the same year as Bogle's birth. He too served an appren-
ticeship in London in the 1760s before going out to India in 1767 to
help in the private trading activities of Richard Becher, the Resident at
Murshidabad. A bout of fever forced him to return to Scotland, but in
1771 he went out to Bengal again as a Writer in the Company's service.
He ended up in 1787 as a member of the Board of Trade which supervised all of the Company's purchases in Bengal. From early in his career
in India he advocated bringing out Christian missionaries.

After his retirement in England he became a prominent member of
the Clapham Sect, the influential Anglican group that sought to bring
Christian values to bear on British policy-making, above all through
their leadership of the campaign to abolish the slave trade. During the
1813 debates in Parliament on the renewal of the Company's charter,
William Wilberforce quoted extensively from Grant's writings on the
need for Christian missionaries in India. By that time, Grant's tract on
the topic "was widely known in evangelical circles, and regarded as an
indispensable and decisive authority."[77] Grant, in short, is a fine example
of the new evangelical culture that was emerging in late eighteenth- and
early nineteenth-century Britain.

Grant's *Observations on the State of Society among the Asiatic Subjects of
Great Britain, particularly with respect to Morals, and the Means of Improving
It. Written Chiefly in the Year 1792* helps us to make a direct connection
between evangelicalism and the imperial attitudes that were to become
common in the nineteenth century. Grant's case is relevant for our purposes because it shows how someone formed in the same time period as
Bogle diverged sharply from Bogle chiefly because of his more intense
religiosity. Bogle was attracted by the sympathetic approach of some
Enlightenment authors to other cultures. In marked contrast, Grant set
out to refute any writer who saw any merit whatsoever in Indian culture.
He did so to justify his case for bringing Christianity to India in order to
save Hindus. In presenting his treatise to the Directors of the East India
Company in 1797, Grant informed them that his was "a tract which

---

[77] Ainslie Embree, *Charles Grant and British Rule in India* (London: G. Allen, 1962),
p. 142.

bears upon a subject pressed by repeated proposals upon your attention, namely, the communication of Christianity to the natives of our possessions in the East . . . for making known to our Asiatic subjects the pure and benign principles of our divine religion."[78]

To justify this call for a missionary campaign in India Grant had to show the failings of Hinduism. He went to work with a will. His second chapter, titled "View of the State of Society among the Hindoo Subjects of Great Britain particularly with regard to Morals," opened with an assessment which took aim at writers and travelers who had found things to admire in Indian culture. Grant dismissed such points of view:

It has suited the views of some philosophers to represent that people as amiable and respectable; and a few late travellers have chosen rather to place some softer traits of their characters in an engaging light, than to give a just delineation of the whole. The generality however of those who have written concerning Hindustan appear to have concurred in affirming what foreign residents have as generally thought, nay, what the natives themselves freely acknowledge of each other, that they are a people exceedingly depraved.[79]

Grant's residence in India had only added to his antipathy. Based on that experience he was "obliged to add his testimony to all preceding evidence, and to avow that they exhibit human nature in a very degraded, humiliating state and are at once objects of disesteem and commiseration." His years in Bengal had shown to his satisfaction that "they [Bengalis] want truth, honesty and good faith in an extreme of which European society furnishes no example. In Europe these principles are the standard of character and credit . . . It is not so in Bengal."[80]

Lying was endemic amongst Indians: "The want of veracity especially is so habitual," Grant informed his readers. In a reference to Tipu Sultan's alleged breach of the treaty of Coimbatore, he cited "the scandalous conduct of Tippoo [Tipu Sultan] in recently denying to Lord Cornwallis, in face of the world, the existence of that capitulation which he had shamefully broken, [which] was merely an example of the manners of the country where such things occur in common life every day." In Bengal, he insisted, "a man of real veracity and integrity is a great phenomenon; one conscientious in the whole of his conduct, it is to be feared, is an unknown character." Indian participation in commerce did not apparently have the same salutary effects as it did in Europe. From Mysore to Bengal the picture was the same:

---

[78] Charles Grant, *Observations on the State of Society among the Asiatic Subjects of Great Britain, particularly with respect to Morals, and the Means of Improving It. Written Chiefly in the Year 1792*, pp. i, ii, BL.

[79] *Ibid.*, p. 43.   [80] *Ibid.*, pp. 43, 44.

Selfishness, in a word, unrestrained by principle, operates universally; and money, the grand instrument of selfish gratifications, may be called the supreme idol of Hindoos. Deprived for the most part of political power, and destitute of boldness of spirit, but formed for business, artful, frugal and persevering they are absorbed in schemes for the gratification of avarice.

The people, he summed up, "seek their ends by mean artifices, low cunning, intrigue, falsehood, servility, and hypocritical obsequiousness."[81]

In seeking the causes of this woeful state of affairs, Grant identified two minor and one major causes. The minor ones were to become familiar elements in imperial ideologies of Europeans. The first was the weather in India. Grant agreed that "the climate of India, particularly in the south-east provinces, must be allowed to be less favourable to the human constitution than the more temperate regions of Europe." While this was a pertinent factor, he thought that "too much seems sometimes to have been imparted to the climate." The other possibility was Eastern despotism. "The despotic mode of government which is generally prevalent in the East, and appears at all times to have subsisted among Hindoos has undoubtedly had a very considerable influence in the formation of their character . . . Despotism is not only the principle of government of Hindustan but the original, fundamental, and inevitable principle in the very frame of society." But as with the Indian weather, despotism was not the root cause of the problem. It was Hinduism itself that was the main culprit. "This whole fabric is the work of a crafty and imperious priesthood," Grant asserted, "who feigned a divine revelation and appointment to invest their own order in perpetuity with the most absolute empire over the civil state of the Hindoos, as well as over their minds."[82]

An embedded defect of Hinduism was imputed to the fatalism it allegedly instilled in its devotees. Grant argued that the notion of re-birth into a status determined by one's actions in a previous life meant that no one took full moral accountability for their own lives: "The doctrine of transmigration tends likewise to weaken the idea of future responsibility." There was no sense of personal identity, no understanding of the reasons for suffering, "but merely passive temporary endurance" of this current existence. Grant was also appalled by what he saw as the rampant promiscuity of Hindu texts and temples. The Vedic texts were an abomination in his eyes. "As connected with this subject, it may be added in illustration of the cruel genius which pervades the Hindoo code that the Vedas undoubtedly enjoin human sacrifices." He cited as an example another image from India that was to become a familiar presence in popular European discourses about India – "Kallee, the Goddess

[81] *Ibid.*, pp. 44, 45, 47.   [82] *Ibid.*, pp. 72, 73, 83.

of Destruction, one of whose terrific ornaments is a necklace of human skulls."

The bewildering array of gods and goddesses were added to the list of Hindu iniquities:

The Character of the whole multitude of Hindu deities, male and female, is another source of immorality. The legends and histories of their actions are innumerable, and in the highest degree extravagant, absurd, ridiculous, and incredible . . . The abandoned wickedness of their divinities . . . the most villainous frauds and impostures, the most detestable cruelties and injustice, the most filthy and abominable conceits, every corrupt excess and indulgence are presented to us in their histories, varied in a thousand forms.

It was unendurable enough to read about all this in religious texts, but Hindus did not stop there. Their temples were covered in riotous stone sculptures illustrating many of these gods and goddesses in action. "Representations which abandoned licentiousness durst hardly imagine within the most secret recesses of impurity," Grant expostulated, "are there held up in the face of the sun to all mankind, in durable materials, in places dedicated to religion."[83]

Grant used another line of argument that was to become a common feature of the justification of colonial rule in India by the 1820s and 1830s – the treatment of women, dramatically encapsulated in the practice of the burning of widows. "The truth," he began authoritatively, "is that the Hindoo writers, and the Hindoo laws express the worst opinion of their women, and seem to place all security in vigilance, none in principle . . . Imperious dominion, seclusion, and terror are the means afterwards [i.e. after the marriage] used to enforce the fidelity of the wife." Grant eagerly turned to *sati*:

But the cruelty of the Hindoo people appears in no way more evident than in the whole of the treatment to which their women are subjected in society under the sanction and authority of the code [which] expressly sanctions this inhuman and astonishing custom . . . It is proper for a woman, after her husband's death, to burn herself in the fire with the corpse.

As British officials were to do when they outlawed the practice in 1833, Grant claimed that *sati* was not a rare occurrence but was widely practiced. The number of women "thus annually destroyed in Hindostan probably far exceeds the general conception of Europeans." He had not seen a case himself, he admitted, but he added a helpful note that "by far the greater part takes place in the interior of the country out of the view and the intelligence of foreigners."[84]

---

[83] *Ibid.*, pp. 120, 108, 121, 122.   [84] *Ibid.*, pp. 52, 104, 107.

The difference between Grant's invective on *sati* and Bogle's earnest efforts to understand its salience in Indian culture is one sign of the growing gap between this new religiously informed thinking and the relativistic approach of Enlightenment thinkers. Grant made a direct attack on such thinkers, whose writings, he claimed, were also undermining Christianity in Europe. It was these atheistically inclined intellectuals who were the ones touting the purported virtues in Asian cultures:

> For some modern philosophers, already hinted at, whose aim has been to subvert, together with revealed religion, all ideas of the moral government of the Deity, and of man's responsibility to Him, have exalted the natives of the East, and of other pagan regions, into models of goodness and innocence. Other writers with far better views, indignant at the alleged delinquencies of Europeans in Hindostan, have described the natives of that country as a harmless, kind, peaceable, and suffering race. Others again speak rather from an admiration inscribed by the supposed past state of the Hindoos, mixed with pity for their present situation than from experience of their actual qualities and dispositions.[85]

Although Grant only "hints" at his targets here, it is easy to identify Voltaire (for attacking revealed religion), Jean-Jacques Rousseau (on innocent natives), and Edmund Burke (indignant about European treatment of Indians).

Grant is an interesting transitional figure. Although he was an evangelical Christian he used the discourse of Enlightenment rationality for his analysis of Hinduism. Rather than cite Christian apologists, or quote from the Bible, he preferred to present an organized, apparently well-reasoned case deploying relevant evidence from his own observations in India and from Hindu texts. His style was an Enlightenment style. But his project was completely anti-Enlightenment. While he was reluctant to engage in direct debate, he was occasionally quite open about attacking Enlightenment figures in his *Observations*. Perhaps because he was more familiar with Scottish writers than continental ones, he gave space to a direct refutation of William Robertson, whose *Historical Disquisition concerning the Knowledge which the Ancients had of India* (1791) had praised early Hindu civilization. This made Robertson the fourth target, after Voltaire, Rousseau, and Burke, in the quotation above. Robertson's praise of Indian civilization made a great deal of sense in the context of the stadial theory of history. Ancient India had clearly moved well beyond the hunting-gathering stage while Europe remained in a much more primitive state. The religious ideas, the system of laws, the complex social arrangements, and the artistic achievements of early Indian civilization were all proof for Robertson that laws, morals, and social organization

---

[85] *Ibid.*, p. 53.

reflected the stage of material development. This was a challenge for Grant. How could he deny these achievements of Hindu civilization?

He had two answers. The first returned to the hot Indian climate; the second argued that in so far as any civilization had appeared in India it had come from outside. He had earlier downplayed the climate argument to account for Hindu degeneracy but he took it up again to explain how some achievements had been made in ancient India. His argument now was that India's climate was so conducive to luxuriant plant growth that the population could not help but be successful at agriculture and thus make some cultural advances. It had been the bountiful land rather than the capabilities of the people that explained any previous historical advances:

For countries extremely productive of the bounties of nature seem to ripen the ideas of men in some respects with a quickness analogous to the rapidity of their vegetation; and where enjoyments are profusely offered a certain degree of refinement will easily take place, and the rights of property be understood, though the facility of acquisition will not be favourable to the spirit of improvement and there may be vices in the political constitution which will absolutely limit its progress.[86]

Grant struggled to deal with the impact of the Indian climate in his *Observations*. He had hesitated to blame the hot climate for Indian sloth and sin earlier in his argument, but he was quite prepared to use the heat when it better suited his argument. He now deployed the excessive climate as part of a dismissive explanation of any supposed advances in ancient India. For European commentators like Grant, Indian weather was a versatile variable.

Grant's second explanation for the achievements of ancient Hindu culture reflected the new knowledge emerging from the work of William Jones (1746–1794) and other scholars who were studying Indian languages and history. Jones, already famous as a scholar of Asian languages, went in 1783 as a judge in the newly established High Court in Calcutta. He continued his research while in Bengal and was a founder, along with Hastings, of the Asiatic Society in 1784. His interest in languages had led him to discover the connection between Sanskrit, Greek, and Latin and to understand that there was an Indo-European family of languages that had come from a common source.

This new knowledge was helpful to Grant because it enabled him to suggest that any vigor in ancient India had come from outside. No one knew then where the original Indo-European heartland was, and scholars

[86] *Ibid.*, p. 144.

still debate this issue today (although most agree it was somewhere in western Central Asia).[87] Grant's all-embracing religious framework led him to seize upon this new information in a way that brought the entire matter back to the supreme truths of the Judeo-Christian tradition. He reassured his readers that with respect to

the Brahminical system of religion, law, and science from which the strongest arguments for a long progressive course of refinement are deduced, reason has of late been given us to believe that the elements of them did not spring up in Hindustan but were derived from a source nearer to the original seat of the post-diluvian race.[88]

The poor Hindus had to be brought to understand that they too were children of Noah and that they had gotten badly off track. "Whatever the origins or extent of knowledge among the [ancient] Hindoos might be," Grant summed up, "it was, as we have seen, monopolized and concealed by the Brahmins. It spread little light among the great body of the people and it is incorrect to refer to the whole nation what only priests possessed and guarded as a mystery."[89] Britain's position in Bengal now presented the opportunity to overturn the errors of the past. The British, according to this reasoning, should wrest power from the Hindu authorities, clear away the debris produced by these fatal historical mis-steps, and bring the truth of Christianity to Bengal.

The lives of Grant and Younghusband did not overlap – Grant died in 1823, Younghusband was born in 1863 – but they were both profoundly influenced by the evangelical Christian forces that had such a wide-ranging impact on British culture between the late eighteenth and mid-nineteenth centuries. This religious orientation informed their belittling accounts of Asian cultures, and seems to have been the driving force behind not only their own sense of righteousness but their broader belief in the righteousness of the British empire. A large oil painting by Thomas Jones Barker (1815–1882) hanging in the National Portrait Gallery in London captures this connection between Grant and Younghusband. The canvas depicts Queen Victoria handing a Bible to a nameless, dark-skinned figure (art historians have since identified him as Ali bin Nasr, the governor of Mombasa) who crouches gratefully and obediently, stretching out a hand towards the holy book. The title of this work is "The Secret of England's Greatness." For both Grant and Younghusband that 1863 painting would have represented something true about the British empire.

[87] J. P. Mallory, *In Search of the Indo-Europeans. Language, Archaeology, Myth* (London: Thames and Hudson, 1989).
[88] Grant, *Observations*, p. 144.   [89] *Ibid.*, p. 144.

Such a painting could not have been conceived of in the 1770s; it reflected the religiously permeated imperial outlook of mid-Victorian England. One of the central tasks of the empire was to bring benighted natives to the invigorating light of Christianity. Grant boldly declared, in an observation that could just as easily have been made by Younghusband, that "the natives [of India] were indolent, improvident, fatalists."[90] If Grant's diatribe against Hinduism, and Barker's painting in the National Portrait Gallery, help us to see the bridge from eighteenth-century evangelicalism to the imperial ideologies of the nineteenth century, they also enable us to appreciate better the Enlightenment outlook of Bogle. In "Imperial Eyes in 'the Golden Territories'" we did not let Bogle off the hook with respect to empire, and we have sketched out his partisan views on commerce and empire, but there is clear water between Bogle and Grant in their approaches to other peoples and cultures.

Bogle was a representative of the moderate Enlightenment as defined by Jonathan Israel. As we have seen when Bogle commented on the coarsening effects of social equality in Bhutan, he thought that social hierarchy was a bedrock of civilization because it was necessary for the refinement of manners. The same conservative approach shaped his religious views. The moderate wing of Scottish Presbyterianism, which distanced itself from the notion of a Calvinist God punishing sinful humans, was in the ascendancy when Bogle was being educated in Glasgow and Edinburgh. In Bengal, he participated in all the Christian rituals and ceremonies of the British community – baptizing children, for example. Bogle on one occasion referred to "Almighty God" when he was justifying the Company's role in India. Thus Bogle remained a Christian believer. But God was not invoked as an active presence in his daily life. Bogle was representative of deist thinking of the time which retained belief in a Christian God but viewed that God as a remote sustainer of the universe rather than an active presence. Phrases such as "divine providence" were used to describe God's distant role from day-to-day events.

Bogle would never have contradicted his father openly but the contrast is marked between father and son on these matters. Bogle was tolerant of religions other than Christianity while his father, like Grant, saw only "idolatry" in Bengal. Bogle praised the Panchen Lama for his tolerance of pilgrims of different religions, and added his own considered view that religious narrowness was "a copious source of human misery." Bogle even had positive things to say about Hinduism, in spite of *sati* and the behavior of the *sanyassis*. He spoke of "the humane maxims" of Hinduism. In

[90] *Ibid.*, p. 17.

contrast to Grant and Younghusband, Bogle was not blinkered by the exclusiveness and chauvinism of evangelical Christianity.

If Bogle was an exemplar of tolerant, deist Christianity in Enlightenment-era Britain, Younghusband was an example of Victorian evangelical Christianity in action. Late in his life Younghusband himself recognized that he had been a representative of those values that had shaped middle-class Victorian culture. As he looked back through some of his letters and diaries in 1940, Younghusband noted, in a reflective moment of self-recognition, that "there is much that is priggish and self-righteous, and that has an air of spiritual superiority and complacency. It is all very 'Victorian'."[91] Younghusband's unassailable sense of rectitude during his Tibet mission was an extreme example of the evangelizing, imperialist mentality even at this peak moment of British imperial power. A vigorous extra-parliamentary opposition to the invasion was led by Sir Henry Cotton in a series of newspaper articles, and through letters to the editor of *The Times*. Cotton was a retired Indian Civil Service official who had risen to the post of Chief Secretary to the Bengal government. He argued that Curzon and Younghusband had worked up an overwrought case for the invasion of Tibet.

The Liberal and Radical press was also full of vociferous criticisms of the Tibet escapade. An editorial in the London *Star* described the mission as "an insane and infamous adventure" while the *Daily News* summed it up as "a foolish and wasteful expedition."[92] Even within the Tory government, as we noted in the comments of Hamilton and Brodrick, the forward policy of Curzon and the way in which Younghusband pushed ahead of his instructions were viewed with alarm. At the end of the mission Younghusband was officially censured for imposing terms on the Tibetans which allowed Britain to remain in occupation of the Chumbi valley for seventy-five years. Some contemporaries viewed Younghusband as extreme. But he was a creation of his time and circumstances, and as such tells us something of that period just as Bogle does of his. He appears to us now as a caricature of a late Victorian and Edwardian imperialist.

Younghusband's own religious views were to change dramatically after his time in Tibet (as we shall see in the next chapter) but throughout the 1903–1904 expedition his vigorous condemnation of benighted

[91] Younghusband Note, March 25, 1940, Younghusband Collection, MSS. EUR. F197/323, BL.
[92] *Daily News*, September 10, 1904; *The Star* (London), August 17, 1904. Press Cuttings concerning Sir Henry Cotton's Opposition to the Younghusband Expedition to Tibet in 1903–1904, MSS. EUR. D1202/3, BL.

lamas was the ugly counterpoise to his own Christian piety. In contrast to Younghusband's simplistic comments on Tibetan government and religion, Bogle viewed Tibet as a complex place when he wrote of "the tumble of interests which govern this Nation."[93] For Younghusband there was no complexity – only rule by a monkish oligarchy.

A related contrast with Bogle was the easy way Younghusband put all Asians into one category, as we saw in his correspondence with Curzon. Younghusband had no hesitation in clumping together all those on the other side. He told Dane, in the course of discussing a dispute about seating precedence in meetings at Khamba Dzong, that insisting on proper ceremony "goes down well with the Oriental."[94] When he made judgments about Tibetans, he often relied on "his experience of Asiatics." In the "Character of the People" section of his long memorandum on Tibet he declared that "the Tibetans are also grossly superstitious . . . This sly exclusiveness, this suspiciousness, this faithlessness, and this belief in superstitions are, however, traits which are very common in Asiatic peoples."[95]

This categorical racial thinking was symptomatic of the quasi-scientific approach to race that flourished in the wake of Charles Darwin's *The Origin of Species* (1859) as crude notions about race differentiation began to be applied to human populations round the world. The academic expression of such ideas appeared in books such as Crozier's *Civilization and Progress* which Younghusband had so enthusiastically recommended to Curzon. This kind of dogmatic thinking about race was absent in Bogle but it was beginning to appear in Grant. In Grant's case the racial thinking made its appearance when he tried to account for the role of Moslems in India. His comprehensive condemnation of India had to take into account the impact of Islam, beginning with Mahmud of Ghazni's raids in the 900s and culminating in the establishment of the Mughal empire in the fifty years after Babur's victory at Panipat in 1526.

Grant's case with respect to Islam moved away from religion. Perhaps the overlap between the Bible and the Koran, in contrast to the

---

[93] George Bogle to David Anderson, Tibet, 1775 [?], David Anderson Papers, Add. 45421, f. 30, BL.

[94] Younghusband to L. W. Dane, Tangu, July 8, 1903, Government of India, Foreign Department. Secret-E. Proceedings, August 1903, Nos. 416–647, Negotiations with Tibet, BL.

[95] *Memorandum on Our Relations with Tibet. Both Past and Present. Together with a Forecast of the Future Developments of Our Policy in that region by Colonel F. E. Younghusband* (Simla, 1903), p. 5, MSS. EUR. F197/78, BL.

uncontainable nature of Hinduism, prompted him to take this tack. In any event, he begins and ends with race. Here is how he deals with Islam in India:

Of the Mahomedans who mix in considerable numbers with the former inhabitants of all the countries subdued by their arms in Hindustan it is necessary also to say a few words. Originally of the Tartar race, proud, fierce, lawless; attached also to that superstition which cherished their native propensities; they were rendered by success yet more proud, sanguinary, sensual, and bigotted . . . Breaking through all the restraints of morals which obstructed their way to power, they afterwards abandoned themselves to the most vicious indulgences, and the most atrocious cruelties . . . Every worldly possession, indeed every cause of secular business, was in their avowed opinion (an opinion they still hold) irreconcilable with strict virtue. Commerce and the details of the finances they left chiefly to Hindoos whom they despised and insulted . . . Their perfidy, however, and licentiousness are the perfidy and licentiousness of a bolder people.[96]

Although the Moslems had their own characteristic faults when they came to India, they and the Hindus were now joined together in iniquity. "The vices of the Mahomedans and Hindoos are so homogenous," continued Grant, "that in stating their effects it is not inaccurate to speak of both classes under the description of the one collective body into which they are now formed."[97] Proceeding by this series of contradictory assertions, Grant declared that India was now inhabited by one degenerate "race." Grant's grand conclusion was that "upon the whole then we cannot avoid recognizing in the people of Hindostan a race of men lamentably degenerate and base . . . and sunk in misery by their vices."[98]

So here too, we can see another bridge that leads away from the relative tolerance of the Enlightenment to the explicit racial justifications of imperialism. Grant's mish-mash of reasoning did not possess the false scientific patina of nineteenth-century racism but its Christian triumphalism was one of the origin points for those later imperial ways of thinking. Grant reached his conclusions by making a direct attack on Robertson and other Enlightenment thinkers who had explicated admirable qualities in Indian and other cultures, the very thinkers who had shaped Bogle's sympathetic engagement with Bhutan and Tibet. During his journey Bogle was ready to study Tibetan society and discover the ways in which it might even outdo his own. In that posture he was reflecting an Enlightenment rather than an imperial approach to the world. Younghusband was determined to teach the Tibetans some lessons; Bogle was open to learning something new from Tibetans.

[96] Grant, *Observations*, p. 70.   [97] *Ibid.*, p. 71.   [98] *Ibid.*, p. 71.

The contrast between Bogle and Grant shows how the new evangelical religious outlook, and emerging concepts of race, began to inform imperial ideologies in the nineteenth century. The contrast also shows how attitudes towards the sex and gender issues we looked at in the "wives and concubines" chapter also changed. Just as attitudes on religion and race widened the gap between British and Indians, so evolving attitudes towards interracial sex and marriage contributed to harsher views of colonized Indians. Bogle, Anderson, and their circle of friends shared their lives with Indian women. The sharing was not based on equality but it was sharing nevertheless and some cultural accommodation took place. This kind of sharing came to an end in the course of the 1800s; by the 1890s the thought of an Indian "family" was utterly inconceivable for Younghusband and the other British soldiers and civilians who ran the *Raj*.

This sea change in attitudes was intimately linked to the impact of the new religious and racial thinking that we have traced from Grant to Younghusband. Charles Grant again provides a window through which we can see the beginning moment of these more exclusionary European views on sexual matters. During his time in Bengal Grant was offended by what he took to be the sexual looseness of Indian women. This view contradicted his earlier assertion that Indian women were locked away and under the power of Hindu men, but it suited his purpose of defining India as a comprehensively sinful place. The custom of having female dancers give public performances – the *nautch* shows, often depicting scenes from Hindu mythology or folk tales – drew Grant's ire. "Indecency is the basis of their [female dancers'] exhibitions; yet children and young persons of both sexes are permitted to be present at these shows . . . Licentious connections are therefore most common." Grant complained that the Company authorities encouraged this general licentious atmosphere in Bengal by their indulgent policy of permitting "receptacles for women of infamous character [to be] everywhere licensed."

Matters only began to improve, in Grant's opinion, after Lord Cornwallis became Governor General and made it clear that he would not countenance female dancers. Grant wrote approvingly that Cornwallis "soon after his arrival in Bengal refused to be present at an entertainment of this sort to which he was invited by the Nabob."[99] Grant linked these sinful sexual activities to his argument about the racial failings of all Indians: "It is the universality of great depravity that is here insisted on." Contriving to work race into this issue too, he added that "there is a general moral hue [of Indians] between which and the European moral

---

[99] *Ibid.*, p. 53.

complexion there is a difference analogous to the difference of the natural colour of the two races."[100]

It was these attitudes, reflected in Cornwallis' behavior and Grant's writings, that began to end the cross-cultural "marriages" and "families" that were so much a part of the world of Bogle and Anderson. Younghusband represented the culmination of these trends within the English community in India. His comment on his Victorian priggishness is nowhere more true than in his attitudes towards women, this self-assessment being made when he looked back at his diary entries on Nellie Douglas, a married woman he had befriended in Srinagar.[101] Younghusband agonized over sexual matters, wracked by a sense of guilt about his sexual urges. He also worried about the sexual purity of women he might marry. His stuffily moralistic understanding of male–female relationships comes out in one of his diary entries where he described a brief shipboard encounter on the *Clyde* during a voyage back from India in 1894. He had a conversation with a Miss Beddie ("talking among the boats"), and worried that her evident (in Younghusband's mind) forwardness might lead him to lose his control for just a moment. He feared he

might be carried away, for she can be fascinating and she admires me I know. But I want to keep high above any interaction of the senses and I should like, by giving her the example of a man who can be a friend without making love to her or falling in love with her, to raise her moral standard and give her a higher type to think of. It is a tussle between us in fact whether I shall lower myself to her level or whether I can raise her up to mine.[102]

When he had first gone out to India as a young subaltern in the King's Dragoon Guards in 1882, Younghusband had been shocked by the behavior of his fellow officers. They drank and swore and visited the regimental brothel "which was staffed by Indian women and subsidized from the canteen fund."[103] Younghusband later confessed to Helen Magniac on the eve of their marriage that he had succumbed to the temptations of prostitutes at some moments of his life in India. "Darling, when you are constantly with men who talk so much on that subject – who are constantly intimate with low women – and when the passion comes on very strong . . . when I was away so long from refined society this sexual craving overcame me and I degraded myself."[104] He preferred not to allow such matters to define his life in India. The females were dismissed

---

[100] *Ibid.*, p. 55.   [101] French, *Younghusband*, p. 101.
[102] Younghusband, Private Journal 1894, November 30, 1894, Younghusband Collection, MSS. EUR. F197/257, BL.
[103] French, *Younghusband*, pp. 16, 17.   [104] *Ibid.*, p. 136.

as "low women" and the entire subject matter was to be suppressed if at all possible.

Younghusband's views can also be seen in his thinly disguised auto-biographical novel *But in Our Lives. A Romance of the Indian Frontier.* The protagonist is Evan Lee, "a two-dimensional, saintly character who is brought up in the west of England by strict aunts and sent to Sandhurst, where he resists lewd talk and leads a 'pure, healthy, manly life.'" When Lee is posted to India, the Colonel of his regiment, worried that his men are too often "incapacitated for active service through diseases contracted from women," enlists young Lee's help to keep his fellow soldiers on the straight and narrow. "Intercourse is not a necessity," the Colonel informed Lee, "Containing themselves will be very good discipline for them. They'll be the better for it. I won't have my men defiling themselves." Lee sees games and sports as a solution but understands that the more fundamental cure is to instill a spiritual fervor in the men which will make them abhor defilement:

Every mother must be yearning that her own son should keep himself uncontaminated. And a son should think of his mother's feelings and all that she has gone through to bring him up. He should loathe to tarnish his purity. And besides this, there should be as much care taken to keep his soul unspotted from the world as there is to keep his uniform and accoutrements clean. If religion could see to keep his soul unspotted, his soul would keep his body pure.[105]

So while Younghusband undoubtedly had sex with some Indian women there was always self-degradation attached to such activity. Any connection with Indian women was dangerous, surreptitious, and shameful.

Although Younghusband briefly noted Bogle's commentary on Tibetan women and how they differed from women in other places he did not show any interest in the topic.[106] He never mixed socially with Indian women, and it was utterly beyond the bounds of possibility that he could live with one and have children by her. When Younghusband did marry at age thirty-four it was partly in pursuit of his ambition to climb higher in society. The Younghusbands were upper middle class but Helen Magniac's family "had social links extending to the aristocracy and the Palace." Younghusband thought his marriage to Helen would help him "to get and keep in touch with the very best people of the time."[107]

During his career in India he hoped she would prove useful to him in "society." As he was being briefed by the Viceroy on the proposed

[105] *Ibid.*, pp. 18, 19.
[106] Younghusband, *Memorandum on Our Relations with Tibet*, p. 6.
[107] French, *Younghusband*, p. 137.

Tibet mission, Helen mixed with the top people in Simla. Younghusband encouraged her to develop her friendship with Lady Curzon:

> I am sure too that by making a friend of her you will have helped me greatly in my career. Lord Curzon and I are bound to be associated together for our lives. There may be years intervals now and then when we have not much direct connection but undoubtedly he and I will often have to work together; so it is a great thing that you have been able to make such a friend of Lady Curzon.[108]

Even when he was camped at Khamba Dzong, he was able to read *The Times* (which reached him in twenty days) and exchange views with his wife on "society" events such as the wedding of Lady Muriel Fox-Strangways in London. He assured Helen that "I am pretty *au fait* with everything that goes on."[109] He worried about his wife staying at a Darjeeling hotel where she would perhaps encounter some of the jute-wallahs from Calcutta – "rather a rough shop-keeping, commercial lot." He recommended Rockville which is "supposed to be more refined and the Manageress told me that Colonel Brown IMS always went there, by which she meant to imply that you would be in the very height of Darjeeling society."[110]

This world of male–female relationships is a vast distance from the world of Bogle and Anderson. Many things had changed in religious and racial attitudes, as we have seen, but another key difference which now pushed Indian women well away from the British community (except as servants and prostitutes) was the well-established presence of English women in India. While the English women may not have exercised any formal power in public, their mere presence had a profound impact on the behavior of their menfolk. An incident in Darjeeling at the beginning of this troubled period in relations between British India and Tibet dramatically illustrates the ways in which these gendered aspects of the Indian empire were playing out by the 1890s.

During the controversy over Younghusband's mission this Darjeeling affair was brought up by critics to show British Indian insensitivity towards Tibetans. In 1892 there had been some Tibetan delegates in Darjeeling in connection with the forthcoming trade talks. One of the Tibetan envoys was Shatra Paljor Dorje, a senior official (a deputy

108 Younghusband to Helen Younghusband, Simla, May 29, 1903, Younghusband Collection, MSS. EUR. F197/173, BL.
109 Younghusband to Helen Younghusband, Khamba Jong, September 19, 1903, Younghusband Collection, MSS. EUR. F197/174, BL.
110 Younghusband to Helen Younghusband, Darjeeling, June 14, 1903, *ibid*. On prejudices within the British community in Calcutta against commercial men see Gordon T. Stewart, *Jute and Empire. The Calcutta Jute Wallahs and the Landscapes of Empire* (Manchester University Press, 1998), pp. 174–179, 220–223.

Kalon). According to Patrick French, there is a Tibetan oral history which tells of Shatra's humiliating experience of being thrown into a drinking trough by a group of British soldiers because he had failed to make way for an English woman walking on the Mall.[111] When the matter resurfaced in 1904, the Indian Government was forced to look again at its police records and interview officials and other witnesses in order to respond to their critics. Sir Henry Cotton entered the fray, not only because he was actively engaged in the controversy over Curzon's Tibet policy, but because he had been Chief Secretary to the Bengal Government at the time, and thus had direct knowledge of the 1892 incident.

According to Cotton's version of the affray, "the Tibetan Commissioner was on the Chowrasta... when he met a party of planters... An altercation ensued... The result was that the planters caught hold of the Tibetan by the heels and dragged him bumping along the road all the way to the police station where he lay for the night." In one of his letters to *The Times*, Cotton described this as "the grossest of outrages" against the Tibetans' delegate.[112] Another account was given in a formal statement to the Lieutenant Governor of Bengal by a Mr. A. S. Judge, the Superintendent of the Preventive and Salt Department, who claimed to have witnessed the incident. According to his statement "a party of English ladies and gentlemen were proceeding... to a dinner party in Darjeeling when several natives on horseback rode past rapidly, and one of their number slashed open the hood of a dandy [a kind of sedan chair] or rickshaw in which one of the ladies was seated. The Englishmen at once took notice of this insult." A Darjeeling policeman who was also drawn in as a witness had yet another version: the Tibetan official had been caught "slashing his whip about and striking the dandiwallahs with it, and hitting the dandis, and nearly hitting and frightening the ladies."[113]

It is not clear whether this is the same incident that French refers to from his Tibetan sources. The Tibetan commissioner named in the 1904 re-hashing of the controversy was Kyung-Zam. Even the accounts of the alleged attack on the rickshaws or dandis differ – the Indian witness speaking of a whip, the British witness of a sword. There may have been more than one incident of abuse directed at the Tibetan delegates. The details of what actually happened are not important for the significant

[111] French, *Younghusband*, p. 210.
[112] *The Times*, December 4, 1903 (Sir Henry Cotton's letter to the Editor).
[113] Sir Henry Cotton to Sir Charles Elliot, St. John's Wood, December 6, 1903; Written Statement prepared for His Honour the Lieutenant Governor by Mr. A. S. Judge, n.d., Calcutta; Statement of Haridas Prodham, Darjeeling Police (First Grade), December 30, 1903, India Office Records L/P&S/7/161, BL.

point here. All witnesses – Indian, Tibetan, and British – agreed that an apparent threat to English women was the instigating factor for the actions of the British men. The men rushed to defend "their" women when they seemed to be in danger. The men intervened because the alleged Tibetan offender was "nearly hitting and frightening the ladies" as they sat in their dandis.[114] This 1892 incident shows how the presence of British women in India led British men to act more aggressively towards "natives" – whether Tibetan or Indian.

This is a different world from the world of the Company men in the 1770s. There was certainly sexual exploitation and aggression in both settings but Bogle, Anderson, and their friends were in a more fluid context in which the Englishmen had to make an effort to establish relationships with Indian men and women. They had to interact with Indian men in order to be successful in their careers and successful in business. They had to interact with Indian women if they wanted to have children and families during their time in Bengal. Without according British women a power they did not possess, their increasing presence in India was one factor in bringing Bogle's world to an end.

The more exclusionist ways of thinking about other races and religions that we traced in Grant's *Observations* also lay behind these changing attitudes towards liaisons and marriages between Indians and British. Durba Ghosh, as she teases out the evolving nature of these relationships between British men and Indian women, reminds us that "scientific notions of race were not yet fully developed in the eighteenth century."[115] She also argues that discourses in Britain about Asian cultures in the 1700s were more varied than Edward Said's depiction of settled Orientalist European attitudes in the 1800s. In the 1700s, as an example of this rational approach, cohabitation was accepted as "a reasonable by-product of heterosexual necessity, (because there were very few European women)."[116] The Company accepted this and set up organizations to attend to the consequences of these cross-cultural relationships. Lord Clive's Pension Fund (1770) and the Bengal Military Orphan Society (1783) were established to provide payments for some of the widows and children of Company men and officers. Ghosh shows that many of the Indian women asserted their legal rights by petitioning these Company organizations.

---

[114] C. R. Marindin (Commissioner of the Rajshali Division) to W. C. Macpherson, Darjeeling, September 30, 1903; Statement of Haridas Prodham (Officer in Darjeeling Police Force); W. C. Macpherson to Louis Dane, Calcutta, January 4, 1904; Louis Dane to Richmond Ritchie (Secretary, Political and Secret Department, India Office), Calcutta, January 13, 1904, India Office Records L/P&S/7/161, BL.

[115] Durba Ghosh, *Bibis, Begums, and Concubines*, p. 25.   [116] *Ibid.*, p. 37.

In her studies of the Dutch in Indonesia, Ann Stoler has argued that the sharper separation of the races that took place during the 1800s flowed from the need of the European communities to maintain their distance from the colonized. The social, spatial, and sexual distancing that took hold was to protect European notions of a pure bourgeois society (and the bourgeois body) from native contamination.[117] It was post-Enlightenment values, associated with a highly successful industrial capitalism, and in the British case the emergence of Victorian middle-class morality, that closed down the hybrid possibilities that were still possible in the 1700s.

Younghusband had something else that Bogle did not have. He had the Maxim gun. When camped at Khamba Dzong, he reassured his father that he was perfectly safe because the camp was fortified and "we have a Maxim too."[118] As the London radical newspaper *The Star* bitterly commented just after Younghusband turned back towards India, "that Imperialist Nightmare, the Mission with Maxims to Lhasa has started on its homeward journey."[119] Younghusband's officers, as we have seen, delighted in demonstrating the machine gun's killing efficiency to the Bhutanese and Tibetans. Agents of empire like Younghusband now had additional power because of these technological advances in the British armaments industry. The Maxim was an intimidating practical expression of the military advantage the western European countries and the United States had achieved over the rest of the world as a consequence of the industrialization of their economies beginning in the late eighteenth and early nineteenth centuries.

Things were much more evenly matched in Bogle's time. Some recent interpretations in world history have argued that the balance of power in the world only tilted away from Asia in Europe's favor in the 1790–1840 period.[120] Britain's relationship with China was illustrative of this timing. In 1793 the Chinese had the economic, political, and cultural confidence to turn away the British embassy of Lord Macartney. The Chinese told the British in no uncertain terms that China had no need of any goods from England, and that an English envoy would only be accepted if he

---

[117] Ann Stoler, "Making Empire Respectable. The Politics of Race and Sexual Morality in Twentieth-Century Colonial Cultures," *American Ethnologist* 16 (1989), pp. 634–660.

[118] Younghusband to his Father, Khamba Jong, August 2, 1903, Younghusband Collection, MSS. EUR. F197/145, BL.

[119] *The Star*, October 5, 1904, Press Cuttings concerning Sir Henry Cotton's Opposition to the Younghusband Expedition, MSS. EUR. D1202/3, BL.

[120] Kenneth Pomeranz, *The Great Divergence. Europe, China, and the Making of the Modern World Economy* (Princeton University Press, 2000); André Gunder Frank, *ReOrient. Global Economy in the Asian Age* (Berkeley: University of California Press, 1998).

adopted Chinese ways and lived the rest of his life in China. Forty years later the Chinese navy was utterly destroyed by (partially) steam-powered British ships in the Opium War and the British established themselves in Hong Kong.

In Bogle's India the Company was hard pressed to hold its position in the 1770s. Bruce Lenman has shown what close-run affairs many of the battles were in eighteenth-century India.[121] Max Boot has argued that it was only at the battle of Assaye in 1803 that European armies could claim a decisive technological and disciplinary advantage over Indian opponents.[122] Certainly, the entire British community held its breath in 1781–1782 when Anderson was negotiating with Scindia and the Marathas. The Company needed to stem the Maratha tide in order to hold onto its still tenuous position in India. Reflecting this sense of vulnerability, Claud Alexander wrote with a touch of desperation to Anderson: "You are not very near bringing matters to a conclusion with the Marathas. I am afraid they will not trust us. We have used them D___d ill indeed . . . We want nothing but a Maratha peace to make all go well, and you will have more Credit than any man I know if you can Effect it before it is too late."[123]

The dominating position of European technology, industrial capability, and associated military power that developed in the 1800s encouraged the evolution of a more comprehensive sense of European superiority over other cultures. Younghusband represented the culmination of these trends when British firepower made it safe to be contemptuous of any threat from all potential enemies in colonial settings. The material progress in Europe during the 1800s was, of course, partly attributable to the rational analysis of economic forces begun by Adam Smith. Industrialization was successful because of (among other factors) the systematic application of science and reason to the production and marketing of goods. In that general sense, successful modern economies derived in some ways from the Enlightenment but it is tendentious to present modern industrialization as inevitably the consequence of Enlightenment ways of thinking. The full-blown imperial ideology in place by the

---

[121] Bruce P. Lenman, *Britain's Colonial Wars, 1688–1783* (New York: Longman, 2001), pp. 83–114. Lenman describes the "erratic emergence" of Company military strength in India.

[122] Max Boot, *War Made New. Technology, Warfare, and the Course of History 1500 to Today* (New York: Gotham Books, 2006), pp. 77–102. In Boot's analysis it was the intensifying professionalization of European armies with its accompanying improvement in officer training and battlefield discipline and tactics that finally began to prevail over the "traditional, hit-and-run" methods used by opponents such as the Marathas.

[123] Claud Alexander to David Anderson, Calcutta, May 18, 1782, David Anderson Papers, Add. 45424, f. 79, BL.

time Younghusband set out for Tibet was not shaped by remembrances of the Enlightenment but by Christian triumphalism and by the aggressive pride associated with British technological achievements in the new industrial era.

These new imperial attitudes began to appear in the early decades of the nineteenth century. Jennifer Pitts has shown how liberal thinkers such as Alexis de Tocqueville and John Stuart Mill, who saw themselves as inheritors of the Enlightenment tradition, became advocates of empire by the 1830s and 1840s. She argues that the advent of democracy and a more sharply articulated sense of national identity caused this shift.[124] The colonial projects overseas could be used by aristocratic, business, and intellectual elites in European states to rally the new laboring and professional middle classes to a national cause. Such projects could provide an ennobling mission that would raise the sights of all social classes round a series of national projects overseas. Linda Colley makes a similar observation about the role of imperial ideologies in nineteenth-century Britain. She proposes that from the 1830s onwards the British identity, shaped since the 1600s by antipathy towards the French, now began to be defined by the numerous encounters with colonized peoples in the empire.[125] The European empires were now becoming intertwined at home with national self-images that attempted to reach across social classes. All the modern media – including magazines, pictures, advertisements – were deployed in this cause.[126] It was new dynamics such as these, linked to industrialization, democratization, and nationalism, that shaped the thinking of liberal supporters of empire such as Mill and de Tocqueville. Imperialism was re-shaping the Enlightenment rather than the other way round.

It is a complicated matter to be sure, no one individual thinking person, well known or obscure, being purely enlightened or purely imperialist. In his great biography of Edmund Burke, Conor Cruise O'Brien has held up Edmund Burke as a paragon of Enlightenment virtues who critiqued empire – in America, in Ireland, and in India.[127] During the impeachment proceedings, Burke lambasted Hastings and the East India Company for their nefarious doings in India. He spoke eloquently about the fate of the ordinary Indians under this oppressive yoke. But of course in the end he too supported Britain's imperial position in India. He used the

---

[124] Pitts, *A Turn to Empire*, pp. 8, 9, 15, 247–254.
[125] Linda Colley, "Britishness and Otherness," *Journal of British Studies* 31 (October 1992), pp. 309–329.
[126] John MacKenzie, *Propaganda and Empire* (Manchester University Press, 1998).
[127] Conor Cruise O'Brien, *The Great Melody. A Thematic Biography and Commented Anthology of Edmund Burke* (University of Chicago Press, 1992).

impeachment of Hastings to advocate reform of British rule rather than end it altogether.

In that sense Burke was exactly like Bartolome De Las Casas, who had made a vehement denunciation of an earlier example of European imperialism on the other side of the world from India. In his *Short Account of the Destruction of the Indies* (1542) De Las Casas had been unsparing in his denunciation of Spanish colonists but, as Anthony Pagden notes, this did not lead him to condemn the Spanish imperial takeover in the Americas. "But for all his insistence that the Crown had seriously mismanaged its colonies and that the behaviour of the colonists 'had given reason for the name of Christ to be loathed and abominated by countless people', Las Casas never once denied . . . that the Spanish Crown was the legitimate ruler of the Americas."[128] Similarly, Burke never doubted Britain's right to rule India. Acknowledging the complex, and sometimes contradictory, nature of the Enlightenment we can say that while the Enlightenment did indeed lead to imperial outcomes, as we saw with Bogle and commerce, there was no single "enlightenment project" which led exclusively into the European imperial mentalities of the 1800s. The Enlightenment, as we also saw with Bogle, recognized the worth of other cultures, and valued the capacity to be skeptical of all cultural claims. Enlightenment thinking offered multiple possibilities – including critiques of empire – in its open methods of inquiry.

Bogle died in Bengal in 1781 and never again saw the family estate at Daldowie which he had done so much to save. But Warren Hastings, the patron to whom Bogle was so loyal, did get to Daldowie. Two years after he returned to Britain, in 1787, Hastings set out on a journey to Scotland. He kept a diary and titled it "Journal of a Tour to Scotland," perhaps still harboring hopes he had once shared with Bogle of replicating the success Samuel Johnson had achieved with his *Journal of a Tour to the Hebrides.* Hastings certainly tried to mimic the blustery honesty of Johnson's commentary on this northern part of the British isles. Shortly after crossing the border hills he made this entry: "Halted at Linlithgow, a large, old, and dirty town." He expressed an amused skepticism about the current craze for relics from the heroic age of the Scottish wars of independence. At Dumbarton Castle he was shown "an old sword which we were to believe had been the property of Sir William Wallace." Hastings commented sardonically, hinting at similar incidents in India,

---

[128] Bartolome De Las Casas, *A Short Account of the Destruction of the Indies* (London: Penguin, 1992 [1542]), translated by Nigel Griffin and with an Introduction by Anthony Pagden, pp. xiv, xv, xvi.

that "I have found the people in every place of Antiquity lavish of its memorials, for which they offer no Evidence but their Assurance of their being such."[129]

By September they were in the vicinity of Paisley and within striking distance of Daldowie. Hastings' party was "joined by Mr. Bogle, the elder brother of my late Friend, George Bogle, of Bengal." The following day Hastings was received at Daldowie. Hastings described his arrival at the Bogle family estate:

A fine, clear, warm Day. At 8:45 am left Glasgow and Captain Lennox added to our party, and at 9:45 stopped at Daldovee, Mr. Bogle's, to breakfast. We walked round the grounds, which though well brossed for a farm, were totally devoid of that artificial decoration which requires a constant attention and repair, had yet more natural beauties than any which we had yet seen. The Estate consisted of hills, or Knowls, of easy ascent, and half encompassed by the Clyde, which was one of the boundaries of it, and almost equalled the Tay in the beauty of its Stream.[130]

Hastings took note of the landscaped trees which had been a particular source of pride for Bogle's father. "A double row of Beeches planted by Mr. Bogle's father, and grown to a good size, coasted the river and surrounded the rest of the grounds which require nothing but the plough and solhom [?] to make a neat and sufficient Walk round them."

The visit was only for a morning. "About Noon we took our leave of the Family, Mr. Bogle still accompanying us."[131] The diary entries offered no affectionate afterthoughts about his friend from Bengal. There was no mention of Bogle's two daughters from India. The girls by this time would have been about twelve years old, likely to have still been living at home under the care of George's sisters. But this was, in Scotland as in Bengal, still predominantly a man's world in which wives, sisters, and daughters were not normally deserving of remark.

Hastings' Scottish journal, and his general response to India, offers another example of the contradictory possibilities within the Enlightenment. Hastings is a controversial figure in the history of the empire. On the one hand, by the 1890s he had become the great founding hero of the British empire in India, which is why Curzon and Younghusband tried to associate themselves with him. But during his own lifetime he was held up by Edmund Burke, Charles James Fox, Philip Francis, and other leaders of the impeachment as an example of all that was rotten

---

[129] Journal of a Tour to Scotland, September 13, 1787 and September 15, 1787, Warren Hastings Papers, Add. 39889, fos. 2, 37, BL.
[130] *Ibid.*, September 25, 1787 and September 26, 1787, fos. 39, 42.
[131] *Ibid.*, September 26, 1787, f. 42.

in the British enterprise in India. He can also be viewed as an appealing figure of the Enlightenment era because of his interest in Indian history, languages, religions, and cultures. As we already mentioned in another context, he was a founding member, along with William Jones, of the Asiatic Society whose aim was to bring the achievements of Indian culture to the attention of hitherto ignorant European audiences.

In contrast to Charles Grant who argued that British rule could only become successful if the nature of India was radically altered, Hastings had "a warm tolerance for the customs of India and he sought, in his own striking phrase to create a system for 'reconciling the people of England to the nature of Hindostan.'"[132] In a reflective moment, revealing Enlightenment-era hesitancies about empires, Hastings had written while still in Bengal that

the dominion exercised by the British Empire in India is fraught with many radical and incurable defects... All that the wisest institution can effect in such a system can only be to improve the advantages of a temporary possession, and to protract that decay, which sooner or later must end it.[133]

Hastings recognized the integrity of Indian cultures and, after a sober analysis, which acknowledged British defects, concluded that Britain could only be a passing presence on the subcontinent, expediently tending to its own business.

In defending his harsh revenue-raising measure during war-time Hastings claimed he was merely doing what other rulers of Bengal had done before him. It is possible to see this as evidence that Hastings believed in the notion of Eastern despotism, thus making him an early example of Orientalist modes of thinking. But Hastings had some quite specific precedents in mind when he made such a defense. Peter Marshall has noted that during a decade of war back in the 1740s Aliverdi Khan pursued similar methods: "all restraint in making fiscal demands was abandoned. Zamindars, office holders, bankers, merchants and the European Companies were all harried ruthlessly... The Raja of Burdwan was said to have been forced to yield Rs 10,000,000."[134] It was such practices that Hastings had in mind when he claimed he was simply doing what other "lords of Bengal" had done in times of war. This merciless extractor of revenues was also the sensitive intellectual who admired Indian cultures, and who fought against those who wished to anglicize the regime in Bengal because they thought English ways were best. There was no hint yet in Hastings of the view which had begun to take hold by the 1830s, that Britain's presence in India needed to be indefinite because Indians were

---

[132] Embree, *Charles Grant and British Rule in India*, p. 143.   [133] *Ibid.*, p. 142.
[134] Marshall, *Bengal. The British Bridgehead*, p. 71.

incapable of modernizing and ruling themselves until they had been thoroughly Westernized. For Hastings there could be no civilizing mission in India because India had already been civilized.

These paradoxical qualities informed Hastings' Scottish journal. During his journey Hastings occasionally made cultural comparisons and categorical judgments that put non-English peoples in their places. As he got north of the river Tay into Highland country, for example, he was struck by the poverty of the people and the ruinous state of their homes, describing the "Highland Hutts [as] not much more elegant than Hottentot Kraals," and suggesting that the land on which these improvident people lived should be sold off into lots so that it could be improved.[135] But Hastings also made judgments in favor of other cultures.

Shortly after leaving the Bogle estate at Daldowie he made a comparison between manufacturing in India and Britain, prompted by his visit to a Scottish textile factory. This region was one of the earliest to witness the emergence of new industrial towns – such as Paisley and Lanark – where innovations in production methods were making Britain into the world's first industrial power. Hastings toured one of the new factories, and paid close attention to the machinery used and the cloth that was produced. Here is his assessment:

Every contemplative mind must be pleased with the mechanical Efforts of human Invention, which at the same time abridge labour and give bread and Incitement to Industry. But I think that the Skill which is bestowed upon the Cotton manufactories is misapplied. The simple and rude process which the Inhabitants of Bengal use for the preparation of their Cotton to fit for the reel or spindle, does certainly yield a smoother and more united thread, or (as I think is the term) a better staple, than any that is spun in England or Scotland: or Perhaps the Cotton of India is better in Quality: I suspect too that the west-Indian cotton is gathered before it is sufficiently ripe. From one of these Causes the Difference must arise which is so visible in the manufactories of Cotton in Great Britain and India. The Cloths of the latter are smooth and perfect from the loom. The European are fuzzy, with Ends of broken fibres covering its Surface. To remove this blemish, they singe the nap by passing the Cloth lightly over a red hot roller of Iron, an operation, which, however skillfully performed, must injure the fabrick. In Effect I have been told that the Paisley Cloths grow brown with frequent washing, which may be ascribed to the same causes which produces the Spots in Cloths which are called Iron moulds.[136]

Hastings began by noting the historical significance of these fundamental changes in manufacturing but ended by remarking that Indian textiles remained superior to these new British products.

---

[135] Journal of a Tour to Scotland, September 15, 1787, Warren Hastings Papers, Add. 39889, f. 23.
[136] *Ibid.*, f. 44.

Hastings may have struggled to find fashionable romantic language to describe mountain scenery, but he was eloquent on this practical subject which could be analyzed with evidence based on his long experience in India. He took the time to make a detailed technical comparison between Indian and British ways of producing cotton cloth. The Paisley factories, along with those in Manchester and other British textile towns, were, over the next forty years, to cause severe problems for Indian spinners and weavers as these cheaper factory textiles, aided by Britain's imperial position in India, flooded into Indian markets. (The factory-made "Paisley pattern" cloth, with its tear-drop motif, was copied from Kashmiri originals.) But that had not yet happened. In the 1780s India still accounted for about 20 percent of the world manufacturing output, Britain only about 4 percent.[137] All the European East Indian companies had been created in the 1600s to gain access to these quality goods from India and other Asian producers. Hastings took systematic account of all the factors that might affect quality – the nature of the cotton crop itself, what the hot-rolling machine did to the fabric, and so on. But after paying careful attention to what these new methods entailed, he delivered his firm opinion that Indian cloth was of better quality. He evaluated all the evidence and concluded that India, even as Britain lauded itself for its revolutionary industrial methods, still outperformed Britain when it came to product quality. In Hastings' commentary, Britain's textile production was still somewhat primitive in contrast to the original and superior Indian manufactures. In this passage, for a moment, Britain still seems rather provincial.

During his Scottish tour Hastings also spent time with David Anderson, Bogle's old friend from Bengal. As we have seen, Anderson had returned to his family estate in Lothian a rich and well-esteemed man. He kept up a correspondence with Hastings, and made visits to Hastings at his country estate in England. The two met up again during Hastings' Scottish trip, parting the day that Hastings went to Daldowie. An exchange of letters in the Anderson papers sums up the contradictory impact of the Enlightenment on Anderson and Bogle as they forwarded the Company interests (and their own) in India.

In his early years in Bengal, Anderson had corresponded with Alexander Mackenzie, an old family friend. These letters were full of lively commentary on Indian history and culture. Mackenzie thanked Anderson for writing at such length from India and praised his intellectual efforts: "your good sense, under the direction of Providence, led you

---

[137] Paul Kennedy, *The Rise and Fall of the Great Powers* (New York: Vintage Books, 1989), p. 149.

to the Study of the Persian language by the help of which, the Laws, Customs, and manners of the Different Indian nations . . . are become familiar to you." Mackenzie wrote that Anderson's "minute enquiry into the progress of their arts and sciences pleases me not a little." He was delighted that Anderson did not seem to be all-consumed with making money. He assured Anderson that he could not

express the pleasure I feel on perusal of your modest and manly Letter, which reflects no small Honour on your Understanding as it Evidently shows your greater thirst after Knowledge and Wisdom than after the Golden Calf so generally worshipped . . . Your account of the Arabian Conquest in India seems well founded, for we read that the arts and sciences flourished there long before their Irruption into it.[138]

In this correspondence we have another example of ordinary Enlightenment-era figures giving thoughtful recognition to the cultural achievements of India. There is a clear understanding on Anderson's part that he had come into contact with a culture that had done great things long before any similar European accomplishments. Mackenzie agreed with Anderson's respect for Indian civilizations, and pointed out that "the Primitive [i.e. the ancient] Indians were the first Inventors of Astrology and Astronomy."[139]

But there was another side to the correspondence which dealt with material opportunities in India rather than the cultural achievements of India. Mackenzie anticipated that Anderson's broad intellectual curiosity would enable him to make money in India with a clear conscience – and might helpfully detract from any potential criticism back in Britain of his fortune-making efforts. Mackenzie assured Anderson that his interest in the history and culture of India "raise your stature and earn the esteem of commercial and legislative management . . . by the prudent discharge of which, a plentifull Fortune may be acquired with Reputation and Honour, and without the reproachful Epithet of Nabob lately censured by a British Parliament."[140] Six months later, Mackenzie was even more explicit. "There is neither money nor credit to be had in this country but many estates advertised for Sale. Make haste then dear David and transmitt a round Sum to purchase, for a pleasant Song, a place to be dressed and ornamented for your reception when you chuse to return to your worthy family the stems and branches of which enjoy perfect health."[141]

---

[138] Alexander Mackenzie to David Anderson, Edinburgh, June 5, 1773, David Anderson Papers, Add. 45430, f. 282–f. 285.
[139] *Ibid.* [140] *Ibid.*
[141] Alexander Mackenzie to David Anderson, Stony Bank, December 13, 1773, David Anderson Papers, Add. 45430, f. 297.

In these letters we can see laid out the two aspects of Anderson's career in Bengal. On the one side, there was an opportunity to learn things about the peoples and cultures of India which would contribute to the laudable goals of the Enlightenment – a better understanding of the universal human condition and of the grand unfolding of history. On the other side, there was the opportunity to make money. In Anderson's case, money-making eventually trumped the intellectual quest. He always retained an interest in Indian languages and cultures, as did any servant of the Company who hoped for a successful career, but that aspect receded into the background. The correspondence with Mackenzie about India's cultural heritage had taken place in 1773. When Anderson left India in 1785, with his fortune in hand, there were no final reflections about the richness of Indian civilizations. It was his own riches that mattered as he toted them up in his cabin on the *Barrington*. He never wished to set foot in Bengal again. Anderson's case suggests, when it comes to understanding the underlying forces behind empires, that economic factors, in the final analysis, outweigh the cultural ones.

It is a pity that Bogle did not get back to Daldowie. He might have had time there to reflect on his experiences in Bengal, Bhutan, and Tibet, and written about them in ways which would have answered all the questions that are raised by his career in India. It is also a pity that Hastings, who did get to Daldowie, was silent on those Bogle daughters who had come all the way from India, and that he made no comment about Bogle's possible Tibetan wife. It would also have been revealing if we had some final thoughts on Bogle from his friend Anderson now that he was comfortably ensconced on his Scottish estate. But that is the nature of history – the record of the past is always fragmentary. If Bogle had lived into the 1820s, as his contemporary Charles Grant managed to do, he might have come under the influence of the new ideas on religion and race that were re-shaping British views on India. His early death in 1781 meant he was untouched by these new ways of thinking about empire. Bogle remains for us a laboratory specimen of an ambiguous agent of empire in the Enlightenment era.

In the writings of Bogle that have survived there is a constant tension between an Enlightenment view of the world and an imperial view. The two were intertwined but his Enlightenment orientation did not inevitably lead Bogle into imperial postures. It provided him with a critical perspective on some aspects of his own culture, and encouraged him to respect other cultures he encountered on his travels. Bogle's writings on Tibet and Bhutan show that he genuinely believed (to use Hastings' phrasing from his private commission to Bogle) that "every nation excels others in some particular art or science."[142] Curzon and Younghusband never exchanged such views about the non-British peoples they encountered in their imperial activities.

On the other hand, Hastings and Bogle were fully aware that their position in India ultimately rested on the exercise of military and economic power. The East India Company had established itself in India for trade; it had to fight wars to win and expand its bridgehead in Bengal. It deployed a standing army in numerous campaigns to defend its interests across India. As Peter Marshall has observed, for the British in Bengal "the Army had first call on their resources." He estimates that between 1761 and 1771, 44 percent of total spending was for the army and fortifications, and subsidies for wars in the Madras and Bombay presidencies.[143] This emphasis held true right down to the end of British rule in India with "defence" always taking by far the largest share of the budget, typically accounting for 30 percent or so of expenditures even in the 1920s and 1930s.[144] Bogle's own mission to Tibet was the result of the war between the Company and Bhutan; he was blocked because of Chinese and Tibetan commercial and military concerns.

The circumstances in the daily lives of Anderson and Bogle in Bengal, with the myriad cultural encounters and the new cross-cultural gender issues they negotiated with their Indian "wives" and "families," were ultimately shaped by these basic economic, military, and political factors. As Bogle admitted to his brother, "We have carried things to a great Height [in India]." The acquisitive and aggressive human instincts that led to the British takeover in India had not been invented by the Enlightenment.

---

[142] Private Commission to Mr. Bogle, Fort William, May 16, 1774, Lamb, *Bhutan and Tibet*, p. 48.

[143] Marshall, *Bengal. The British Bridgehead*, p. 135.

[144] Military expenses remained by far the biggest item in the annual budget of British India right down to 1947. For example, the three largest expenditure categories (Provincial and Central together) in the 1923–1924 budget were tallied as follows by the Director of Public Information of the Government of India: Military Services 30 percent, Railways 12 percent, Police, Jails, and Justice 10 percent. L. F. Rushbrook Williams, C. B. E., *India in 1924–1925* (Calcutta: Government of India Central Publication Branch, 1925), pp. 118–119. Such figures, going all the way back to the 1770s, are a revealing commentary on British imperial priorities in India. Education expenditures accounted for 5 percent of the 1923–1924 budget.

6　Tibet lessons

Both Bogle and Younghusband in their different ways contributed to the romantically exotic image of Tibet which has shaped Western responses to that country right down to present times. Bogle's journals and letters left a picture of a simple and happy people protected behind the Himalayan mountains. In Younghusband's book summing up Tibet's relations with British India, he rapturously described a transcendental spiritual moment as he contemplated the bare mountains round Lhasa. In both cases, at the end of the story, Tibet became a uniquely isolated place of contented simplicity and extraordinary human spirituality.

This persistent image of Tibet as a Shangri-La is anathema to those scholars who study Tibet. While other places in the world have been seen by outsiders in mythical ways, the Tibet case is unusual because these images are so pervasive and tenacious that they still shape contemporary discourse about Tibet. In his book *Virtual Tibet. Searching for Shangri-La from the Himalayas to Hollywood* Orville Schell has provided a comprehensive description of how a mythical Tibet has been constructed in the popular imagination of the West.[1] "Fantasies of escape are naturally more powerful when rooted in real geography," Schell observes. "More than any other land, Tibet has provided . . . a corpus of romantic transferences and has continuously fired the imagination of Western escape artists." The reality of Tibet has been replaced by a virtual Tibet "hyperlinked to Hollywood."[2]

Tibet's remarkable hold on the imagination of the West has many consequences. It makes it difficult for many in the West to accept that Tibet might have a complex internal history just like any other country. In his summing up of the state of history writing on Tibet Alex McKay ruefully notes that

---

[1] Orville Schell, *Virtual Tibet. Searching for Shangri-La from the Himalayas to Hollywood* (New York: Henry Holt, 2000).
[2] *Ibid.*, pp. 16, 315.

Tibet is not the first or only place to be seen by outsiders in mythological terms or subject to colonial constructions for political purposes; what is unusual is the survival of these mythological modes of understanding into the modern age and also the complex interrelationship between the mythical and political constructs.[3]

The problem is compounded by the fact that when Tibet is studied in Western universities the scholarly endeavor is most often located in departments of religion rather than history or anthropology or sociology. Even when this scholarship is impeccably done, and broadly conceived, it presents Tibet as a site of exceptional religiosity rather than a country shaped by the usual range of economic, political, cultural, and regional forces. The combined impact of the popular media images of Tibet and the prominence of the religious approach to the study of Tibet creates difficulties for our understanding of Tibetan history. Approaches with a dual focus on the Shangri-La theme and on the densely detailed version of Buddhism that developed in Tibet tend to loom large in Western writings on that country. McKay laments this state of affairs:

> Tibetologists also face the unique problem that the dominant "history" of Tibet in the popular domain remains that which denies Tibetans a history: the historical image of Tibet as "Shangri-la"... As scholars such as Tsering Shakya and Don Lopez have demonstrated, Tibet's Shangri-la image has denied human agency and even humanity to the people of Tibet, marginalizing their real political and spiritual aspirations.[4]

Many of the British responses to the Younghusband mission illustrate the readiness of modern Europeans to treat Tibet in terms of fable rather than history. *The Times* and the *Daily Mail* had their own special correspondents accompanying the invading force. From January to August 1904, Perceval Landon's despatches to *The Times* described the expedition in the style of a serial adventure story, complete with half-page maps "to illustrate the Advance to Lhasa." When the British column arrived in Lhasa, *The Times* ran a lengthy piece headed "Description of the Forbidden City."[5] The titles of some of the books subsequently published, including *The Unveiling of Lhasa* (1905) written by the *Daily Mail* reporter who had accompanied the mission, and Thomas Holdich's *Tibet, the Mysterious* (1906), helped to maintain an alluring, secretive aura about Tibet.[6] An editorial in *The Times* on August 8, 1904 described the invasion as "a very brilliant feat of arms... a conspicuous success

---

[3] McKay, *The History of Tibet*, vol. I, p. 3.   [4] *Ibid.*, p. 6.
[5] *The Times*, August 6, 1904, p. 4; August 8, 1904, p. 3.
[6] Edmund Candler, *The Unveiling of Lhasa* (London: T. Nelson & Sons, 1905); Col. Sir Thomas H. Holdich KCMG, KCIE, CB, *Tibet, the Mysterious* (New York: F. A. Stokes, 1906).

achieved with the minimum of cost, and as such will hold a high place even among the efforts of the British in India." Choosing phrases that would evoke the magic of the moment for British readers, *The Times* editors observed that

It is not without a twinge of sentimental regret that we see opened up to the eyes of the Western world one of the few places on the earth round which still hangs something of the romance of mystery and inviolability. The few isolated travellers who have penetrated the heart of Tibet have not sufficed to dispel the mystery or seriously hamper the imagination.[7]

The "forbidden city" lived up to its reputation apparently, for in September another *Times* editorial commentary, taking its cue from Landon's "graphic letters," declared that "Lhasa the city of mystery, the seat of the strangest government in the world, seems to have satisfied even the eager expectations of its visitors."[8]

The Times' ebullient endorsement of Younghusband was part of its campaign to support the Tory government's Tibet policy against Liberal and Radical critics, but its eagerness to stir the imagination when it came to reporting on Tibet was typical of the romantic response to that country in the West. A perfect example of this orientation was on display in February 1905 in the middle of a debate in Parliament on the Younghusband mission. In the King's Speech at the opening of the new parliamentary session the government had set out a justification of its Tibet policy. It now had to defend that justification. Speaking on behalf of the Government, Lord Oranmore and Browne, the Irish peer, summed up the British invasion in the following astonishing language:

The expedition naturally created much interest in the public mind. It was felt that this was not a mere frontier war in which we were engaging to punish some marauding tribe. It was something much more serious, and much more wonderful than that. It was going into an unknown land, into Tibet the Mystical, the Mysterious, of which strange travellers' tales were told, but of which little or nothing was known with certainty. It was a visit to be paid to the Grand Lama in his palace-fortress to convince his ignorant and superstitious followers that not even a Buddha re-incarnate could resist the power of Britain. My Lords, we followed with intense interest the steps of our soldiers as they crossed the snow-clad passes of the forbidden land. We saw them attacked and attacked again, and, ever victorious, pursuing their way till the goal was reached, and Lhasa, the Unknown, the Holy City, lay before them. The description, my Lords, reads like a page from some fairy tale.[9]

In such ways did historical events in Tibet – in this case an invasion by an overwhelming military force equipped with modern weapons –

[7] *The Times*, August 8, 1904, p. 7.   [8] *The Times*, September 6, 1904, p. 6.
[9] *Parliamentary Debates*, vol. CXLI (1905), col. 12, February 14, 1905.

become transformed into a fabulous tale. As *The Times* nonchalantly acknowledged, when the subject of Tibet came up in the West there was little to "seriously hamper the imagination."

In view of Younghusband's extreme animosity towards lamas in 1903 and 1904, it is surprising that his mission contributed to this image of Tibet. But during and after the invasion both he and O'Connor wrote about Tibet in ways which evoked the kind of responses that defined Tibet in the Western imagination. An example of this inclination to make Tibet an exotic place was apparent during the early stages of the expedition when both men gave a semblance of credence to the possibility that reincarnated lamas had preternatural powers of memory which enabled them personally to recall an historical event that had taken place 130 years ago. To be sure, this portrayal of Tibetan lamas was deployed for expedient diplomatic purposes, but the fact that Younghusband chose this tactic revealed a readiness to retail incredible anecdotes about Tibet. When he wrote to his wife and father, and to the Foreign Department of the Government of India, about reincarnated Lamas and historical memory – how "the present man" might have been able to remember "his" meeting with Bogle – he furthered the impression of Tibet as a place of strange religiosity. It was akin to a non-Christian traveler in Roman Catholic Europe purveying shallow comments, without providing any theological context, about Catholic believers claiming to be eating the body and drinking the blood of Christ, and of bishops thinking themselves personally touched by the hands of St. Peter.

Younghusband's epiphany inside Tibet after the completion of his military mission added to this sense that Tibet was above all a place of extraordinary spirituality. It was a moment that had a lasting impact on how Younghusband has been viewed by his biographers, softening his image as an obsessed imperialist. Although he kept up a public observance of the Church of England conventions of his time, and of his social class, Younghusband had been on an intense religious quest for much of his adult life. He read widely in books that challenged conventional beliefs. Like many thinking men and women in Victorian England, his first questioning was prompted by the impact of the new theory of evolution on biblical accounts of history. "As a boy I accepted everything on authority," he wrote in 1940. "What made me think was an article in 1888 or 1889 by, I think, Huxley on Evolution."[10] Like many contemporaries, including the young Mohandas Gandhi, he had also been profoundly

---

[10] Younghusband Note, March 25, 1940, Younghusband Collection, MSS. EUR. F197/ 323, BL.

moved by Tolstoy's *The Kingdom of God is Within You* (1894).[11] Ever since reading Tolstoy he had wanted to write a book explaining his own spiritual insights. It was in Tibet that he finally crossed the spiritual threshold he had been longing to reach all his adult life.

There were intimations of this transformation in the Chumbi valley in December 1903 when he read Annie Besant's theosophical ruminations about the all-encompassing spiritual nature of the cosmos. He wrote to his wife that he had also just read "a beautiful book on 'Cosmic Consciousness' which I will explain to you sometime and which gives a most intensely beautiful and peaceful idea of the universe."[12] But the great transformation took place as he rode away from Lhasa. He paused, turned, and as he looked back over the bare Tibetan mountains the exquisite moment of spiritual fulfillment occurred:

I gave myself up to all the emotions of this eventful time. My task now over and every anxiety passed . . . and as I now looked towards that mysterious purply haze in which the sacred city was once more wrapped . . . I was insensibly suffused with an almost intoxicating sense of elation and good-will. This exhilaration of the moment grew and grew until it thrilled me with overpowering intensity . . . All nature and all humanity were bathed in a glowing radiancy; and life for the future seemed nought but burgeoning and light . . . That single hour on leaving Lhasa was worth all the rest of a lifetime.[13]

The landscape of Tibet seemed to have exerted a strange power over Younghusband, as though the geographical location itself had spiritual properties. Back in 1774 Bogle had described the religious ceremonies made by his Tibetan and Bengali traveling companions at the foot of Chomalhari. Younghusband made no references in this passage to Buddhist and Hindu beliefs in a spiritualized landscape. His thinking at this moment was instead a harbinger of a Western response to Tibet that was to become widespread in the following decades – a response in which Tibet's remoteness itself became a source of inspiration, cleansing Europeans from all the baleful influences associated with industrialization, urbanization, and consumerism.

Much of the rest of Younghusband's life was devoted to exploring the new spiritual world that had opened before him in the Tibet mountains. He abandoned the traditional Christian concept of a father-like creator of the world and adopted the view that there was some animating spirit

---

[11] French, *Younghusband*, p. 109.
[12] Younghusband to Helen Younghusband, Chumbi, December 30, 1903, Younghusband Collection, MSS. EUR. F197/174, BL; French, *Younghusband*, p. 206.
[13] Younghusband, *India and Tibet. A History of the Relations which have subsisted between the two countries from the time of Warren Hastings to 1910 with a particular account of the Mission to Lhasa of 1904* (London: J. Murray, 1910), pp. 326, 327.

suffusing all living and material things in the universe. Instead of treating his Christianity in exclusionist terms he now looked for commonalities across all human expressions of spirituality. All religions were attempts to comprehend this spiritual force which sustained nature and humans alike. He believed he had now finally grasped the true nature of the cosmos: "I regard the whole universe as living, as animated by a Creative Spirit which is for me God." This spirit appeared in many forms and had been "manifested in special degree in certain men, Buddha, Jesus, Mohamed."[14] During the 1920s and 1930s Younghusband was an enthusiastic member of the World Congress of Faiths, an organization he had helped to create, devoted to bringing together the common spiritual insights shared by religions round the globe.[15] His image of Tibet as a land dominated by bigoted monks had been transformed into an image of Tibet as a deep spiritual pool from which thirsty souls could drink.

After Younghusband's death the obituary notice in the *New York Times* linked him to the burgeoning Hollywood myths about Tibet which had begun with the film version of James Hilton's novel *Lost Horizons* (1933). The protagonist in Hilton's novel was a veteran British diplomat, Robert Conway, who journeyed into the Himalayas looking for the enchanted land where he would find inner peace and an understanding of his place in the universe. The obituary began by identifying Younghusband as the man "who opened Lhasa to the British after the expedition to the Forbidden City in 1904" and proceeded to place him in the context of the popular depictions of Shangri-La:

> If, as James Hilton strongly suggests in *Lost Horizons*, Shangri La is somewhere in Tibet ... then Sir Francis Younghusband probably came closer than anyone else to being Robert Conway ... the fictional hero who reached the strangest of cities beyond the Himalayan storms – and who, leaving through an error of judgment, insisted on fighting his way back, where he presumably took over the job of the Methuselah-like high lama who had chosen him as an heir.[16]

As was to be the case for many Westerners in the twentieth century, mythological Tibet had cast its spell on Younghusband, and on those who wrote about him.

The ways in which Europeans could become entranced by these aspects of Tibet also comes out in O'Connor's writings in the aftermath of the 1904 invasion. He convinced himself that the real Panchen

---

[14] Younghusband Note, March 25, 1940, Younghusband Collection, MSS. EUR. F197/323, BL.
[15] French, *Younghusband*, pp. 365, 367.
[16] *New York Times*, August 2, 1942, p. 39.

Lama he had met was just like the fictional "Teshoo Lama" in Rudyard Kipling's *Kim* (1901). That famous novel of empire told the story of the young orphan Kimball O'Hara who worked with a venerable Tibetan lama to forestall Russian designs along India's northern border. Who was Kipling's inspiration for his lama? The literary critic Laurie Hovell McMillan suggests that Kipling's lama may even have been inspired by Bogle's 1774 description of Tibet – "it is as if the novel has swallowed Bogle whole."[17] It is interesting to note, too, that Kipling used the same spelling as Samuel Turner's 1800 narrative *An Account of an Embassy to the Court of the Teshoo Lama in Tibet*. But Peter Hopkirk who has written an entire book on the search for the possible historical inspirations for the characters in *Kim* does not cite either Bogle or Turner as potential sources.[18]

Moreover, the lama in *Kim* is quite different from the two Panchen Lamas whom Bogle and O'Connor met. Kipling's lama was a wandering ascetic who crossed and re-crossed the Himalayan passes picking up valuable snippets of information about the nefarious activities of Russian agents. The Panchen Lamas encountered by the British envoys in 1774 and 1904 were revered holy men with highly advanced expertise in Buddhist theology and cosmology, but they also had important political, administrative, and diplomatic roles. They remained most of the time at their monastic seat at Tashilhunpo, or occasionally, as in the 1780 journey of the Third Panchen Lama to Peking, on diplomatic visits. Kipling seems simply to have borrowed the name of his lama (without thinking at all about the real Panchen Lama) from the general British usage, which began with Bogle and Hastings, of referring to the Panchen Lama as the "Tashi" or "Teshoo" Lama.

When he returned to Britain, O'Connor met Kipling and the two of them compared notes on Tibetan lamas. O'Connor, a self-confessed admirer of Kipling, was introduced to him by Perceval Landon whom he had befriended when Landon had served as *The Times* correspondent accompanying the 1904 invading force. Landon's *Opening of Tibet. An Account. . . of the Mission sent there by the English Government in the Year 1903–1904* (1905) had become one of the most popular descriptions of the expedition that had "unveiled the forbidden city" to Western eyes. In his memoirs O'Connor recalled that

---

[17] Laurie Hovell McMillan, *English in Tibet, Tibet in English. Self-Presentation in Tibet and the Diaspora* (New York: Palgrave, 2001), p. 79; Teltscher, *The High Road to China*, p. 260.

[18] Peter Hopkirk, *Quest for Kim. In Search of Kipling's Great Game* (Ann Arbor: University of Michigan Press, 1996).

Kipling was especially interested in meeting someone who had been to Tibet and was a personal friend of a Lama! *Kim* had been published only a few years before and we discussed it at great length. Needless to say, I am a devoted admirer of the book and more impressed every time I read it by his amazing grasp of detail . . . [Kipling] sketched a real Lama to the life – in fact the poor Tashi Lama as I knew him.[19]

O'Connor thought "his" Panchen Lama was just like the one in *Kim*. He allowed himself to be rather carried away here – as the exclamation mark suggests.

O'Connor was perfectly aware of the difference between Kipling's mendicant lama, traveling the pilgrim trails of north India and the Himalayas in search of the sacred river, and the real Panchen Lama. While he was serving as the British Trade Agent at Gyantse O'Connor had played a key role in arranging a trip to Calcutta in 1906 for the Panchen Lama to meet the Prince of Wales during his state visit to India. He understood that there were political tensions between the Dalai Lama, who had fled to Urga in Mongolia ahead of Younghusband's invasion, and the Panchen Lama. The Dalai Lama, as we have noted, had been suspicious of the Panchen Lama's friendship with the British ever since those first meetings at Khamba Dzong, and remained concerned about his continuing dealings with the British regime in India after 1904.[20]

O'Connor was part of the diplomatic effort to cultivate a friendly relationship with the Panchen Lama designed to build up a rival authority to the Dalai Lama inside Tibet who would be better disposed towards the British. He reported to the Foreign Department of the Government of India in October 1904 that during their first meeting the Panchen Lama "referred to the high-handed proceedings of the Lhasa Government and asked me whether we should be able to assist him should they try to act oppressively towards him in the future."[21] O'Connor had replied encouragingly that if the Panchen Lama responded to British diplomatic overtures "he would find us good and friendly neighbours."[22] In spite of O'Connor's involvement in these political maneuvers, and his by now extensive knowledge of Tibetan politics, he could not resist, when writing his memoirs, conflating the real Panchen Lama with the mystery-laden character in Kipling's *Kim*.

[19] O'Connor, *Things Mortal*, p. 235.
[20] Parshotam Mehra, *Tibetan Polity, 1904–1937. The Conflict between the 13th. Dalai Lama and the 9th. Panchen Lama* (Wiesbaden: Otto Harrassowitz, 1976), pp. 13, 22–42.
[21] O'Connor to Secretary of the Foreign Department, Government of India, October 26, 1904, FO 17/1753, National Archives, Kew.
[22] O'Connor, *Things Mortal*, p. 98.

Perhaps the most remarkable moment of cultural exchange in these two British encounters with Tibet took place in 1774 without Bogle even being aware of it. In one of his letters Bogle described his journey to Tibet as "this Strange Trip" and in a very strange way his mission became a small thread in the fabric of Tibetan Buddhism. In 1775 the Panchen Lama wrote a guide for those who wished to attempt the journey to Shambala, the sacred kingdom which later became transformed in Western readings into the enchanted land of Shangri-La.[23] The text described "the magical hazards and symbolic trails encountered en route to the hidden land." Its title was *An Explanation of Shambala together with a Narrative of the Holy Land.* According to Edwin Bernbaum, this version of the journey, although "it clearly follows the route description of an earlier guidebook found in the Tengyur, the commentary section of the Tibetan canon," became the most respected of all Tibetan writings on the subject. This 1775 version of the journey to Shambala remains even today "the most popular and widely read guidebook... When speaking about the journey to the hidden kingdom, Tibetans usually refer to this text which has tended to supersede all others."[24]

In the Kalacakra tradition of Tibetan Buddhism, within which Lobsang Palden Yeshes was working, Shambala is both an ideal and an actual place. As Donald Lopez vividly explains,

in the texts associated with the Kalacakra Tantra the kingdom of Shambhala is said to be located north of the Himalayan range. It is a land devoted to the practice of the *Kalacakra Tantra* which the Buddha himself had entrusted to Shambhala's king. Shambhala is shaped like a giant lotus and is filled with sandalwood forests and lotus lakes, all encircled by a great range of snowy peaks. In the center of the kingdom is the capital of Kalapa, where the luster of the palaces, made from gold, silver, and jewels, outshines the moon; the walls of the palaces are plated with mirrors that reflect a light so bright that night is like day. In the very center of the city is the mandala of the Buddha Kalacakra. The inhabitants of the 960 million villages of Shambhala are ruled by a beneficent ruler, called the Kalkin. The laypeople are all beautiful and wealthy, free of sickness and poverty; the monks maintain their vows without the slightest infraction. They are all naturally intelligent and virtuous, devoted to the practice of the Vajrayana, although all

---

[23] The version of this guidebook which I read was the German translation made by Albert Grünwedel in 1915 – "Der Weg nach Sambhala des dritten Gross-Lama von bKra sis lhun po bzan dPal ldan Yeses aus dem tibetischen Original ubersetzt und mit dem Texte herausgegeben." It was published in the *Abhandlungen der Königlich Bayerischen Akademie der Wissenschaften Philosophisch-philologische und historische Klasse* 29 (Munich, 1915), pp. 1–118. I am grateful to Burkhard Quessel, Curator of the Tibetan Collections of the British Library, for helping me track it down.

[24] Edwin Bernbaum, *The Way to Shambhala. A Search for the Mythical Kingdom beyond the Himalayas* (Garden City, NY: Anchor Press, 1980), p. 182.

authentic forms of Indian Buddhism are preserved. The majority of those reborn there attain buddhahood during their lifetime in Shambhala.[25]

Those who are devotees of this tradition within Tibetan Buddhism

believe there are various ways of going to Shambhala ... The prevalent belief in these degenerate times is that it can only be achieved through death and rebirth because it is no longer possible to develop the superhuman powers needed to follow the guidebooks, but a number of Tibetans still believe it is possible to make the journey in this lifetime. There are stories of yogis or lamas with exceptional powers who have taken the journey; some tell of actually going there in their physical bodies.[26]

But Tibetans also speak in terms of "dream journeys which are sometimes difficult to distinguish from the visionary journeys of meditation."[27]

By whatever means the journey is made, it requires a highly advanced level of theological and mythological knowledge if it is to be completed successfully. The Panchen Lama's guidebook was written to help seekers who wished to reach the spiritually pure land attain the necessary level of religious knowledge and self-discipline.[28] In so far as there is a notional geographical location for the land of Shambala, it is situated somewhere north of the Himalayan range. It is extremely difficult to reach, and "the journey is fraught with dangers, both natural and supernatural: the traveller must cross vast deserts, forests full of wild beasts, mountains inhabited by beautiful goddesses, demons, flesh eaters, and hungry ghosts. Only those who are neither tempted nor terrified may reach the perfect land of Shambala."[29]

The Panchen Lama devoted the first half of his book to the geography and history of India, the birthplace of the historical Buddha and hence the holy land of the title. In writing his account of India he drew on material provided by various informants, and one of those informants was none other than George Bogle. In his journal Bogle mentioned a moment during their conversations when the Panchen Lama quizzed him about Bengal and "desired me to inquire particularly about the situation of a town called Shambul about which he said the pundits of Bengal would be able to inform me."[30] As Albert Grünwedel, the German scholar who first translated the Panchen Lama's text from Tibetan in 1915, explained in his introduction, "the book was written in 1775 ... In the winter of

---

[25] Donald S. Lopez Jr., *Prisoners of Shangri-La. Tibetan Buddhism and the West* (University of Chicago Press, 1998), p. 182.

[26] Bernbaum, *The Way to Shambhala*, p. 157.   [27] *Ibid.*, pp. 159, 161.

[28] *Ibid.*, pp. 159, 161.   [29] Teltscher, *The High Road to China*, p. 140.

[30] Bogle's Journal, Negotiations with the Tashi Lama at Tashilhunpo, December 1774–April 1775, Lamb, *Bhutan and Tibet*, p. 268.

1774–75 the English envoy George Bogle was at his court...What the Panchen Lama wrote about India comes from the conversations with Bogle Sahib."[31]

The Panchen Lama directly incorporated Bogle's benign account of the East India Company's role into his description of the Indian holy land. The Mughal emperor had given the Company "a merchant house at the place called Kalikata." At first things had gone well but as the Mughal state "through internal discord began to disintegrate, the Company had to make arrangements for its own protection...No longer protected by the Mughal peace, and under threat of being killed, the Company brought soldiers out of their own land. From Varendra and Bengal they took everything up to Varanasi and brought it under their protection."[32] Contemporary Bengal appears briefly in the narrative and is described just as Bogle said it was. The English king lived on an island across the sea; the English merchants were murderously attacked when living peacefully in Calcutta.[33]

In this manner Bogle made his way into the most popular Tibetan guidebook for the journey to Shambala. Such surprising borrowing of information evokes a wonderful moment of encounter between Tibetan and British cultures as each man brought to their convivial meetings a thirst for knowledge. Bogle and Lobsang Palden Yeshes liked each other enormously. They talked at length about politics, diplomacy, geography, and trade. They talked about even larger things as they shared ideas on astrology and the nature of the universe. In the Panchen Lama's case he was attempting to make sense of the human condition using concepts from the Kalacakra tradition within Buddhism. This particular Buddhist system became popular in Tibet but, as David Snellgrove notes, "it appears to remain more closely attached to recognizable Hindu terminology than other tantras."[34] It may have been that feature of the Panchen Lama's Buddhism that impelled him to pay so much attention to the Indian holy land – and which enabled Bogle to follow along with his rudimentary understanding of Hinduism.

As with the numerous gods and goddesses within Hinduism there "are a bewildering variety of Buddha names" within tantric Buddhism. In the same way as many ordinary Hindu believers worship their particular gods, so "the simple Tibetan believers" treat these many representations of the

---

[31] Grünwedel, "Der Weg nach Sambhala," p. 5.
[32] Ibid., p. 44.   [33] Ibid., pp. 44, 45.
[34] David Snellgrove, Indo-Tibetan Buddhism. Indian Buddhists and their Tibetan Successors (London and Boston: Shambhala, 1987), p. 264.

Buddha as the gods of their religion. But a true adept recognizes that these representations are "mere expressions of absolute buddhahood" just as sophisticated Hindus see all their gods and goddesses merely as ways to help believers approach the ultimate mysteries of the unknowable creative force of Brahma. For the highly trained believer within Tibetan Buddhism "all these divine forms are absorbed by him into the luminous state of the Void, and it is out of the Void that they are duly summoned by meditative practice."[35]

The main texts in the Kalacakra tradition "contain sermons delivered by the Buddha in which he describes Shambala and the role it will play in history." As Bernbaum sums up this version of Buddhism:

All three parts of the Kalacakra Tantra come together in the principal of a Primordial Buddha who underlies everything covered by their separate teachings – the external world, body and mind, and the realm of the deities. Although he comes close to monotheistic conceptions of God, he does not create the universe as a creator distinct from his creation but is, instead, the very essence of it. All things and beings, from stones to Buddhas, are his manifestations. Each in its true nature is the Primordial Buddha. Beyond form and emptiness, he lies somewhere in the unity of the two. According to the Kalacakra, he is ultimate reality, empty even of emptiness.[36]

The challenging complexity of the Kalacakra texts stems from their attempt "to embrace all phenomena, from the workings of the mind to the layout of the universe, in one all-encompassing system of knowledge and practice."[37]

This attempt to understand all phenomena in the human and the natural worlds was also what European thinkers of the Enlightenment era were attempting to do. The Panchen Lama was a highly trained thinker within his culture. He was deeply enough informed about theology and the history of thinking on these profound matters, and so self-confident about his knowledge, that he wrote the guidebook to ensure a wide circulation of his ideas and to serve the millions of believers who looked to him for guidance in such matters. Bogle and Lobsang Palden Yeshes were not intellectual equals in their separate worlds. As we have agreed from the outset, Bogle was not at the top level of European thinkers whereas the Panchen Lama was in the first rank of Buddhist philosophers in his era. But Bogle was interested in acquiring a broader understanding of the human condition and of the world he saw around him. We can imagine these two men in their long conversations in the winter and spring of 1774–1775 enjoying each other's company so much because they both

---

[35] *Ibid.*, p. 206.   [36] Bernbaum, *The Way to Shambhala*, p. 127.   [37] *Ibid.*, p. 122.

saw themselves as embarked on a similar quest to gain an understanding of the universe and all life in it.

Bogle certainly responded warmly to the world-view of the older (if only by eight years) and wiser man. When he returned to Calcutta, he wrote that "I have learnt a great deal of Philosophy by my Pilgrimage."[38] It is tempting, but probably pushing too far, to interpret Bogle's comment that "the scenes ... I have met with [in Tibet] ... seem a perfect illusion ... as in a fairy dream" as a sign that he had picked up some knowledge of these Buddhist spiritual-dream journeys to far-off lands during his conversations with the Panchen Lama.[39] But it is consistent with all the evidence to say that both men were seeking enlightenment. Bogle attempted to understand different societies, cultures, and religions by means of the Enlightenment approaches he had absorbed from his reading – by observing, gathering evidence, and systematically comparing. The Panchen Lama pursued his enlightenment through spiritual discipline and by means of a religious epistemology. Both men viewed all humankind as connected. Both thought they could acquire knowledge and work their way towards a higher understanding. The serendipity of history had brought two human experiments in enlightenment together.

The fact that the Panchen Lama included information from Bogle in his *magnum opus* shows how much he trusted his new-found friend as an informant. The Panchen Lama apparently accepted Bogle's version of the Company's role in recent Indian history. He even tells us in his *Explanation of Shambala* that "these English were the best of all of them [the other Europeans in India]."[40] This exchange of information gives us a sense of two quite different world-views coming into contact. Bogle had come to forward the diplomatic and economic interests of the East India Company. The Panchen Lama listened to him on those matters. He told Bogle frankly about the opposition to his mission from Lhasa. He explained Tibet's relationship to China. He discussed trade. But at the same time as the Panchen Lama engaged, as a highly competent and fully informed participant, in these mundane issues, he was always thinking about spiritual matters which were of critical importance to him. As Bogle described Bengal and sketched out some facts about England, the Panchen Lama was listening with a religious as well as a practical curiosity. For the Panchen Lama the visit of this young British emissary

---

[38] George Bogle to David Anderson, Calcutta, October 26, 1775, David Anderson Papers, Add. 45421, f. 45, BL.

[39] Extract from Bogle's letter to one of his sisters, March 10, 1775, Lamb, *Bhutan and Tibet*, p. 276; Teltscher, *High Road to China*, p. 159.

[40] Grünwedel, "Der Weg nach Sambhala," p. 44.

presented an opportunity for him to ask questions about the current situation in Bengal and add some up-to-date details to his description of the Indian holy land in the important book he was writing about the perilous journey to Shambala.

Thus was Bogle infiltrated into a famous Tibetan Buddhist treatise. The equivalent on the other side to the Panchen Lama's theological quest was Bogle's earnest searching for knowledge during his own perilous journey through the mountains. In contrast to Bogle, however, the Panchen Lama managed to write his book before he died.

In following the trail to Shambala we are in danger of contributing to the image of Tibet as an enchanted spiritual land. These two encounters between Britain and Tibet in 1774–1775 and 1903–1904 were not about religion either for the Tibetans or for the British. They were about empires and resistance to empires. The British version of imperialism was not the only one at work in this part of the world. Looking at the variety of imperialisms that have swirled around Tibet provides some illuminating lessons about the relationship of Enlightenment and empire that we have been exploring.

On the British side the motives were clear enough. The Bogle mission was a tentative effort to gain access to the China market which, if successful, would have strengthened the position of the Company in Bengal and throughout India and much of Asia. The Younghusband mission was more explicit about its imperial goals. The British Indian government in 1903 was interested to some extent in trans-Himalayan trade, especially in getting tea from the estates in northern Bengal and Assam into the Tibet market. In his general memorandum on Tibet, Younghusband declared that "there is not the slightest doubt that Indian tea . . . could supplant Chinese tea" in Tibet.[41] There was even still some talk of Tibetan gold that can be traced back in Western writings about Tibet to Herodotus. During his mission Younghusband received a letter from Sir Thomas Holdich, who had retired from the Survey of India in 1898 and was to become President of the Royal Geographical Society in 1917. Holdich informed Younghusband "that he was a member of a syndicate formed for the purpose of starting an expert examination into the capabilities of Tibet . . . in the matter of minerals, especially gold."[42] Holdich added excitedly that "gold has been worked there from the days

[41] Younghusband, *Memorandum on Our Relations with Tibet*, pp. 32, 33.
[42] Younghusband to Louis W. Dane, Khamba Jong, September 2, 1903, Government of India, Foreign Department. Secret-E. Proceedings, November 1903, Nos. 118–158, Tibet Negotiations, BL.

of Herodotus!"[43] But the driving force behind the 1903–1904 mission was Curzon's obsessive conviction that Russia was about to establish a presence in Tibet which would threaten the British position in India and be a significant Russian gain in the Great Game for imperial control in Central Asia.

While the British had their imperial plans in 1774–1775 and 1903–1904 there were much more consequential imperial factors on the other side of the Himalayan mountains. Tibet could fend off British attempts at colonial interference but they had a far more formidable challenge to face from the Chinese empire. When Bogle first made contact with the Panchen Lama and his officials he was told directly that Tibet was subject to the authority of the Chinese emperor. He reported this information to Hastings in simple Western terms: "the Emperor of China is paramount sovereign."[44] By 1903, when Younghusband crossed into Tibet, Chinese authority had diminished almost to the point of non-existence. For the British, as we have seen, that was the nub of their problem with Tibet. The disintegrating influence of the Chinese meant that when the British negotiated treaties with the Chinese, the Chinese were unable to force the Tibetans to meet the treaty obligations.

One of the unanticipated consequences of the Younghusband invasion was to reinvigorate Chinese claims of sovereignty over Tibet.[45] The new Liberal Government in London, disturbed by the forward policy that the Younghusband expedition represented, conducted negotiations with Russia and China to review, amend, and clarify the convention made in Lhasa at the end of the invasion. China viewed these tripartite negotiations as an opportunity "to assert its sovereignty in Tibet and to replace the Tibetan officials in all dealings with the British government."[46] In

---

[43] Sir T. H. Holdich KCMG to Younghusband, Pall Mall, July 27, 1903, Government of India, Foreign Department. Secret-E. Proceedings, November 1903, Nos. 159–234, Tibet Negotiations, BL. In his *Histories*, Herodotus described giant ants which unearthed gold dust as they made their burrows. Once dismissed as a typically bizarre story from Herodotus there is now some evidence that he may have been right. He had got hold of some account of how gold was collected from ancient alluvial deposits in the high mountainous desert in the western Himalayas. See Michel Peissel, *The Ant's Gold. The Discovery of the Greek El Dorado in the Himalayas* (London: Collins, 1984) and "Himalayas Offer Clue to Legend of Gold-Digging Ants," *New York Times*, November 25, 1996.

[44] Bogle to Warren Hastings, Desheripgay, December 5, 1774, quoted in D. B. Diskalkar, "Bogle's Embassy to Tibet," *Indian Historical Quarterly* 9 (June 1933), pp. 420–438.

[45] Melvyn C. Goldstein, *A History of Modern Tibet 1913–1951* (Berkeley: University of California Press, 1989), p. 46.

[46] Jennifer Siegel, *Endgame. Britain, Russia and the Final Struggle for Central Asia* (London: I. B. Tauris, 2002), p. 45.

the course of those diplomatic agreements between Britain, China, and Russia in 1906 and 1907, Chinese suzerainty over Tibet was formally recognized for the first time in modern international law. As Hugh Richardson put the matter, "Chinese rights in Tibet were thus recognised to an extent to which the Chinese had been wholly unable to exercise them."[47]

These developments in the aftermath of the Younghusband expedition confirm an old lesson from history, that invasions of far-off countries by great powers often have unintended consequences. The Dalai Lama stopped off at Peking on his way back from Mongolia as part of his effort to clarify the current status of the relationship (although he did not perform the kow tow).[48] It was only the collapse of Manchu dynastic power following the 1911 revolution, and the subsequent period of internal disorder in China, that allowed the Thirteenth Dalai Lama to claim a *de facto* independence for Tibet. Hugh Richardson's stint as the British–Indian envoy at Lhasa in the 1930s and 1940s – the first European diplomat to be stationed in Lhasa – was one sign of this Tibetan attempt to distance their country from the Chinese empire.

The China–Tibet relationship is described in the West as a case of imperialism but it was different in significant ways from Western examples of imperialism. It "was expressed in what is popularly designated a 'patron–client' relationship in which the Tibetans acted as religious advisers to the emperor, who serves as the secular patron and military protector of the Tibetan 'priest'."[49] As Alex McKay notes, "the nature of the relationship was to have continuing and complex implications in regard to the post-1912 Tibetan claim to independent status."[50] China did indeed act as a protector to Tibet on occasion, as for example when a Chinese imperial army expelled the Nepalese invaders in 1792.

When the British tried to understand the relationship they used such phrases as "Chinese suzerainty" but that did not quite capture all the religious and cultural ideas in play. The lack of congruence between Asian and European terminology was apparent when Sir Ernest Satow, the British Ambassador in Peking, tried to get officials in the Ministry of Foreign Affairs to tell him the correct language to use for China's relationship to Tibet. Satow explained to Prince Ch'ing (Qing) that in English diplomatic usage "China was described as the 'suzerain' of Tibet" and he asked "what was the proper technical term in Chinese" to express

---

[47] Hugh Richardson, *Tibet and its History* (Oxford University Press, 1962), p. 94.
[48] Tsepon W. D. Shakabpa, *Tibet. A Political History* (New Haven: Yale University Press, 1967), p. 222.
[49] McKay, *History of Tibet*, vol. II, p. 13.   [50] *Ibid.*

that concept. Prince Ch'ing (Qing) replied that in Chinese "there was no proper word to express this."[51]

Thus while the Chinese claimed authority over Tibet they knew that it was not simply another province within their empire. In the aftermath of the Younghusband invasion, which had driven the Dalai Lama into exile, the Chinese thought about getting rid of all these historical ambiguities by bringing Tibet into the empire as another province. As Satow reported in November 1904, Chinese officials were now considering "whether they could not cut the Gordian knot by declaring their dependency [Tibet] a province, and so an integral part of the Empire of China."[52] But Prince Ch'ing (Qing) subsequently told Satow that they had decided not to attempt that radical solution because "to accomplish it [make Tibet a province within the empire] would be difficult."[53] Although not an integral part of the empire, Tibet was viewed by the Chinese as a dependency in the context of their shared traditional religio-political obligations; the two Ambans stationed in Lhasa were symbols of that claimed authority. Chinese officials also argued in diplomatic meetings with Western representatives like Satow that their eighteenth-century military operations in Tibet had effectively taken over the country. As Prince Ch'ing (Qing) explained to Satow: "We have conducted military operations in Tibet in Chi'ien Lung's reign [Qianlong, 1736–1795] and may be said to have subjugated it."[54]

There were many examples of Chinese behavior in Tibet which suggested they thought they had the right to act in an imperial manner. One such incident was reported by Sarat Chandra Das, the Bengali scholar and teacher who spent six months at Tashilhunpo and Shigatse in 1879, and visited Lhasa in 1882 where he had an audience with the Dalai Lama. In the course of his 1879 journey from Shigatse to Lhasa, Das saw what he referred to as "Chinese tyranny" at first-hand:

Today at nine a.m., the junior Amban with a retinue of 300 men on horseback, left for Lhasa. The owners of the relay ponies followed them on foot, keeping pace with the ponies, or if they lagged behind they were whipped by the men on horseback; so that some dropped out and disappeared, abandoning their property to the Chinese rather than undergo their ill-treatment.[55]

[51] Sir Ernest Satow to the Marquess of Landsdowne, Peking, November 17, 1904, Further Correspondence Respecting Tibet, FO 17, 1753, National Archives, Kew.
[52] Same to Same, Peking, November 1, 1904, Further Correspondence Respecting the Affairs of Tibet, October–December 1904, FO 535/5, National Archives, Kew.
[53] Same to Same, November 11, 1904, *ibid.*
[54] Same to Same, Peking, November 17, 1904, Further Correspondence Respecting the Affairs of Tibet, FO 17/1753, National Archives, Kew.
[55] Sarat Chandra Das, *Journey to Lhasa and Central Tibet* (New Delhi: Manjusri, 1970 [1902]), p. 87.

Das was witnessing the application of a small dose of state violence committed by an imperial official who thought himself to be superior to the Tibetans. When Younghusband reached Lhasa he reported that the Chinese Amban told him that "the Tibetans are impossible to deal with, that kindness is thrown away upon them, and nothing but force produces any effect."[56] Younghusband certainly had his own axe to grind at that moment as he tried to justify his own use of force against Tibetans, but the Amban's words ominously anticipated how China might act in Tibet if it ever regained the power to do so.

The China–Tibet relationship was deeply intertwined with Buddhism and general cultural attitudes. The imitation Potala at Chengde was an architectural expression of this cultural and religious dynamic at work. The Qing (Manchu) emperors in the 1700s "organized in Chengde a territory intended to display a system of symbolic landmarks that would contribute to justifying the newly established rule of the Qing dynasty in Tibet and Mongolia." They portrayed themselves as the protectors of Lamaist Buddhism. The Potala and other temples at Chengde "contributed to the symbolic control that the expanding empire sought to exert on the cultural landscapes of South China and Central Asia."[57]

An even more direct example of the intertwining of religion and empire was Tibet itself. Tibet had its own moment of imperial expansion when it sent conquering armies beyond its borders in the eighth and ninth centuries. "The assumption that Buddhism and imperium might be incompatible is one that would not have occurred to these [Tibetan] Buddhists," notes Matthew Kapstein, "and, indeed, it is one that few serious students of Buddhist history would countenance today."[58] The Tibetans "converted to Buddhism in the very process of their warlike activities."[59] As Hugh Richardson has drily observed,

the outburst of religion with the building of monasteries, the ordination of monks and the translation of religious texts, did nothing to abate the military ardour of the Tibetans. Their armies were steadily conquering a wide expanse of Chinese territory in the northeast right up to and including the fortress cities of the Silk

---

[56] Younghusband to Government of India, Camp Lhasa, August 17, 1904, Further Correspondence Respecting Tibet, October–December 1904, FO 535/5, National Archives, Kew.

[57] Foret, *Mapping Chengde*, p. 15; Gray Tuttle, *Tibetan Buddhists in the Making of Modern China* (New York: Columbia University Press, 2005), pp. 222–224, sketches out the range of ideological, religious, and racial arguments used by the Chinese authorities to justify their case that Tibet was part of China.

[58] Matthew Kapstein, "Plague, Power, and Reason. The Royal Conversion to Buddhism Reconsidered," in McKay, ed., *History of Tibet*, vol. I, p. 403.

[59] Snellgrove, *Indo-Tibetan Buddhism*, p. 328.

Road, and well into the border provinces of China itself. There they established a well-organized, efficient colonial government with administrative centres in strategic places complete with a large hierarchy of military and civil officials including some local Chinese.[60]

An early form of Tibetan Buddhism came in the wake of those conquests and formed the "dominant high culture of northern Eurasia" for the ensuing millennium, as the ancient Tibetan manuscripts in the Dunhuang caves still testify to this day.[61] Matthew Kapstein points out that "religion became a means for the representation of political difference" in this Tibetan empire.[62]

It would be reductionist to conclude from this Tibetan history that Buddhism causes imperialism. A more reasonable conclusion is that people shaped by a particular culture will use aspects of that culture to justify their seizing of territory, their expansion of trade, and their claims of cultural superiority. The commentaries provided by Alex McKay in his *History of Tibet* volumes help us work our way through to an understanding of the dynamics behind these Asian examples where religion could become a handmaiden of imperialism:

> It is characteristic of these developed Asian forms of religio-political theory that they were explicitly expansionist to an unlimited degree . . . Tibetan understandings of their polity as a divine realm, and Chinese understandings of the emperor as the centre of the world were not bounded by the fixed borders of the European nation state concept. Rather they allowed for the entire world to be envisaged as within a potential sphere of control, whether in secular or divine guise. In this sense they may be better equated to Western doctrines such as imperialism and even Christianity than those of nationalism and the nation state. These elite expansionist ideologies – Asian and European – shared an implicit aspect: they embodied and justified state violence.[63]

In similar ways to these Asian examples where religion was used to legitimize expansion, Europeans used the Enlightenment to justify their colonial projects round the world. That does not mean the Enlightenment was the tap-root of European imperialism any more than Buddhism was the tap-root of Tibetan imperialism, but simply that some of the tenets of the Enlightenment provided ideological legitimacy at particular moments. To reach the core of the conceptual issue at stake here, it is useful to borrow the notion of the Primordial Buddha and apply that

---

[60] Hugh Richardson, "Political Aspects of the Snga-Dar, the First Diffusion of Buddhism in Tibet," in McKay, ed., *History of Tibet*, vol. I, p. 302.
[61] McKay, ed., *History of Tibet*, vol. I, p. 25.
[62] Kapstein, "Plague, Power, and Reason," *ibid.*, p. 403.   [63] *Ibid.*, p. 18.

mode of thinking to empires. There is a Primordial empire, as it were, that informs all of world history. Since the earliest period of recorded history humans have forged empires. The forces that create empires have been broadly similar in all epochs. Empires have been driven by the human desire for riches, the lure of new territory, the pressures of climate change, the enticement to deploy superior military power, the belief that your culture is superior to others, and the longing to achieve some sort of lasting place in history.

The Enlightenment did contribute to imperialism because some of its propositions were used to justify state violence in the name of progress. But the Enlightenment had many sides to it – just as Buddhism does in its various Asian settings. Buddhism has been implicated in empire, but Buddhism has also (to stick with the Tibet case) launched critiques of imperialism. Buddhism and the Enlightenment have both been adapted for imperial purposes but those adaptations can be separated from their basic epistemologies. The fundamental principle of Buddhism, that the material world is an illusion which obscures the ultimate spiritual nature of existence, was not destroyed because some regimes used Buddhism to justify their very real empires. A fundamental feature of the Enlightenment, that knowledge about the natural and human worlds can be gained through evidence and reason, did not disappear when the Enlightenment was used to justify empire.

The periodic connections between religion and imperialism in these Asian settings brings us back to the general issue of the role of religion in justifying empires. As the contrast between Bogle and Younghusband vividly demonstrates, evangelical Christianity played a major role in the re-shaping of British imperial attitudes throughout the 1800s. The Maxim-armed Younghusband was convinced that the Christian God was at his side as he fought his way to Lhasa. George Bogle, Charles Grant, and William Jones were all born in 1746 and went to serve the nascent British empire in India. In this trio it was the one shaped by dogmatic evangelical Christianity who expressed an open contempt for Indian people and Indian cultures, and foreshadowed the more arrogant imperial ideologies of the nineteenth century. Grant was dismissive of everything about India, and convinced "that British rule in India must be accepted as permanent."[64]

On the other hand, Grant was a critic of the military campaigns that resulted in British territorial conquests in India during the

---

[64] Ainslie Embree, *Charles Grant and British Rule in India* (London: G. Allen, 1962), p. 142.

1793–1818 years. This was not out of any sympathy for Indian peoples, but because he preferred a policy of consolidating the British position in Bengal so that the thorough anglicization and Christianization that he advocated could take hold. Still, he can be separated from the aggressive military imperialism that was mounted by Governor General Wellesley (1798–1805) and his brother, the future Duke of Wellington, and some of their like-minded successors. And, of course, evangelical Christians like Grant played a prominent role in ending the slave trade within the empire in 1807. Some of these same evangelical impulses, as E. P. Thompson has shown, also played a creative role in the formation of English working-class culture in this period.[65] The evangelical Christian movement in Britain had other sides to it than the bigotry we noted in Grant's views on Hinduism.

Evangelical Christianity certainly contributed in many ways to the arrogant imperial ideologies of the nineteenth century but that was only one aspect of the movement's impact in Britain and the empire. If even narrow evangelical Christianity had a variety of possibilities within it, then how much more so is that the case with the broad, self-questioning intellectual movement that we now designate as the Enlightenment. It contained opposites within itself just as Hindu and Buddhist cultures see opposites in their gods and buddhas.

When George Bogle got back to Calcutta he reflected on his travels. As he did so, he mused about the impression he had left behind in Bhutan and Tibet. He thought he had taken a big responsibility on his shoulders for, quite aside from the Company business upon which he was embarked, he believed that nothing less than the reputation of European culture as a whole was at stake as he made his way across the Himalayas:

As I was the first European who ever travelled to Bootan, I have sometimes considered that the character not only of the English but of all the people of Europe depended on me. This Idea of being shown as a Specimen of my Countrymen has often given me a world of Uneasiness, and I don't know that I ever wished so heartily to have been a dull, personable Man as upon this Occasion. It was some Comfort to have Mr. Hamilton with me, and I left it entirely to him to give a good Impression of the Persons of Fringies. But from a national, and perhaps excusable, vanity I was anxious also to give the people whom I visited a favourable Opinion of the dispositions of the English.[66]

---

[65] E. P. Thompson, *The Making of the English Working Class* (New York: Vintage, 1964).
[66] Remarks on his Mission to Bhutan and Tibet, Calcutta, 1775 [made when Bogle submitted his accounts to the Council], Warren Hastings Papers, Add. 29233, f. 388, BL.

This is Bogle at his most appealing. There is a generous compliment to his traveling companion and a wry, amused, self-mocking speculation that the Bhutanese and Tibetans would probably make generalizing judgments about English and European culture based on the impressions they formed of him.

He noted that such judgments by one country of another were often initially based on personal interactions: "Nations cannot converse together as Man to Man, [so] that Opinion which the People of one country entertain of those of another is formed from an Acquaintance with a few Individuals."[67] Bogle thought he was representing England and Europe to Asian audiences who were fully entitled to make judgments in return. Because he thought in those terms, he was a European on his best behavior during his Tibet mission. In contrast, Younghusband was totally dismissive of any Asian capabilities and was a European on his worst behavior during his Tibet mission.

In Alan Bennett's play *The History Boys* the lone female character, Mrs. Lintott, becomes exasperated with the various definitions of history that are being cleverly tossed about during the mock examination interviews for entry to Oxford and Cambridge. She suddenly delivers a heartfelt indictment of what, after a lifetime of teaching history, she sees as an enduring feature of the subject: "Can you, for a moment, imagine how dispiriting it is to teach five centuries of masculine ineptitude?" To further edify the momentarily bewildered boys (and her surprised male colleagues), she adds, for good measure, that "History is a commentary on the various and continuing incapabilities of men."[68] When reading Mrs. Lintott's lament it is hard not to think of Younghusband's mission to Tibet in 1904. With his unquestioning sense of entitlement, with his pompous posturing, and with his occasionally stupid and violent actions, Younghusband seems to sum up the entire range of masculine ineptitude in one fell swoop. Bogle wished to be "a dull, personable Man" to convey some impression of his cultural sensitivity while Younghusband strutted like a peacock in his determination to display the superiority of British power and British civilization.

Curzon and Younghusband, as we have seen, convinced themselves that they were invading Tibet for the good of the Tibetans just as Britain had taken over in India for the good of the Indians. They would have agreed with one of their contemporary cheerleaders of empire, the Canadian historian George M. Wrong, who declared in 1909 that

[67] *Ibid.*, f. 388.
[68] Alan Bennett, *The History Boys* (London: Faber and Faber, 2004), pp. 84, 85.

Britain controls today the destinies of some 350,000,000 alien people, unable as yet to govern themselves, and easy victims to rapine and injustice unless a strong arm guards them. She is giving them a rule that has its faults, no doubt, but such . . . as no conquering state ever before gave to a dependent people.[69]

Hastings and Bogle would have been taken aback by this declaration of supreme cultural certainty. The outlook on the world represented by Edwardian pro-empire advocates such as Wrong, and by the views of Curzon and Younghusband during their Tibet mission, show how imperial ideologies had shifted along to the more extreme end of the spectrum since Bogle's time.

This hardening of imperial attitudes on the part of the British that we traced in the chapter "From Enlightenment to Empire" was evident in the revised British response to Bhutan by the mid-nineteenth century. In 1863, for example, Sir Ashley Eden, after his failed mission to Bhutan, described it as "a country in which there is no ruling class, no literature, no national pride in the past or aspirations for the future; there is, as a matter of course, no reliable history and very little tradition."[70] Eden was in a sour mood when he gave that assessment for he had been summarily dismissed and insulted by Bhutanese negotiators but his views were not unusual for the time. We are well on the way towards Younghusband's and Curzon's views of feckless Asiatics when we read that summing up of Bhutan. What a contrast this is with Bogle's 1774 commentary.

The story of these two Tibet missions is an odd tale of empire. Younghusband invoked the 1774 mission when he crossed into Tibet in 1903. Having introduced the linkage he used it for all it was worth to pressure the Tibetans and make his mission more palatable for British audiences. Once the linkage was in play even the Panchen Lama took it up enthusiastically when it suited his diplomatic strategy of making friends with the British. But the 1774 mission had taken place 130 years previously and had been forgotten or mis-remembered both in Tibet and Britain.

---

[69] Quoted in Niall Ferguson, *Empire. The Rise and Demise of the British World Order and the Lessons for Global Power* (London: Allen Lane, 2002), p. xii. As this choice of a framing quotation suggests, Ferguson presents a very favorable view of the British empire.

[70] *Political Missions to Bootan comprising the Reports of the Honble. Ashley Eden . . .* (Calcutta: Bengal Secretariat Office, 1865), p. 108; B. Chakravarti, *A Cultural History of Bhutan*, 2 vols. (Chittaranjan, India: Hilltop Publishers, 1980), vol. II, p. 106; Aris, *The Raven Crown*, p. 44. The British went to war with Bhutan in 1863 following the Bhutanese rejection of the treaty terms and the direct insults to Eden. So Eden's evaluation can be read as an example of propaganda by an ill-treated official to justify another local war on the subcontinent. By this time British officials in India viewed Bhutan as a dysfunctional country beset by endless civil wars. It had to be shaped up.

While the dramatic comparison may have surged so conveniently into Younghusband's inventive and romantic mind the two missions were not cut from the same cloth. Although Bogle and Younghusband were both agents of the British empire they were very different in their responses to Tibet. But like some of the strange but true stories in Herodotus this one tells us something about history and how history is presented. In examining the comparison itself, and then following the ideological transformations from Bogle to Younghusband, we have opened out the multifaceted nature of the British empire.

In its two journeys to the roof of the world in 1774 and 1904 the empire revealed many of its contradictory aspects. It was sympathetic and tolerant; it was prejudiced and aggressive. The opposites represented by Bogle and Younghusband in the course of their Tibet missions reveal the Sufi (and Shakespearean) insight that the perspectives of the sage and the fool are both necessary when it comes to plumbing the depths of human history. The insight is so powerful because sages are not always sagacious and fools are not always foolish. Bogle's sensitive and measured outlook on the world disappeared when he dressed down Indians who challenged British rule and when he advocated the conquest of Assam. Younghusband postured in a crude and aggressive manner during his Tibet mission but ended his life as a religious mystic who sought to "mediate between East and West."[71]

To recapture its abundant complexity, empire history needs to be written in ways which incorporate its sages and its fools in all their changing phases. The history of the British empire is often written in ways that appeal to nationalist or communal identities. It is presented from opposing sides, each locked into its own framing of the past – the empire flourished because of slavery and exploitation of other lands; the empire led the anti-slavery crusade and brought about beneficial modernization round the world. Comprehensive praising of the empire from a metropolitan perspective or comprehensive dumping on the empire from the perspective of colonized peoples are both limiting in their different ways, and neither accurately reflects the permanent contradictions in the empire's history. Similarly, condemning the Enlightenment as the cause of imperialism or extolling the Enlightenment as a critical voice against imperialism both misrepresent the complicated nature of the Enlightenment. Such one-dimensional historical narratives may even create barriers between communities now living in a country whose diverse population has been created by the unanticipated working out of the history of the empire.

---

[71] French, *Younghusband*, p. 357.

There is nothing new in trying to capture all the contradictions of the past when it comes to writing history – it is how Herodotus wrote the first history book in the Western world over two thousand years ago. Herodotus was respectful, even admiring at times, of Persians, Egyptians, and other non-Greek peoples, just as Bogle was of the Bhutanese and Tibetans he met on his travels. He was later roundly condemned for that approach to writing history. Plutarch, that high-minded, Greek-born, Roman patriot, derided Herodotus as a "philobarbaros" (a barbarian-lover) as he ruminated about the uses of history during another moment of imperial power.[72] In the British case the only way to satisfactorily incorporate imperial history into the contemporary national narrative is to embrace all the contradictions within the empire – as we have done with these two utterly different missions to Tibet. It is a trickier proposition to approach history writing in this way but using such a "compass of truth" guides us a bit closer to what the past was actually like. An empire full of opposites also makes the empire more interesting for everyone involved.

[72] Herodotus, *The Histories*, ed. Walter Blanco (New York: W. W. Norton, 1992), pp. 272–274.

Bibliography

PRIMARY SOURCES BY ARCHIVES AND LIBRARIES

BRITISH LIBRARY, LONDON

Manuscript

Ampthill Papers, MSS. EUR. E233
Bogle Papers, MSS. EUR. D532, E226
Cotton Papers, MSS. EUR. D1202
Curzon Collection, MSS. EUR. F111–112
David Anderson Papers, Add. 45417–45441
Hamilton Collection, MSS. EUR. F123
India Office Records, Bengal Administrations, 1774–1799, L/AG/34/29/1
India Office Records, Correspondence, Home Miscellaneous, 1774, 1775, H/118
India Office Records, Tibet Mission Correspondence, 1904, L/PS/7/162
Philip Francis Papers, MSS. EUR. E15
Warren Hastings Papers, Add. 29117, 29134, 29144, 29145, 29146, 29233, 39871, 39889, 39892
Younghusband Collection, MSS. EUR. F197

Printed

A List of the Company's Civil Servants at their Settlements in the East Indies (London, 1770–)
Bolts, William, *Considerations on India Affairs Particularly Respecting the Present State of Bengal and its Dependencies to which is prefixed a Map of those Countries chiefly from actual Surveys* (London, 1772)
Buckland, C. E., *Dictionary of Indian Biography* (London, 1906)
Firminger, W. K., ed., *Bengal District Records. Rangpur*, vol. I *1770–1779*, vol. II *1779–1782* (Calcutta, 1914)
Glazier, E. G., ed., *Further Notes on the Rungpore Records*, 2 vols. (Calcutta, 1876)
Government of India, Foreign Department. Secret-E. Proceedings, Tibet Negotiations, February 1903–March 1905
Grant, Charles, *Observations on the State of Society among the Asiatic Subjects of Great Britain, particularly with respect to Morals, and the Means of Improving It. Written Chiefly in the Year 1792* (London?, 1797?)
Grünwedel, Albert, "Der Weg nach Sambhala des dritten Gross-Lama von bKra sis lhun po bzan dPal ldan Yeses, aus dem tibetischen Original übersetzt und

mit dem Texte herausgegegeben," *Abhandlungen der Königlich Bayerischen Akademie der Wissenschaften. Philosophisch-philologische und historische Klasse* 29 (Munich, 1915), pp. 1–118

Memoranda on the Indian States 1940 (Government of India, New Delhi, 1940)

O'Connor, Captain W. F., *Report on Tibet* (Calcutta, 1903)

The Bengal Obituary or A Record to Perpetuate the Memory of Departed Worth, being a Compilation of Tablets and Monumental Inscriptions from various parts of the Bengal and Agra Presidencies to which is added Biographical Sketches and memoirs of such as have distinguished themselves in the history of British India since the formation of the European Settlement to the Present Time (Calcutta, 1848)

Williamson, Captain Thomas, *The East India Vade-Mecum; or Complete Guide to Gentlemen intended for the Civil, Military or Naval Service of the East India Company* (London, 1810)

PUBLIC RECORD OFFICE (NATIONAL ARCHIVES), KEW

Foreign Office, FO 535/5 (1904), FO 17/1753–1754 (1904, 1905)

MITCHELL LIBRARY, GLASGOW

Bogle Family Papers

NATIONAL ARCHIVES OF INDIA, NEW DELHI

Government of India, Foreign Department. Secret-E. Proceedings, Tibetan Affairs, February 1903, Nos. 1–88; February 1903, Nos. 38–95; April 1903, Nos. 192–194; July 1903, Nos. 18–19; July 1903, Nos. 288–289

Government of India, Foreign Department. Secret-E. Proceedings, Account of Lecture by Captain Koskoff at St. Petersburg, June 1903, Nos. 274–275

Government of India, Foreign Department. Secret-E. Proceedings, British Policy Towards Tibet, April 1903, Nos. 130–172

Government of India, Foreign Department. Secret-E. Proceedings, Tibet Nego-tiations, September 1903, Nos. 189–235; November 1903, Nos. 118–158

Government of India, Foreign Department. Secret-E. Proceedings, Sikkim Diaries, September 1903, Nos. 85–94

Government of India, Foreign Department. Secret-E. Proceedings, Darjeeling Confidential Frontier Reports, April 1903, Nos. 192–194; November 1903, Nos. 40–80

Government of India, Foreign Department. Secret-E. Proceedings, Notes of Conversations between Lieutenant-Colonel C. W. Ravenshaw, Resident in Nepal, and Colonel Mahabir Singh regarding Tibet, November 1903, No. 117

Government of India, Foreign Department. Secret-E. Proceedings, Status of Nepal, July 1903, Nos. 20–21

Government of India, Foreign Department. Secret-E. Proceedings, Newsletters from the Nepalese Representative at Lhasa regarding Tibetan Affairs, July

1904, Nos. 403–411; August 1904, Nos. 82–92; October 1904, Nos. 646–666

Government of India, Foreign Department. External-B. Appointment of Captain W. F. O'Connor as Intelligence Officer with Tibet Frontier Commission, October 1903, Nos. 117–120

Government of India, Foreign Department. Secret-E. Proceedings, Frontier Commission Diaries, December 1903 – March 1904, July 1904, Nos. 388–402; Diaries, March–July 1904, August 1904, Nos. 231–246

Government of India, Foreign Department. Secret-E. Proceedings, Tibet Negotiations, July 1904, Nos. 258–387

Government of India, Foreign Department. External-B. Proceedings, Allegations against Tibet Commission with Regard to Looting, August 1904, Nos. 254–254(a)

Government of India, Foreign Department. External-B. Proceedings, Tibet Mission General Series, Part XII, Nos. 12–88, Correspondence December 1903–January 1904

Government of India, Home Department. Proceedings, Collection of Tibetan Books, Block Prints, and Manuscripts for the India Office Library, July 1904, Nos. 90–96

PRIMARY SOURCES, PRINTED

OFFICIAL RECORDS

Askari, Syed Hasan, ed., *Fort William-India House Correspondence*, vol. XVI *Foreign, Secret and Political 1787–1791* (Delhi: National Archives of India, 1976)

Gupta, Hira Lal, ed., *Fort William-India House Correspondence*, vol. VIII *1777–1781* (Delhi: National Archives of India, 1981)

Patwardhan, R. P., ed., *Fort William-India House Correspondence*, vol. VII *1773–1776* (Delhi: National Archives of India, 1971)

Prasad, Amba, ed., *Fort William-India House Correspondence*, vol. XIV *1752–1781* (Delhi: National Archives of India, 1985)

Prasad, Bisheshwar, ed., *Fort William-India House Correspondence*, vol. VI *Public, Select and Secret 1770–1772* (Delhi: National Archives of India, 1960)

Saletore, B. A., ed., *Fort William-India House Correspondence*, vol. IX *1782–1785* (Delhi: National Archives of India, 1959)

Williams, L. F. Rushbrook, *India in 1924–1925* (Calcutta: Government of India Central Publication Branch, 1925)

TRAVEL ACCOUNTS, MEMOIRS, AND TEXTS WRITTEN AT THE TIME OF THE TWO MISSIONS

Candler, Edmund, *The Unveiling of Lhasa* (London: T. Nelson & Sons, 1905)

Holdich, Thomas, *Tibet, the Mysterious* (New York: F. A. Stokes, 1906)

Lamb, Alastair, ed., *Bhutan and Tibet. The Travels of George Bogle and Alexander Hamilton 1774–1777*, vol. I *Bogle and Hamilton Letters, Journals and Memoranda* (Hertingfordbury, Hertfordshire: Roxford Books, 2002)

Landon, Perceval, *The Opening of Tibet. An Account of Lhasa . . . and the Progress of the Mission sent there by the English Government in the Year 1903–1904* (London and New York: Doubleday, 1905)

Markham, Clements, ed., *Narratives of the Mission of George Bogle to Tibet and of the Journey of Thomas Manning to Lhasa* (New Delhi: Manjusri, 1970 [1876])

Marshall, P. J., ed., *The Writings and Speeches of Edmund Burke*, vol. V *India; Madras and Bengal 1774–1785* (Oxford University Press, 1981)

O'Connor, Lieutenant-Colonel Sir Frederick, CSI, CIE, CVO, *Things Mortal* (London: Hodder, 1940)

Turner, Samuel, *An Account of an Embassy to the Court of the Teshoo Lama in Tibet* (London: W. Bulmer & Co., 1800)

Younghusband, Francis, *India and Tibet. A History of the Relations which have subsisted between the two Countries from the time of Warren Hastings to 1910 with a particular Account of the Mission to Lhasa of 1904* (London: J. Murray, 1910)

The Light of Experience (London: Constable, 1927)

NEWSPAPERS AND PERIODICALS

The Annual Register (London), 1774–1785

The Times (London), 1903–1906

New York Times, 1903–1904, 1942

Black, C. E. D., "The Trade and Resources of Tibet," *Imperial and Asiatic Quarterly Review* [*IAQR*] 26 (July–October 1908), pp. 87–104

Bruce, Captain George E., "Our Relations with Tibet," *IAQR* 18 (July–October 1904), pp. 28–43

Crosby, Oscar T., "England and Russia in Tibet," *North American Review* 178 (1905), pp. 711–716

Keene, H. G., "Rulers of India – Review of Captain L. J. Trotter's *Warren Hastings*," *The Academy* 968 (November 22, 1890), pp. 471–472

Lawrence, Sir Walter, "The British Mission to Tibet," *North American Review* 177 (1904), pp. 869–881

[Macaulay, Thomas Babington,] "Review of G. R. Gleig's *Memoirs of the Life of Warren Hastings*," *Edinburgh Review* 74:149 (October 1841), pp. 160–255

Malcolm, Ian, "Thibet and the India Office. A Blazing Indiscretion," *Nineteenth Century* 57 (April 1905), pp. 577–584

"Tibet" [review article of 5 books], *Edinburgh Review* 201:412 (April 1905), pp. 338–360

"Tibet and the Scotsman Who First Opened It," *The Scotsman* (March 7, 1892), p. 9

Waddell, L. A., LL.D., CB, Archaeologist to the Mission, "Tibetan Manuscripts and Books etc. Collected During the Younghusband Mission to Lhasa," *IAQR* 34 (July–October 1912), pp. 80–113

Younghusband, Sir Frank, KCIE, "The Geographical Results of the Tibet Mission," *Scottish Geographical Magazine* 21 (1905), pp. 229–245

PARLIAMENTARY PAPERS

"Papers Relating to Tibet," Command Papers 1904 [Cd. 1920], vol. LXVII, p. 779

"Further Papers Relating to Tibet," Command Papers 1904 [Cd. 2054], vol. LXVII, p. 1103

"Further Papers Relating to Tibet," Command Papers 1905 [Cd. 2370], vol. LVIII, p. 403

The Parliamentary Debates, 4th and 5th Sessions of 27th Parliament, vol. CXXVI (1903), vol. CXXIX (1904), vol. CXXX (1904), vol. CXXXIII (1904), vol. CXXXIV (1904), vol. CXXV (1904), vol. CXLI (1905)

MISCELLANEOUS

Casas, Bartolome De Las, *A Short Account of the Destruction of the Indies*, edited and translated by Nigel Griffin with an introduction by Anthony Pagden (London: Penguin Books, 2004)

Dalzel, Andrew, *History of the University of Edinburgh from its Foundation* (Edinburgh: Edmonston and Douglas, 1862)

Das, Sarat Chandra, *Journey to Lhasa and Central Tibet* (New Delhi: Manjusri, 1970 [1902]) [ed. W. W. Rockhill]

Encyclopedia Britannica or A Dictionary of Arts and Sciences Compiled upon a New Plan... by a Society of Gentlemen of Scotland, 3 vols. (Edinburgh: A. Bell and C. MacFarquhar, 1771)

Gould, B. J., *The Jewel in the Lotus. Recollections of an Indian Political* (London: Chatto and Windus, 1957)

Grant, Alexander, *The Story of the University of Edinburgh* (London: Green & Co., 1884)

SECONDARY SOURCES CITED OR REFERRED
TO IN THE TEXT

Addy, Premen, *Tibet on the Imperial Chessboard. The Making of British Policy towards Lhasa 1899–1925* (London: Sangam Books, 1985)

Archer, Mildred, *India and British Portraiture 1770–1825* (London: Sotheby Parke Barnet, 1979)

Aris, Michael, *The Raven Crown. The Origins of Buddhist Monarchy in Bhutan* (London: Serindia Publications, 1994)

Armitage, David, *Theories of Empire 1450–1800* (Aldershot: Ashgate, 1998)

Ballhatchet, Kenneth, *Race, Sex and Class under the Raj. Imperial Attitudes and Policies and their Critics 1793–1905* (London: Weidenfeld and Nicolson, 1980)

Barrow, Ian J., *Making History, Drawing Territory. British Mapping in India c.1756–1905* (Oxford University Press, 2003)

Bayly, C. A., *Indian Society and the Making of the British Empire* (Cambridge University Press, 1988)

   Rulers, Townsmen, and Bazaars. North Indian Society in the Age of British Expansion 1770–1870 (Cambridge University Press, 1983)

Bennett, Alan, *The History Boys* (London: Faber and Faber, 2004)
  Untold Stories (London: Faber and Faber, 2005)
Bernbaum, Edwin, *The Way to Shambhala. A Search for the Mythical Kingdom beyond the Himalayas* (Garden City, NY: Anchor Press, 1980 [2001])
Bernstein, Jeremy, *Dawning of the Raj. The Life and Trial of Warren Hastings* (Chicago: Ivan R. Dee, 2000)
Bhuyan, S. K., *Anglo-Assamese Relations 1771–1826* (Gauhati, Assam, 1949)
Boot, Max, *War Made New. Technology, Warfare, and the Course of History 1500 to Today* (New York: Gotham Books, 2006)
Bose, Sugata, *Peasant Labour and Colonial Capital. Rural Bengal since 1770* (Cambridge University Press, 1993)
Bowen, H. V., *Revenue and Reform. The Indian Problem in British Politics 1757–1773* (Cambridge University Press, 1991)
Bowen, H. V., Margaret Lincoln, and Nigel Rigby, eds., *The Worlds of the East India Company* (Leicester University Press, 2002)
Brunero, Donna, *Britain's Imperial Cornerstone in China. The Chinese Maritime Customs Service 1854–1949* (London: Routledge, 2006)
Cain, Alex M., *The Cornchest for Scotland: Scots in India* (Edinburgh: National Library of Scotland, 1986)
Cameron, Ian, *To the Farthest Ends of the Earth. 150 Years of World Exploration by the Royal Geographical Society* (New York: E. P. Dutton, 1980)
Cammann, Schuyler, *Trade through the Himalayas. The Early British Attempts to Open Tibet* (Princeton University Press, 1951)
Carnall, Geoffrey, and Colin Nicholson, eds., *The Impeachment of Warren Hastings* (Edinburgh University Press, 1989)
Chakravarti, B., *A Cultural History of Bhutan* (Chittaranjan: Hilltop Publishers, 1980)
Colley, Linda, "Britishness and Otherness," *Journal of British Studies* 31 (October 1992), pp. 309–329
  Britons. Forging the Nation 1707–1837 (New Haven and London: Yale University Press, 1992)
Cooper, Frederick, and Ann Laura Stoler, eds., *Tensions of Empire. Colonial Cultures in a Bourgeois World* (Berkeley: University of California Press, 1997)
Dalrymple, William, "Plain Tales from British India," *New York Review of Books*, April 26, 2007, pp. 47–50
  The White Mughals. Love and Betrayal in Eighteenth-Century India (London: HarperCollins, 2002)
Das, Nirmala, *The Dragon Country. The General History of Bhutan* (Bombay: Orient Longman, 1974)
Dilks, David, *Curzon in India*, 2 vols. (London: Rupert Hart-Davis, 1969)
Diskalkar, D. B., "Bogle's Embassy to Tibet," *Indian Historical Quarterly* 9 (June 1933), pp. 420–438
Edney, Matthew H., *Mapping an Empire. The Geographical Construction of British India 1765–1843* (University of Chicago Press, 1997)
Embree, Ainslie Thomas, *Charles Grant and British Rule in India* (London: G. Allen, 1962)

Farrington, Anthony, *Trading Places. The East India Company and Asia 1600–1834* (London: British Library, 2002)

Feiling, Keith, *Warren Hastings* (London: Macmillan, 1954)

Ferguson, Niall, *Empire. The Rise and Demise of the British World Order and the Lessons for Global Power* (London: Allen Lane, 2002)

Fleming, Peter, *Bayonets to Lhasa. The First Full Account of the British Invasion of Tibet in 1904* (New York: Harper, 1961)

Forêt, Philippe, *Mapping Chengde. The Qing Landscape Enterprise* (Honolulu: University of Hawaii Press, 2000)

Frank, André Gunder, *ReOrient. Global Economy in the Asian Age* (Berkeley: University of California Press, 1998)

French, Patrick, *Younghusband. The Last Great Imperial Adventurer* (London: HarperCollins, 1994)

Fry, Michael, *The Scottish Empire* (Edinburgh: Birlinn Ltd., 2001)

Ghosh, Durba, *Colonial Companions: Bibis, Begums, and Concubines of the British in North India, 1760–1830* (Ph.D. dissertation, University of California, Berkeley, 2000)

    Sex and the Family in Colonial India. The Making of Empire (Cambridge University Press, 2006)

Ghosh, J. M., *Sanyassi and Fakir Raiders in Bengal* (Calcutta, 1930)

Ghosh, Suresh Chandra, *The Social Condition of the British Community in Bengal 1757–1800* (Leiden: E. J. Brill, 1970)

Gilmour, David, *Curzon* (London: John Murray, 1994)

Goldstein, Melvyn C., *The Snow Lion and the Dragon. China, Tibet, and the Dalai Lama* (Berkeley: University of California Press, 1997)

Goldstein, Melvyn (with the help of Gelek Rimpoche), *A History of Modern Tibet, 1913–1951. The Demise of the Lamaist State* (Berkeley: University of California Press, 1989)

Gordon, Stewart, *The Marathas 1600–1818* (Cambridge University Press, 1993)

Hawes, Christopher, *Poor Relations. The Making of a Eurasian Community in British India 1773–1833* (Richmond, Surrey: Curzon Press, 1996)

Herman, Arthur, *How the Scots Invented the Modern World* (New York: Crown Publishers, 2001)

Herodotus, *The Histories*, ed. and trans. Walter Blanco (New York: W. W. Norton, 1992)

Hopkirk, Peter, *Quest for Kim. In Search of Kipling's Great Game* (Ann Arbor: University of Michigan Press, 1996)

    Trespassers on the Roof of the World. The Race for Lhasa (Oxford University Press, 1982)

Horn, D. B., *A Short History of the University of Edinburgh 1556–1889* (Edinburgh University Press, 1967)

Hutchins, Francis, *The Illusion of Permanence. British Imperialism in India* (Princeton University Press, 1967)

Hyam, Ronald, *Empire and Sexuality. The British Experience* (Manchester University Press, 1990)

Israel, Jonathan, *Enlightenment Contested. Philosophy, Modernity, and the Emancipation of Man 1670–1752* (Oxford University Press, 2006)

Radical Enlightenment. Philosophy and the Making of Modernity (Oxford University Press, 2001)

Kadian, Rajesh, *Tibet, India and China* (New Delhi: Vision Books, 1999)

Kennedy, Dane, "Imperial History and Post Colonial Theory," *Journal of Imperial and Commonwealth History* 24 (1996), pp. 345–363

Islands of White. Settler Society in Kenya and Southern Rhodesia 1890–1939 (Durham, NC: Duke University Press, 1987)

The Highly Civilized Man. Richard Burton and the Victorian World (Harvard University Press, 2005)

The Magic Mountains. Hill Stations and the British Raj (Berkeley: University of California Press, 1996)

Kennedy, Paul, *The Rise and Fall of the Great Powers* (New York: Vintage Books, 1989)

Kidd, Colin, *Subverting Scotland's Past. Scottish Whig Historians and the Creation of an Anglo-British Identity 1689–1830* (Cambridge University Press, 1993)

Kors, Alan Charles, ed., *Encyclopedia of the Enlightenment*, 4 vols. (Oxford University Press, 2003)

Lamb, Alastair, *Britain and Chinese Central Asia. The Road to Lhasa 1767 to 1905* (London: Routledge and Kegan Paul, 1960)

British India and Tibet 1766–1910 (London: Routledge and Kegan Paul, 1980)

The China-India Border. The Origins of the Disputed Boundaries (Oxford University Press, 1964)

The McMahon Line. A Study in the Relations between India, China and Tibet 1904–1914 (London: Routledge and Kegan Paul, 1966)

Lawson, Philip, *The East India Company* (London: Longman, 1993)

Lenman, Bruce P., *Britain's Colonial Wars, 1688–1783* (Harlow and New York: Longman, 2001)

Lopez, Donald S., *Prisoners of Shangri-La. Tibetan Buddhism and the West* (University of Chicago Press, 1998)

MacGregor, John, *Tibet. A Chronicle of Exploration* (London: Routledge and Kegan Paul, 1970)

McKay, Alex, *Tibet and the British Raj. The Frontier Cadre 1904–1947* (Richmond: Curzon Press, 1997)

McKay, Alex, ed., *The History of Tibet*, 3 vols. (London: Routledge Curzon, 2003)

MacKenzie, John, *Propaganda and Empire* (Manchester University Press, 1998)

McMillan, Laurie Hovell, *English in Tibet, Tibet in English. Self-Preservation in Tibet and the Diaspora* (New York: Palgrave, 2001)

Mallory, J. P., *In Search of the Indo-Europeans. Language, Archaeology, Myth* (London: Thames and Hudson, 1989)

Maraini, Fosco, *Secret Tibet*, translated by Eric Mosbacher and Guido Waldman (London: The Harvill Press, 1998 [1951])

Marshall, Julie G., *Britain and Tibet 1765–1947. A Select and Annotated Bibliography of British Relations with Tibet and the Himalayan States including Nepal, Sikkim and Bhutan* (London and New York: Routledge Curzon, 2005)

Marshall, P. J., *Bengal. The British Bridgehead. Eastern India 1740–1828* (Cambridge University Press, 1987)

East Indian Fortunes. The British in Bengal in the Eighteenth Century (Oxford University Press, 1976)

May, Henry F., *The Enlightenment in America* (New York: Oxford University Press, 1976)

Mehra, Parshotam, *The McMahon Line and After. A Study of the Triangular Contest on India's North-eastern Frontier between Britain, China and Tibet 1904–1947* (Madras: Macmillan of India, 1974)

The Younghusband Expedition. An Interpretation (Bombay: Asia Publishing House, 1968)

Tibetan Polity 1904–1937. The Conflict between the 13th. Dalai Lama and the 9th. Panchen Lama (Wiesbaden: Otto Harrassowitz, 1976)

Metcalf, Thomas, *Ideologies of the Raj* (Cambridge University Press, 1995)

Meyer, Karl E., and Shareen Blair Brysac, *Tournament of Shadows. The Great Game and the Race for Empire in Central Asia* (Washington DC: Counterpoint, 1999)

Misra, B. B., *The Central Administration of the East India Company 1773–1834* (Manchester University Press, 1959)

Moon, Penderel, *Warren Hastings and British India* (New York: Macmillan, 1949)

Muthu, Sankar, *Enlightenment Against Empire* (Princeton University Press, 2003)

Neilson, Keith, *Britain and the Last Tsar. British Policy and Russia 1894–1917* (Oxford University Press, 1995)

Nussbaum, Felicity, ed., *The Global Eighteenth Century* (Baltimore: Johns Hopkins University Press, 2003)

O'Brien, Conor Cruise, *The Great Melody. A Thematic Biography and Commented Anthology of Edmund Burke* (University of Chicago Press, 1992)

O'Brien, Karen, *Narratives of Enlightenment. Cosmopolitan History from Voltaire to Gibbon* (Cambridge University Press, 1997)

Petech, Luciano, *Aristocracy and Government in Tibet 1728–1959* (Rome, 1973)

"The Missions of Bogle and Turner according to the Tibetan Texts," *T'oung pao* 39 (1950), pp. 330–346

Pitts, Jennifer, *A Turn to Empire. The Rise of Imperial Liberalism in Britain and France* (Princeton University Press, 2005)

Pocock, J. G. A., *Barbarism and Religion*, 4 vols. (Cambridge University Press, 1999–2005)

Virtue, Commerce and History (Cambridge University Press, 1985)

Pomeranz, Kenneth, *The Great Divergence. Europe, China and the Making of the Modern World Economy* (Princeton University Press, 2000)

Prakash, Gyan, "Inevitable Revolutions," *The Nation*, April 30, 2007, pp. 25–30

Ramusack, Barbara N., *The Indian Princes and their States* (Cambridge University Press, 2004)

Richardson, Hugh, "George Bogle and His Children," *Scottish Genealogist* 29 (September 1982), pp. 73–83

High Peaks, Pure Earth. Collected Writings on Tibetan History and Culture (London: Serindia, 1998)

Tibet and Its History (Oxford University Press, 1962)

Said, Edward, *Culture and Imperialism* (New York: Alfred A. Knopf, 1993).
  Orientalism (New York: Pantheon, 1978)
Schell, Orville, *Virtual Tibet. Searching for Shangri-La from the Himalayas to Hollywood* (New York: Henry Holt, 2000)
Schwartz, Stuart, ed., *Implicit Understandings. Observing, Reporting and Reflecting on the Encounters between Europeans and Other Peoples in the Early Modern Era* (Cambridge University Press, 1994)
Sen, Sudipta, *Distant Sovereignty. National Imperialism and the Origins of British India* (New York: Routledge, 2002)
  Empire of Free Trade. The East India Company and the Making of the Colonial Marketplace (Philadelphia: University of Pennsylvania Press, 1998)
Shakabpa, Tsepon W. D., *Tibet. A Political History* (New Haven: Yale University Press, 1967)
Siegel, Jennifer, *Endgame. Britain, Russia and the Final Struggle for Central Asia* (London: I. B. Tauris, 2002)
Snellgrove, David, *Indo-Tibetan Buddhism. Indian Buddhists and their Tibetan Successors* (Boston: Shambhala, 1987)
Snellgrove, David, and Hugh Richardson, *A Cultural History of Tibet* (Boston: Shambhala, 1995 [1968])
Spear, T. G. P., *The Nabobs. English Social Life in Eighteenth Century India* (Oxford University Press, 1963 [1951])
Spivak, Gayatri, "The Rani of Sirmur. An Essay in Reading the Archives," *History and Theory* 24 (October 1985), pp. 247–272
Stewart, Gordon T., *Jute and Empire. The Calcutta Jute Wallahs and the Landscapes of Empire* (Manchester University Press, 1998)
  "The Russo-Japanese War and the British Invasion of Tibet 1904," in Rotem Kowner, ed., *Rethinking the Russo-Japanese War 1904–1905* (Hong Kong: Global Oriental, 2007), pp. 430–443
Stoler, Ann, "Making Empire Respectable. The Politics of Race and Sexual Morality in Twentieth-Century Colonial Cultures," *American Ethnologist* 16 (1989), pp. 634–660
  Race and the Education of Desire (Durham, NC: Duke University Press, 1995)
Strobel, Margaret, *European Women and the Second British Empire* (Bloomington: Indiana University Press, 1991)
Teltscher, Kate, *The High Road to China. George Bogle, the Panchen Lama, and the First British Expedition to Tibet* (London: Bloomsbury, 2006)
Tobin, Beth F., *Picturing Imperial Power. Colonial Subjects in Eighteenth-Century British Painting* (Durham, NC: Duke University Press, 1999)
Todorov, Tzvetan, *The Conquest of America. The Question of the Other*, translated by Richard Howard (New York: Harper & Row, 1984)
Tuttle, Gray, *Tibetan Buddhists in the Making of Modern China* (New York: Columbia University Press, 2005)
Verrier, Anthony, *Francis Younghusband and the Great Game* (London: Jonathan Cape, 1991)
Walia, Shelley, *Edward Said and the Writing of History* (Duxford, Cambridge: Icon Books, 2001)
Waller, D. J., *The Pundits. British Exploration of Tibet and Central Asia* (Lexington: University of Kentucky Press, 1990)

Webster, Mary, *Johan Zoffany 1733–1810* (London: National Portrait Gallery, 1976)

Wilson, Kathleen, ed., *A New Imperial History. Culture, Identity and Modernity in Britain and the Empire 1660–1840* (Cambridge University Press, 2004)

Winks, Robin, ed., *The Oxford History of the British Empire*, vol. V *Historiography* (Oxford University Press, 1999)

Woodcock, George, *Into Tibet. The Early British Explorers* (London: Faber and Faber, 1971)

Index